TECHNOLOGY AND LEGAL SYSTEMS

To the memory of my late mother Dorothy Sophia Cox, who passed away during the writing of this book

Technology and Legal Systems

NOEL COX
Auckland University of Technology, New Zealand

ASHGATE

Published by
Ashgate Publishing Limited
Gower House
Croft Road
Aldershot
Hampshire GU11 3HR
England

Ashgate Publishing Company
Suite 420
101 Cherry Street
Burlington, VT 05401-4405
USA

Ashgate website: http://www.ashgate.com

British Library Cataloguing in Publication Data
Cox, Noel
Technology and legal systems
1.Constitutional law 2.Technology and law
I.Title
342

Library of Congress Control Number: 2006922513

ISBN-10: 0 7546 4544 4
ISBN-13: 978 0 7546 4544 3

Printed and bound in Great Britain by TJ International Ltd,
Padstow, Cornwall

Contents

Preface

The twentieth century was one of the most profoundly significant in the recorded history of mankind. Although relatively few of the technological changes which occurred in the course of the century were revolutionary, per se, in that they changed the cultural paradigm in which they were set, taken as a whole the twentieth century saw more significant and widespread change than any previous century. Across political, economic, social, military, and technological fields the twentieth century saw enormous evolutionary and occasionally revolutionary shifts in paradigms.

One vital aspect of the societal construct which reflected and in part aided these developments was law. Individual laws encouraged, allowed, tolerated, or prescribed certain activities or undertakings. Laws, and the legal regimes or systems through which these operate, have had to change dramatically across many areas of human endeavour. New fields of legal regulation have developed in response to these changes. But law, because it is often prescriptive or regulatory, and because of the complex process through which it is developed or created, is not ideally suited to respond to profound changes, nor is it generally pro-active. This is especially so where the changes are unexpected or unanticipated, or their scope and nature is uncertain. Its ability to pre-empt change, or influence the direction of developments, is even more limited.

This limitation is particularly true of constitutional laws, which govern the law-making entities (generally sovereign states, but also including sub-state entities, and international legal entities), and the regimes through which specific substantive and procedural laws are made. These establish the frameworks in which the discourse proceeds, but challenges to the framework may come from paradigmatic changes to technologies, or the societies, or of the cultures which they serve.

This book is an attempt to integrate what has been for me a long-standing interest in constitutional law. This is done through identifying some of the dynamics which constrain and regulate the development of specific constitutional laws. Expressed another way, why does country A have a particular form of legislature, and country B does not? There are numerous studies of the constitutions of individual countries, and many comparative studies of constitutions and constitutional arrangements. One field which, it seemed to me, is ripe for exploration – and this book does not pretend to be anything more than a preliminary foray into the field – is the influence of technology upon legal systems (upon constitutions, if one prefers, though it is in reality rather broader than that). This is especially important today as the so-called knowledge revolution threatens – or so we are told by some – to undermine the pre-existing political, legal, and economic paradigms.

What I set out to achieve in this book – and which I hope I have succeeded in achieving, at least in part – is to show that this form of influence is neither new nor especially threatening. There have been many instances in the past when technology – either new technologies, or the new application of old technologies – have had profound effects upon nations. Some of these are relatively obvious (such as the advent of the printing press, or of gunpowder), while others may be less so, and are therefore more controversial. The controversy lies in the degree of influence, and in the degree to which the technology was influenced by the contemporary legal system, rather than vice versa.

If we accept that technology, however broadly defined, has been a profound influence upon legal systems, then we may use case studies of how this has happened in the past in order to identify some possible guidelines, principles or indicators for the nature of this influence in the future.

This book began as a research project undertaken while I was in residence as a visiting fellow at The Australian National University, Canberra. I wish to acknowledge the assistance of members of the Faculty of Law, and of the Law Programme of the Research School of Social Sciences, of The Australian National University, in particular Professor Peter Bailey, Professor Suzanne Corcoran, and Mr Daniel Stewart.

The remainder of the work was undertaken at the Auckland University of Technology, which (as its name suggests) has a particular interest in the implications of changing technology on law, business, society and government.

I would also like to thank the other scholars, commentators, reviewers and myriad other people who are inevitably involved to some degree in the production of any work of this sort. As always, any errors and omissions remain mine alone.

Noel Cox

Introduction

Any attempt to understand the structure of contemporary law and society cannot fail to consider the roles technological innovation and change play in the development of law, and in the relationship of law and society respectively. This influence extends to not merely the detail or minutiæ of the law, but also to what might be called the meta-structure of law and society, as well as to the constitution of a country. The latter term should be understood in this context to refer, not to a single written document, but to the complex amalgam of rules, regulations, conventions and practices which comprise the governing constitution of a country. A narrower definition would do a disservice to the inquiry, as we are here concerned with the dynamics of constitutionalism, not the narrow details of constitutions or of individual laws, however important they may otherwise be.

The constitution is a flexible and changing instrument, and the real constitution is not only created but also only fully known by its actors, those who take part in the day-to-day operation of its institutions. The differences in perception – and in aspirations – between these actors and the general public can be significant. A constitution does not have an objective existence, in that it is more than merely individuals and legal structures, particularly in respect of what might be called policy legacies. It exists in the imagination of those who create it, use it and thus know it. Thus the actions of politicians, judges and public servants – and even of members of the public – provide the key to understanding the constitution. This constitution provides a framework for governance, and in turn is the product of the society and environment in which it is based.

It is axiomatic that law is a product of society, indeed of the cultural inheritance, structures, norms, and economies of a specific society. This is true at both the domestic level, and at the regional, supra-national, and international levels (at which levels the specific societies are generally progressively more complex and less homogeneous). Law is also primarily organic in nature, and is not purely a conscious or deliberate coherent system of man-made rules. In general, analyses of law and society have tended to concentrate upon social and political influences within individual jurisdictions, or historical traditions. This is an almost inevitable consequence of the complexity of such studies and the difficulty of undertaking a comparative study which is not grounded in the cultural tradition of the author. The weakness here, if such it be, is that it is more difficult to perceive international, or generic, dynamics, than those of a single country.

Though the effect of technology upon society has been subject to a considerable amount of scholarly study, there has been comparatively little consideration of the generic influence of technology upon law, and in particular, upon legal norms, governance, and constitutions. This is especially unsatisfactory in light of the significant technological, economic, and social effects of technology, and particularly as a result of those changes occurring within the last 150 years. In recent years it has become necessary for law reformers and policy makers to take into account the affects of information technology, and the advent of the knowledge economy and knowledge society, upon the law, and upon legal and political processes. It is difficult enough ascertaining the legal implications of specific technological changes; it is quite another matter to appreciate the overall effect of technological change upon the political grundnorm. The information technology revolution has been lauded as profound and bringing in its wake a paradigmatic change. It is as yet too early to be certain of the importance of the information technology revolution, if indeed it should be styled a revolution, but it is likely to be significant.

However there is nothing especially new in technology influencing the development of law, or in law itself retarding, promoting, or otherwise influencing the development of technology. Indeed, these processes have occurred repeatedly throughout recorded history (and doubtless for as long as humans have known systems of laws, however primitive those systems might be), though certain periods may be categorized as being more changeful – and more juridical – than others. It would be inexplicable if laws did not influence technology and vice versa. Evolution is a process of steps (some of which may be sideways, or even backwards), whether that evolution is of the law, or of natural organisms.

The current international obsession with the 'information society', and with various aspects of globalization, indicates that this influence (of technology on law), while not novel, may be in some respects distinct from that in earlier eras. This may be so (though this is not certain), even if only in its comprehensiveness, both geographically and culturally. Thus, not only is much of the world almost simultaneously affected by the new technology, but this technology affects societies and economies at multiple levels. It is these latter respects – the breadth and depth of information technology – that seems to place the current technology revolution on a different level to previous technological revolutions, and may demand a broader approach to understand the dynamics of change, and thus the legal and policy implications.

The social conditions which constitute the conditions of a given society include political, cultural, economic, and technological influences. Separating these, or determining which (if any) may be pre-eminent at a given time, is a highly complex exercise. However, there is little doubt that technology has had a strong on-going influence on legal systems and constitutions, and upon the economic structure and operation of societies. This book seeks to explore some aspects of technology's relationship with law and government, and in particular the effects changing technology has had on constitutional structures and upon business.

Part I considers the legal normative influence of constitutional structures and political theories. This includes the rule of law, and legitimacy, both of which inhibit the freedom of action of political organs. The interrelationship between law and political entities in the constitution is dynamic and multi-directional, so that the substantive and procedural laws are the product of their context. This also means that these laws also influence the subsequent development of the constitution itself – in some cases in a form of self-fulfilling prophecy. Technology is also both inhibited and directed by these laws and by the constitutional systems in which they are embedded. But technology also affects the laws and the legal processes, especially when there are significant shifts of technological paradigms.

Part II concentrates upon the relationship of government and technology. The constitution – always here broadly defined – responds to significant shifts in technology. This may be reflected domestically, or through states' relationships with one another at a global level. Such changes are not of course new, and historical studies illustrate how technology has both shaped past civilizations and been the product of their political and constitutional environment.

In the twenty-first century the most significant new technologies – significant in their potential for constitutional change – are the information technologies, including telecommunications, and also genetic engineering. These are already having discernible affects upon laws, and their eventual affects upon legal systems may be predicted – with greater or lesser accuracy.

Technology must be contextualised within a constitution. As a human creation it is sensitive to the political and economic conditions of the time and location in which it is placed. But constitutions are equally influenced by their time and place, and by technology.

PART I
THE NATURE OF LAW AND TECHNOLOGY

Technology, and technological changes, affects the legal system. These effects are partly direct, and partly indirect. The former include those comparatively rare instances where the process or form of government is directly affected by technological change, or by the advent of new technology. A simple example would be the creation and introduction of electronic voting for use in political elections, which might have significant implications for the electoral process, and on political campaigning. Indirect effects are those which occur via changes to the economy and in society, and may well be very much more wide-ranging, if more difficult to identify and measure, than the direct effects. Technological changes are altering the relationship of governed and government, and between government and government, and between government and the world legal order. But these changes are neither new in nature, nor are the changes always clearly discernible.

Legal systems also affect the development of technology, and changes in legal systems (whether wrought by technological changes or otherwise) can have significant effects upon business. This part of the book discusses the nature of law and technology, and the general relationship between government and business, as a specific sector of society which can be particularly sensitive to technological change, and also itself a source of many of the technological changes.

Chapter 1

The Nature of Law and Government

1.1 Introduction

What is the relationship between law and government? How does law evolve, and how does government evolve? What are some of the influences upon this relationship? These are extremely broad questions which have taxed theorists in a number of academic disciplines, and across jurisdictions – as well as politicians and others more directly concerned with the application of theory to practice – for many centuries. This Chapter will not presume to attempt to directly answer these questions, but will consider some aspects of the relationship, particularly as it affects law, business and technology.

Let us start with a brief definition of law – one which is neither comprehensive nor necessarily valid for all purposes, but which will suffice for this limited purpose. Law may be defined as the procedural and substantive environment through which rights, wrongs and responsibilities are assigned, judged and enforced by some external agency.[1] Thus it may be seen as being at once an externally-imposed environmental element, within which individuals and communities must operate, and at the same time the internal product of that community – though the degree to which the individual and even communities influence the substance of the law may be strictly limited by various factors.[2] Generally these laws are created, and interpreted, and judgements are enforced, by some element of the government of a state. There are of course other forms of law, but for the purposes of this book we will confine ourselves to this more formal and narrow concept of law.

Having provided a definition of law with which to work, we will now consider how this relates to government. This analysis will be based upon a case study of an actual government, so as to illustrate some aspects of the dynamics of the relationship.

1.2 Government – a Case Study

Government is, in its loosest definition, merely that process or apparatus which governs a given political entity. This of course immediately involves consideration of such controversial and contentious concepts as territoriality and sovereignty. These concepts are especially important because they concern the relationship of state to state, and are not purely domestic or national in nature. They are thus particularly important when considering the development of technological changes which have a global reach – as, increasingly, many do.

The Montevideo Convention of 1933 is generally regarded as articulating the modern requirements for statehood. According to the requirements of this Convention (strictly binding only on the party states, but generally accepted since then as representative of customary international law), a state must have a permanent population; it must have a defined territory; it must have a government; and it must have the capacity to enter into diplomatic relations.[3] No other entity could be regarded as a state, whatever its *de facto* power. Leaderless populations or ethnic groups within states generally lacked sovereign status and, accordingly, the recognition and protection of public international law. However, having identified a given political entity as a state (and that may be a far from easy task, despite the apparent simplicity of the Montevideo requirements), much yet remains unsettled – primarily because there are few, if any, internationally valid norms of domestic law with respect to statehood. In other words, though a sovereign state may appear much the same externally, from within there are marked structural differences between one state and another.

The precise nature of the authority of a state within its own territory is not within the scope of international law, and is heavily influenced by the particular constitutional, political, historical, social and economic heritage of individual states. It is therefore difficult to generalize about the nature and form of government. However, there are certain common elements, at least among the modern legalistic entities which we call states. In earlier times, that is, before the advent of modern juridical states, there was a greater element of flexibility and consequently a lesser degree of similarity, in statehood.

We will consider one case study of a constitution (or constitutional structure), in order to show some aspects of the relationship between law and government. This example is New Zealand, which – almost uniquely – enjoys the advantages and disadvantages of an unwritten and unentrenched constitution. Its constitutional arrangements, and hence the relationship between law and government, are not controlled by what may be categorized as artificial constraints. They are rather the product of evolutionary political, social and economic forces which have been at work since 1840.[4] No other country offers the opportunity to study an organic constitution of this sort.

New Zealand has a constitution which contains what might appear at first glance to be a dichotomy. It is a democratic monarchy, with executive power (and elements of legislative and judicial authority) vested in the Sovereign – or Crown, as the entity which the Sovereign represents is styled. Yet it has a government responsible to Parliament and thence to the electorate. This arrangement, typical of the nineteenth century British genius for improvisation and compromise (or what has also been described as muddle and hypocrisy), seems to work despite – or perhaps because of – its apparent weakness in principle.

New Zealand statutes have tended to use the terms ‘Her Majesty the Queen’ and ‘the Crown’ interchangeably and apparently arbitrarily.[5] There appears to have been no intention to draw any theoretical or conceptual distinctions. This may simply be a reflection of a certain looseness of drafting, but it may have its foundation in a certain lack of certainty felt by legal draftsmen as much as by the general public.[6] 'The Crown' itself is a comparatively modern concept in Commonwealth jurisprudence. As Maitland said, the king was merely a man, though one who does many things.[7] For historical reasons the king or queen came to be recognized in law as not merely the chief source of the executive power, but also as the sole legal representative of the state or organized community.

According to Maitland, the crumbling of the feudal state threatened to break down the identification of the king and state, and as a consequence Coke recast the king as the legal representative of the state. It was Coke who first attributed legal personality to the Crown.[8] He recast the king as a corporation sole, permanent and metaphysical.[9]

The king's corporate identity[10] drew support from the doctrine of succession that held that the king never dies[11] – so that there might be no interregnum or lacuna of authority. It was also supported by the common law doctrine of seisin of land, where the heir was possessed at all times of a right to an estate even before succession.[12] Blackstone explained that the king:

> is made a corporation to prevent in general the possibility of an interregnum or vacancy of the throne, and to preserve the possessions of the Crown entire.[13]

Thus the role of the Crown was eminently practical. In the tradition of the common law constitutional theory was subsequently developed which rationalized and explained the existing practice – as, for example, in the development of the law of succession to the Crown.[14]

Generally, and in order to better conduct the business of government, the Crown was accorded certain privileges and immunities not available to any other legal entity.[15] Blackstone observed that '[t]he King is not only incapable of doing wrong, but even of thinking wrong; he can never mean to do an improper thing, in him is no folly or weakness'.[16] Mathieson has proffered the notion that the Crown may do whatever statute or the royal prerogative expressly or by implication authorizes, but that it lacks any natural capacities such as an individual or juridical entity may possess.[17]

In the course of the twentieth century the concept of the Crown has succeeded the king as the essential core of the corporation, which is now regarded as a corporation aggregate rather than a corporation sole.[18] In a series of cases in both the United Kingdom and New Zealand, we can see the courts struggling to categorize the nature of the Crown.[19]

In *Re Mason*[20] Romer J stated that it was established law that the Crown was a corporation, but did not indicate whether it was a corporation sole (as generally accepted) or a corporation aggregate (as Maitland argued). Maitland believed that the Crown, as distinct from the king, was anciently not known to the law but in modern usage had become the head of a 'complex and highly organized "corporation aggregate of many" – of very many'.[21] In *Adams v Naylor*,[22] the House of Lords adopted Maitland's legal conception of the Crown.[23]

Although the House of Lords in 1977, in *Town Investments v Department of the Environment*,[24] accepted that the Crown did have legal personality, it also adopted the potentially confusing practice of speaking of actions of the executive as being performed by 'the government' rather than 'the Crown'.[25] The practical need for this distinction is avoided if one recognizes the aggregate nature of the Crown.[26] 'The government' is something which, unlike the Crown, has no corporate or juridical existence known to the constitution. Further, its legal definition is both legally and practically unnecessary.

In *Town Investments*[27] Lord Simon, with little argument, accepted that the Crown was a corporation aggregate, as Maitland had believed. This appears to be in accordance with the realities of the modern state, although it was contrary to the traditional view of the Crown. Thus, the Crown is now seen, legally, as a nexus of rights and privileges, exercised by a number of individuals, officials and departments, all called 'the Crown'.

More recently, in *M v Home Office*,[28] the English Court of Appeal held that the Crown lacked legal personality and was therefore not amenable to contempt of court proceedings.[29] But it is precisely because in the Westminster-style political system we do not have the Continental notion of a state, nor an entrenched constitution,[30] that the concept of the Crown as a legal entity with full powers in its own right arose. *Town Investments* must in any event be regarded as the definitive statement of current English law.

The development of the concept of the aggregate Crown from the corporate Crown provides sufficient flexibility to accommodate the reality of government, without the need for abandoning an essential legal grundnorm[31] in favour of a very undeveloped and inherently vague concept of 'the government'.[32] Thus, for reasons principally of convenience, the Crown became an umbrella beneath which the business of government was conducted.

The Crown has always operated through a series of servants and agents, some more permanent than others. The law recognizes the Crown as the body in whom the executive authority of the country is vested, and by which the business of executive government is exercised.

Whether New Zealand has a Crown aggregate or corporate, the government is formally that of the Sovereign,[33] and the Crown has the place in administration held by the state in other – principally civil law – legal traditions. The Crown, whether or not there is a resident Sovereign, acts as the legal umbrella under which the various activities of government are conducted, and with whom, in the specifically New Zealand context, the indigenous Maori people may negotiate as treaty partner with the Crown.[34] Indeed, the very absence of the Sovereign has encouraged this modern tendency for the Crown to be regarded as a concept of government quite distinct from the person of the Sovereign.[35]

The monarchy does, however, have a role beyond the symbolic. In his analysis of the British Crown in his own day (1865), Bagehot seriously underestimated its surviving influence.[36] His famous aphorism, that a constitutional Sovereign has the right to be consulted, to encourage, and to warn,[37] can hardly express the residual royal powers of even the late nineteenth century.[38] It may describe the royal powers today – in the United Kingdom if not the overseas realms of Queen Elizabeth II – but does not explain why the inherited concept of the supremacy of the Crown should leave the constitution apparently centred upon an institution lacking real power.

But Bagehot, like Palmerston and Gladstone, wanted the monarchy relegated to the status of a museum piece, despite the Sovereign‘s ‘right to be consulted, to encourage, and to warn’.[39] This passive role was not that envisaged by George IV, William IV, Victoria or Edward VII (though the latter's sons and granddaughter were each to later study Bagehot in their schooldays), nor that held by the majority of statesmen and text-book writers over this period. They felt that the Sovereign's role as head of state in a popular parliamentary system had still to be satisfactorily defined, and might well be rather wider than that assigned to it by Bagehot.[40]

Dicey and Anson, the leading authorities of their own day, were inclined to advocate a stretching of the royal discretion (or rather to acknowledge a broader discretion than Bagehot had done), and, to some extent at least, the monarchy ostensibly operated at a political level under Edward VII in much the same way as it did under George IV.[41] But there had been a clear change in the basis of royal authority. This was now almost totally dependent upon parliamentary support. But there has been no study which offers evidence to show that the exercise by the Crown of the rights to be consulted, to encourage, and to warn, has influenced the course of policy.[42]

The Crown is more than just the mechanism through which government is administered. It is also itself one of the sources of governmental authority, as a traditional source of legal sovereignty. Not only is government conducted through the Crown (as discussed above), but some governmental authority is derived from the Crown as the legal focus of sovereignty.

‘Sovereignty’ put simply, is the idea that there is a ‘final authority within a given territory’.[43] Foucault identified four possible descriptions of the traditional role of sovereignty:

(i) to describe a mechanism of power in feudal society;
(ii) as a justification for the construction of large-scale administrative monarchies;
(iii) as an ideology used by one side or the other in the seventeenth century wars of religion; and
(iv) in the construction of parliamentary alternatives to the absolutist monarchies.[44]

Whatever rationale applied to the embryonic English Crown, the old theory of sovereignty has been democratized since the nineteenth century into a notion of collective sovereignty, exercised through parliamentary institutions. The fundamental responsibility for the maintenance of society itself is much more widely dispersed throughout its varied institutions and the whole population. To some degree this equates to the concept of the aggregate Crown favoured by the more recent jurists.[45]

But the concept of sovereignty, however understood, is especially important because it has become part of the language of claims by indigenous people, as in New Zealand, where Maori claims are based on the conflicting concept of *tino rangatiratanga*, or chiefly authority.[46] The particular problems this causes in New Zealand are that it represents the claims of an antecedent regime to juridical survival despite apparently ceding sovereignty to the Crown in the Treaty of Waitangi in 1840. Indeed, it is significant that most talk of 'sovereignty' in the second half of the twentieth century concentrated upon the sovereignty of racial groups, and particularly, the so-called indigenous peoples.[47]

Sovereignty has assumed different meanings and attributes according to the conditions of time and place, but at a basic level it requires obedience from its subjects and denies a concurrent authority to any other body.[48] In New Zealand, the Sovereign is responsible for the executive government, and indeed is specifically so appointed by the Constitutions of most Commonwealth countries of which Her Majesty is head of state.[49]

It will be immediately apparent that there is a divergence between abstract law and political reality, for substantial political power lies in politicians rather than the Sovereign. Political orthodoxy also appears to hold that for a constitution to be legitimate it must derive from the people. Yet, our constitution is not apparently based legally on the sovereignty of the people, but rather on that of the Queen-in-Parliament.

In the Westminster tradition, it is Parliament, in contrast to the Crown, which is widely regarded as being the focus of political power.[50] Joseph assumes therefore that it is the people rather than Parliament who is sovereign.[51] But it would seem that sovereign authority is legally vested in the Crown-in-Parliament, politically in the people.[52] Legally, this can be seen as less than ideal, or even confused. However, a constitution is more than merely a legal structure.[53]

The authority of government is based upon several sources. Even were authority legally derived from the people, as it appears to now be in Australia,[54] it is not clear how the position of the Maori can be reconciled,[55] in particular, the preservation of their *tino rangatiratanga*, or chiefly authority. For the Maori retained for themselves at least some degree of political power under the Treaty of Waitangi, power which has its origins in traditional sources rather than the popular will. The Crown also claims some degree of authority based upon traditional sources, including mystique and continuity.[56]

The origins and nature of constitutional authority, whether in a monarchy or a republic, are important. But although a formal constitution can say, as does that of Papua New Guinea, that it is derived from the popular sovereignty of the people,[57] this may be confusing legal authority with political authority.[58] Where the Crown exists, and no formal entrenched Constitution has been adopted, difficult questions of the basis of governmental authority can be avoided.

There has been to date comparatively little theoretical analysis of the conceptual basis of governmental authority in countries with informal constitutions such as New Zealand.[59] There has been much discussion focused on the legitimacy of government derived from written constitutions, and in New Zealand, from the Treaty of Waitangi[60] – since it is a written document of apparent if not formal legal authority. But there has been little work done towards an understanding of the nature of governmental authority in New Zealand, except by those who argue that there is too much (or too little) involvement of government in individual lives.[61] This dearth of work may be due to apathy,[62] but it could also be influenced by an underlying suspicion of abstract theory which can be traced in British tradition of political thought from the seventeenth century, if not earlier.[63]

In Canada, in contrast, there have been several major studies of the conceptual basis of government. In particular, in 1985 the Law Reform Commission of Canada released a working paper which called for a re-examination of the concept of the Federal Crown in Canadian law.[64] The working paper called for the recognition of a unitary federal administration in place of the legal concept of the Crown.[65] The paper specifically asked:

> to what extent should Canada retain the concept of the Crown in federal law? Should we replace the concept of Crown with the concept of State or federal administration?

The Commission briefly described what it termed the chaotic and confusing historical treatment of 'the Crown' in English and Canadian law. Historical inconsistencies and contradictions in the treatment of the concept of the Crown cannot and need not be rationalized. Judges, legislators, and writers are not always talking about the same thing. They may mean the Sovereign herself, the institution of royal power, the concept of sovereignty, the constitutional head of state, judicial instructions, or actors.[66]

To recognize the political reality the authors of the working paper suggested that the concept of the Crown should be abolished, and the Sovereign relegated to the status of constitutional head of state.[67] Discarding monarchical terminology and limiting the Crown to its purely formal role would, in the opinion of the Commission 'reduce terminological confusion, historical biases, and anti-democratic and non-egalitarian concepts so far as they affect individuals in the relationships between bureaucrats and the majority'.[68] The Crown would be replaced by the 'administration'. The authors of the working paper wanted to recognize the executive branch of the state.[69] The legal nature of the Crown or state in Canada has also been considered by others,[70] but the issue is not yet settled.[71]

Cohen believed that the methodology of the working paper itself was flawed because it focused on theoretical and abstract analyses of the state.[72] Essentially, the difficulty is that there is no developed concept of the state or nation in Commonwealth constitutional theory.[73] Moore attributes this to parliamentarian mistrust inspired by the association between civil law and Baconian theory.[74] But it is equally true that modern theoretical studies of the state have been limited even in Continental Europe.[75]

In New Zealand executive authority is also, like that of Canada, formally vested in the Crown.[76] The government does not require parliamentary approval for most administrative actions; nor need it show popular approval or consent for these actions – though the rule of law, a long tradition of political restraint, political expediency, and the strictly limited range of powers held by the Crown, prevent authoritarian Crown government.[77]

The executive authority of a country could be vested in a president, the Governor-General, or the Queen irrespective of the basis of sovereignty. But in the constitutional arrangements of New Zealand the principal if not indeed the sole focus of legal authority is the Crown-in-Parliament (there remains some debate over the role of the indigenous Maori people). This institution enjoys full legal sovereignty or supremacy. The Crown itself is allocated executive functions, and, within a limited field, requires no other legal authority than its own prerogative.[78]

This approach has the advantage of simplicity, leaving broader questions of sovereignty unanswered.[79] As such it owes much to the British tradition of a constitution as something which evolves, and for which theory is sometimes developed subsequent to the practice.[80] One aspect of this paucity of theory, if it may be so called, is the weakness – or absence – of a general theory of the state.[81]

In Canada, problems with the place of the French-speaking minority, and the federal nature of the country, meant that difficult questions of the location and nature of governmental authority had to be addressed. Thus, claims by Quebec for special status within the federation required an analysis of the nature of power exercised by federal and provincial governments. The existence of an entrenched constitution also meant that this could substitute for the Crown, as in the United States of America, as a conceptual focus of government.

Clarke argues that in Canada the marriage of the parliamentary form of government to the federal principle makes the determination of legislative authority problematic, at least in part, because it fails to develop an adequate conceptualization of sovereignty. In the absence of a better understanding authority is described merely in terms of a division of power.[82]

There have been neither technical nor practical reasons for these difficult questions of the sources of governmental authority to be answered in New Zealand. To some extent, the asking of such questions was also avoided.[83] Thus, the existence of the Crown, whilst providing a convenient legal source for executive government, has also acted as an inhibitor of abstract constitutional theorizing. As a consequence, in Laski's view, the Crown covered a 'multitude of sins'.[84] Whilst this might not be desirable, it provides a convenient and pragmatic cover behind which the business of government is conducted, unworried by conceptual difficulties.

The principal reason why the Crown has been regarded in New Zealand as a legal source of executive authority is historical. Not only is the Crown a source of legal authority, it serves to personify the political community. Thus the legal role of the Crown is important at three conceptual levels. First, and most fundamentally, it is a metonym for state. Secondly, it is a source of legal authority. Third, it is the means through which government is conducted. In most political systems the executive power and the state are synonymous.[85] The state may be classified as that which refers to some or all of the legal administrative or legislative institutions operating in a community.[86] In the British system, and those derived from it,[87] it is questionable whether there is a state, at least as a formal constitutional entity or concept. Most legal commentators had traditionally given it little treatment, or simply answered in the negative. Political scientists considered the question from a different perspective, though not one which is necessarily any more complete.[88] These differing approaches to understanding the constitution are rooted in the different constitutional histories of countries. There was a common element to many, especially in Europe, but experiences were not identical, and affected the relationship of law and government.

The character of communities in the central Middle Ages was rooted and grounded in older traditions than those created by the study of Roman and canon law, which was the basis for much later conceptualizations of the state in continental Europe.[89] Nor did the rediscovery of Aristotle by western scholars, the development of modern government,[90] or demographic and economic changes significantly affect them. The traditional bonds of community owed much to ties of kinship, much to loyalties of war-bands, very much to Christianity, and perhaps most strongly, from legal practices and values.[91] In these communities the king was representative of the people, to whom his people owed allegiance, and who, in turn, was held responsible for the government of a nation.[92]

Hobbes, with Bodin, Machiavelli, and Hegel did much to stimulate European state theory, a theory which had not been fully reconsidered in the context of the British constitution since Hobbes and his contemporaries, though recent work has sought to correct this imbalance. Hobbes' *Leviathan* (1651) was perhaps the greatest piece of political philosophy written in the English language. Like Machiavelli's *The Prince* (1532), it offered a dramatic break with the usual apologies for the Christian feudal state of the Middle Ages.

The modern territorial state, the concept of political absolutism, and the principle of *quod principi placuit, legis nabet vigorem*[93] spelled the end of the mediæval nexus of rights and duties, counterbalanced powers, and customs. Hobbes excluded religion as a source of morality, and based ethical values, as well as political theory, on the human impulse toward self-preservation.[94] The reality of early modern government throughout Europe was that it was essentially driven by political realists or pragmatists, who sought the centralization of power for the good of the country.[95]

Since the modern states inherited the papal (and imperial) prerogative, it must, then, govern all within the geographical confines of the country. Speculation in France was centred on a sovereign state with a royal organ to declare its sovereign purposes. This regime collapsed because in eighteenth century France the political and social atmosphere was similar to that which caused such profound changes in

England a century earlier, and the unity of the state failed when the strain proved too much for one institution to survive.

Inspired by the political changes in England, and in part directed by the theories of such as Rousseau[96] and Montesquieu,[97] the French people had become the masters of the state. This example was followed elsewhere in the course of the nineteenth century, though usually with less overt violence.[98]

However, for two interrelated reasons, the state never became a legal concept in English law. Most countries have a date at which they can be said to have begun their constitutional existence, but not the United Kingdom.[99] The need to create (or recreate) a concept of the state has not been generally felt since 1688,[100] and even then the feeling was half-hearted.[101] Nor was there a general reception of the Roman civil law, with its concept of the state. The common law, through common law courts and judges, was always happier developing theories to describe the realities of the law, rather than moulding the law around abstract theories.[102] 'The supreme executive power of this kingdom', as Blackstone knew, was vested in the king;[103] and there the matter was allowed to rest.

As a consequence of this jurisprudential weakness, if it can be so called, there had been in the Commonwealth (excepting perhaps in Canada) comparatively little thought given to theories of the structure of the state. In particular, there had been little consideration of the theory of government in New Zealand beyond questions of 'state responsibility', and the proper role of the state.[104] Yet, the history of this country, and in particular, the existence of the Treaty of Waitangi, makes this a curious deficiency.[105]

Since the 1980s, however, there has been more consideration given in New Zealand to the more abstract notions of governmental authority.[106] Inspired by the predominantly neo-liberal market-economy reforms initiated by the 1984 Labour Government,[107] commentators saw a resurgence of the state as a subject worthy of serious study.[108] In the writings of Mulgan[109] and Sharp,[110] for example, are seen the formulation of new conceptions of the state – though not ones which necessarily have much direct influence on politicians or the general public. The disputes between neoliberals,[111] pluralists,[112] feminists,[113] Marxists[114] and others in the 1980s and 1990s[115] have however begun a process towards developing a comprehensive theory of government.

Few of these studies have considered the Crown as an entity of government, let alone a pivotal one. The ideological dominance of neo-liberalism may be in part responsible for this, for whatever its advantages and disadvantages, neo-liberalism is largely ahistorical. Pluralism, at least in its classical form, considers more fully the historical evolution of governmental institutions,[116] and this is critical to an understanding of a political construct like the Crown.

Jacob has postulated that the notion of the state has now begun to evolve in the United Kingdom, as a consequence of the development of public law in place of an emphasis on Crown immunities. His thesis is that since the Franks Report and the consequent Tribunals and Inquiries Act 1958 (United Kingdom), judicial activism has developed an embryonic state.[117] This has been due, so his argument goes, to the increasingly common platform between those politicians who desired to 'roll back the frontiers of the state',[118] or at least placed their emphasis on individual rights, and the attitude of judges asserting the inherent power of the common law. It was not fashioned out of a desire for centralized power. It was, according to Jacob, both judicially and politically created in order to limit it.[119]

Modern Anglo-American constitutional theory is preoccupied with the problem of devising means for the protection and enhancement of individual rights in a manner consistent with the democratic basis of our institutions. In the United Kingdom the focus is on the need for, or the advisability of, imposing restraints on the legislative sovereignty of Parliament – though this latter concept has suffered significantly from the devolution of power in the United Kingdom.[120]

But it would be precipitate to claim the development of a state has been universally accepted in either New Zealand or the United Kingdom. More in keeping with the tradition of historical development found in those two countries[121] would be an acceptance of the evolution of a new form of aggregate Crown, one in which the distinction between person and office is increasingly great.[122]

Allegedly right-wing elements in New Zealand opposed the use of the term 'state', and sought alternatives, such as the pre-existing concept of the Crown, not because of any attachment to monarchy, but because of opposition to anything evocative of interventionist government.[123] In part because of the neo-liberal attempt to 'roll back the state', there was also a corresponding weakening of the legal status of the Crown in late twentieth century New Zealand.[124] However, there has been some work done on the Crown in its continuing important role as signatory of the Treaty of Waitangi, some of which has led to tentative discussion of concepts of government.[125] It is in this symbolic role that the modern function of the Crown appears to lie.

It may be that the Sovereign lacks personal power, but the organs of royal government, whether they are Ministers or departments, enjoy the benefit of the residual power of the Crown, as an institution in which the *maiestas* of law and government is vested. This institution is more important than the person of the Sovereign.[126] The Crown can be seen as a living thing, personified by the Queen and the Governor-General, and distinct from any obscure concept of governmental state. This was the basis of Bagehot's analysis of the British constitution,[127] and it remains important in New Zealand today. The exact definition of the Crown may at times be uncertain, but it has the advantage over the state of being the structure of government which is actually utilized in New Zealand, and therefore somewhat better known, if not well understood.

In both Canada and Australia the existence of entrenched constitutions have resulted in at least a partial shifting of emphasis from the Crown to the entrenched written constitution. Indeed, revolutionary necessity required this in the United States more than two hundred years ago. But the technical and legal concept of the Crown continues to pervade the apparatus of government and law in New Zealand.

No new generally accepted theory of government has been postulated in New Zealand, nor would such a project be likely to attract the attention which it deserves. In so far as such matters have been considered, the focus has been on the sovereignty, or supremacy of Parliament, and the possibility that there may be limits to such sovereignty.[128] For Dicey, sovereignty of Parliament was matched by the rule of law, or supremacy of law.[129]

Political sovereignty may lie in practice with the people,[130] but legally this is less certain,[131] though legitimacy derives principally from the people. Indeed, as a constitution characterized by its uncodified (or 'unwritten') nature, the New Zealand constitution cannot be anything but a traditional evolutionary Burkean type.[132] Yet, whether this remains the basis of the constitution in New Zealand is uncertain, for two major reasons.

First, the non-Maori population seems, by and large, influenced by basically Lockean ideas of government as a direct compact.[133] Though they may not directly question the basis of governmental authority, the possibility of such questioning in the future cannot be discounted. This is particularly so because of the impetus to reform given by the introduction of a system of proportional voting in 1996.[134]

By contrast, Maori tend to see government, and society, in more evolutionary terms.[135] Most importantly, however, claims to Maori sovereignty do not rest upon claims to popular sovereignty as such, but upon the cession, or non-cession, of kawanatanga and *tino rangatiratanga* to the Crown in 1840. The sovereignty of the Crown, in the context of the Treaty of Waitangi, is more than merely a legal doctrine; it has a continuing political relevance. Merely redefining the location of sovereignty as the people, a reconstituted Parliament, or a president, would not necessarily satisfy the other party to the Treaty, for it would constitute the removal of one party to the Treaty.[136] The difficult task of determining what constitutional structures will satisfy both perspectives remains.[137] This task may not be urgent.

It might be said that there are two constitutional imperatives in a democratic country, the government's legitimacy, and its continuity. Its continuity can be seen in institutional continuity. In the words of a former Governor-General of New Zealand, 'continuity of government is more than usually important in New Zealand, because our nation was founded when the Treaty of Waitangi was signed'.[138] This continuity is also symbolized by the descent of the Crown through generations of hereditary Sovereigns, from the original party to the Treaty, Queen Victoria.[139] This continuity is an important aspect to the legitimacy of the Crown, not simply in New Zealand.

Legitimacy is a more supple and inclusive idea than sovereignty, or of continuity.[140] Legitimacy offers reasons why a given state deserves the allegiance of its members. Weber identifies three bases for this authority – traditions and customs; legal-rational procedures (such as voting); and individual charisma.[141] Some combination of these can be found in most political systems – and often all three.

With the dominance of democratic concepts of government, it might be thought that if the people believe that an institution is appropriate, then it is legitimate.[142] In other words, the structure influences the process, which determines the substance – and vice versa. But this scheme leaves out substantive questions about the justice of the state and the protection it offers the individuals who belong to it.[143] It is generally more usual to maintain that a state's legitimacy depends upon its upholding certain human rights.[144]

Three current alternative definitions of legitimacy are firstly, that it involves the capacity of the system to engender and maintain the belief that the existing political institutions are the most appropriate ones for the society.[145] Second, in the tradition of Weber, legitimacy has been defined as 'the degree to which institutions are valued for themselves and considered right and proper'.[146] Third, political legitimacy may be defined as the degree of public perception that a regime is morally proper for a society.[147]

Whichever definition is preferred, all are based on belief or opinion, unlike the older traditional definitions which revolved around the element of law or right.[148] These traditional concepts of legitimacy were built upon foundations external to and independent of the mere assertion or opinion of the claimant.[149] These normative or legal definitions included laws of inheritance, and laws of logic. Sources for these included immemorial custom, divine law, the law of nature, or a constitution.[150]

Legitimacy is sought through the advancing and acceptance of a political formula, a metaphysical or ideological formula that justifies the existing exercise or proposed possession of power by rulers as the logical and necessary consequence of the beliefs of the people over whom the power is exercised.[151] Just what this formula is depends upon the history and composition of a country.

In modern democratic societies, popular elections confer legitimacy upon governments. But legitimacy can also be independent of the mere assertion or opinion of the claimant. This has been particularly important in late twentieth century discussion of indigenous rights.[152]

There is a tendency to undervalue the Crown, because its legitimacy is regarded as of minimal significance compared with that derived from the ballot box. But, in the view of observers such as Smith and Birch, the most important of the defects of the liberal political model of the Westminster-type constitution – the view of the political theorist rather than the lawyer or politician, is its failure to depict the role of the Crown in the system of government, and the implications of the interrelated independence of the executive.[153]

The legitimacy of the Crown includes that owed to the established regime. While the modern democratic ethos might regard such a basis of authority as weak, it does have its value. In Tuvalu respect for the Crown was regarded as instilling a high sense of respect for whoever was occupying the position of Governor-General, not so much because of the incumbent but rather for the durability of a system which had stood the test of time.[154]

The Crown itself provides some governmental legitimacy, simply because it is a permanent manifestation of authority, a proto-state as some would argue.[155] Smith has suggested that in Canada the Crown provides the necessary underlying structure for government. This is equally true in New Zealand, arguably even more so, since there is no entrenched written Constitution upon which constitutional or political thought may focus.[156] Although electoral support might suffice for much of the legitimacy of government, this is reinforced by the historical continuity of the Crown, particularly in respect of the Treaty of Waitangi, but also as the principal apparatus of government which dates from 1840 – and (more importantly) – for much longer.

In contrast to a common political theorists' view – which concentrates upon the political actors[157] – official terminology (the view of the administrator) had in the past tended to emphasize the importance of the Crown. Thus the formal role played by the Sovereign in Parliament conveys a totally different view to that played by the political realist. It is arguably even more inaccurate, as the Sovereign's legislative role has been largely nominal for three hundred years.

According to Barker, the principal function of the theory of the Crown is to provide a legal person who can act in the courts, to whom public servants may owe and own allegiance, and who may act in all those exercises of authority, such as the making of treaties or the declaration of war, which do not rest upon the legislative supremacy of Parliament.[158] In this view, and in the United Kingdom at least, the legitimacy involved here is quite independent of any popular authorization, and the idea of the Crown as a legitimizing principle is articulated and employed within the personnel of government, but little outside.

Much of the legal basis of executive power derives from the Crown,[159] though for political reasons this has not been emphasized. Indeed, in the Commonwealth political independence has often been equated with the reduction of the Crown to a position of subservience to the political executive.[160] What remains important is the position of the Crown as an organizing principle of government (the framework upon which the structure of government is built[161]), as a source of legitimacy, and as a symbol.

The popular conception of the Crown was often as uncertain as that of the theorists, but tended to focus more on the person of the Sovereign, rather than on the legal institution. This is, of course, precisely what Bagehot meant when he wrote that it was easier to conceive of an individual or family rather than a constitution.[162]

The extent to which contemporary democratic political systems are legitimate depends in large measure upon the ways in which the key issues which have historically divided the society have been resolved. Not only can regimes gain legitimacy, but they can lose it also.[163]

As symbolic of the permanent apparatus of government, the Crown represents constitutional continuity and legitimacy. The Crown can exercise powers not specifically conferred upon it to preserve constitutional order.[164] But time, and fresh elections, can confer new legitimacy upon usurpers.[165]

If a regime is both legitimate and effective (in the sense of achieving constant economic growth), it will be a stable political system. From a short-range point of view, a highly effective but illegitimate system is more unstable than regimes which are relatively low in effectiveness, and high in legitimacy.[166] Prolonged effectiveness can give legitimacy.[167] Yet legitimacy cannot be determined solely by majoritarian principles alone, though democratic states tend to emphasize this aspect of their authority.[168]

In normal times it may be hard to distinguish feelings about legitimacy from routine acquiescence. But it has been often said that legitimate authority is declining in the modern state, and all modern states are well advanced along a path towards a crisis of legitimacy.[169] Obedience looks more like a matter of lingering habit, or expediency, or necessity, but no longer a matter of reason and principle, and of deepest sentiment and conviction.[170]

One main source of legitimacy lies in the continuity of important traditional integrative institutions during a transitional period in which new institutions are emerging.[171] This applies equally where there is a re-alignment of power, as in the development of responsible government, or the granting of economic or political benefits to certain sectors of society, in the New Zealand context, Maori.

Crises of legitimacy occur during a transition to a new social structure, if the status of major established institutions is threatened during the period of structural change, and all the major groups in the society do not have access to the political system in the transitional period, or at least as soon as they develop political demands.[172] These transitional periods occur when for example decolonization takes place without a nationalist struggle, and where interstate conflict is absent – in other words, when a colonial power freely confers independence upon a colony.[173]

A crisis of legitimacy is afflicting all countries whose origins lie in colonial conquest and settlement. This is due in part to the justification for colonialization being largely discredited. As Mulgan has observed, the critical issue posed by the anti-colonial critique and revisionist history is whether a society and government founded in illegitimate conquest can ever hope to acquire legitimacy.[174]

Challenges to legitimacy from claims for Maori sovereignty are a more serious question than any dangers of authoritarian rule. Ironically, the former may serve to strengthen the case for royal legitimacy, because of the link between Crown and Maori in the Treaty of Waitangi.[175] Brookfield has considered this relationship, and concluded that one and a half centuries of government may have been at least partly legitimated through this relationship.[176]

A more serious challenge to continued legitimacy comes from the changing popular perceptions of government. A regime which was once legitimate, in that the popular perception was that it was the proper government for that country, can potentially become illegitimate. This might be because it ceases to follow the principles of the rule of law, or otherwise departs from the accepted conduct.[177] Or, it might be because doubts arise over the suitability or appropriateness of the particular form of government.[178] In this later case however, dissatisfaction should lead to legal change, not violent change. Only if justifiable attempts at change are unjustly blocked would more extreme measures be justified.[179]

Such a situation would be unlikely, as a lack of popular (or political) support would result in positive steps being taken to adopt a republican form of government, as in Tuvalu. However, those Maori who reject the authority of the

Crown might well argue that already the Crown lacks legitimacy, because it lacks legal title, since (in this argument) the Treaty of Waitangi did not confer sovereignty, only an uncertain form of oversight.[180]

The authority of the regime in New Zealand is based, at least in part, upon the assumption of legal sovereignty by the British Crown and Parliament in the middle of the nineteenth century. But clearly legitimacy based upon an act of state by the United Kingdom in 1840 is insufficient of itself to be a basis for modern governmental legitimacy. This authority has been called into question, in particular by those who claim that Maori sovereignty survives, or ought to be re-established.[181]

Whether the present regime can be called illegitimate depends upon one's perspective, and the weight which one attaches to European political and legal concepts of authority. As Hayward has said:

> [T]he Treaty of Waitangi is a fundamental document in New Zealand, because it allowed for the settlement by Pakeha and the establishment of legitimate government by cession (as opposed to by military conquest).[182]

Yet this is only partly true, for legally, the acquisition of sovereignty, and the settlement of this country by Europeans, can be ascribed (in traditional European terms) to an act of state,[183] though one which was made conditional upon the agreement of the indigenous inhabitants of the islands.

The authority of the Crown was legally imposed by Governor William Hobson by proclamation of 21 May 1840, under authority vested in him by the British Government.[184] But this was based to some degree, morally at least, on the Treaty of Waitangi. However, the Maori version of the Treaty gave rather less authority to the Crown than did the English-language version, and retained rather more for the Maori chiefs. Nor did all the chiefs sign the Treaty.

The post-1840 evolution of Maori–Pakeha [indigenous people–European settler population] relations has been at times difficult. But, even in terms of European legalism, the evolution of the constitution since 1840 has presented problems for its legitimacy. The Crown of the United Kingdom having assumed sovereignty over New Zealand by an act of state or cession, the United Kingdom Parliament never formally renounced power to legislate for New Zealand,[185] nor did New Zealand legislate to end this power until 1986. This was due rather to inertia than to any lingering sentiment of imperial unity.[186]

Where a constitution is established by a revolutionary break in the line of authority, it may be easier to see the new regime as autochthonous[187] – and its legitimacy based upon an expression of popular will. This is less easy to see in cases where there has been no legal break, though Wade believed that this continuity was merely 'window-dressing for a revolutionary shift in power'.[188] If New Zealand has a legal legitimacy separate from that of the United Kingdom, it is not clear when this occurred. This is particularly so in respect of the Crown, which is less readily distinguishable than the respective Parliaments of the United

Kingdom and of New Zealand. Yet it would appear that such concerns have not proven significant, as the Crown developed distinct identities in the course of the twentieth century.[189]

While the acquisition of power may be legitimated by treaty or similar action, its subsequent conduct must also conform to appropriate standards to maintain that legitimacy. This constitutional principle – that of the rule of law – is based upon the practice of liberal democracies of the Western world.[190] It means that what is done officially must be done in accordance with law.[191] In Europe, where an entrenched Constitution is widely regarded as the touchstone for the legitimacy of government,[192] there might be a general grant of power to the executive, and a bill of rights to protect the individual. In the British tradition public authorities must point to a specific authority to act as they do.[193] The state sees itself as the source of both law and power. Instead of law, legality prevails.[194] Thus the emphasis lay on formal objective laws rather than subjective justice. Procedure rather than substance dominates.

The notion of the rule of law is important in the concept of the Crown because the Crown, as a concept, forms a constitutional model, a proto-state. This 'Crown in Treaty' derives at once political legitimacy in a post-colonial environment, as well as technical authority, both prerogative and otherwise.[195] The executive government cannot act except with some identifiable authority, which is derived, in this model, at least in part from the Treaty of Waitangi.

It may be seen, at least in a state untainted by an entrenched constitution or a developed public law, that the constitution is very much a product of the historical, political and cultural environment of the country. The legal system of which the constitution is a reflection is both evolutionary and subject to the influence of the contemporary environment in which it is located. Yet the constitution is also playing a significant role in forming a framework which determines the practical limitations which are imposed on the development of specific law and policies. As Foucault might have argued, the pre-existing constitutional structure imposes controls upon the social and political discourse – and the social and political environment itself affects the constitutional discourse.

1.3 The Rule of Law

Much of the legitimacy of a political system derives from the impartiality and objectivity with which it is administered.[196] Thus the very exercise of authority legitimates that authority.

Dicey defined rule of law to encompass the liberty of the individual, equality before the law, and freedom from arbitrary government.[197] The scope of the concept is however rather fluid. As Joseph observed, it includes such meanings as government according to law; the adjudicative ideal of common law jurisdictions; and a minimum of state intervention and administrative power. It also includes the need for fixed and predictable rules of law controlling government action;

standards of common decency and fair play in public life; and the 'fullest possible provision by the community of the conditions that enable the individual to develop into a morally and intellectually responsible person'. It includes the principles of freedom, equality, and democracy.[198] Most writers now distance themselves from Dicey, and believe that his ideas of the rule of law should be subject to reappraisal,[199] as being too broad and insufficiently nuanced.

The rule of law is symbolic. It is a transcendent phenomenon in that it is almost always shorthand for some interpretation of the inner meaning of a polity. It is highly connotative. In the fifteenth century it meant that the king was always subordinate to a higher law of somewhat uncertain provenance. After the 1688 Revolution, it became clearly associated with the idea of a Lockean ideal state. The old idea of the unity of the state dominated till the classical liberal tradition overtook the older habit of mind in the eighteenth and nineteenth centuries. The post-Lockean version of the rule of law was associated with the views of the classical liberal theorists, who combined the concepts of legitimacy, legality and legal autonomy.[200] The rule of law was used by the Whigs to confer legitimacy upon their dominance of politics during the eighteenth and nineteenth centuries.

If the rule of law means an absence of arbitrary power, then, as was inherent in the mediæval concept of government, the law, whether human or divine, was pre-eminent. King James I, in *The Trew Law of Free Monarchies* (1598)[201] and the *Basilikon Doron* (1599)[202] outlined a fairly simple assertion of divine right kingship. Legal authority, though vested in the king as it always had been, was founded on long-established religious principles.

Theories of divine right were outlined by writers such as Sir Robert Filmer in *Patriarcha* (1680).[203] Hobbes and Filmer argued that the will is the source of all law and the form of all authority. They believed in the necessity of a perpetual and absolute submission to the arbitrary dictates of an indivisible sovereign, and in the impossibility of mixed government (or pluralism). They were criticized by Whig theorists of contract such as Sidney and Locke. It would seem that Locke wrote his *Two Treatises of Government* to refute Filmer rather than Hobbes. Hobbes was politically the least important of the absolutist writers, although his impact as an analytical thinker was more profound over time. Locke, however, succeeded in seriously undermining Filmer's arguments.[204]

The doctrine of the divine right of kings was not an academic but a popular doctrine. It satisfied deep instincts and fulfilled a function. In its classic definition, it was said that the monarchy is a divinely ordained institution; that hereditary right is indefeasible; that king's are accountable to God alone; and that non-resistance and passive obedience are enjoined by God. The doctrine was supported by the authority of the *Bible*.[205]

Examples of this support are Samuel's description of a king, on the Jewish nation demanding one,[206] and David's refusal to touch 'the Lord's anointed'.[207] The passage describing the vision of Nebuchadnezzar;[208] 'render unto Cæsar';[209] Christ's words to Pilate;[210] the behaviour of the primitive Christians; are further examples. Above all we have the direct enjoining by both Saint Peter and Saint

Paul to obedience to constituted authority.[211] The theory belongs to an age when politics and theology were closely connected.[212]

Critics of the doctrine generally were content to argue on the same lines as its supporters.[213] They argued that scripture was misunderstood, especially texts which inculcate the right and duty of resistance; that early Christians exhibited the virtue of passive obedience because they could not do otherwise; that the *Bible* provided an alternative theory in the original compact – the 'law of the Kingdom' of Samuel.[214] Political theory in the twentieth and twenty-first centuries tends to be utilitarian, we must not judge the seventeenth century by our standards. Sovereignty in the Austinian sense was unknown in any single nation in the Middle Ages. Bracton knew of no sovereign which was above the laws because it made them. It is also certain that the notion of a single ultimate authority is a modern one[215] – provided we discount a divine authority.

The origin of the theory of the divine right of kings is to be found in the conflict between the Papacy and the Empire. But even in England, which was only on the periphery of this dispute, the king, who had a strong sacred character and became, with the advent of Christianity God's vicars on earth, obedience to the king was a religious duty. The effect of the Norman Conquest was to some extent muted because there was no theory of sovereignty.

With the accession of King Edward II the election of the king fell into disuse, while the royal prerogative grew. Indeed the whole constitutional struggle of the fourteenth century raged around the prerogative, as the king developed his sovereignty. In 1322 the right of Parliament to petition for new laws was made exclusive.[216] The distinction between the personal and political capacity of the king was also caused by the growth of Parliament. But even in the time of Edward II it was a matter of controversy, and was apparently one of the arguments for the banishment of Gaveston. An ordinance of 1311 accused him of 'encroaching to himself royal power and royal dignity and lording it over the state of the king and the people'. Later on, in the trial of the De Spensers, the doctrine that there is any distinction between the king and the Crown was condemned.[217]

Not surprisingly this view, very similar to that held by the Long Parliament, was criticized by Coke in *Calvin's Case*[218] as a 'damnable and damned opinion'. The formation of a theory of sovereignty in England in the Middle Ages was effectively prevented by feudalism, and the unwritten common law did not encourage it either. Bracton did not ascribe sovereignty to the king, nor made him absolute, as was believed by royalist writers of the seventeenth century.[219] The theory was advanced that resistance to the Crown was only lawful if enjoined by the inferior magistrates. Thus Parliament could pretend that they only took up arms against Charles I the person, but were in support of his authority.[220]

The divine right of kings is the form taken in the seventeenth century by the theory of sovereignty.[221] Jean Bodin's *Les Six Livres de la République* (1576)[222] stressed the indivisibility of sovereignty and the consequent impossibility of limited or mixed monarchies. The primary attribute of sovereignty was the power to give laws to subjects without their consent. Consultation was a matter of prudence rather than a legal requirement. This theory was simple but its application to all monarchies on principle was peremptory and indiscriminate. In practice the English monarchy relied more on finance than on political theory – upon practice than theory, about which there was comparatively little debate.

The difficulty in assessing the nature of constitutional developments when the principle is developed to suit the apparent situation is seen in the divergent views of the early modern monarchy. Stubbs thought that promising constitutional progress was arrested by the vigour of Tudor rule, while Pollard (as well as Elton and Neale) thought that the foundation of later parliamentary rule was laid under that dynasty.[223] There has moreover been a swing back towards Stubbs' view more recently, such as with Roskell.[224]

Locke attacked the idea of sovereignty, than on the idea of absolute monarchy; although the legislature is supreme, it has limitations.[225] Sidney's *Discourses concerning Government* and even Milton's *Tenure of Kings and Magistrates* exhibit similar limitations. The definite ground assumed is that of Rousseau, that the people are sovereign, that this sovereignty comes from God and is inalienable. All governments are in their view merely officials carrying out the will of the sovereign people, and they may therefore be removed at any time. This view is apparently also that of Mariana and Suarez, and is more consistent and logically defensible than the common Whig theory. But in comparatively few states is the sovereignty legally and formally vested undiluted in the people[226] – perhaps to avoid heightening the risk of demagoguery.

Hobbes was vehemently opposed by the believers in divine right. His system of politics is pure utilitarian, and was largely devoid of religious content. He also, almost alone for his time, realised that politics is not, and cannot be, a branch of theology. His theory of government was based upon the original compact, which lay at the root of such consistency as the opponents of the theory of divine right had. To those believing in the compact, the state was an artificial creation. To Filmer, Hickes or Leslie it is a natural growth.

To Locke, Sidney or Milton the original compact limits all forms of government and reduces the state to a mechanical instrument that may with ease be destroyed and manufactured afresh. In the view of Hobbes the machine of state, when created, is indeed to last for all time, but it has no quality of life, no principle of internal development. The popular theories of the seventeenth century were a survival of the notion proclaimed by Hildebrand, but hinted at by Aquinas.[227] It was more or less dominant in all the 'Papist' writers. It was simply that the state is a consequence of the fall, existing because in our imperfection we have need of it.[228]

To the believers in the divine right, political society is natural to man. Government and therefore obedience are necessities of human nature. No theory of government was ever more untrue to the reality of political life than is that of Locke, and the difference between him and Filmer is in this respect all in favour of the latter. Even Filmer's theory is based upon the notion that what has always existed must be natural to man and of divine authority, and therefore immutable.[229]

The theory forms the necessary transition between mediæval religious and modern secular politics.[230]

Theories of divine right outlined by such as Sir Robert Filmer in *Patriarcha* (1680) were criticized by Whig theorists of contract such as Algernon Sidney and John Locke. A doctrine which relied heavily upon biblical authority was bound to suffer damage in the Age of Reason.[231]

Sir Julius Cæsar had doubts about the abortive Great Contract between the king and Parliament, which would have seen the king give up purveyance's and modify wardship, in return for a parliamentary grant of £200,000. To abandon prerogative rights in exchange for parliamentary revenue, would lead to democracy. Yet the old concept of the Crown living off its own resources made sense no longer. The old constitution was close to stalemate, and the Crown eventually collapsed due to the exigencies of the Bishops' War in Scotland in 1641–42.[232]

With the last of the Stuarts disappeared, in the British Isles at least, strict indefeasible hereditary right and much of the mystical power of kingship.[233] The theory lost its popularity because its work was done – the independence of the state had been attained.[234] But where did this leave the Crown, and the rule of law?

Rarely was theory and practice so far apart as in the Stuart monarchy, yet it was the practice which had changed, not the theory,[235] which was neglected. In the seventeenth century theorizing about the constitution evolved between models of law which were not always empirically-based.

Ironically, in the absence of a developed constitutional theory, great reliance is placed on legal form as a substitute. Such is the present situation in New Zealand. Certainly, recognizing that the acquisition of sovereignty was based on a compact in 1840 would bring this country to a more principled constitutional position, one indeed much discussed in the seventeenth century, that of the compact.[236]

That such a recognition has not yet been fully made is indicative of what Kelsey calls the integration ethic and the self-determination ethic,[237] a desire to accommodate the separateness of Maori culture but also a desire to integrate that culture into mainstream Pakeha society. The future direction of the constitution is not clear, but concepts of Western liberalism require at least the resolution of grievances resulting from breaches of the Treaty of Waitangi.[238]

Brookfield has looked at what he calls the Crown's seizure of power over New Zealand from 1840, the challenges of Maori, and the establishment of the separate New Zealand Crown. Developing from his earlier writings on law and revolution and on Waitangi matters and indigenous rights, he has examined how a revolutionary taking of power by one people over another may be at least partly legitimated.[239] This process relies heavily upon redressing grievances and upon the development of new concepts of authority. There is no doubt that, as part of this process, during the 1980s in particular the Treaty of Waitangi was constitutionalized, and, in some views at least, the basis of government is now founded upon it.[240]

By using the example of one country, New Zealand, it may be seen that government is both the product of history, and a significant ongoing influence upon the development of both constitutional law, and substantive and procedural laws. Even where the form of constitution is unique or unusual – as in a colonial or post-colonial state – this is apparent. In the context of a country without the restrictions of an entrenched constitution this justification for government action is particularly clear.

1.4 The Relationship between Law and Government

We may now ask 'what is the relationship between law and government?' In essence this may be categorized as regulatory. To Machiavelli the state was an organized force, supreme in its own territory and pursuing a conscious policy of aggrandisement in its relations with other states. The distinction could be drawn by European theorists between the state in the exercise of its legal functions and the state in the exercise of activities carried out by or in common with subjects. In the latter case, the state, having entered into competition with private citizens, is deemed to waive the advantages of its public character, something which the Crown, in the British tradition, does not do. This may result in injustices, as for example with the Crown's priority over debts. However this is a natural consequence of the historical origin of the Crown. To correct these there has been a significant move towards the development of public law, and an awareness of civil law principles (and in some cases their reception), in common law jurisdictions.

The supremacy of the law is an idea we owe to the early Middle Ages.[241] There was then no concept of the sovereign state, at least in part because everyone had a different lord to whom they owed allegiance.[242] To many in the seventeenth century the law was the true sovereign. With the Reformation a true theory of sovereignty became possible, because of the vast increase in the powers and activity of the legislature. Judges, as professors of the common law, claimed for it supreme authority. Had this been admitted they would have been the ultimate authority in the state,[243] as perhaps they are in the United States, where the Supreme Court is the final arbiter of the law.

All parties in the seventeenth century British constitutional disputes united to respect law, but differed as to the nature of law and sovereignty. Whigs saw law as the product of custom and ancient statute little removed from custom. Tories saw that in no state could there be law without a lawgiver, so deduced the necessity for a true legal Sovereign.[244]

By early in the nineteenth century analytical jurists had made parliamentary sovereignty the pivot of the British legal system.[245] The constitution depended upon the common law, whose creature it was. The legal expression of the power of the state was always through the Crown. But there is nothing which transcends the power of an Act of Parliament.[246] The Sovereign could suspend the law – to some extent at least – and Parliament's power to do so was absolute. But this position was reached comparatively recently, and is not necessarily immutable.

The law alone remained permanent and ever-present, in a way similar to the later conceptualization of the Crown.

Oresme argued that legislative power was vested in the people as a whole, since they alone could judge the common good.[247] This view was roughly compatible with the English constitutional position in the latter Middle Ages, when Parliament was regarded as the indispensable forum for the production of statute law.[248] Fortescue arrived at a similar conclusion, though by a very different route. This was a result of his experience in the English law courts, where he concluded that:

> The statutes of England ... are made, not only by the Prince's will, but also by the assent of whole realm, so they cannot be injurious to the people nor fail to secure their advantage.[249]

Fortescue's doctrine of English kingship was that it was *dominium politicum et regale*, in contrast with the French *dominium regale*.[250] Continental rulers ruled on the basis of the civil law of their stronger Roman legal heritage.[251] They relied especially on the maxim *quod principi placuit legis habet vigorem* ('what hath pleased the prince has the force of law'). English kingship was superior, at least, according to the chancellor in Fortescue's fictitious disputation which comprises the basis of *De Laudibus Legum Anglia*, because the monarchy was limited by a requirement for the assent of Parliament. In Fortescue's conception of the constitution this was despite the fact that the power of kings was everywhere the same, but authority differed because of differences in their origins. The laws of England were more venerable, and must be deemed to be the best obtainable. This was because they were not enacted at the sole behest of the prince, but by the prudence of 300 members of Parliament.[252]

The Reformation Parliament settled the conventional view of the English constitution so clearly expounded in Sir Thomas Smith's *De Republica Anglorum* (1565) and so hard to find even obscurely stated before 1530s.[253] As a result of the Reformation the doctrine of parliamentary supremacy was developed.[254] But a long fight was waged by King Charles I in defence of his prerogative. He was committed to the traditional symbiosis of prerogative and law rather than any new theory of the state.[255]

In the course of time the King-in-Parliament, the legislature, became supreme over the law. On the Continent the lawyers – and courts – were antagonistic to representative assemblies, and there courts persisted in maintaining the predominance of the law over the authority of such assemblies, and so encouraged the growth of absolutism. In England after 1688 no claim was made that any rule of the common law was too fundamental to admit of change. The course of our constitutional and legal development must have been profoundly different had it been otherwise.[256] It is unclear just when parliamentary sovereignty triumphed over the supremacy of the Crown, but Parliament took control of the succession in 1689, and asserted it in 1701.[257]

The law remained supreme over all organs of government as well as people, and legislative power (properly expressed) extended over the whole field of law.[258]

The growth of the territorial state brought about the need for one supreme authority. As a consequence a more modern doctrine, a doctrine embodying a conception that was widely held, was developed. This was the supremacy of the Crown as the mystical holder of the sovereignty of the state. Continental Europe found in kingship the state's source of unity and power. This was to remain the lynch-pin of constitutional theory until modern times.

The early mediæval legal thinkers had to reconcile three distinct systems of thought – Roman, Christian, and Germanic. Perhaps the most difficult task was to accommodate a conception of kingship that rested on divine foundations, derived in part from Roman and in part from Christian thought, with Germanic and feudal kingship, which based its claim to legitimacy on the relationship of the King to his barons and people.

German custom subjected the King to the law, and limited his authority to govern without the consent of his subjects.[259] Christian thought and classical jurisprudence and philosophy stressed the divine origins of kingship and the sacral nature of political authority. This tension led the lawyers to distinguish between the prince's private body, that was subject to the law, and his public body that was not.[260] As a consequence, the canonists became the first lawyers in the western tradition to establish law as an essential element of political theory.[261]

The early twelfth century Norman cleric known as Anonymous of Rouen re-affirmed the dual personality of the King.[262] Inspired by the liturgy, a King was 'by nature an individual man, by grace [through his consecration] a *Christus*, that is, a God-man'.[263] This idea appears exceptionally modern, but was in fact in line with Carolingian tradition.[264]

In the mid-twelfth century Gratian completed his *Concordia Discordantium Canonum*.[265] This was a direct consequence of the revival of legal studies in the late eleventh century. Gratian's understanding of law and its sources was shaped by the *Digest*, which described the emperor's supreme legislative authority.[266]

The majesty of the Holy Roman Emperor had spread all over Europe in the thirteenth century. To this doctrine of the divine right of kings habits of thought of the greatest consequences have been traced. These include a deep sense of the majesty of the law, and the duty of obedience.[267] When the competing focal points of sovereignty were reconciled in the course of the seventeenth and eighteenth centuries, the splendour of the Crown remained as the legal expression of the sovereignty of the nation. The supremacy of the Crown necessarily had to give way under the inexorable advance of the supremacy of Parliament.

The aims of the late mediæval and early modern state were negative and disciplinary. The extreme emphasis on property rights carried with it an emphasis on law – a lawyer's rather than a politician's view of government. By Fortescue's time if not earlier, men felt strong monarchy upheld their rights (a mass of technical rules and practices), rather than Parliament.[268]

De Laudibus Legum Angliæ[269] written 1468–71 was one of the first coherent exercises in comparative law. It was strongly influenced by the French experience of Sir John Fortescue. It had a direct influence on the constitutional thinkers of the seventeenth century. Fortescue's successors in that century argued more precisely that the ancient constitution was Anglo-Saxon – and prerogative was the right of conquest of William the Conqueror.[270]

Fortescue supports the doctrine of constitutional monarchy found in St Thomas, but really his support is derived from his own liberal sentiments and the experience of England.[271]

A main theme of English constitutional history was the question of whether the *communitas regni* had a right to force an unwilling King to take cognisance[272] of the legitimate interest in the Crown of the *communitas regni*.[273] The contention, most clearly expressed by Aquinas, that the King was not restrained by law because he controlled coercion, was widely rejected in thirteenth century England. Royal jurisdiction depended on co-operation.[274] In both England and France Giles of Rome's view that 'laws are laid down by the prince and established by princely authority'[275] was disputed.[276] Bracton regarded the magnates as having an essential role in legislation.[277]

John Locke and later commentators rationalized the notion that the Sovereign stood above the law and acted in trust for his subject, whose rights he should be as sedulous to guard as his own.[278] Few in the seventeenth century ever doubted that government was a trust.[279] But where they differed was whether it was a trust created by God or man.[280] That the trust might be from the people, rather than from God was a novel idea.[281]

Although he was primarily a writer of the interregnum and died in 1653, Sir Robert Filmer provided the most spectacular defence of royal powers in the 1680s. His best work was *Patriarcha*, written before the civil war but first published only in 1680.[282] Although Filmer's ideas are now outmoded, his views were a product of his time. He argued that God had given sovereignty over the earth to Adam, which was then passed by hereditary descent through the sons of Noah and the heads of the nations into which mankind was divided at the Confusion of Tongues, to all the modern rulers of the world.

Filmer's great merit was in seeing government as conforming to the generally accepted pattern of social organization in his time. This saw the King as the father of his people, and entitled to the obedience of his family. The idea that there was a sovereign authority did not supersede the older idea of 'natural law' which reason would lead men to acknowledge.[283]

The common law, by which we mean that body of laws common to all, and which are to be distinguished from local custom, royal prerogative and all other exceptional or special law,[284] is remarkable historically for its formulary nature. The history of the common law is the history of the writ. Yet in its origins English law drew from two distinct traditions, neither of which was overly concerned with niceties of form. The Anglo-Saxon law, from the *Lex Salica*,[285] the laws of Ine[286] and the dooms of Æthbert,[287] to the code of Canute and the ordinances of Ælfred, constitute one of these. The other is the French or Frankish tradition, the capitularies of the Carlovingian emperors and the Merovingian kings to Chloding, who led the Franks to Gaul.

The King of the English was expected to publish laws at a time when hardly anyone else was attempting any such feat – the dooms of Canute are probably the most comprehensive of any code in eleventh century Europe.[288] The Normans by contrast had little if any written law to bring with them, and had perforce to rely on the relatively well-developed Saxon legal and administrative structure. Yet in the first half of the twelfth century one could still speak of Wessex law, Danish law, Mercian law, and the law of the King's own court apart from and above all these partial systems, though in a way more significant than ever in the Saxon kingdom. The local customs were those of the shires and hundreds, and the King's law came to be ever more pre-eminent, especially as the royal judicial system developed. Royal authority was founded on the constitutional history and structure of society, including the role of the king as the official representative of the community.

Yet even the Saxon kings were more than mere officials, as popular reverence for their real or imagined pedigree shows. Feudalism added to their power by formalising in a legal structure the already significant ties of fealty. As the tendency of feudalism was to connect jurisdiction with land, so the right to hold the Crown, and to its prerogatives, came to be regarded as a proprietary right. The king was also not just the chosen of the people, but the chosen of God. He was also able to command greater resources than any potential rival, unlike the King of France, who was dominated by over-powerful vassals.[289] Yet he remained in essence no different from any of his subjects, who might exercise juridical functions of their own, though on a much smaller scale than those of the King.

Thus the scope of public law in the English model is not distinct from the private law because the Sovereign as the representative of the state possessed few if any powers which were inherently unavailable to the subject. Ironically however, The Queen's Courts have now generally placed greater restrictions upon the working of the executive, by classifying as prerogative powers those powers of action which the Crown shares with the public.

The example of Carolingian kingship brought a tradition of royal war-leadership and an idea of empire.[290] English developments were influenced by Carolingian models, in political ideas as in institutions and royal ritual. Yet it retained its own traits, and was especially king-centred. The king was in the place of a father, as Christ's representative.[291] Royal peacekeeping was a distinctive feature, as was drafting laws. The old insular ideas of imperial kingship gained new impetus, not only from the extension of the West Saxon power, but also from English acquaintance with Ottonian and Salian courts.[292]

Ælfred promoted education so that his laws could be understood more widely, but also so that religious works reached a wider readership. The function of the king as law-giver and judge was gradually emphasized at the expense of self-regulation by leading figures in the community, as a consequence of the Christianising of kingship, with the *Bible*'s stories about great judges and Christian law. From Ine to Æthelred II the tradition of assembling the pronouncements, administrative regulations and laws of their predecessors led to the development of a recognizable body of Anglo-Saxon law. To make and proclaim the law became a mark of kingship.[293]

The Norman Conquest brought few changes in the ideal or practice of English rulership, rather these could strengthen the Conqueror's authority in the face of an alternative Norman tradition of aristocratic freedom.[294]

The law served to develop the powers of kings, and to direct and limit their action.[295] The balance between the king and the community as the fount of law and the dispenser of justice was perceptibly altered in favour of the king by Ælfred's time.[296] Kings and their subjects were increasingly made aware of the king's religious and moral responsibilities.[297] The Europe-wide Papal investiture contest led to King John being excommunicated in 1209. Although the king and pope were reconciled in 1213, a Christian king had been declared unworthy of kingship.[298] The Church modified and restrained the scope of the king's authority.[299] The king's duty to maintain the peace in his kingdom and provide justice for his subjects underwent a major transformation in the twelfth century which emphasized the king's authority throughout England and made more explicit his obligations and the parameters within which he ruled. His role as judge and law-maker was revolutionised.[300]

The change during the twelfth century was more one of availability and effectiveness rather than new laws as such. Under Henry I especially, new royal officials, including roving or itinerant justices, were introduced. The law itself developed significantly under Henry II, with new formula making new remedies available.[301] The Statute of Marlborough 1267[302] was a review of the relations between the king and his subjects and of the working of the common law. So comprehensive was the statute that contemporaries wrote of the constitutions or the statutes of Marlborough, rather than of the statute. At this time legislation meant an explicit statement of what the force of existing custom or the ruling of divine law provided for in particular instances. Mostly statutes were non-controversial.

As the monarchy grew more authoritarian in the eleventh and twelfth centuries, flaws and weaknesses were exposed which ultimately produced major changes in the course of the thirteenth century. Under the influence of the Crown's continental dominions the monarchy changed from a West Saxon kingdom writ large to a transmarine monarchy whose main arteries of royal communications and travel were the Thames Estuary and the south-eastern ports.[303]

Henry II established permanent government[304] Legal memory extends only as far back as the coronation of Richard I,[305] by a technical doctrine whose scope was concerned merely with prescriptive rights. It does however illustrate the longevity of the common law, whose roots indeed go back centuries earlier than that date.

The English was by the end of the twelfth century the most sophisticated and effective monarchy in Europe.[306]

Because of the uncomfortable paradox of monarchy and the unsuitability of some kings it came to be believed over the course of the thirteenth and fourteenth centuries that one could separate the Crown from the wearer, so that it became possible to correct or even remove the king. Discussion along these lines tended to decline in the fifteenth century because of the weak title of the usurpers in that century. There was no real alternative to hereditary rule, and force of arms was not really conducive to stability and order.[307]

In the time from Henry VIII to the accession of William and Mary the court was at the very centre of political power. But the power of the king was limited by a tradition of consultation, though this may not have been much more a feature of the English monarchy than the French, despite the belief to the contrary held by Fortescue and Smith.[308]

The repudiation of papal authority and the insistence upon the Crown's imperial status, though of great symbolic importance, did not in themselves materially alter the Crown's position.[309]

Royal authority was founded on the constitutional history and structure of society, including the role of the king as the official representative of the community. Unlike, in some degree, in the French model of constitutionalism, influenced as it was by Roman concepts of statehood, the English conception of monarchy was limited. Although England was unified from a comparatively early time, and did not suffer from the over-mighty magnates found in France, or indeed in the German lands of the Holy Roman Empire, it was nevertheless spared the growth of a dominant kingship. While this may have been due to the accidents of history, such as the Wars of the Roses, rather than to principled belief in sharing power, it was to have great significance in the later constitutional development of the country.

We can see that, not only was there an ongoing political and legal debate about the nature of authority in the early modern state, but in practice the tendency was for centralisation, however unjustified, as the most efficient. It was no coincidence that much of the importance of the British revolutions of 1642–60 and 1688, the French revolution of 1789–99, the American revolution of 1776–89 (and the Civil War of 1861–65),[310] and other significant events has been in their determination of the locus of authority. This tendency to centralize was as much for pragmatic functional reasons as for theoretical. The king was long seen as the keeper of the peace – and this role required an iron fist. Government was regulatory.

An understanding of the regulatory role of the state must be built upon a conceptual and functional analysis of sovereignty, the organizing and political principle upon which national economic policy making and regulation, as well as international economic co-ordination and regulation are based.[311] Further, proper appreciation of the internal dimension of sovereignty requires an understanding of the relationship between the state and the society it governs.[312] As Tshuma has emphasized, the relationship between the state and civil society over which it exercises sovereignty is historically specific and the manner in which sovereign power is exercised is shaped by the configuration of social forces.[313] These forces include legal and constitutional rights and limitations. The external dimension of sovereignty is equally circumscribed by an international system where sovereign states are *de jure* equal, but not, of course, *de facto* equal. The reality is of course that states are not equal politically, economically, military or even socially. This reality means that the legal systems of countries are not all equal in economic or political importance.

The relationship between law and government may also be seen from an economic perspective – indeed it may be that this is its primary nature. It is especially important at a time when technology has caused a reappraisal of the role of law and state. The liberal interventionist approach to economic policy and regulation in the context of globalization would hold that global problems require international collective action. But, as Matthews has asserted, a shift in power from hierarchical state organizations to multi-layered networks of supra-states, sub-state, and non-state entities, has broken the dominance of hierarchy, and enjoined a revival of the network-based society.[314] This argument has been said to resemble technological determinism which overlooks or downplays the role of politics in the development and diffusion of technology.[315] But that is not a charge which could be laid at Castells' door.

Manuel Castells attempted an analysis of contemporary society which extended beyond the concept of the information society.[316] He postulated that society is not purely defined by our technology. Cultural, economical, and political factors contribute to what he styled the Network Society.[317] He stressed the importance of networks rather than hierarchy-ranked global cities. Networks are the basis of one of the most important new technologies – information technology. Those who classify themselves as Internet realists would minimize the extent and breadth of the societal and constitutional influences of the information technology revolution, but it is clear that technology has a major influence, if not a determinate one, upon the shape of future society. Government operates through laws, but technology also operates through laws.

1.5 The Nature of Law and Technology

An understanding of the nature of the relationship of law and technology is crucial to understanding modern societies and governments. Law regulates technology, both by prohibiting and regulating certain forms of technology, and also by encouraging or protecting other forms. The forms of technology which are prohibited are those which involve risk or the potential to cause serious harm, and those over which there may be ethical, religious or cultural concerns. Certain armaments are banned outright – such as biochemical weapons,[318] while the use of others is strictly controlled by international agreements.

Certain technologies are restricted directly or indirectly. For instance, nuclear power, due to its dangerous by-products and potential for highly damaging accidents, is strictly regulated, both nationally and internationally (the latter through the International Atomic Energy Agency). In the United States the Nuclear Regulatory Commission (NRC) has detailed regulations that apply to all United States' power plants. NRC regulations require nuclear plants to have conservative safety margins, strict procedural controls and multiple safety systems to protect public health and safety. Special regulatory controls – rigorous design qualifications, record-keeping, maintenance and testing requirements – are used to ensure that systems necessary to safely shut down a nuclear reactor and prevent radioactivity from travelling off-site will function effectively during and after an accident. The inspection and reporting regime thus established ensures a high level of safety, but at a considerable cost to the user of the technology. There is thus both a direct (through licensing) and indirect (through compliance costs) regulation.

The general laws also encourage certain technologies, directly or indirectly. The whole range of intellectual property laws may be seen as being, in some respects at least, as the result of an ongoing tension between the encouragement of individual effort through the protection of original ideas and effort, and the encouragement of industry through dissemination of those ideas. Competition, or anti-trust laws, may have a similar effect, though more usually to inhibit developments, or to force them to develop in a particular direction. Recent examples have included the *Microsoft* case, and a few years earlier the *AT&T* case. Both of these had, or have the potential to have, technological implications.

In December 1999, United States District Court Judge Thomas Penfield Jackson issued a far-reaching 'findings of fact' that found for the plaintiffs in almost all the allegations. Jackson found, among other things, that Microsoft had a monopoly in the personal computer (PC) operating systems market where it enjoys a large and stable market share; Microsoft used its monopoly power in the PC operating systems market and harmed competitors; Microsoft unduly restricted the innovation process; various Microsoft contracts had anti-competitive implications; and Microsoft's actions harmed consumers. The case proceeded through a number of hearings and decisions, but the final result and the consequences remain uncertain. However, Microsoft has already suffered from the process, and development, design and marketing of its products underwent a noticeable change during the course of the case. Even without being broken up, Microsoft was compelled to change the course of development of its products.

The earlier case also illustrated how government-imposed legal requirements affect technology and businesses which operate technology. In 1982 AT&T was found to be in breach of United States anti-trust laws, and compulsorily broken up. In 1981, AT&T was a 100-year-old company with many layers of management. For historical reasons, the local phone companies within the old AT&T, such as New York Telephone, were managed separately from the 'long lines' division. Thus it was not difficult to separate the divisions since they functioned on many levels as separate companies. AT&T's rigid management structure and abundance of managers helped it avoid managerial problems in the break-up.[319]

The company was divided into the long-distance company (AT&T), and seven regional operating companies, each of which remained a regulated local telecommunications monopoly. The destruction of AT&T's long-distance technological monopoly encouraged competition, which brought sharply lower prices and immense consumer benefits – but a less homogenous system.

Telecommunications companies in the United States are regulated as public utilities. In the 1930s, all phone companies were forced by the government to interconnect so that anyone could place a call to anyone else. The companies emerging from the AT&T break-up were guaranteed this interconnectivity.[320] The technological consequences of regulation were less pronounced than those in the *Microsoft* case may yet prove to be.

1.6 Conclusion

In this first Chapter we have considered the relationship of law and government. Government is both a product of society, history and environment, but is also instrumental in determining the form and direction of laws. While the notion that governmental actions should be constrained by law has gained widespread, if not universal, acceptance, such principles reflect only one of the influences upon society and thus upon technology. Law both constrains and encourages developments both of technology and of other social and economic change, but is itself also a product of its environment.

Society influences law, for law is but a reflection of the society of which it is a product. The following Chapter considers the response of business to changes in the legal environment. Business is a broad sub-set of society. It is as sensitive to legal change – and technological change – as any part is. An appreciation of the relationship of business and changes in political or technological environment is therefore instructive.

Notes

1 The extent to which this is general, rather than the product of definite cultural inheritance, has long been subject of study, see, for instance, Sir Henry Sumner Maine, *Early Law and Custom* (London, 1890).

2 For example, in the principle of *quod principi placuit, legis nabet vigorem* ('what hath pleased the prince has the force of law'). The reality of early modern government throughout Europe was that it was essentially driven by political realists, who sought the centralisation of power for the good of the country. This was typified by Niccolo Machiavelli, *The Prince*, ed. Quentin Skinner and Russell Price (Cambridge, 1988).

3 *Montevideo Convention on the Rights and Duties of States*, 26 December 1933, 49 Stat 3097; USA Treaty Series 881, entered into force 26 December 1934, in *International Legislation*, ed. M.O. Hudson (6 vols, Washington, 1931–50), vol. 6, p. 620; Ian Brownlie, *Principles of Public International Law* (5th edn, New York, 1998),

ch. 5. Although the application of the Convention is confined to Latin America, it is regarded as declaratory of customary international law. See also *Island of Palmas Arbitration Case* (1928) No xix (2) Reports of International Arbitral Awards 829; (1928) 22 *American Journal of International Law* 986; 4 Arbitration Decisions 3.

4 The constitutional position of New Zealand prior to 1840 was tribal and non-unitary, and is therefore outside the scope of this study.

5 The word 'Sovereign' appears in New Zealand statutes only in the Sovereign's Birthday Observance Act 1952. Otherwise the usage is generally such as is found in s 2 of the Public Finance Act, where 'Crown' is defined as 'Her Majesty the Queen in right of New Zealand; and includes all Ministers of the Crown and all departments'.

6 For this conceptual uncertainty, see Janine Hayward, 'In search of a treaty partner' (1995) Victoria University of Wellington PhD thesis; Interview with Sir Douglas Graham, 24 November 1999.

7 'The Crown as a Corporation', *Law Quarterly Review*, 17 (1901) 131–46.

8 Maitland, 'The Crown as a Corporation'.

9 It was as late as 1861 that the House of Lords accepted that the Crown was a corporation sole, having 'perpetual continuance'; *Attorney-General v Kohler* (1861) 9 HL Cas 654, 671.

10 'A corporation is a number of persons united and consolidated together so as to be considered as one person in law, possessing the character of perpetuity, its existence being constantly maintained by the succession of new individuals in the place of those who die, or are removed. Corporations are either aggregate or sole. A corporation aggregate consists of many persons, several of whom are contemporaneously members of it. Corporations sole are such as consist, at any given time, of one person only'; *Mozley and Whiteley's Law Dictionary*, ed. E.R. Hardy Ivamy (10th edn, London, 1988), p. 109.

11 It was at the time of Edward IV that the theory was accepted that the king never dies, that the demise of the Crown at once transfers it from the last wearer to the heir, and that no vacancy, no interregnum, occurs at all; William Stubbs, *The Constitutional History of England* (4th edn, Oxford, 1906), vol. 2, p. 107.

12 Howard Nenner, *The Right to be King – The Succession to the Crown of England, 1603–1714* (London, 1995), p. 32.

13 Sir William Blackstone, *Commentaries on the Laws of England*, ed. E. Christian (New York, 1978), book 1, p. 470. That Blackstone was at least partly incorrect can be seen in the development of a concept of succession to the Crown without interregnum of the heir apparent. Since this concept had fully developed by the time of Edward IV, this cannot have been the principal reason for the development of the concept of the Crown as a corporation sole.

14 Noel Cox, 'The Law of Succession to the Crown in New Zealand', *Waikato Law Review*, 7 (1999): 49–72.

15 Bruce Harris, 'The "Third Source" of Authority for Government Action', *Law Quarterly Review*, 109 (1992): 626–51.

16 Blackstone, book 1, p. 254.

17 'Does the Crown have Human Powers?', *New Zealand Universities Law Review*, 15 (1992): 118–42. Contrary case law includes *Sutton's Hospital Case* (1613) 10 Co Rep 23a; *Clough v Leahy* (1905) 2 CLR 139, 156–7; *New South Wales v Bardolph* (1934) 52 CLR 455, 474–5; *R v Criminal Injuries Compensation Board* [1967] 2 QB 864,

886; *Malone v Metropolitan Police Commissioner* [1979] Ch 344, 366; *Attorney-General of Quebec v Labrecque* [1980] 2 SCR 1057, 1082; *Davis v Commonwealth* (1988) 166 CLR 79 (HCA).

18 Philip Joseph, 'Suspending Statutes Without Parliament's Consent', *New Zealand Universities Law Review*, 14 (1991): 282, 287.

19 To the question, 'What is the Crown?', there have been what Wade calls 'some extraordinary answers'; Sir William Wade, 'The Crown, Ministers and Officials: Legal Status and Liability', in Maurice Sunkin and Sebastian Payne (ed.), *The Nature of the Crown: A Legal and Political Analysis* (Oxford, 1999), p. 23, referring to *Town Investments Ltd v Department of the Environment* [1978] AC 359; *M v Home Office* [1992] 1 QB 270 (CA); [1993] 3 All ER 537 (HL).

20 [1928] 1 Ch 385, 401.

21 Maitland, 'The Crown as a Corporation'.

22 [1946] AC 543, 555 (HL).

23 It has also been accepted by the Supreme Court of Canada: *Verreault v Attorney-General of Quebec* [1977] 1 SCR 41, 47; *Attorney-General of Quebec v Labrecque* [1980] 2 SCR 1057, 1082.

24 [1978] AC 359, 400 per Lord Simon of Glaisdale (HL).

25 *Town Investments Ltd v Department of the Environment* [1978] AC 359, 380–1 per Lord Diplock.

26 Some writers, following *Town Investments*, have preferred the expression 'government' rather than 'Crown' or 'State', for example Harris, 'The "Third Source" of Authority for Government Action', 634–5. The government has never been a juristic entity, so in trying to abandon one legal fiction in *Town Investments*, their Lordships adopted a new one; Philip Joseph, 'Crown as a legal concept (I)', *New Zealand Law Journal*, (1993): 126, 129.

27 *Town Investments v Department of the Environment* [1978] AC 359, 400 (HL).

28 [1992] 1 QB 270.

29 However, in the House of Lords, Lord Templeman spoke of the Crown as consisting of the monarch and the executive, and Lord Woolf observed that the Crown had a legal personality at least for some purposes; [1993] 3 All ER 537.

30 That is, one which claims for itself legal paramountcy, and which limits executive and legislative powers in such a way that the constitution itself, rather than any institution of government, becomes the focus of critical attention.

31 In Kelsen's philosophy of law, a grundnorm is the basic, fundamental postulate, which justifies all principles and rules of the legal system and which all inferior rules of the system may be deduced; Michael Hayback, 'Carl Schmitt and Hans Kelsen in the crisis of Democracy between World Wars I and II' (1990) Universitaet Salzburg DrIur thesis.

32 For a critique of these propositions generally see Joseph, 'The Crown as a legal concept (I)'; and Philip Joseph, 'The Crown as a legal concept (II)', *New Zealand Law Journal* (1993): 179; F.M. Brookfield, 'The Monarchy and the Constitution today', *New Zealand Law Journal* (1992): 438.

33 A concept which is alive today, in part as a substitute for a more advanced concept of the constitution; Interview with Sir Douglas Graham, 24 November 1999.

34 Generally, see Janine Hayward, 'In search of a treaty partner' (1995) Victoria University of Wellington PhD thesis.

35 See, for instance, Noel Cox, 'The Theory of Sovereignty and the Importance of the Crown in the Realms of The Queen', *Oxford University Commonwealth Law Journal*, 2(2) (2002): 237–55.

36 Following the example set by Bagehot, British historians since 1945 have very largely neglected the continuing political influence of the monarchy under George VI and Elizabeth II; Peter Hennessy, 'The throne behind the monarchy', *Economist*, 24 December 1994, pp. 77–9.

37 'The English Constitution', in the *Collected Works of Walter Bagehot*, ed. Norman St John-Stevas (5 vols, London, 1974), vol. 5.

38 Frank Hardie, *The Political Influence of Queen Victoria, 1861–1901* (London, 1935), pp. 23–7.

39 Bagehot, 'The English Constitution', vol. 5, p. 253.

40 The limitations of the distinction between dignified and efficient, so central to Bagehot's model, can be seen in Laura Jackson, 'Shadows of the Crown' (1994) University of Chicago PhD thesis.

41 H.J. Hanham, *The Nineteenth Century Constitution, 1815–1914* (Cambridge, 1969), p. 24.

42 David E. Smith, 'Bagehot, the Crown, and the Canadian Constitution', *Canadian Journal of Political Science*, 28 (1995): 622–37. An example of the use of influence through an 'exchange of views' has been given in Kenneth Rose, *Kings, Queens and Courtiers: Intimate Portraits of the Royal House of Windsor from its foundation to the Present Day* (London, 1985), p. 92.

43 F. Hinsley, *Sovereignty* (2nd edn, Cambridge, 1986), p. 1; Stephen Krasner, 'Sovereignty', *Comparative Political Studies*, 21(1) (1988): 66–94, 86.

44 From Michel Foucault, *The Foucault Effects: Studies in Governmentality*, ed. Graham Burchell, Colin Gordon and Peter Miller (London, 1991), pp. 97–8, 101–2. See also David Held, *Political Theory and the Modern State* (Cambridge, 1989), pp. 216–25.

45 Sovereignty is always limited in some way. Genesis 1.26–30 makes it clear that God created mankind to subdue the earth and to exercise dominion over it under God; Rousas John Rushdoony, *The Institutes of Biblical Law* (Philadelphia, 1973), pp. 448–51.

46 P.G. McHugh, 'Constitutional Theory and Maori Claims', in Sir Hugh Kawharu (ed.), *Waitangi: Maori and Pakeha Perspectives of the Treaty of Waitangi* (Auckland, 1989), p. 25.

47 Sir Elihu Lauterpacht, 'Sovereignty – Myth or Reality?', *International Affairs*, 73(1) (1997): 137–50.

48 Daniel Philpott, 'Sovereignty', *Journal of International Affairs*, 48(2) (1995): 353–68.

49 See, for example, the Barbados Independence Order 1966, the Schedule of which is the Constitution of Barbados. Section 63(1): 'The executive authority of Barbados is vested in Her Majesty'.

50 See Allan Kornberg and Harold Clarke, *Citizens and Community – Political Support in a Representative Democracy* (Cambridge, 1992); Carol Harlow, 'Power from the People?', in Patrick McAuslan and John McEldowney (ed.), *Law, Legitimacy and the Constitution: Essays marking the Centenary of Dicey's Law of the Constitution* (London, 1985); J.R. Mallory, 'The Appointment of the Governor General', *Canadian Journal of Economics and Political Science*, 26 (1960): 96.

51 Philip Joseph, *Constitutional and Administrative Law in New Zealand* (Sydney, 1993), pp. 284–5.

52 In early America, there was no question, whatever the form of government, that all legitimate authority was derived from God. The influence of the classical tradition revived the authority of the people, which historically is equally compatible with monarchy, oligarchy, dictatorship, or democracy, but is not compatible with the doctrine of God's authority; Rushdoony, p. 214.

53 Particularly in respect of what might be called policy legacies; Theda Skocpol, *States and Social Revolution* (Cambridge, 1979), p. 27. Indeed, a Constitution exists in the imagination of those who create it, use it, and thus know it; Joseph Jacobs, *The Republican Crown*: *Lawyers and the Making of the State in Twentieth Century Britain* (Aldershot, 1996), p. 6.

54 The Australian Constitution has been held to be based on popular sovereignty, as it was adopted by popular vote; *Australian Capital Television Pty Ltd v Commonwealth* (1992) 177 CLR 106, 138 per Mason CJ; *Theophanous v Herald & Weekly Times Ltd* (1994) 182 CLR 104, 171 per Deane J; *McGinty v Western Australia* (1996) 186 CLR 140, 230, 237 per McHugh, J.

55 Canada has the same type of conceptual difficulty; Peter Russell, *Constitutional Odyssey*: *Can Canadians become a Sovereign People*? (Toronto, 1992).

56 The Australian Labour Party wanted a republic partly for symbolic nationalist reasons, but partly also to deprive the Governors-General of their association with royal legitimacy; R. Lucy, *The Australian Form of Government* (Melbourne, 1985), p. 17.

57 Constitution of the Independent State of Papua New Guinea 1975.

58 See Harold Laski, 'The Theory of Popular Sovereignty', *Michigan Law Review*, 17 (1919): 201–15.

59 Indeed, it has been said that few care for such esoteric matters; Interview with Sir Douglas Graham, 24 November 1999.

60 For example, F.M. Brookfield, *Waitangi and Indigenous Rights*: *Revolution, Law and Legitimation* (Auckland, 1999); Andrew Sharp (ed.), *Leap into the dark*: *the changing role of the state in New Zealand since 1984* (Auckland, 1994); Andrew Sharp, *Justice and the Maori*: *the philosophy and practice of Maori claims in New Zealand since the 1970s* (2nd edn, Auckland, 1997); Richard Mulgan, 'Can the Treaty of Waitangi provide a constitutional basis for New Zealand's political future?', *Political Science*, 41(2) (1989): 51–68.

61 See, for example, the recent writings on the State; Jane Kelsey, *Rolling Back the State*: *Privatisation of Power in Aotearoa/New Zealand* (Wellington, 1993); Richard Mulgan, *Democracy and Power in New Zealand*: *A study of New Zealand politics* (2nd edn, Auckland, 1989).

62 As former Prime Minister David Lange believed; Interview with David Lange, 20 May 1998.

63 See Michael Foley, *The Silence of Constitutions*: *Gaps, 'Abeyances' and Political Temperament in the Maintenance of Government* (London, 1989). The wars of the seventeenth century were, to no small degree, between competing conceptions of the State, and engendered a suspicion for such speculation. It is probable that the long dominance of Whig ideology also contributed to this attitude.

64 Law Reform Commission of Canada, *The Legal Status of the Federal Administration* (Ottawa, 1985).

65 *Bank voor Handel v Slatford* [1952] 1 All ER 314, 319 per Devlin J:
The Crown is a convenient term, but one which is often used to save the asking of difficult questions. It is a description of the powers that formerly at common law were exercised by the king in person, and that latterly have been bestowed by statute on the king in council or on various Ministers.

66 In this, parallels may be seen with the position of the Crown in New Zealand, in the Maori–Crown context. In Australia debate on whether The Queen is head of state continues.

67 The King of Sweden, for instance, has been so relegated; Constitution of Sweden (1975). Note the Canadian paper spoke of the Crown as an institution, rather than of the person of the Sovereign, or of their representatives.

68 David Cohen, 'Thinking about the State', *Osgoode Hall Law Journal*, 24 (1986): 379–409.

69 In effect a republican form of government.

70 Neil Komesar, 'Taking Institutions seriously', *University of Chicago Law Review*, 51 (1984): 366; P.W. Hogg, *Liability of the Crown in Australia, New Zealand and the United Kingdom* (Sydney, 1971); Law Reform Commission of British Columbia, *Legal Position of the Crown* (Vancouver, 1972).

71 Because Canadians never severed their ties with Britain, they never found it crucial to define themselves in a way which rendered them distinct from the 'mother country'; Smith, 'Empire, Crown and Canadian Federalism', 471.

72 Cohen, 'Thinking about the State'.

73 Sir William Moore, 'Liability for the Acts of Public Servants', *Law Quarterly Review*, 23 (1907): 112; Sir William Corbett, '"The Crown" as representing the State', *Commonwealth Law Review*, 1 (1903): 23, 145; H.T. Postle, 'Commonwealth and Crown', *Australian Law Journal*, 3 (1929): 109; Harold Laski, 'The Responsibility of the State in England', *Harvard Law Review*, 32 (1919): 447–72, 472; Maitland, 'The Crown as a Corporation', 136.

74 Sir William Moore, 'Law and Government', *Commonwealth Law Review*, 3 (1905): 205.

75 J. Dearlove, 'Bringing the State Back In', *Political Studies* (1989): 521–39.

76 Harris, 'The "Third Source" of Authority for Government Action'.

77 For an example of the application of such limits on government see *Fitzgerald v Muldoon* [1976] 2 NZLR 615.

78 Harris, 'The "Third Source" of Authority for Government Action'.

79 Which suits most political leaders and the general public alike; Interview with Sir Douglas Graham, 24 November 1999.

80 By contrast Australia's Constitution may be described as a social covenant drawn up and ratified by the people; J.A. La Nauze, *The Making of the Australian Constitution* (Melbourne, 1972).

81 The sovereignty of the Crown is not merely a legal fiction, as Bercuson argued, since it has practical consequences, including a measure of public perception as a source of authority; David Bercuson and Barry Cooper, 'From Constitutional Monarchy to Quasi Republic', in Janet Ajzenstat (ed.), *Canadian Constitutionalism, 1791–1991* (Ottawa, 1992); cf David E. Smith, *The Republican Option in Canada, Past and*

Present (Toronto, 1999), p. 18; Interview with Sir Douglas Graham, 24 November 1999.

82 Gregory Clarke, 'Popular Sovereignty and Constitutional Reform in Canada' (1997) Acadia University MA thesis.

83 At least, by Pakeha. Maori showed a greater willingness, if only because they saw thereby a means of increasing their share of authority; Interview with Hon Georgina te Heuheu, 7 December 1999.

84 Laski, 'Responsibility of the State in England'.

85 Sir Ernest Barker defined a modern State as:

generally a territorial nation, organized as a legal association by its own action in creating a constitution ... and permanently acting as such an association, under that constitution, for the purpose of maintaining a scheme of legal rules defining and securing the rights and duties of its members.

This is to be distinguished from a nation, which 'is a society or community, whose unity is based primarily on space ... and in that common love of the natal soil (or *patria*) which is called patriotism'; and 'on time, or the common tradition of centuries, issuing in the sense of a common participation in an inherited way of life, and in that common love for the inheritance which is called nationalism'

– Sir Ernest Barker, *Reflections on Government* (London, 1942), p. xv.

86 Held; J.R. Strayer, *On the Mediæval Origins of the Modern State* (Princeton, 1970).

87 Excepting those countries, such as the USA, which were compelled to address this often difficult issue, because of the republican and federal nature of their government.

88 Bernard Susser (ed.), *Approaches to the Study of Politics* (New York, 1992), p. 180. In recent decades State-centred theorists have sought to bring the State back, arguing that it is more autonomous than society-centred theorists have claimed. As Bogdanor found, it is necessary to range across law, politics, and history to understand a historic constitution; Vernon Bogdanor, *The Monarchy and the Constitution* (Oxford, 1995).

89 Ernst Kantorowicz, 'Kingship under the impact of scientific jurisprudence', in Marshall Clagett et al (ed.), *Twelfth century Europe* (Madison, 1961), p. 89.

90 Strayer.

91 Susan Reynolds, 'Law and Community in Western Christendom', *American Journal of Legal History* (1981): 206.

92 Dark Age kings were expected to hold fast the territory of their own communities, to master or conqueror their neighbours, and to protect their own people and enable them to live securely; Kantorowicz, 'Kingship under the impact of scientific jurisprudence', pp. 89–111.

93 'What hath pleased the prince has the force of law'.

94 Thomas Hobbes, *Leviathan* (New York, 1962); Quentin Skinner, 'Conquest and Consent: Thomas Hobbes and the Engagement Controversy', in G.E. Aylmer (ed.), *The Interregnum – The Quest for Settlement, 1640–1660* (Hamden, 1972).

95 Typified by Machiavelli.

96 He argued for a version of sovereignty of the whole citizen body over itself; Jean-Jacques Rouseau, *The Social Contract and other later political writings*, trans. and ed. Victor Goureatres (Cambridge, 1997).

97 He outlined what he believed was the equilibrium of the British political system, which he compared to the French – to the disadvantage of the latter; Charles de

Secondat Baron de Montesquieu, 'The Spirit of the Laws', in Arend Lijphart (ed.), *Parliamentary versus Presidential Government* (Oxford, 1992), p. 48.

98 Harold Laski, *Authority in the modern State* (New Haven, 1919), pp. 21–4.

99 The United Kingdom can, of course, be dated to the Union with Ireland Act 1800. British constitutional law has been essentially that of England – though not without dispute; Sir Thomas Smith, 'Pretensions of English Law as "Imperial Law"', in *The Laws of Scotland* (Edinburgh, 1987), vol. 5, paras 711–19.

100 Though in recent decades there have been some movements in this direction, for legal rather than political reasons; see Jacobs.

101 Vernon Bogdanor, 'Britain and Europe' in R. Holme and Michael Elliott (ed.), *1688–1988 Time for a New Constitution* (London, 1988), p. 81.

102 Indeed, a Continental observer would find two of the distinguishing characteristics of English law (and by extension that of the common law world) to be its antiquity and continuity, and its predominantly judicial character and the absence of codification; Henri Levy-Ullmann, *The English Legal Tradition: Its Sources and History*, trans. M. Mitchell rev. and ed. Frederick Goadly (London, 1935), pp. xlvi–liii.

103 s 8: 'The Queen's excellent Majesty, acting according to the laws of the realm, is the highest power under God in the kingdom, and has supreme authority over all persons in all causes, as well ecclesiastical as civil'; see *The Canons of the Church of England* (London, 1969) Canon A7; *Thirty-Nine Articles of Religion* (1562, confirmed 1571) Art. 37.

104 Kelsey, for example, speaks of the State where constitutional lawyers would traditionally speak of the Crown, or some political scientists the government; Kelsey, *Rolling Back the State*. See also Sharp, *Leap into the dark*.

105 Or, perhaps not so curious, given the uncertainty felt by many Maori about the scope of *kawanatanga* and *tino rangatiratanga*; Interview with Sir Douglas Graham, 24 November 1999.

106 See, for example, the 'Building the Constitution' conference held in Wellington in 2000; Colin James (ed.), *Building the Constitution* (Wellington, 2000).

107 Shaun Goldfinch, 'The State', in Raymond Miller (ed.), *New Zealand Government and Politics* (Melbourne, 2001), pp. 511–20, 516–17.

108 For example, in the chapters devoted to the various interpretations of the State in Miller, *New Zealand Government and Politics*.

109 *Democracy and Power in New Zealand.*

110 *Leap into the dark*; *Justice and the Maori.*

111 John Morrow, 'Neo-Liberalism', in Miller (ed.), *New Zealand Government and Politics*, pp. 521–32.

112 Richard Mulgan, 'A pluralist analysis of the New Zealand State', in Brian Roper and Chris Rudd (ed.), *State and Economy in New Zealand* (Auckland, 1993), pp. 128–46.

113 Rosemary Du Plessis, 'Women, Feminism and the State', in Brian Roper and Chris Rudd (ed.), *The Political Economy of New Zealand* (Auckland, 1997), pp. 220–36.

114 Chandra Dixon, 'Marxism', in Raymond Miller (ed.), *New Zealand Politics in Transition* (Auckland, 1997), pp. 350–8.

115 Sharp, *Leap into the dark*; Kelsey, *Rolling Back the State*; Pat Moloney, 'Pluralist Theories of the State', in Miller, *New Zealand Politics in Transition*, pp. 317–28.

116 Pat Moloney, 'Neo-Liberalism: A Pluralist Critique', in Miller, *New Zealand Government and Politics*, pp. 533–43, 542.

117 Jacobs.

118 See Kelsey, *Rolling Back the State*.

119 Jacobs, p. 24.

120 Gavin Little, 'Scotland and Parliamentary Sovereignty', *Legal Studies*, 24(4) (2004): 540–67.

121 This evolutionary and legalistic approach has been remarked upon regularly by Continental observers; Levy-Ullmann, *The English Legal Tradition*.

122 A conclusion in accordance with the findings of Janine Hayward, 'In search of a treaty partner' (1995) Victoria University of Wellington PhD thesis.

123 Gordon McLauchlan, 'Of President and Country', *New Zealand Herald*, 17 February 1995.

124 Joseph, 'The Crown as a legal concept (I)'; 'The Crown as a legal concept (II)'. See also Kelsey, *Rolling Back the State*.

125 See Janine Hayward, 'In search of a treaty partner' (1995) Victoria University of Wellington PhD thesis; Margaret Wilson, 'The Reconfiguration of New Zealand's Constitutional Institutions: The Transformation of Tino Rangatiratanga into Political Reality', *Waikato Law Review*, 5 (1997): 17.

126 There was a real interregnum between the death of one king and the election and coronation of another. The hereditary right to be considered eventually became the right to be elected. As the conception of hereditary right strengthened the practical inconvenience of the interregnum was curtailed; Frederic Maitland and Sir Frederick Pollock, *History of English Law before the Times of Edward I* (2nd edn, Cambridge, 1895), vol. 1, p. 507.

127 'The English Constitution'.

128 This question has been called 'the most puzzling constitutional conundrum of all'; Andrew Sharp, 'Constitution', in Miller, *New Zealand Government and Politics*, pp. 37–47, 40. *Taylor v New Zealand Poultry Board* [1984] 1 NZLR 394, 398 per Cooke P.

129 With the courts supervising the exercise of a common law power of government, as in *Wolfe Tone's Case* (1798) 27 State Tr 614.

130 Laski, 'The Theory of Popular Sovereignty'.

131 Though the Australian Constitution has been held to be based on popular sovereignty, as it was adopted by referendum, and may only be changed by referendum: *Australian Capital Television Pty Ltd v Commonwealth* (1992) 177 CLR 106, 138 per Mason CJ; *Theophanous v Herald & Weekly Times Ltd* (1994) 182 CLR 104, 171 per Deane J; *McGinty v Western Australia* (1996) 186 CLR 140, 230, 237 per McHugh J.

132 Edmund Burke saw a constitution as based on a social contract which evolved from generation to generation; Russell, *Constitutional Odyssey*, pp. 10–11.

133 The Prince of Wales was reported as believing that a referendum on the monarchy in the United Kingdom would provide a new and lasting legitimacy for the Crown; 'Prince wants British to choose', *New Zealand Herald*, 8 November 1999.

134 Alan Simpson (ed.), *Constitutional Implications of MMP* (Wellington, 1998).

135 Dona Awatere, *Maori Sovereignty* (Auckland, 1984).

136 See Janine Hayward, 'In search of a treaty partner' (1995) Victoria University of Wellington PhD thesis.

137 Jock Phillips, 'The Constitution and Independent Nationhood', in James, *Building the Constitution*, pp. 69–76.

138 Dame Catherine Tizard, *Crown and Anchor*; *the present role of the Governor-General in New Zealand* (Wellington, 1993), pp. 7–8.

139 There was a strong feeling in Tuvalu that a system which had stood the test of time must have something good about it; Tauassa Taafahi, *Governance in the Pacific*: *the dismissal of Tuvalu's Governor-General* (Canberra, 1996), p. 1.

140 Rodney Barker, *Political Legitimacy and the State* (Oxford, 1990), p. 4. For a general discussion of aspects of legitimacy in relation to the Crown, see F.M. Brookfield, 'Some aspects of the Necessity Principle in Constitutional Law' (1972) University of Oxford DPhil thesis; and Brookfield, *Waitangi and Indigenous Rights*.

141 See Randall Collins, *Weberian Sociological Theory* (Cambridge, 1986).

142 Penelope Brook Cowen, 'Neo-Liberalism' in Miller, *New Zealand Politics in Transition*.

143 Which is illustrated by the study of the application of the model to Mummar Qadhafi's Libya; Saleh Al Namlah, 'Political legitimacy in Libya since 1969' (1992) Syracuse University PhD thesis.

144 John Rawls, *Political Liberalism* (New York, 1993); Ted Honderich (ed.), *The Oxford Companion to Philosophy* (Oxford, 1995), p. 477; Matthew Swanson, 'The Social extract tradition and the question of political legitimacy' (1995) University of Missouri–Columbia PhD thesis.

145 Seymour Martin Lipset, *Political Man*: *The Social Bases of Politics* (New York, 1960), p. 77.

146 Robert Bierstedt, 'Legitimacy', in Julian Gould and William Kolb (ed.), *A Dictionary of the Social Sciences* (London, 1964), p. 386.

147 Richard Merelmen, 'Learning and Legitimacy', *American Political Science Review*, 60(3) (1966): 548–61.

148 In an extreme form, the divine right of kings; J.N. Figgis, *The theory of the Divine Right of Kings* (2nd edn, Cambridge, 1914).

149 John Schaar, 'Legitimacy in the Modern State', in William Connolly (ed.), *Legitimacy and the State* (Oxford, 1984), p. 108; Jonathan Waskan, 'De facto legitimacy and popular will', *Social Theory and Practice*, 24(1) (1998): 25–56.

150 Hannah Arendt, 'What was authority', in Carl Friedrich (ed.), *Authority* (Cambridge, Massachusetts, 1958), p. 83.

151 Fatos Tarifa, 'Quest for legitimacy and the withering away of utopia', *Social Forces*, 76 (1997): 437–74.

152 See, for example, Sir Elihu Lauterpacht, 'Sovereignty'.

153 David E. Smith, *The Invisible Crown*: *The First Principle of Canadian Government* (Toronto, 1995); Anthony Birch, *The British System of Government* (9th edn, London, 1993).

154 Taafahi, *Governance in the Pacific*, p. 1.

155 Jacobs.

156 The Treaty of Waitangi might serve a similar purpose, though it is perhaps unlikely that it would achieve this alone, as opinion polls suggest that it lacks the general support of the non-Maori population; see Paul Perry and Alan Webster, *New Zealand Politics at the Turn of the Millennium*: *Attitudes and Values about Politics and Government* (Auckland, 1999), pp. 74–5.

157 Note the emphasis in such works as Jonathan Boston, Stephen Levine, Elizabeth McLeay, Nigel Roberts and Hannah Schmidt, 'Caretaker governments and the

evolution of caretaker conventions in New Zealand', *Victoria University of Wellington Law Review*, 28(4) (1998): 629, where the institutional role of the Crown is given relatively little coverage.

158 Barker, *Political Legitimacy and the State*, pp. 143–4.

159 Harris, 'The "Third Source" of Authority for Government Action'.

160 Smith, 'Bagehot, the Crown, and the Canadian Constitution'.

161 Recent examples include Crown Health Enterprises.

162 'The English Constitution', vol. 5, p. 253.

163 F.M. Brookfield, *The Constitution in 1985: The Search for Legitimacy* (Auckland, 1985), p. 5.

164 As in Grenada in 1983, and Fiji in 1987; *Mitchell v Director of Public Prosecutions* [1986] LRC (Const) 35; P.StJ. Smart, 'Revolution, Constitution and the Commonwealth: Grenada', *International and Comparative Law Quarterly*, 35 (1986): 950.

165 See F.M. Brookfield, 'Some aspects of the Necessity Principle in Constitutional Law' (1972) University of Oxford DPhil thesis.

166 The principle of popular sovereignty, hitherto vague, has acquired sufficient determinacy to serve, in a limited range of circumstances, as a basis for denial of legal recognition to putative governments; Brad Roth, 'Governmental illegitimacy in international law' (1996) University of California, Berkeley PhD thesis.

167 Seymour Lipset, 'Social Conflict, Legitimacy, and Democracy', in Connolly, *Legitimacy and the State*, p. 92.

168 A. Passerin d'Entrèves, *The Notion of the State: An Introduction to Political Theory* (Oxford, 1967), p. 141 and following.

169 See, for example, Tarifa, 'Quest for legitimacy and the withering away of utopia'.

170 Schaar, 'Legitimacy in the Modern State', pp. 104–6.

171 Lipset, 'Social Conflict, Legitimacy, and Democracy', pp. 89–90.

172 Ibid., pp. 88–90.

173 Collins, *Weberian Sociological Theory*.

174 Mulgan, 'Can the Treaty of Waitangi provide a constitutional basis for New Zealand's political future?', 53–4.

175 Briefly, Maori sovereignty involves the dispute over precisely what the Maori relinquished in the Treaty of Waitangi with the Crown in 1840.

176 Brookfield, *Waitangi and Indigenous Rights*.

177 Thus the German government after 1933, while still adhering to legal form, departed from accepted standards of behaviour and so lost its legitimacy.

178 This could perhaps occur in Australia, were a second republican referendum to fail to achieve the necessary overall majority, but enjoy a popular majority nonetheless.

179 See, for examples, Matthew Strickland, 'Against the Lord's anointed', in George Garnett and John Hudson (ed.), *Law and Government in Mediæval England and Normandy* (Cambridge, 1994), p. 56.

180 Or even less authority. See, for example, Jackson, 'Maori Law, Pakeha Law and the Treaty of Waitangi', p. 19.

181 Awatere, *Maori Sovereignty*; Jane Kelsey, 'Legal Imperialism and the Colonization of Aotearoa', in Paul Spoonley (ed.), *Tauiwi: Racism and Ethnicity in New Zealand* (Palmerston North, 1984).

182 Janine Hayward, 'In search of a treaty partner' (1995) Victoria University of Wellington PhD thesis 2.

183 An act committed by the sovereign power of a country which cannot be challenged in the courts. At least, this had been the attitude of the courts from 1877; Wayne Attrill, 'Aspects of the Treaty of Waitangi in the Law and Constitution of New Zealand' (1989) Harvard University LLM thesis 39–54.

184 For the text of the proclamation, see the despatch of Hobson to the Secretary of State for the Colonies, 25 May 1840, in *British Parliamentary Papers – Colonies, New Zealand* (Shannon, 1970) Sessions 1841/311, pp. 15, 18–19.

185 F.M. Brookfield, 'Parliamentary Supremacy and Constitutional Entrenchment', *Otago Law Review*, 5 (1984): 603; Bruce Harris, 'Law-making powers of the New Zealand General Assembly', *Otago Law Review*, 5 (1984): 565.

186 Brookfield, *The Constitution in 1985*, p. 9.

187 This is illustrated by Canada's continued difficulties in identifying its own constitutional grundnorms; Carl Berger (ed.), *Imperialism and Nationalism, 1884–1914: A Conflict in Canadian Thought* (Toronto, 1969).

188 Sir Henry Wade, 'The Basis of Legal Sovereignty', *Cambridge Law Journal* (1955): 172–97, 190 onwards.

189 See Noel Cox, 'The control of advice to the Crown and the development of executive independence in New Zealand', *Bond Law Review*, 13(1) (2001): 166–89.

190 Robert Heuston, *Essays in Constitutional Law* (2nd edn, London, 1964), pp. 40–1.

191 *Arthur Yates and Co Pty Ltd v Vegetable Seeds Committee* (1945) 72 CLR 37, 66 per Latham CJ.

192 I. Hardin and N. Lewis, *The Noble Lie: The British Constitution and the Role of Law* (London, 1987), p. 7.

193 *Entick v Carrington* (1765) 19 State Tr 1030 per Lord Camden.

194 Rushdoony, p. 61.

195 Harris, 'The "Third Source" of Authority for Government Action'.

196 Royal Commission on the Electoral System, *Report of the Royal Commission on the Electoral System "Towards a better democracy"* (Wellington, 1986), p. 27.

197 *Introduction to the Study of the Law of the Constitution*, introduction and appendix by E.C.S. Wade (10th edn, London, 1959).

198 Joseph, *Constitutional and Administrative Law in New Zealand.*

199 Hardin and Lewis, p. 3.

200 Ibid., pp. 30–2.

201 Written 1598, collection published 1616.

202 King James I, *Basilikon Doron* (Menston, 1969, first published 1599).

203 Sir Robert Filmer, *Patriarcha and other writings*, ed. J.P. Sommerville (London, 1991).

204 See, for example, John Dunn, *The Political Thought of John Locke: An historical account of the Two Treatises of Government* (London, 1969), ch. VII.

205 This idea, not unknown in earlier times, was most explicitly and universally expressed after the Restoration. The divine right, the impiety of resistance, and of the subjects' duty to render at least passive obedience to royal commands. If the king recovered only an attenuated authority, he possessed it by the most august and sacred of titles.

206 Sam vii.10–18.

207 Prov viii.15.

208 Daniel iv.

209 Luke xx.25.

210 John xix.11.

211 Rom xiii.1–7; 1 Pet ii.13–17. The Roman Pontiff, in orders a bishop, is in jurisdiction held to be by divine right the centre of all Catholic unity, and consequently Pastor and Teacher of all Christians. There is no recourse against the judgement or decree of the Pontiff, who is regarded in canon law as being the supreme judge for the whole world: *The Code of Canon Law: in English Translation* prepared by the Canon Law Society of Great Britain and Ireland (London, 1983), canons 333 §3, 1442.

212 Figgis, pp. 3–11.

213 Although John Hall did reject biblical arguments – John Hall, *The Grounds and Reasons of Monarchy* prefixed to *The Political Works of James Harrington*, ed. J.G.A. Pocock (Cambridge, 1977).

214 The first function of Locke's First Treatise of Government was to show that Scripture did not show that God had given any man, or order of men, superiority over other men: John Locke, *Two Treatises of Government*, ed. Peter Laslett (Cambridge, 1988), treatise I.

215 *Revocatio Novarum Ordinationum* 1322 Statutes of the Realm (Printed by command of His Majesty King George the Third in pursuance of an address of the House of Commons of Great Britain, London, 1810–1822), vol. 1, p. 189.

216 Ibid.

217 Ibid., vol. I, p. 182. The trial criticized the passage which said that:

Homage and the Oath of Allegiance is more by reason of the Crown than by reason of the person of the king, and it bideth itself more unto the Crown than unto the person; and this appears in that before the Estate of the Crown hath descended, no allegiance is belonging to the person; wherefore if the king by chance be not guided by Reason, in right of the Crown, his Liege Subjects are bound by the Oath made to the Crown to guide the king and the Estate of the Crown back again by reason, or otherwise the oath would not be kept. Nor were it to be asked, how they ought to guide the king? Whether by course of law, or by violence? By course of law a man will not be able to get redress, for he will have no judges but such as are the king's, in which case, if the will of the king be not according to reason he certainly will have only Error maintained and confirmed; wherefore it behoveth, in order to save the Oath, that when the king will not redress the matter and remove that which is hurtful to the people at large, and prejudicial to the Crown, it is to be determined, that the king be removed by violence, for he is bound by his oath to govern the people and his liege subjects, and his liege subjects are bound to govern in aid of him and in his default.

218 (1608) 7 Co Rep 1a; 77 ER 377.

219 Figgis, pp. 11–32.

220 Ibid., p. 223. The king was also above the law in the sense that the courts, being his courts, could not try him. A special High Court of Judicature was set up to try Charles I. Henry VI's judges also refused to advise him regarding the claim of the Duke of York, on the grounds that it was not justiciable – Rot Parl V 375–9 in *English Historical Documents* vol. 4, 1327–1485, ed. A.R. Myers (London, 1969), pp. 416–17.

221 Figgis, p. 237.

222 Jean Bodin, *Les Six Livres de la République* (‘*The Six bookes of a Commonwealth*’), trans. M.J. Tooley (Oxford, 1955).

223 John Cannon and Ralph Griffiths, *The Oxford Illustrated History of the British Monarchy* (Oxford, 1988), p. 301.

224 Cannon and Griffiths, p. 302.

225 Figgis, p. 242.

226 Ibid., p. 243.

227 St Thomas Aquinas, *Summa theologiæ* (London, 1963).

228 Figgis, pp. 249–51.

229 Ibid., p. 252.

230 Ibid., p. 258.

231 Cannon and Griffiths, p. 415.

232 Ibid., pp. 370–76.

233 Ibid., p. 459.

234 Figgis, p. 263.

235 Cannon and Griffiths, p. 357.

236 The original compact – the ‘law of the Kingdom’ of Samuel. All political theory in the twentieth century was arguably utilitarian. We must not judge the seventeenth century by our values and standards, any more that we should that of the nineteenth century. See Locke, *Two Treatises of Government*; Jonathan Scott, *Algernon Sidney and the Restoration Crisis, 1677–1683* (Cambridge, 1991).

237 Jane Kelsey, ‘Restructuring the Nation’, in Peter Fitzpatrick (ed.), *Nationalism, Racism and the Rule of Law* (Aldershot, 1995), p. 185; See also Bruce Clark, *Native liberty, Crown Supremacy – the Existing Aboriginal Right of Self-Government in Canada* (Montreal, 1990), pp. 191–219. That traditional structures and modern institutions each owe their validity and authority to distinct criteria is obvious. Where a constitution is based on such a pluralistic basis tension is inevitable; Bekithemba Ralph Khumalo, ‘Legal Pluralism and constitutional tensions’ (1993) York University LLM thesis.

238 Interview with Sir Douglas Graham, 24 November 1999.

239 Brookfield, *Waitangi and Indigenous Rights*.

240 P.G. McHugh, ‘Constitutional Myths and the Treaty of Waitangi’, *New Zealand Law Journal* (1991): 316; David Williams, ‘The Constitutional Status of the Treaty of Waitangi: an historical perspective’, *New Zealand Universities Law Review*, 14 (1990): 9–36.

241 In England, Reginald Pecock and John Fortescue, and on the Continent, Pierre D’Ailly, Nicholas of Cusa; Reginald Pecock, *Donet*, ed. Elsie Vaughan Hitchcock EETS OS 156 (1921 for 1918, repr. 1971), p. 76; Sir John Fortescue, *In Praise of the laws of England (De Laudibus Legum Angliæ)*, ed. Stanley Chrimes (Cambridge, 1942), c. 36, p. 87; Sir Robert Carlyle and A.J. Carlyle, *A History of Mediæval Political Theory in the West* (6 vols, Edinburgh, 1928–36), vol. 6, pp. 138, 141.

242 Maitland and Pollock, vol. 1, p. 182.

243 Figgis, p. 230.

244 Ibid., p. 245.

245 See William Hearn, *The Government of England: Its Structure and its Development* (London, 1867), which was a major influence on Dicey.

246 Sir Owen Dixon, 'The Law and the Constitution', *Law Quarterly Review*, 51 (1935): 590, 593–5. Nor will the courts be eager to question the authority of an Act of Parliament, a principle cited as early as 1455; P 33 Hen VI 17, 8 at 18 per Fortescue, CJKB.

247 Nicole Oresme, *Le livres de Politiques d' Aristotle*, ed. A.D. Menut (1970) Transactions of the American Philosophical Society 137–8.

248 He followed Masilius, drawing on Roman law and Aristotelian utility; Jean Dunbabin, 'Government', in J.H. Burns (ed.), *The Cambridge History of Mediæval Political Thought c.350–c.1450* (Cambridge, 1988), p. 507.

249 *Sed non sic Angliae statuta oriri possunt, dum nedum principis voluntate sed et totius regni assensu ipsa conduntur, quo populi laesuram illam efficere requeunt vel non corum commodum procurare.* – Fortescue, *In Praise of the laws of England*, p. 41.

250 A limited monarchy, in contrast to an absolute monarchy; Sir John Fortescue, *The Governance of England*, notes by Charles Plummer (reprint Westport, Connecticut, 1979).

251 The extent to which the common law resisted the reception of Roman law has been much disputed, though recent research suggests that the mediæval common law, though surviving in an organic sense, actually underwent a substantial reformation in the Renaissance period, especially in the 1490s to 1540s; See the introduction to *The Reports of Sir John Spelman* (2 vols, London, 1978), vol. 2 Seldon Society vol. 94; Sir John Baker, 'English Law and the Renaissance', *Cambridge Law Journal* (1985): 46.

252 *In Praise of the laws of England*, pp. 12–98.

253 Sir Thomas Smith was a civil lawyer who stood analytically outside the constraints of the common law tradition.

254 Sir Geoffrey Elton, *Reform and Reformation, 1509–1558* (London, 1979), pp. 199–200.

255 Kevin Sharpe, *The Personal Rule of Charles I* (New Haven, 1992), p. 930.

256 Sir Owen Dixon, pp. 590–2.

257 See, for example, H.T. Dickinson, 'The Eighteenth-Century Debate on the "Glorious Revolution"', *History*, 61 (1976): 28–45; H.T. Dickinson, 'The Eighteenth-Century Debate on the Sovereignty of Parliament', *Transactions of the Royal Historical Society (5th Series)*, 26 (1976): 189–210.

258 I.R. Christie, *Wars and Revolutions: Britain, 1760–1815* (Cambridge, Massachusetts, 1982), p. 21.

259 Kenneth Pennington, 'Law, Legislative authority and theories of government, 1150–1300', in Burns, *The Cambridge History of Mediæval Political Thought c.350–c.1450*, pp. 426–7.

260 Part of this problem is discussed in Ernst Kantorowicz, *The King's Two Bodies: A Study in Mediæval Political Theology* (Princeton, 1957), pp. 42–61.

261 Pennington, 'Law, Legislative authority and theories of government, 1150–1300', p. 427.

262 Anonymous of Rouen, *Die Texte des Normannischen Anonymous*, ed. K. Pellens (Stuttgart, 1966) p. 130.

263 *Itaque in unoquoque gemina intelligitur fuisse persona: una ex natura, altera ex gratia ... In una quippe erat naturaliter individuus homo, in altera per gratiam christus, id est, deus-home.* – Anonymous of Rouen, p. 130.

264 See Kantorowicz, *The King's Two Bodies*, pp. 42–61.

265 Gratian of Bologna, *Concordia discordantium canonum* (or *Decretum magistri Gratiani*), in A. Friedberg (ed.), *Corpus Iuris Canonici* (2 vols, Tauchnitz, 1879), vol. 1. Better known simply as the *Descretum*.

266 Pennington, 'Law, Legislative authority and theories of government, 1150–1300', pp. 424–5.

267 Figgis, p. 266.

268 J.R. Lander, *The Limitations of English Monarchy in the Later Middle Ages* (Toronto, 1989), pp. 4–6.

269 *In Praise of the laws of England.*

270 Robert Brady argued that Parliament and the common law were not part of an ancient and immemorial constitution, but traceable instead to the Conquest and the institution of feudalism; J.G.A. Pocock, *The Ancient Constitution and the Feudal Law; A Study of English Historical Thought in the Seventeenth Century* (2nd edn, Cambridge, 1987), pp. 3–8.

271 Fortescue, *The Governance of England*, p. 172.

272 To recognize the truth of something without the need for that thing being proven.

273 In 1311 the ordainers thought that they were acting only to subordinate an erring King to the obligations imposed by the Crown, but in doing so they risked the accusation that they had separated the King from the Crown. This fault was in fact committed in 1308, with the opposition to Gaveston; Stanley Chrimes and A.L. Brown, *Select Documents of English Constitutional History 1307–1485* (London, 1961), p. 30.

274 Dunbabin, pp. 505–6.

275 Giles of Rome, *De regimine principum* (2 vols, Rome, 1556), vol. 1, ch. 2, p. 10, 1556 fol. 44v.

276 Aquinas in particular was not convinced by the Latin tag; St Thomas Aquinas, vol. 1, book IIae, qu. 90, art. 3.

277 Henry de Bracton, *On the Laws and Customs of England* ('*Henri de Bracton de Legibus et Consuetudis Angliæ*'), ed. G.E. Woodbine, trans. S.E. Thorne (2 vols, Cambridge, Massachusetts, 1968), vol. 2, p. 21.

278 See John Dunn, 'The concept of trust in the politics of John Locke', in R. Rorty (ed.), *Philosophy in History* (Cambridge, 1984), pp. 279–302.

279 In the fifteenth century words of Sir John Fortescue, 'the king is given for the kingdome, and not the kingdome for the king': Fortescue, *In Praise of the laws of England*, p. 87.

280 In the Remonstrance of 1648 the army called for 'no king be hereafter admitted, but upon the election of, and as upon trust for the people'; William Cobbett (ed.), *The Parliamentary History of England* (12 vols, London, 1806–20), vol. 3, p. 1125.

281 Robert Bennet, *King Charle's Trial Iustified* (London, 1649), p. 4.

282 Filmer.

283 J.R. Western, *Monarchy and Revolution – the English State in the 1680s* (London, 1972), pp. 7–14. For Locke's concept of the state of nature see Robert A. Goldwin, 'Locke's state of nature in political society', *Western Political Quarterly*, 31 (1976): 126–35.

284 Including the statute law because that was formerly rare.

285 c.500.

286 c.690.

287 c.600.

288 In western Europe law codes were rare until the twelfth century, when a whole new jurisprudence appeared, as the Roman law of Justinian became better understood and diffused: F.L. Attenborough (ed.), *Laws of the earliest English kings* (Cambridge, 1922); A.J. Robertson, *Laws of the Kings of England* (Cambridge, 1925). The real distinction between law and custom only arose from the twelfth century, as a clear distinction must depend on the monopoly of law enforcement and on a procedure of legislation, and of recording legislation: M. Gluckman, *Politics law and ritual in tribal society* (Oxford, 1977), pp. 196–202.

289 Sir William Anson, *The Law and Custom of the Constitution*, ed. A.B. Keith (5th edn, 1922, Oxford; 3rd edn, 1907), vol. 2, Part 1, pp. 16–17.

290 Janet L. Nelson, 'Kingship and empire', in Burns, *The Cambridge History of Mediæval Political Thought c.350–c.1450*, pp. 213–29.

291 Wulfstan of York, *An Werk Erzbischof Wulfstans von York – Die 'Institutes of Polity, Civil and Ecclesiastical'*, ed. K. Jost (Tübingen, 1959), pp. 40–2.

292 Nelson, pp. 239–40.

293 Cannon and Griffiths, p. 32.

294 Nelson, p. 241.

295 Cannon and Griffiths, p. 34.

296 Ibid., p. 66.

297 Ibid., p. 104.

298 Ibid., p. 106.

299 Ibid., p. 108.

300 Ibid., p. 110.

301 Ibid., pp. 111–12.

302 52 Hen III.

303 Cannon and Griffiths, pp. 148–9.

304 Ibid., p. 156.

305 3 September 1189.

306 Cannon and Griffiths, p. 158.

307 Ibid., p. 217.

308 Ibid., p. 299.

309 Ibid., p. 322.

310 These dates are approximate, since the events contained within these revolutionary periods were often loosely conjoined.

311 Lawrence Tshuma, 'Hierarchies and Government versus Networks and Governance: Competing Regulatory Paradigms in Global Economic Regulation', *Law, Social Justice and Global Development* (1999) <http://elj.warwick.ac.uk/global/issue/2000-1/tshuma.html>.

312 W.H. Reinicke, 'Global Public Policy', *Foreign Affairs* (1997): 127–38, 129.

313 Tshuma, 'Hierarchies and Government versus Networks and Governance: Competing Regulatory Paradigms in Global Economic Regulation'.

314 J. Matthews, 'Power Shift', *Foreign Affairs*, 76(1) (1997): 50–71.

315 Tshuma, 'Hierarchies and Government versus Networks and Governance: Competing Regulatory Paradigms in Global Economic Regulation'.

316 Susan Hornby and Zoë Clarke (ed.), *Challenge and change in the information society* (London, 2003).

317 Manuel Castells, *The Rise of the Network Society* (2nd edn, Oxford, 2000).
318 Illegal under the 1992 Chemical Weapons Convention and the 1928 Geneva Protocol.
319 *United States v. AT&T*, 552 F. Supp. 131 (D.D.C. 1982), affirmed *sub nom Maryland v. United States*, 460 U.S. 1001 (1983).
320 R.G. Noll and B.M. Owen, 'The Anticompetitive Use of Regulation: *United States v. AT&T*', in J.E. Kwoka and L.J. White (ed.), *The Antitrust Revolution* (Glenview, 1989), pp. 290–337.

Chapter 2

The Response of Business to Changes in the Legal Environment

2.1 Introduction

The consequences of changes in the legal environment, whether caused by technological developments, political reform or otherwise, can be particularly severe for businesses. Managers often start with an attitude that separates legal issues from the strategic and operational concerns of the business. However, in a global economy where goods, services and investments move across political (and less tangible economic) borders, subjecting businesses to the growing complexity of regulation and liability in other countries, this conventional approach to legal concerns is no longer very realistic.[1] The development of business is heavily influenced by the legal environment, including the global legal environment, and by technology.

This Chapter considers how business responds to changes in legal systems, whether wrought by technological changes, or otherwise. Significant changes are being wrought by developments in technology (especially information technology in its widest definition), so the focus is upon the relevance of past and current example of change to the current technological environment. It is not concerned with the social or economic implications of these technological revolutions – profound as they may be.[2] Nor is it concerned with the effect of technological change upon the structure of government – upon the legal system (except briefly) – nor on how the structure of governments may have in turn effected technological changes (or changes of any other sort).[3] Rather this Chapter is concerned with the possible response of businesses to paradigmatic[4] changes to the legal system caused by technological or other changes external to the businesses.

We begin with a brief look at some of the ways in which technology affects legal systems, whether at the constitutional level, or less fundamentally, at the legislative, regulatory or administrative level. We will also look at ways in which technology is altering the relationship of governed and government, and between government and government. After a brief discussion of what is meant by business – and what its role is, we then consider how legal systems also affect technology. We then proceed to consider how business responds to changes in the legal systems, whether wrought by technological changes, or otherwise.

For the purposes of this Chapter, business is to be seen as having a broad rather than a narrow definition. It may be defined is a commercial activity engaged in by an actor as a means of livelihood or profit, or an entity which engages in such activities,[5] as well as a commercial activity engaged in otherwise than for profit.[6] This concept of business includes both public and private manifestations, and combines legal and sociological aspects. This broad definition matches the wide definition given to technology, both of which are chosen in order to maximise the range of activities covered, and avoid excluding activities due to unduly artificial definitions or criteria.

The role of business in society depends, to some extent at least, upon the degree of economic development of the society, as well as its homogeneity.[7] A highly industrialised, or post-industrial society, will present subtly different forms of business enterprise than pre-industrial, or less developed societies. Such classifications can be little better than indicative at best – though such writers as Marx[8] have developed important and influential models and theorems based around them. However, whether an economy may be characterised as industrial, post-industrial, partially industrialised, or otherwise, individuals and groups will see (and seek to exploit) commercial opportunities.[9] These opportunities may arise as a result of many developments, some of which are internal and others external to both the business and the economy, but will include changing technology, or changing laws.

Business (or capital as Marx would have called it, though his definition is rather more formal than that used here) takes advantage of opportunities afforded by the economic, political, social, and technological environment. Business practices must change to meet changing environment – including the legal environment. If the legal system is too rigid the economy is restricted.[10] This may be seen in traditional societies where the legal code restricts property ownership or the succession to property, and limits the opportunities for collective business enterprise. This could be, for example, by not recognizing the concept of the company, or placing limitations upon the exploitation of capital by limiting the use of interest on loans.

It may also be that certain fields of technological endeavour are more restricted by laws than others. For example modern genetic research is generally subject to close and highly restrictive government regulation – at least in the industrialised west.[11] There is, of course, little homogeneity in this. Certain business undertakings – for example the cultivation of genetically modified crops[12] – are illegal in some countries though not in others.[13] Sometimes the individual state follows the lead of the scientists, developers and businesses, and sometimes the state alone determines the pace and direction of development.[14] The approach may be varied depending upon the economic and political conditions of the time, and varies depending upon the particular prevailing philosophy of each country.

When there is a profound change in the legal system, as by political, economic, or social upheaval, or a seminal technological breakthrough which has the potential to affect the whole of society, then business is directly affected. The ways in which businesses respond to these challenges – and opportunities – are also a reflection of the prevailing cultural ethos of the country concerned, as well as of the company culture or ethos. The former has been the subject of detailed study,[15] the latter rather less so.

2.2 Business Response to Changes in Legal Systems

Just as legal systems may be categorised as being primarily national and international (discounting for the moment the question of regional legal systems within countries, and supra-national legal systems), so business responses to changes in legal systems may be seen as having national and international aspects. Changes at each level may have significant effects on businesses, but the effects will differ, depending upon the degree of exposure the particular business faces to international economic or regulatory developments.

At the national level, economic liberalization – especially through industry regulation or deregulation, the creation or dismantling of tariff protection, or the establishment or removal of subsidies, may offer both opportunities for business realignment, and incentives to change. Such reforms may have significant social and economic effects, such as were seen as a result of economic liberalization in the United Kingdom and elsewhere in the 1980s,[16] and throughout much of the world in the 1990. To a large extent businesses are reactive rather than pro-active in this respect, constrained by their relatively limited ability to influence these developments.

However, even where there are few if any obviously significant changes, it may be possible for profound changes in business to occur. As observed earlier, this may be seen in the development of intellectual property laws. As Drahos and Braithwaite have argued,[17] the intellectual property laws, especially patents, copyright and trademarks, were instrumental in creating cartels and monopolies throughout the twentieth century. These have been created at both national and international levels, and have been of particular benefit to the larger western economies, which enjoyed the significant advantages of pre-existing infrastructures, complex but highly efficient economies, and well-developed legal regimes.

These monopolies or business dominance has been apparent in numerous areas of industry, including chemical, pharmaceutical, electronics, biotechnology, software and entertainment. It has created what Drahos and Braithwaite have called 'information feudalism'. They categorise this as a regime of property rights that is not economically-efficient, and which does not get the balance right between rewarding innovation and diffusing it, being unduly skewed towards the former. Whether it is possible to achieve such a balance when intellectual property laws are at once primarily national (and heterogeneous) in origin, and at the same time international in application, is another question.

Intellectual property rights are those rights that our law recognizes as attaching to ideas, concepts, designs, inventions and creations of the mind or intellect, all of their very nature are intangible and which typically co-exist with other property rights, especially personal property rights. The term 'industrial property' rights refers to a sub-grouping namely trade marks, patents and rights of that nature. However, though classed as a single category of laws, they have little in common except their concern for protecting information.

The history of intellectual property law has been one of an ongoing conflict between protection and dissemination. This can be seen, for instance, in the history of patents. A patent is a right, granted to a person by the Crown (in the British context), to enjoy a monopoly in an invention, for a limited period. Rights of this nature are called 'patents' because they are granted by Letters Patent ('open' letters). English patent law really began with the passing of the Statute of Monopolies 1623. The Tudor monarchs and King James I had constantly granted all manner of rights of monopoly to favoured individuals. The statute put an end to this practice, but permitted the Crown to grant monopolies to the 'first inventors' of 'manufactures'. This exception was permitted because the public has an interest in the stimulation which new inventions give to commerce.

Basically copyright also confers a negative right. This is a negative right which is owned by the person producing an original work (whether as author, composer, artist and so on) which allows the holder to prevent others from copying the work for their own commercial advantage. As a broad rule any 'work' which is not itself a copy attracts a copyright.[18] It covers literary, artistic, and musical works, films, video productions, photographs, and designs of all types.[19] The aim of the law in this area is to protect the honest efforts of a person who produces an original work, regardless of their intention in doing so.[20] But in so doing it also restricts free dissemination. Economies of scale, improved communications, and a constant demand for greater efficiency, have all led to the development of copyright dominance by an increasingly small group of major publishing houses.

Like feudalism, Drahos and Braithwaite argue that 'information feudalism' rewards guilds instead of inventive individual citizens. This is because it limits access to what might be called the common heritage of humankind, their educational birthright. This can be ideas, but includes unique resources such as plants varieties. Drahos and Braithwaite conclude that information feudalism, by abandoning the public nature of knowledge, will eventually rob the knowledge economy of much of its productivity. This outcome would, of course, prove the validity of their claim that information feudalism is an inhibiting influence.

This modern feudalism – perhaps an unfortunate choice of term since it raises images of feudal allegiance and fealty which are not particularly helpful in this context – is especially potent on an international scale (where the term is perhaps even more inapplicable). Globalization, especially through trade liberalization,[21] has offered opportunities without parallel for economic growth, but also for the creation of globally dominant businesses. Multi-national companies, now commonly called trans-national corporations (TNC), are the vehicles through which these are most commonly developed. The definition of TNCs made by the United Nations Conference on Trade and Development (UNCTAD) is a parent company and its foreign subsidiaries with a share in the ownership of 10% of the shares or equivalent ownership structure.[22]

The development of global business has been a particular study of Drahos and Braithwaite. Looking at contract, intellectual property and corporations law, and the mechanisms and processes of trade, telecommunications, labour standards, drugs, food, transport and environment, Drahos and Braithwaite have considered the question of how the regulation of business has shifted from national to global institutions. They examined the role played by global institutions such as the World Trade Organization (WTO), the Organization of Economic Cooperation and Development (OECD), the International Monetary Fund (IMF), Moody's, and the World Bank, as well as various non-governmental organizations (NGOs) and significant individuals. They argue that effective and decent global regulation depends on the determination of individuals to engage with powerful agendas and decision-making bodies that would otherwise be dominated by concentrated economic interests.[23] This tendency to dominance is harmful at once to the smaller business entities, and to less sophisticated or powerful economies.

This has been very much a political fight, with business dominance based as much – or more – on successful lobbying than on inherent economic efficiency. For example, Drahos and Braithwaite have examined the Agreement on the Trade-Related Aspects of Intellectual Property Rights 1994 (the TRIPS Agreement). They concluded that representatives from a small number of multinational corporations were able to persuade developing nations to adopt policies which were to the advantage of the companies, through political lobbying in Washington for trade sanctions against their trade opponents.[24]

Developments have not all been one-sided, however. Article 27.3(b) of the TRIPS Agreement requires WTO Members to provide for the protection of plant variety rights (PVR) either by patents or by an effective sui generis system, or by any combination thereof. The grant of a PVR gives the owner the exclusive right to produce for sale and to sell reproductive material of the variety concerned. A variety that is the subject of a PVR is referred to as a 'protected variety'. The International Union for the Protection of New Varieties of Plants (UPOV) has established an international framework for PVRs through the UPOV Convention, which has a similar effect to TRIPS.

This procedure has provided some protection for the protection of locally developed plant varieties. However, it also offers the larger laboratories and research stations opportunities for protecting their work, potentially at the expense of the countries and regions to which the plants are native. Smaller-scale businesses almost inevitably failed to compete with the larger companies, and especially those with international capital upon which to draw.

The business response to legal change is inhibited by the discourse in which it is set. It is not independent of it. This is especially so when the change in the legal environment are not technical or sectional, but general and widespread, as in the political, legal, social and economic upheavals of Eastern Europe at the end of the twentieth century.

2.3 Political Collapse and Laissez-Faire Economies

The case study of the response of business to major changes in the legal system is the collapse of Communism in Eastern Europe. This was primarily a politically-driven change to legal system, rather than a technology-driven change.[25] However, it was a paradigm shift for the legal systems concerned.

The Communist era was marked by a history of inefficient industrialisation in Eastern Europe,[26] guided by the region's centralised political leadership. It was chiefly responsible for a long inventory of environmental disasters, and has left a legacy of pernicious, long-term ecological contamination.[27] Economies however can evolve more quickly, giving opportunities for business entrepreneurs, including privatization.[28]

The fall of Communism and the rise of nationalism in Central and Eastern Europe created a large number of new states that qualify as developing countries economically while they undergo this political transition. They have begun interacting with the industrialised countries accordingly.[29] For many observers, the recent transition phenomenon represents one of the two most important economic developments of the twentieth century, the other being the Great Depression of the 1930s.[30] According to Stern, transition involves 'the establishment of a competitive market economy where central planning once prevailed, including the full range of institutions that are required to support a decentralized economy.'[31] But it has not been wholly successful.[32]

Business takes advantage of privatization – but most of all of opportunities to embark on new ventures hitherto prohibited. The more marginal the greater the return. However, this is rarely productive investment. The encouragement of longer-term investment might require deregulation to be gradually implemented. However, this has rarely been the case in Eastern Europe since the late 1980s.

One example of an Eastern European country undergoing the process of marketization is Bulgaria. Since the fall of Communism in 1989 Bulgaria embraced economic reform and is gradually becoming a viable investment market. The goal was to achieve 'complete intellectual and moral reconstruction' for total economic restructuring to occur and for the establishment of a new institutional system.[33] Bulgaria's strategic geographic location provides easy access to the European, Asian and North African markets. The lack of ethnical tensions makes the country a centre of economic and political stability in the Balkans. The costs of Bulgarian labour are significantly lower than the European average and various trade agreements with neighbouring countries ensure a duty-free movement of goods and services within a market of 550 million consumers.[34]

Yet, Bulgaria's favourable geographic location and low labour cost failed to attract foreign investors. Despite the great advantages Bulgaria offers, there were concerns based on recent political and economic history. Internally, fears of inflation, an inefficient judiciary, an uncertain legislative framework, inefficient government bureaucracy, a protracted privatization process, and corruption continued to deter foreign investment.[35] Internally, however, the picture was slightly different. As in most of post-Communist Eastern Europe, domestic businesses flourished, often sporadically,[36] but in a relatively unregulated manner similar to the growth of the US economy during the nineteenth century.

Even in areas not normally thought of as 'commercial' there were opportunities for business models and for business in post-Communist Eastern Europe. With the old hierarchical structures disintegrating and cultural policy largely dismantled throughout Central and Eastern Europe, the issue of privatization and the concomitant threat of a commercialisation or 'marketization'[37] of the arts and culture began to dominate the policy debates.[38] As Schuster has argued, privatization became a 'buzzword' indiscriminately used for a whole range of processes and rationales for policy action.[39]

Although the arts and culture were subject to governmental control and censorship in the party-states of the Warsaw Pact, the supply of artistic and cultural goods and services was plentiful, heavily subsidised, and widely accessible. With the demise of socialism and the fall of the Berlin Wall, perceived as the victory of the capitalist West, concerns arose as to what the change of systems might mean for the future of the arts in Central and Eastern Europe and in the Newly Independent States (NIS) of the former Soviet Union.[40]

Because of the tremendous political, economic, and social challenges of the transition, a widespread privatization of cultural assets, if not a complete abandonment of culture by the state, was the logical if undesired outcome of the revolution after the immediate post-1989 euphoria had subsided. Many countries in the region saw 'the march through the "valley of death" [take] its toll'[41] with the initial dismantling of certain cultural institutions such as cultural centres, movie houses, theatres, and youth and music clubs.[42]

Although the cultural industries[43] have mostly been transferred to the private or market sector, the state has not relinquished its primary responsibility for the institutions of high culture in the region. Moreover, a third, or non-profit, sector has also developed between the state and the market as a result of the loss of certain forms of state patronage and of pre-existing, less institutionalised venues of cultural activity and production in the socialist era.[44] These cultural industries have been relatively successful because for such enterprises, generally speaking, the degree of economic success seems to depend upon the infrastructure – political, social, economic, and legal.

A decade of experience with the transition from centrally planned to market economies has shown that the strength of a country's market-supporting 'institutions' have powerfully affect the transition success.[45] The decisions made by former countries of the Soviet Union – Newly Independent States ('NIS') – to build free-market economies require appropriate legal structures. New civil codes have been successfully adopted in many of the NIS. Work on the new Civil Code in Ukraine based on free-market principles is still in progress.[46] The form of the legal system may not be influenced by the business community, but business is still able to take advantage of the reforms which have occurred, particularly privatization.

The legal codes entrench 'Western'-style free market models, including private ownership of business enterprises. Over the past decade, privatization has been advanced, as these countries have moved to dismantle their previous, dominantly state-owned, economies.[47]

Massive redistribution of property occurred that reshaped not only their economic systems but their political and social systems as well.[48] However, in the absence of significant restructuring, privatization alone could not solve the underlying problems facing the previously state-owned enterprises.[49] A hurdle that had to be overcome in privatization was the fact that Communist rule was long intertwined within the countries of Eastern Europe, and that the judicial system was directly affected by it. Consequently, it has become very hard to find judges who are qualified to rule on the actions and policies of their former Communist rulers.[50] Nor was the rule of law necessarily fully embedded.[51]

However, more significantly, mass privatization left new owners and managers with the responsibility of implementing the investments and reforms necessary to make their enterprises viable.[52] These investments and reforms were created through free trade in the newly capitalized markets.[53] Some of the new enterprises were run by the 'old guard' – bureaucrats from the Communist era. But most passed to the new business elite.

Post-Communist Eastern Europe, for example, saw business reacting feverishly to the relaxation of previously strict and prohibitive legal regulation. The immediate consequence, especially where political uncertainly remained, was frequently unregulated growth. But it was often not in productive sectors – such as industry and agriculture – but rather where large short-term profits could be most readily made.[54]

The potential for profits were greatest when embarking on new enterprises, rather than reviving inefficient Communist-era enterprises. Unfortunately, this meant decay in what were often the more productive sectors of the economy (such as heavy industry), while the ephemeral grew. But business reacted to deregulation by seizing any opportunity now allowed to make money,[55] in preference to maintaining the old economies. This encouraged an opportunistic spirit of laissez faire, the almost inevitable result of the ending of centralised planning.

2.4 Conclusion

This Chapter asked how business responds to changes in legal systems, whether wrought by technological changes, or otherwise. It will be seen from the examples discussed that this response varies depending on the pre-existing state of the economy and of the legal system. Where there is already a thriving private sector, the advent of new technologies (and new legal rules) will be seen as an opportunity for long-term investment – even though they may be tightly regulated. But investment requires sufficient legal protection for intellectual property.

Where there is a less well developed private sector, and where the economy tightly controlled, the ending of control also offers opportunities. But here the outcome will be influenced by the weakness of the private sector. Short-term gains will be preferred to long-term gains, and the smaller the business the less the potential for risk-taking.

Business, as a sub-set of society, is dependent upon environmental factors, including the technological and legal grundnorms. It is no more nor less dependent upon technology than is government, which is also both a contributor to the discourse and is influenced by it.

Notes

1 See George J. Siedel, *Using the Law to Gain Competitive Advantage* (San Francisco, 2002).

2 For a discussion of the nexus between social change and the law, see Alan Watson, *Society and Legal Change* (2nd edn, Philadelphia, 2001). It has also been observed that recent finance scholarship finds that countries with legal systems based on the common law have more developed financial markets than civil-law countries; See Robert G. King and Ross Levine, 'Finance and Growth: Schumpeter Might Be Right', *Quarterly Journal of Economics*, 108 (1993): 717–37. This may be due to the common law's association with limited government; Paul G. Mahoney, 'The Common Law and Economic Growth: Hayek might be right', *Journal of Legal Studies*, 30 (2001): 503–25.

3 There is a considerable body of work on the nexus between constitutions and social and economic change; from the United States' perspective, for example, see John R. Vile, *The Constitutional Amending Process in American Political Thought* (New York, 1992), pp. 137–56; Daniel Lazare, *The Frozen Republic: How the Constitution is Paralysing Democracy* (New York, 1996); David E. Kyvig, *Explicit and Authentic Acts: Amending the United States Constitution* (Lawrence, 1996), pp. 216–314; Richard Kay, 'Constitutional Chrononomy', *Ratio Juris*, 13 (2000): 31–48, 33.

4 A paradigmatic is a technical concept derived from linguistics and semiotics, used in anthropological theories of meaning, to denote the stable, rule-governed aspect of communication (opposite of syntagmatic, that which flows and moves in time). The concept is often used more loosely about basic premises underlying communication (as grammar underlies language). 'Paradigmatic shifts' should thus be understood as fundamental changes in the premises of communication; Thomas Kuhn, *The Structure of Scientific Revolutions* (Chicago, 1962).

5 See, for example, the definition at Investorwords.com, at <http://www.investorwords.com/623/businesses.html> (as at 19 December 2003).

6 See, for instance, the definition of business in the Fair Trading Act 1986 (NZ):
'Business' means any undertaking –
(a) That is carried on whether for gain or reward or not; or
(b) In the course of which –

(i) Goods or services are acquired or supplied; or

(ii) Any interest in land is acquired or disposed of – whether free of charge or not.

7 And upon which economic model is preferred; see for instance, R.J. Holton, *Cities, capitalism, and civilization* (London, 1986), cf. Michael Perelman, *Classical political economy: primitive accumulation and the social division of labour* (Totowa, 1984).

8 As in *Das Kapital: Kritik der politischen Ökonomie* (*Capital: A Critique of Political Economy*), ed. Frederick Engels (New York, 1967).

9 Robert R. Locke, *The end of the practical man: entrepreneurship and higher education in Germany, France, and Great Britain, 1880–1940* (Greenwich, 1984); Paul Klep and Eddy Van Cauwenberghe (eds), *Entrepreneurship and the transformation of the economy (10th–20th centuries): essays in honour of Herman Van der Wee* (Leuven, 1994).

10 During the second millennium, the Middle East's commerce with Western Europe fell increasingly under European domination. Two factors played critical roles. First, the Islamic inheritance system, by raising the costs of dissolving a partnership following a partner's death, kept Middle Eastern commercial enterprises small and ephemeral. Second, certain European inheritance systems facilitated large and durable partnerships by reducing the likelihood of premature dissolution. The upshot is that European enterprises grew larger than those of the Islamic world. Moreover, while ever larger enterprises propelled further organizational transformations in Europe, persistently small enterprises inhibited economic modernisation in the Middle East; See Timur Kuran, 'The Islamic Commercial Crisis: Institutional Roots of Economic Underdevelopment in the Middle East', *The Journal of Economic History*, 63(2) (2003): 414–46.

11 See Charles F. De Jager, 'The Development of Regulatory Standards for Gene Therapy in the European Union', *Fordham International Law Journal*, 18 (1995): 1303–39, 1304, 1305.

12 Emily Marden, 'Risk and regulation: U.S. regulatory policy on genetically modified food and agriculture', *Boston College Law Review*, 44(3) (2003): 733–87; Michael R. Taylor and Jody S. Tick, 'An incomplete picture: consideration of environmental laws to address problems that may arise from genetically engineered crops and food', *The Environmental Forum*, 20(4) (2003): 19.

13 New Zealand Law Commission, *Liability for loss resulting from the development, supply or use of genetically modified organisms* (Wellington, 2002).

14 See Helen Szoke, 'The nanny state or responsible government', *Journal of Law and Medicine*, 227(83) (2002): S-1.

15 See, for a practical example, Roger Harrison, *Diagnosing organizational culture: trainer's manual* (San Diego, 1993).

16 Nicholas Woodward, *The management of the British economy, 1945–2001* (Manchester, 2004).

17 Peter Drahos and John Braithwaite, *Information Feudalism – Who owns the Knowledge Economy?* (New York, 2003).

18 *University of London Press v University Tutorial Press* [1916] 2 Ch 601, 608–9 (Petersen J); *Macmillan & Co v Cooper* (1923) 40 TLR 186, 190 (Lord Atkinson); *Ladbroke Ltd v William Hill Ltd* [1964] 1 WLR 273, 289 (Lord Devlin), 292 (Lord Pearce).

19 That is, dress templates: *Thornton Hall Manufacturing Ltd v Shanton Apparel Ltd* (Unreported, High Court, Auckland, Hillier J, 9 December 1988, CL 15/87).

20 The question of originality is a question of fact and degree in each case: *International Credit Control Ltd v Axelsen* [1974] 1 NZLR 695, 699 (Mahon J).

21 See, for instance, Martin Richardson (ed.), *Globalization and international trade liberalisation: continuity and change* (Cheltenham, 2000).

22 United Nations Conference on Trade and Development, *UNCTAD World Investment Report 2000: Cross-border mergers and acquisitions and development* (New York, 2000).

23 Peter Drahos and John Braithwaite, *Global Business Regulation* (Cambridge, 2000).

24 Peter Drahos and John Braithwaite, *Information Feudalism*.

25 Cynthia B. Schultz and Tamara Raye Crockett, 'Economic development, democratization, and environmental protection in Eastern Europe', *Boston College Environmental Affairs Law Review*, 18 (1990): 53.

26 See Vlad Sobell, 'The CMEA's Future: The Demise of the Soviet-Centered Model', RAD Background Report/17, Radio Fred Europe Research Reports, 17 January 1989, at 2.

27 See Cornelius van der Veen, 'Facts and figures on Rhine pollution', *International Business Lawyer*, 9(2) (1981): 41–52; D.J. Peterson, *Troubled lands: the legacy of Soviet environmental destruction* (Boulder, 1993).

28 Bruno Dallago, Gianmaria Ajani and Bruno Grancelli (eds), *Privatisation and entrepreneurship in post-socialist countries: economy, law, and society* (New York, 1992). Privatization is a set of policies designed to curtail the size and influence of the public sector through the sale of public assets; Mariusz Mark Dobek, *The Political logic of privatisation* (Westport, 1993) 1.

29 Vinod Rege, 'Economies in transition and developing countries: prospects for greater co-operation in trade and economic fields', *Journal of World Trade (Law–Economics–Public Policy)* 27(1) (1993): 83–115.

30 Nauro Campos and Fabrizzio Coricelli, 'Growth in Transition: What We Know, What We Don't, and What We Should', *Journal of Economic Literature*, 40 (2002): 793–836.

31 Nicholas Stern, *Transition: Private Sector Development and the Role of Financial Institutions* (London, 1994) Working paper no 13. XY/N-1.

32 Martin Krygier and Adam Czarnota (eds), *The Rule of Law After Communism: Problems and Prospects in East–Central Europe* (Brookfield, 1998); P. Sarcević, *Privatisation in Central and Eastern Europe* (London, 1992).

33 See Csaba Varga, 'Transformation to Rule of Law From No-Law: Societal Contexture of the Democratic Transition in Central and Eastern Europe', *Connecticut Journal of International Law*, 8 (1993): 487, 488.

34 Bulgarian Foreign Investment Agency, 'Bulgarian Business Guide: Legal, Tax, and Accounting Aspects' 6 (2002), available at <http://www.bfia.org> (as at 19 December 2003).

35 Dora Djilianova, 'To be or not to be: What went right in the Bulgarian foreign investment climate after 1997', *Thomas Jefferson Law Review*, 25 (2002): 223.

36 As in the growth of the opportunist 'black market'.

37 That is, a movement away from a centrally planned economy and toward a market system integrated with the world economy; Emily Stoper and Emilia Ianeva, 'Democratisation and women's employment policy in post-Communist Bulgaria', *Connecticut Journal of International Law*, 12 (1996): 9.

38 A. van Hemel and N. van der Welen (eds), *Privatisation/desetatisation and culture. Conference reader for the Circle Round Table 1997* (Amsterdam, 1997).
39 J. M. Schuster, 'Deconstructing a Tower of Babel: Privatisation, decentralisation and devolution as ideas in good currency in cultural policy', *Voluntas*, 8(3) (1997): 261–82.
40 Stefan Toepler, 'From Communism to civil society? The arts and the nonprofit sector in Central And Eastern Europe', *Journal of Arts Management, Law and Society*, 30(1) (2000): 7.
41 O. Novotny, 'Key issues in the transformation of culture in the post-socialist countries: With particular reference to the Slovak Republic', *European Journal of Cultural Policy*, 1(2) (1995): 217–23, 218.
42 G. Muschter, 'Kunstlerforderung in der Bundesrepublik Deutschland', in R. Strachwitz and S. Toepler (eds), *Kulturforderung: Mehr als Sponsoring* (Wiesbaden, 1993), pp. 35–40.
43 Including publishing, cinema, recording, and the media.
44 See Toepler, 'From Communism to civil society? The arts and the nonprofit sector in Central And Eastern Europe'.
45 Bernard S. Black and Anna S. Tarassova, 'Institutional reform in transition: A case study of Russia', *Supreme Court Economic Review*, 10 (1993): 211.
46 Alexander Biryukov, 'The Doctrine of Dualism of Private Law in the Context of Recent Codifications of Civil Law: Ukrainian Perspectives', *Annual Survey of International and Comparative Law*, 8 (2002): 53–4.
47 See Varga, 'Transformation to Rule of Law From No-Law: Societal Contexture of the Democratic Transition in Central and Eastern Europe'.
48 Ibid.
49 See International Labour Organisation, *World Labour Report* (London, 1995), p. 64. See Mariusz Mark Dobek, *The Political logic of privatisation* (Westport, 1993), p. 68 (discussing the steps that Poland made in privatizing its economy).
50 See Mark Gibney, 'Decommunization: Human Rights Lessons from the Past and Present, and Prospects for the Future', *Denver International Law and Policy*, 23 (1994): 7, 88.
51 See Varga, 'Transformation to Rule of Law From No-Law: Societal Contexture of the Democratic Transition in Central and Eastern Europe'.
52 See International Labour Organisation, *World Labour Report* (London, 1995), p. 64.
53 See Varga, 'Transformation to Rule of Law From No-Law: Societal Contexture of the Democratic Transition in Central and Eastern Europe', 492 (discussing how the transition period enabled former Communist countries to set historic new directions for their future).
54 This was often in marginally legal or illegal activities, such as gambling, drugs, and prostitution.
55 And some not allowed.

Chapter 3

Technology's Effect on Legal Systems

3.1 Introduction

Having looked briefly at some aspects the relationship of law and government, and of the response of business to changes in the legal environment, we now begin to consider the specific question of the effect of technology on legal systems. First we will begin with a definition of technology. Common dictionary definitions include 'the practical application of knowledge especially in a particular area', or 'a manner of accomplishing a task especially using technical processes, methods, or knowledge'.[1] There are both wide and narrow definitions, from technology as objects (tools, machines, instruments, weapons, appliances – the physical devices of technical performance), to technology as a sociotechnical system (the manufacture and use of objects involving people and other objects in combination). Each definition has its specific uses, its advantages and its disadvantages. But, just as business was defined broadly in the previous Chapter, so technology is given a broad definition here.

Technology is marked by different purposes, different processes and different relationships to established knowledge and a particular relationship to specific contexts of activity. Change in the material environment is the explicit purpose of technology, and not, as is the case with science, the understanding of nature. Technology is a means to an end, not an end in itself. At the centre of technology lies design. The motivating factor behind all technological activity is the desire to fulfil a need. Not only may design and production involve co-operation between different specialisms, but it may also involve 'technologists' in performing a multitude of functions, such as working with others.

Technology is informed by values at every point. Value decisions may be called for not only in relation to the specific design criteria (such as aesthetic, ergonomic and economic judgements, suitability for purpose and ease of manufacture) but also in relation to the rightness or wrongness of a particular solution in ethical terms. Technological enterprises are determined, not by advances in knowledge, nor simply by the identification of needs, but by social interests. Of the potential new technologies available at any one time only a few are developed and become widely implemented. Technology is shaped by society, by consumer choice, yet it can also be argued that technology itself (or perhaps some technologies) shapes society.

The definition for technology which will be used in this book is 'human innovation in action that involves the generation of knowledge and processes to develop systems that solve problems and extend human capabilities'. This is both broad and specific enough to cover information technology in both its tangible and intangible forms.

As a generality, technology affects the legal system of a given society in that the generation of knowledge and processes to develop systems that solve problems and extend human capabilities result, almost inevitably, in changes to the society which conceives and implements the processes and systems. Changes to society changes law and the legal system. This is, however, a relatively indirect effect.

The effect of different forms of technology will, however, be different. Technology as objects and as sociotechnical systems will differ in their effects. This presents some difficulties in identifying and understanding the nature of the relationship between law and technology, and technology and society. But no single definition of technology would suffice to produce a coherent understanding, nor would it adequately reflect the changing nature of the relationship, temporally and spatially. Biotechnology technology, which raises profound ethical and religious questions, many of which are of greater influence on ethics and social policy than other technologies, such as telecommunications. Yet the latter may have equally great socio-political effects, and certainly threatens specific fields of law, such as intellectual property law and privacy law.

3.2 The Nature and Type of Technologies

Technology is not uniform in structure and implications. This is scarcely surprising, give the wide range of technologies. Classifications may be useful as a means of guidance, though care must be taken. The forms of technology as objects are the physical devices of technical performance. These tools, machines, instruments, weapons, appliances may have profound effects, depending upon the context. Firearms spelt the end of many pre-industrial social orders and societies. Radio and television has had profound implications upon the way in which countries conduct their foreign affairs. But the effect of individual tools might generally be regarded as less likely to have significant effects on legal systems than other forms of technology might have.

Technology as a sociotechnical system is more complex, and therefore more likely to have direct social, economic and political effects. The very process of the manufacture and use of objects involving people and other objects in combination necessitates a different organizational approach to that which preceded it. The arrival of the manufacturing factories, for instance, had a profound and revolutionary effect on economies, social structures, and governments. The development of modern forms of democracy is in large part the consequence of the seemingly inexorable advance of industrialization and globalization.

3.3 The Effect of Technological Change on Law

The current technological revolution[2] brings with it seminal advances across a multitude of disciplines, and linked – if linked at all – by the distinction of belonging to what has been called the 'knowledge revolution.'[3] This new revolution brings with it challenges to legal systems, and to constitutions, which cannot lightly be underestimated.[4] But as yet we are unsure of the economic, social, and legal effects of this technological revolution.[5]

Some facets of the revolution[6] offer opportunities for internationalization – or globalization[7] – on a scale previously unimaginable.[8] Globalization is both a result of technological change and a consequence of it. But it is also independent of technology. This poses challenges to states, as well as offering almost unprecedented opportunities for business expansion.[9] Globalization[10] is now an economic fact,[11] if still far from uniform.[12] It is not yet a political reality – indeed it may never be so – and all law is *prima facie* territorial.[13] Nor is the nature of globalization universally agreed, with different economic and political models being proposed. However globalization is defined, its consequences are not hard to find, because individuals have unparalleled access to information and commerce across the globe,[14] allowing them to both buy and to sell products and services globally,[15] and to take part in a global commons.[16] This affects their relationship with national governments.

It is relatively clear that technology affects legal systems.[17] This is partly directly, for example, in the advent of telecommunications which allowed state-to-state diplomatic negotiations to be conducted at a governmental level, thereby reducing the role of diplomatic representatives.[18] But it is mainly indirect, via changes to the economy and to society.[19] Technology is also altering the relationship of governed and government, and between government and government.[20] It is changing specific technical rules – such as the alteration to copyright laws which occurred as a result of the advent of electronic technologies.[21] But it is also having a wider effect. The globalizing effect of the Internet,[22] in particular, is affecting legal systems. Technology is causing and facilitating globalization – though the latter is economic and political as well as technology-driven.

But legal systems themselves also affect technology, in that the development and utilization of technology may be controlled to a greater or lesser extent by laws and by the legal system.[23] Thus businesses, and those involved in the development of technology, must be aware of the effect changes to the legal system may have,[24] for it may affect their activities. They must be conscious of all aspects of the legal environment in which they operate.[25]

All new technologies, whether mechanical, biotechnology,[26] production, communications, or any other form, challenge existing legal concepts.[27] This is true both with respect to specific laws, as well as the structure of the state legal system, and of the constitution.[28] For instance, copyright law has been seriously affected globally by the advent of the Internet,[29] and is in the process of adjusting to this new medium.[30] Technological changes can produce – or assist – relatively dramatic changes in economic and social organization in a short span of time.[31]

Technological changes may also affect constitutions – particularly where the technological changes are profound.[32] Social and economic acceleration also affects constitutions because these latter are expected (by the community at large) to provide stable rules suited to long-term use.[33] The Lockean constitution was perceived as one which would be unalterable because it encompassed all that was needed for a sound constitution,[34] but this conception of a constitution has been challenged.[35] Constitutions are normative in nature and also reflect the history of the particular country, as related in Chapter 1. More importantly, perhaps, social and economic acceleration conflicts with the traditional expectation that constitutional law-makers can be expected to predict future trends with some measure of competence.[36] For moral as well as economic reasons, sound constitutions aim at promoting exchange and constraining hierarchy.[37] This is difficult if there is disparity between less sophisticated constitutions and more sophisticated society, economy, or technology.

Technological advances in fields other than the Internet challenge the boundaries of law, science, public policy, and ethics.[38] Biotechnology in general is highly controversial,[39] and particularly so is embryonic stem cell research,[40] and all work on human genetics.[41] Important developments are also occurring in artificial intelligence,[42] nano-technology,[43] and cryonics.[44] All of these raise legal, religious and moral, if not constitutional, questions. In an age where technological and medical advances are developing at what sometimes appears to be exponential rates, the law may shape or follow advances.[45] In large part this is because although we speak of a revolution, in reality there are a number of interrelated changes, each of which must be considered – to some degree at least – as separate. There have been warnings that decisions with respect to government involvement in high technology industries should be on a case-by-case basis and not of a general nature.[46] It has not been possible to avoid this. For law, this means a piecemeal approach to reform, and for the constitution[47] – where this is affected – potentially a lack of the coherency and consistency which should be the hallmark of a good constitution.[48] This coherency is desirable even if a true Lockean constitution is not possible.

Fundamentally, at an abstract level, this technological revolution raises questions about the role of state and society,[49] and the place of the individual, and the state, within this structure,[50] as well as the relationship between state and state.[51] Modern state institutions, and the principal western models of state structures themselves,[52] were established or consolidated during the fifteenth to early twentieth centuries; an era of nation-state building.[53] That time was also a revolutionary one in its own way, one which saw the decline of the Middle Ages and the growth of the modern era – and much of that political and legal change can be seen as grounded on technological change.[54] But generally the economic development of capitalism and later socialism did not greatly change the relationship.[55] It remains to be seen whether a post-industrial, globalized world will do so.

Technology is altering the relationship of governed and government, and between government and government. Technology does not change the essential problems that legal systems seek to address, because these go much deeper, being rooted in the enduring nature of humanity.[56] Technology can transform the human environment,[57] but, as Burke recognized, the key to sound structures of governance in every age and place is to understand the intersection of humanity's enduring nature with its particular circumstance.[58]

Economic and technological changes eventually alter legal systems, because they change society, which legal systems reflect to a greater or lesser degree.[59] Economic growth affects labour patterns, disposable incomes, population distribution, even population size – all of which affect social behaviour. Technological changes may have equally significant effects – and indeed this has been predicted as a consequence of Internet development[60] (though this has also been disputed).

One reason for this profound change, according to McGready, is that the new rights which aim to respond to opportunities and risks arising from new information and communication technologies, biotechnological or other technology-based industrial development, are not grounded in the nation-state.[61] Generally, established civil, economic, social and political rights,[62] were predicated upon the existence of the nation-state, and indeed were constructed within the framework of the nation-state.[63] Globalization, and a concurrent individualization (or the enfranchisement of the individual) has led to additional rights, desires and pressures.[64] It has also led to international business (and others operating globally) facing an environment of greater complexity than was previously the case. One example will suffice. A business operates from country X, selling to customers worldwide via a website hosted in country X. They may be subject to the laws of country Y – in which the website may be accessed – even though country Y was not the target market.[65] Never before has business faced this potentially oppressive multiple liability. But the consequences of globalizing technology, such as the Internet, are not limited to business alone. The development of the Internet is simply part of the evolution of the global information system.

Cortada examined the historical, cultural, and (to some degree) legal aspects of interaction between society and information.[66] He maintained that the information age is not really a new phenomenon, but rather is the most recent manifestation of a long-standing process of historical evolution.[67] Yet Lessig suggests that the historical evolution of the information society is a foundational preamble for what he characterizes as one of the most critical battles of our time – the battle for the future of the Internet.[68] Both views may be correct, for while the knowledge technology may be grounded in an earlier Industrial Revolution, so evolution has its periods of stagnation, and its periods of fundamental change. We may be entering just such a latter phase now. This is as critical for business and for society as it is for government.

Technological changes also offer significant challenges internationally, as distinct from those to national companies, individuals and groups. Abbott has argued that international society of the twenty-first century will be highly integrated. He argues that the World Trade Organization (WTO) governance structure should be adapted to account for more diverse interests, including those of marginalised developing countries, non-governmental organizations (NGOs), and individuals.[69] This view has also been advanced by McGinnis,[70] who envisaged the prospect of international federalism through the WTO and other global economic organization.[71] While this may appear overly ambitious, even utopian, it is true that (for most countries at least) legislation is no longer overwhelmingly domestic in origin, even though it may still be enacted by domestic legislative bodies,[72] due to an increasing number of treaties and conventions. Fundamentally, the challenge – or threat – of techno-globalism to sovereign states[73] has profound implications for jurisprudence,[74] and for laws, as well as for society and business. Some of these changes are a consequence of technological change alone, but others are a direct consequence of globalization (which itself is often driven by technology).

The development of information technology-driven e-government, through a relatively simple provision of information on the Internet, through the conducting of simple transactions such as paying taxes online, to more inter-active and comprehensive relationships may ultimately affect the structure of government. This may increase governmental centralization, in that citizens might make contract with governmental agencies through a single portal.

The challenge for governments is to respond to the ongoing – and possibly long-term[75] – technological revolution,[76] and not become victims of it.[77] The more inflexible the state – or the more economically or politically dogmatic – the greater the risk of failure.[78] Failure by governments to respond fully and effectively to changing paradigms can result in loss of competitive advantage[79] – or even the existence of that state (through loss of economic viability). This ability to respond is not merely political, social or economic. It is also constitutional.

But not only does technological change affect (and sometimes even threaten)[80] the legal system, the legal system itself also affects the development of technology. Some legal systems have traditionally been laissez-faire, inclined to leave technology and business to develop alone – at least so long as it did not cause undue harm.[81] They also sought to protect the intellectual property of authors, inventors and originators of novel ideas.[82] McGinnis argues that the United States constitution (to be understood as a broader concept than 'the Constitution') was at the heart of the steady growth of the United States, helping it to become an economic superpower by the beginning of the twentieth century.[83] His explanation for this was that the balance between federal and state powers prevented excessive government intervention in business, while also providing a strong central government where this was essential – in foreign policy and defence.[84] In such an environment there is no disincentive to develop and market technological innovations. Yet, even here, public health concerns has a role to play – the pharmaceutical and nuclear power industries, for instance, are usually heavily regulated.[85]

The legal system affects technology because technology involves (amongst other things) the creation, utilization, and protection, of intellectual property,[86] the exploitation of capital,[87] and the protection of consumers,[88] and of the environment[89] – all of which are generally controlled by laws. Where certain areas of law are weaker or ill-developed, there will be technological consequences.[90] More rigid legal systems, and industries which inherently involve higher risk, or potentially higher liability, are more strictly controlled.[91]

3.4 Conclusion

Technology is simply a process, or tool, through which mankind alters his environment. It may be complex or it may be simple. The consequences of the existence of the technology, and of its use, will be correspondingly great or small. But it will often be difficult to identify any clear instance of technology directly affecting legal systems. That is not, however, to suggest that this never occurs. As we will see in later Chapters, there are many instances where profound, indeed paradigmatic changes have occurred, primarily as the result of the development and the utilization of a new technology, or the new use of an old technology. But first we will consider in more detail the nature of constitutional responses to paradigmatic shifts in technology.

Notes

1 Merriam-Webster Online Dictionary <http://www.m-w.com/cgi-bin/dictionary>.

2 Here 'technology' is defined as processes and things people create for the purpose of using them to alter their lifestyle or their surroundings.

3 See Graciela Chichilnisky, 'The Knowledge Revolution', *Journal of International Trade and Economic Development*, 7 (1998): 39–45.

4 See, for an ecological perspective, L. Ali Khan, *The Extinction of Nation-States: A World without Borders* (The Hague, 1996), p. 1.

5 See, for instance, Michael H. Shapiro, 'Thinking about biomedical advances: The role of ethics and law: On the possibility of "progress" in managing biomedical technologies: Markets, lotteries, and rational standards in organ transplantation', *Capital University Law Review*, 31 (2003): 13–127.

6 Particularly the Internet, and the telecommunications revolution in general; see Michael Leventhal, 'The Golden Age of Wireless', *Intellectual Property and Technology Law Journal*, 14 (2002): 1.

7 For some of the effects of this, see Masatsugu Tsuji, 'Transformation of the Japanese system towards a network economy' in Emanuele Giovannetti, Mitsuhiro Kagami and Masatsugu Tsuji (eds), *The Internet revolution: a global perspective* (Cambridge, 2003); Ian Tunstall, *Taxation and the Internet* (Pyrmont, 2003); Brian Kahin and Charles

Nesson (eds), *Borders in cyberspace: information policy and the global information infrastructure* (Cambridge, 1997); Adam Czarnota, 'A few reflections on Globalization and the constitution of society', *University of New South Wales Law Journal*, 24 (2001): 809–16.

8 Location remains important, but it is virtual location, rather than physical location – there is no necessary connection between an Internet address and a physical location.

9 Pippa Norris, *Digital Divide: Civic Engagement, Information Poverty, and the Internet Worldwide* (New York, 2001), p. 40.

10 This might be defined as those processes which tend to create and consolidate a unified world economy, a single ecological system, and a complex network of communications that covers the whole globe, even if it does not penetrate every part of it; William Twining, *Globalization and Legal Theory* (London, 1998), pp. 4–10.

11 And it is also an extremely broad subject of study; Doron M. Kalir, 'Taking Globalization Seriously: Towards General Jurisprudence', *Columbia Journal of Transnational Law*, 39 (2001): 785–821, 821.

12 Though it might be noted that even Bhutan, one of the poorer and more remote countries, established a mobile telephone network in late 2003; Richard Taylor, 'Himalayan kingdom goes mobile', BBC News, 21 December 2003, at <http://news.bbc.co.uk/2/hi/technology/3335417.stm> (as at 22 December 2003).

13 *American Banana Co v United Fruit Co*, 213 US 347, 357 (1909), and international law has a limited – though growing – role in business activities. See also Guy Arnold, *World government by stealth: the future of the United Nations* (New York, 1997); Bertrand Earl Russell, *Towards world government* (London, 1947); Clarence Brinton, *From many one: the process of political integration, the problem of world government* (Cambridge, 1948); Howard O. Eaton, *Federation: the coming structure of world government* (Norman, 1944).

14 See also Walter B. Wriston, *The Twilight of Sovereignty: How the information revolution is transforming our world* (New York, 1992).

15 The 'knowledge revolution' is based on the acquiring, processing, and dissemination of knowledge, just as the last great technological revolution, the Industrial Revolution, concerned the mass production, and distribution of commodities; Charles More, *Understanding the Industrial Revolution* (London, 2000).

16 The global commons is the common heritage of all humanity – though commonly limited to those features of the geo-biosphere – such as forests, bio-diversity, oceans and global atmosphere – that in combination form the global climate system; Global Commons Institute, at <http://www.gci.org.uk/> (as at 21 December 2003).

17 See, for example, Wriston.

18 Geoffrey Moorhouse, *The diplomats: the Foreign Office today* (London, 1977).

19 Such as the Internet. Sunstein has argued that, by increasing the possibility of community, the Internet has undermined the American republic. In his view, the printing press helped create modern nationalism, as books and newspapers came to be written in the vernacular, encouraging a conception of a shared community among groups of people who would never actually meet. His concern is that through the Internet we may choose to find only 'echo chambers' of our own opinions, magnifying and confirming our inclinations and resulting in a deeply polarised society; Cass R. Sunstein, *Republic.com* (Princeton, 2001).

20 For instance, it has been said that the Internet poses a threat to state sovereignty; Georgios Zekos, 'Internet or Electronic Technology: A Threat to State Sovereignty', *Journal of Information, Law and Technology*, 3 (1999), available at <http://elj.warwick.ac.uk/jilt/99-3/zekos.html> (as at 28 November 2003); David G. Post and David R. Johnson, '"Chaos Prevailing on Every Continent": Towards a New Theory of Decentralised Decision-Making in Complex Systems', Social Science Research Network Electronic Library (14 June 1999), available at <http://papers.ssrn.com/sol3/delivery.cfm/99032613.pdf?abstractid=157692> (as at 1 December 2003). See also Dan L. Burk, 'Federalism in Cyberspace', *Connecticut Law Review*, 28 (1996): 1095–1127; Joel R. Reidenberg, 'Governing Networks and Rule-Making in Cyberspace' in Brian Kahin and Charles Nesson (eds), *Borders in Cyberspace* (Cambridge, 1997), pp. 84, 85–7.

21 For instance, in the United States, the Digital Millennium Copyright Act (1998), Pub L No 105-304, 112 Stat 2860, 2905; in New Zealand the Electronic Transactions Act 2000 (NZ).

22 Though it has other causes, partly economic, partly social, and partly political.

23 See Remigius N. Nwabueze, 'Ethnopharmacology, patents and the politics of plants' genetic resources', *Cardozo Journal of International and Comparative Law*, 11 (2003): 585–632; Henrique Freire de Oliveira Souza, 'Genetically Modified Plants: A Need for International Regulation', *Annual Survey of International and Comparative Law*, 6 (2000): 129–74.

24 Janet L. Dolgin, 'Embryonic discourse: Abortion, stem cells, and cloning', *Florida State University Law Review*, 31 (2003): 101–62.

25 Including private, domestic, national, transnational, supranational, and international.

26 This may be defined as 'any technique that uses living organisms or substances from those organisms to make or modify a product, to improve plants or animals, or to develop microorganisms for specific uses'; Office of Technology Assessment, U.S. Congress, Biotechnology in a Global Economy (1991), app. f, at p. 268.

27 See Nasheri Hedieh, 'The intersection of technology crimes and cyberspace in Europe: The Case of Hungary', *Information and Communications Technology Law*, 12 (2003): 25–48.

28 See Tom W. Bell, 'Free speech, strict scrutiny, and self-help: how technology upgrades constitutional jurisprudence', *Minnesota Law Review*, 87 (2003): 743–78; Mark S. Kende, 'Technology's future impact upon state constitutional law: the Montana example', *Montana Law Review*, 64 (2003): 273–94; Deborah Jones Merritt, 'The Constitution in a brave new world: a century of technological change and constitutional law', *Oregon Law Review*, 69 (1990): 1–45.

29 See Neil Weinstock Netanel, 'Copyright and a democratic civil society', *Yale Law Journal*, 106 (1996): 283–387; David Friedman, 'Does technology require new law?', *Harvard Journal of Law and Public Policy*, 25 (2001): 71–85.

30 See Mihály Ficsor, *The law of copyright and the Internet: the 1996 WIPO treaties, their interpretation and implementation* (Oxford, 2002).

31 See Manuel Castells, *The Rise of Network Society* (London, 1996); William E. Scheuerman, 'Constitutionalism in an age of speed', *Constitutional Commentary*, 19 (2002): 353–90, 359–60.

32 They may indeed have revolutionary consequences. See, for instance, the Industrial Revolution's contribution to the 1848 political revolutions in Europe; Rudolf

Stadelmann, *Social and political history of the German 1848 revolution*, trans. J.G. Chastain (Athens, 1975).

33 Scheuerman, 360.

34 John Locke, 'Fundamental Constitutions for Carolina' in David Wootton (ed.), *Political Writings of John Locke* (London, 1993), p. 232.

35 Scheuerman, 361.

36 Ibid., 362.

37 John O. McGinnis, 'The Symbiosis of Constitutionalism and Technology', *Harvard Journal of Law and Public Policy*, 25 (2001): 3–14, 4.

38 See Christine C. Vito, 'State biotechnology oversight: the juncture of technology, law, and public policy', *Maine Law Review*, 45 (1993): 329–83; Organization for Economic Co-operation and Development, *Bio technology and the changing role of government* (Paris, 1988); Robert H. Blank, *The political implications of human genetic technology* (Boulder, 1981); E. Donald Elliott, 'The Genome and the law: Should increased genetic knowledge change the law?', *Harvard Journal of Law and Public Policy*, 25 (2001): 61–70.

39 The mapping of the human genome allows doctors to screen out embryos with a genetic predilection for Alzheimer's disease. Genetic engineering may permit scientists to alter the genes of embryos and negate predilections for certain illnesses; See Kathy Hudson, 'The Human Genome Project, DNA Science and the Law: the American Legal System's Response to Breakthroughs in Genetic Science', *American University Law Review*, 51 (2002): 431–45; Cass R. Sunstein, 'Keeping Up with the Cloneses' (1 May 2002), The New Republic Online at <http://www.tnr.com/doc.mhtml?i=20020506&s=sunstein050602&c=1> (as at 9 December 2003); Gregory Stock, *Redesigning Humans, Our Inevitable Genetic Future* (Boston, 2002); Lee M. Silver, *Remaking Eden: How Genetic Engineering and Cloning will Transform the American Family* (New York, 1998), p. 266.

40 See Denise Stevens, 'Embryonic stem cell research: will President Bush's limitation on federal funding put the United States at a disadvantage? A comparison between United States and international law', *Houston Journal of International Law*, 25 (2003): 623–53.

41 See, for example, Elliott, 'The Genome and the law: Should increased genetic knowledge change the law?'.

42 See John McCarthy, 'What is Artificial Intelligence?', at <http://www-formal.stanford.edu/jmc/whatisai/whatisai.html> (as at 9 December 2003).

43 See Glenn Harlan Reynolds, 'Environmental Regulation of Nanotechnology: Some Preliminary Observations', *Environmental Law Reports*, 31 (2001): 10681–8; Joel Rothstein Wolfson, 'Social and ethical issues in nanotechnology: Lessons from biotechnology and other high technologies', *Biotechnology Law Report*, 22 (2003): 376–96.

44 See Michael Janofsky, 'Even for the Last .400 Hitter, Cryonics is the Longest Shot', (10 July 2002) available at <http://www.nytimes.com/2002/07/10/science/10WILL.html?> (as at 9 December 2003).

45 See James E. Bowman, 'Symposium Genetics and the Law: the Ethical, Legal and Social Implications of Genetic Technology and Biomedical Ethics: The Road to Eugenics', *University of Chicago Law School Roundtable*, 3 (1996): 491, 495–6, 501; Herbert Hovenkamp, 'Technology, politics, and regulated monopoly: an American historical perspective', *Texas Law Review*, 62 (1984): 1263–312.

46 See Genevieve Kirkwood and Michael Purdue, 'High technology; role and status of central government policy', *Journal of Planning and Environmental Law* (1988): 111–18.

47 The point must be here made that the term "constitutions" is not to be taken to refer to the formal written constitutional documents of a country, but rather to include all aspects of its governance, including the state's underlying relationship with its people. It is not confined to the narrower modern definition of a constitution, such as exemplified by Lassalle (the written constitution of the modern state collects together and determines 'in one instrument, on one piece of paper, all the country's institutions and principles of government' (Ferdinand Lassalle, 'Uber Verfassungswesen' in E. Bernstein (ed.), *Gesammelte Reden und Schriften* (Berlin, 1919), vol. 2, pp. 38, 46), but rather the more ancient and open definition, namely of a characteristic power structure and a minimal amount of legal norms about the structure of power; Hermann Heller, 'The Decline of the Nation State and its Effect on Constitutional and International Economic Law', *Cardozo Law Review*, 18 (1996): 1139, 1206.

48 It has been suggested by Scheuerman that we should see constitutions as expressive of a broadly-defined set of abstract moral principles; Scheuerman, 366.

49 See Judith D. Ahrens and Gerardo A. Esquer, 'Internet's potential as a global information infrastructure: A case study and assessment', *Journal of Global Information Management*, 1 (1993): 18–27.

50 See Kevin G. DeNoce, 'Internet privacy jurisdiction begins to develop; courts and legislators address e-mail confidentiality and other New Age constitutional issues', *The National Law Journal*, 19 (1997): B11.

51 It should come as no surprise then that an emerging international law dimension of the Internet has been identified; Franz C. Mayer, 'The Internet and Public International Law – Worlds Apart?', *European Journal of International Law*, 12 (2001): 617–22; Ruth Wedgwood, 'The Internet and Public International Law: Cyber-Nations', *Kentucky Law Journal*, 88 (2000): 957–65; Klaus W. Grewlich, *Governance in 'Cyberspace' – Access and Public Interest in Global Telecommunications* (The Hague, 1999); Makoto Ibusuki (ed.), *Transnational Cyberspace Law* (Oxford, 2000); Sylvia Ostry and Richard R. Nelson, *Techno-nationalism and techno-globalism: conflict and cooperation* (Washington, c.1995).

52 At least those of the European model.

53 Philip Cooke, 'Globalization of economic organization and the emergence of regional interstate partnerships' in Colin H. Williams (ed.), *The Political Geography of the New World Order* (London, 1993), pp. 46–58, 47.

54 See Steven McGready, 'The Digital Reformation: Total Freedom, Risk, and Responsibility', *Harvard Journal of Law and Technology*, 10 (1996): 137–48.

55 See Max Weber, *The Protestant Ethic and the Spirit of Capitalism*, trans. Talcott Parsons (London, 1992).

56 See McGinnis, 'The Symbiosis of Constitutionalism and Technology'.

57 Including the economic and social environment.

58 Edmund Burke, *Selected Writings and Speeches*, ed. Peter J. Stanlis (Washington, 1997), cited by McGinnis, 'The Symbiosis of Constitutionalism and Technology'.

59 See, generally, J. Woodford Howard Jr, 'Constitution and society in comparative perspective', *Judicature*, 71 (1987): 211–15.

60 See Sunstein, *Republic.com*.

61 See McGready, 'The Digital Reformation'.

62 See, for instance, the Universal Declaration of Human Rights, as passed and proclaimed by the General Assembly of the United Nations on the tenth day of December 1948 (Wellington, 1951).

63 See Maria Eduarda Goncalves, 'Technological change, Globalization and the Europeanization of rights', *International Review of Law, Computers and Technology*, 16 (2002): 301–16.

64 Such as raised economic and political expectations in poorer and less democratic countries.

65 See, for example, *Yahoo! Inc v La Ligue contre Le Racisme et L'Antisemitisme*, 145 F Supp 2d 1168; 169 F Supp 2d 1181 (2001); Andreas Manolopoulos, 'Raising "Cyber-Borders": The Interaction Between Law and Technology', *International Journal of Law and Information Technology*, 11 (2003): 40–58.

66 See James W. Cortada, *Making the Information Society: Experience, Consequences and Possibilities* (Paramus, 2001).

67 Ibid.

68 See Lawrence Lessig, *The Future of Ideas: The Fate of the Commons in a Connected World* (New York, 2001).

69 Frederick M. Abbott, 'Distributed governance at the WTO–WIPO: An evolving model for open-architecture integrated governance', *Journal of International Economic Law*, 3 (2000): 63.

70 McGinnis, 'The Symbiosis of Constitutionalism and Technology', 9; John O. McGinnis and Mark L. Movsesian, 'The World Trade Constitution', *Harvard Law Review*, 114 (2000): 511–605, 514–15.

71 McGinnis, 'The Symbiosis of Constitutionalism and Technology', 9–10.

72 Unless, of course, they have relinquished legislative authority, in part or whole, as have members of the European Union. See Trevor C. Hartley, *Constitutional Problems of the European Union* (Oxford, 1999).

73 See Ostry and Nelson.

74 See Catherine Dauvergne (ed.), *Jurisprudence for an interconnected globe* (Aldershot, c.2003); Richard Warren Perry and Bill Maurer (eds), *Globalization under construction: governmentality, law, and identity* (Minneapolis, c.2003); Jean Stefancic and Richard Delgado, 'Outsider jurisprudence and the electronic revolution: Will technology help or hinder the cause of law reform?', *Ohio State Law Journal*, 52 (1991): 847–58.

75 It is, of course, impossible to predict what further developments are likely to occur, which makes it necessary that the legal system – and the constitution – is sufficiently flexible so as to allow this development, and yet restrict or prohibit developments which are deemed unsuitable.

76 See Ilene K. Grossman, 'The new Industrial Revolution: meeting the challenge', *Public Law Forum*, 4 (1985): 419–26; Thomas W. Rudin, 'State involvement in the "new Industrial Revolution"', *Public Law Forum*, 4 (1985): 411–17.

77 See Maurice Pearton, *The knowledge state: diplomacy, war, and technology since 1830* (London, 1982).

78 See Bruce Parrott, 'Technology and the Soviet polity: the problem of industrial innovation, 1928 to 1973' (1976) Columbia University PhD thesis; Rensselaer W. Lee, 'The politics of technology in Communist China' (1973) Stanford University PhD thesis.

79 For example, see House of Representatives Standing Committee for Long Term Strategies, *Government response: Australia as an information society: grasping new paradigms* (Canberra, c.1992); Nick Moore and Jane Steele, *Information-intensive Britain: an analysis of the policy issues* (London, 1991), where the emphasis of both is upon information technology. See also James Botkin, Dan Dimancescu, Ray Stata and John McClellan, *Global stakes: the future of high technology in America* (Cambridge, c.1982); Thomas L. Friedman, *The Lexus and the Olive Tree* (London, 2000), p. 9.

80 For example, the Internet potentially threatens the monopoly of the Communist regime in mainland China, which partly explains their efforts to regulate access to and use of the Internet; Jack Linchuan Qiu, 'Virtual Censorship in China: Keeping the Gate between the Cyberspaces', *International Journal of Communications Law and Policy*, 4 (1999–2000): 1–25; Renee M. Fishman, Kara Josephberg, Jane Linn, Jane Pollack and Jena Victoriano, 'China issues rules on content enforcement', *Intellectual Property and Technology Law Journal*, 14(10) (2002): 24. China has regulated access to the Internet through centralised filtered servers, and by requiring filters for in-state Internet service providers and end-users; Timothy Wu, 'Cyberspace Sovereignty? – The Internet and the International System', *Harvard Journal of Law and Technology*, 10 (1997): 647, 652–4.

81 See, for instance, Arthur J. Taylor, *Laissez-faire and state intervention in nineteenth-century Britain* (London, 1972); Sir Norman Chester, *The English administrative system, 1780–1870* (Oxford, 1981).

82 Alison Firth (ed.), *The prehistory and development of intellectual property systems* (London, 1997).

83 See McGinnis, 'The Symbiosis of Constitutionalism and Technology'.

84 Ibid.

85 For instance, the pharmaceutical and nuclear power industry; See Ivette P. Gomez, 'Beyond the neighbourhood drugstore: United States regulation of online prescription drug sales by foreign businesses', *Rutgers Computer and Technology Law Journal*, 28 (2002): 431–62; Michael R. Fox, 'Nuclear regulation: the untold story; poor management? Yes, but lay the blame on too much regulation', *Public Utilities Fortnightly*, 133 (1994): 37–41.

86 Andrew Brown and Anthony Grant, *The law of intellectual property in New Zealand: an exposition of the New Zealand law relating to trade marks, passing off, copyright, registered designs, patents, trade secrets and the Fair Trading Act 1986* (Wellington, 1989); Hilary Pearson and Clifford Miller, *Commercial exploitation of intellectual property* (London, 1990); Allen Consulting Group, *Economic perspectives on copyright law: research paper* (Strawberry Hills, 2003).

87 Joseph W. Bartlett, *Venture capital: law, business strategies, investment planning* (New York, 1988).

88 Thomas Wilhelmsson, Salla Tuominen and Heli Tuomola (eds), *Consumer law in the information society* (Boston, 2001).

89 David M. Driesen, *The economic dynamics of environmental law* (Cambridge, 2003); Chris Miller (ed.), *Planning and environmental protection: a review of law and policy* (Oxford, 2001).

90 For example, in the rampant industrialization in Eastern Europe under Communism, and the resulting environmental catastrophe; F.W. Carter and David Turnock (eds), *Environmental problems in Eastern Europe* (London, 1993); Gretta Goldenman (ed.),

Environmental liability and privatisation in Central and Eastern Europe (London, 1994).

91 Law, economics, and risk are the subject of an ongoing debate. See, for instance, Christopher K. Braun, 'Alternative rhythms in law and economics: the Posner–Malloy dialectic', *The Legal Studies Forum*, 15 (1991): 153–65.

PART II
THE RELATIONSHIP OF GOVERNMENT AND TECHNOLOGY

The technological revolution affecting the global economy has profound implications not merely for society, but also for national and even global legal systems – insofar as the international legal environment can be described as being a system. The various aspects of the influence of technology upon society include affecting the nature of governmental and business relationships, as well as the substantive and procedural law per se. In this part of the book we will consider the more profound aspects of the influence of technology on constitutional paradigms, and then consider the wider implications of this.

This part of the book will consider some aspects of the nature of constitutional responses to paradigmatic shifts in technology. This includes an examination of the extent to which the structure or institutions of government has reacted to technological change, and the extent to which technology itself has responded to the nature and form of constitutions. It considers the nature of constitutions and of their relationship with technology. It then proceeds to briefly examine several seminal technological changes which have occurred in the past, in order to identify common elements in relation to constitutions and technology. It then looks at several contemporary technological revolutions, with a similar purpose. Finally, it seeks to draw some common themes from these examples, with the intention of identifying some lessons which may serve to guide law and policy-makers.

Chapter 4

Constitutional Responses to Paradigmatic Shifts in Technology

4.1 Introduction

As has been observed elsewhere, the world is in the midst of a new technological revolution.[1] Though this might be a simplistic or even crass observation, yet it appears to remain essentially true. This is a revolution in that the pace of change in technology, and the implications of that change, is threatening to destabilise societies, legal systems and economies alike, whether they choose to embrace it or not. This is through its tendency to undermine traditional power structures and create new allegiances and new networks (especially global interconnectivity).

It is a revolution which is seeing significant advances across a multitude of disciplines. Like some of the earlier cultural and economic revolutions which have punctuated the rise and fall of human civilization this revolution is one of knowledge – the so-called 'knowledge revolution'.[2] This revolution is based on the acquiring, processing, and dissemination of knowledge, just as the last great technological revolution, the Industrial Revolution, concerned the mass production, and distribution of commodities,[3] through the acquisition of the knowledge associated with applied technology.

Governments are directly affected by these developments because knowledge is power,[4] and power in turn is acquired through the control of knowledge. This occurs concurrently at multiple levels of society, from the state (which might enforce and justify its monopoly or near monopoly of political power through the control of political, cultural and economic information), through the businesses (whose success or failure depends as much on the control of information as it does on the production, sales and distribution of products and services). When knowledge is acquired by non-government entities governments can be threatened, though this threat is normally indirect rather than overt and direct.

It is for this reason, amongst others, that a revolution based on knowledge should have, and in the present situation, may well be shown to have, significant constitutional effects. The acquisition and control of knowledge has never been a monopoly of governments – though it has been found to be a useful prop and support for arbitrary or dictatorial regimes especially, and has also been used to bolster the authority of democratic governments,[5] especially at times of crisis or tension.[6]

There are a number of reasons why the present high technology revolution is of crucial importance to governments. As observed earlier, some facets of the revolution (particularly the Internet, but the telecommunications revolution in general)[7] offer opportunities for internationalization – or globalization[8] – on a scale previously unimaginable.[9] Globalization[10] is not merely a notion; it is an economic fact,[11] and increasingly of political and cultural significance. This significance is particularly noticeable in the economic sphere, as legal systems are still (despite increasing cross-jurisdictional ties[12]) largely separate and distinct, as the products of the sovereign state.[13]

As Zekos has written, the real jurisdictional novelty of cyberspace[14] (which is perhaps the most frequently considered aspect of the technological revolution), is that it will give rise to more frequent circumstances in which effects are felt in multiple territories at once.[15] This has implications for all states, and particularly so because it is an ongoing process,[16] one whose eventual impact is unknown. At times it is unclear that there is movement at all, and its direction may always be uncertain. At the same time that the Internet provides states with tools through which they could potentially increase the level of control or oversight which they exercise over their populations,[17] it also is allowing individuals, communities, and other sub-state groups unparalleled access to information and commerce across the globe.[18] All of these effects have constitutional implications, or will have in the future, or have potential effects upon the very structure of government itself, both in its domestic and international aspects.

Technological advances in fields other than the Internet and information technology are also significant. They also have the potential to challenge the boundaries of law, science, public policy, and ethics.[19] Biotechnology in general is highly controversial,[20] and particularly so is embryonic stem cell research.[21] This form of research raises the type of issues which Mary Shelley addressed in her novel *Frankenstein*.[22] What are the proper limits to mankind's inquiry into, and tampering with, the forces of nature. If this was a legitimate theme of literary endeavour for early nineteenth century English writers it was doubly important today, when the potential of gene manipulation is only now being explored. The Churches and ethicists are also deeply concerned, though not necessarily dismissive of all technological innovation. Important developments are also occurring in the fields of artificial intelligence,[23] nano-technology,[24] and cryonics.[25]

All of these developments raise legal and moral, if not constitutional questions. In an age where technological and medical advances are developing at what sometimes appears to be exponential rates, the law may shape or follow advances.[26] It may follow because, by its very nature, most law is reactive to identified events, situations and problems. Laws are enacted to meet identified situations. For this reason each nation's scientific community must generally wait for approval, guidance, or funding to continue genetic research.[27] In some cases such research is illegal under pre-existing laws which governed the production, distribution and sale of produce, especially that intended for human consumption. In other cases the law was more permissive. Because of consumer concerns about the risks of generically manipulated foodstuffs regulations on the development of such products were introduced in a number of countries, but such laws were almost inevitably reactive, and limited in their potential for influencing the direction of future research.

But it is not clear whether the state should follow or lead these developments.[28] A generic approach to technological changes is rendered difficult by the diverse nature of change. High-technology industries are no different to earlier technologies, where the nature of the influence upon the constitution, as upon society and the economy, is uncertain. This almost inevitably makes the legal approach a reactive one, rather than pro-active, and therefore potentially lacking in principle and coherence. The question of whether this is a serious problem for a constitution remains another question, the answer to which depending, perhaps, upon the inherent nature of the particular country and its constitution. The inherent problem with reactive legislation to respond to individual technological concerns is that it is unprincipled, uncertain, and potentially subject to interest group lobbying. None of these drawbacks mean, of themselves, that governments should not legislate in response to technological innovation. But it does suggest that such legislation should be based on broader principles than has hitherto generally been the case.

Law cannot however be silent, whether at the constitutional level, or with respect to what may be called matters of ordinary legislation, that is, those dealing with specific technical details, and not the structure of the state or fundamental rights and responsibilities. There are risks inherent in any new technology. Sometimes errors are made – though these do not necessarily have to involve the very latest technology to have devastating consequences for societies. A relatively simple mistake at a petrochemicals or fertiliser plant can have serious consequences for an entire community.[29] These risks are particularly significant in respect of technology transfer,[30] where the nature of the technology applied may be maladjusted to the underlying technological base of the society and economy – and legal regime – of the society to which it is transplanted.

To leave all to chance may well be dangerous. In some cases governments have chosen to act to regulate technologies, in others they have chosen to not do so. Obviously dangerous technologies are almost universally regulated. But the choice of regulation, or non-regulation, and the choice of regulatory model, is often more difficult. There have been debates – which have raged now for more than a decade – over whether the Internet is unique and should be governed (if regulated at all) by a *sui generis* 'cyberlaw',[31] or is simply an extension of existing technology and can be regulated by existing laws. It may well be asked how there can be agreement on a common approach, when laws, and public policy in general, are the product of the nation-state, and agreement between them is often difficult to achieve, even if it is desirable. It might also be questioned whether there is a need for a common approach, or whether the current combination of state regulation, co-operation and self-regulation is sufficient.[32]

Fundamentally, this technological revolution raises questions about the nature and role of state and society, and the place of the individual, and the state, within this structure, as well as the relationship between state and state. Had the speed of development of technology in the late twentieth century been less rapid these questions would have remained academic but not especially material for the day-to-day operation of government. However, not only is the speed of development very great, but more has been learnt in the last hundred years about the world in which we live than in the last thousand years. It is almost inevitable that this should lead to a reappraisal of the nature of government.

Modern state institutions, and the principal Western models of state structures,[33] were established or consolidated during the fifteenth to early twentieth century era of nation-state building.[34] It was a period which saw relatively steady technological development across the Europe, and a lesser degree of technological evolution in other parts of the world. This asymmetrical development itself had implications for the then contemporary society – colonialization, and the growth of colonial empires of the European states being prime examples.

The present revolution is also asymmetrical, but rather less so in some respects, and (crucially), it is much more fluid and less tied to existing nation-states. This revolution raises questions about the nature of the state, just as earlier revolutions have often done.

4.2 Technological Challenges to Constitutional Paradigms

Technology, as defined earlier, is not limited to the physical tools through which we affect our environment. It includes the processes and systems through which this is done. This can include worldviews or philosophies where they have a direct practical application. Though less obviously a 'technology', if such a view manifests itself in a series of new innovations in art, learning, culture, and government, then it may qualify as a technology in this broad sense. We can look at one example of this form of 'technology'.

Weber's *The Protestant Ethic and the Spirit of Capitalism*[35] has been described as 'a polemic that links the Protestant Revolution (the Reformation) and the Industrial Revolution, in particular, Calvinism and the rise of entrepreneurial capitalism.'[36] In this model a paradigm shift away from religious conceptions which had shaped the European world for over a thousand years brought with it a renewed interest in the physical world – and a new approach to observing and understanding it. This was more than a mere revolution; it was a new approach to life, a change as profound as that which punctuated the end of the classical world and the beginning of the modern world.[37] The Reformation led at once to new governmental structures and to new innovations in technologies. A revolution changes political systems and governments; the Reformation changed almost every aspect of western European society, including religion, government, scholarship, education, and business.[38] But whether the Reformation should be seen as a technological revolution which led to further technological revolutions as well as to constitutional revolutions remains to be seen. It may equally validly – perhaps more so – be seen as the constitutional revolution which led to technological revolution. Either way, the process was multi-directional throughout, with law, government, society and technology influencing each other.

McGready has argued that the advent of the personal computer (PC), the Internet (and the World Wide Web – often included in the term Internet) is causing a reformation rather than a revolution.[39] He argues that the changes being wrought by the knowledge revolution will be as far-reaching as those of the Reformation.[40] Like the Reformation, it will be a series of revolutions, and not simply a single discrete change. Whilst this view is not necessarily shared by all – indeed it may be seen as radical by the Internet realists – nevertheless it is worth careful consideration.

One reason for this profound change, according to McGready, is that the new rights which aim to respond to opportunities and risks arising from new information and communication technologies, biotechnological or other technology-based industrial development, are not grounded in the nation-state. Generally, established civil, economic, social and political rights,[41] were predicated upon the existence of the nation-state, and indeed were constructed within the framework of the nation-state.[42] Globalization, and a concurrent individualisation (or the enfranchisement of the individual) has led to additional rights, desires and pressures.[43] These threaten the state, not to its very existence,[44] but in its relationship with its people and with other states.

The concept of the state is not necessarily unassailable, as has been seen in the few modern examples we have of supra-national political entities. Indeed the concept of the autonomous sovereign state is a relatively modern one. The state's potential loss of power and autonomy to regulate economic and social activity, as well as to protect individual rights, has been accepted by the member states of the European Union. They have voluntarily relinquished some of their sovereignty – and will gradually lose more of it, some powers passing to the Union, and some being delegated to regional authorities.

The creation of this supra-national entity is as the result of a process that to a certain degree anticipated contemporary global tendencies,[45] but which is so far the best (if not the only) example of a modern multi-national quasi-state. The members of the European Union enjoyed a certain shared heritage, including significant cultural, historical and legal links – though Christianity was rejected as a core principle.[46] Such common elements are not found throughout the world, thus making truly global government rather more complex a proposition. Economic and cultural globalization can continue regardless, but it will have an uncertain effect on states.

In 1996 Khan argued that the evolution of a world without borders seemed unavoidable.[47] He postulated a theory of a Free State, relying on Hugo Grotius, most particularly *The Law of War and Peace*.[48] Khan argued that the globalizing tendencies of the late twentieth century, when he was writing, rendered the state effectively obsolete, as it was no longer the efficient player which justified its creation.

Yet it is possibly very premature to consign the nation-state to the scrap heap of history.[49] This is not least because, despite continued falls in the costs of transport and communications in the first half of the twentieth century, integration actually reversed course – for predominantly political and related sociological reasons.[50] But it may well be necessary to re-examine the place of the state in the new world technological order.[51] It is information, not transportation (though that is one aspect of communications, a sub-set of information), that is crucial to globalization, and the biggest potential threat to the state.

Cortada examined the historical, cultural, and (to some degree) legal aspects of interaction between society and information.[52] He maintained that the information age is not really a new phenomenon, but rather is the most recent manifestation of a long-standing process of historical evolution.[53] This would seem both logical and correct – so far as it goes. As McGready might argue, this is a reformation, a series of revolutions, and so the apparent continuity is masking a deeper, more profound, underlying change.

Lessig suggests that the historical evolution of the information society is a foundational preamble for what he characterises as one of the most critical battles of our time – the battle for the future of the Internet.[54] Both views may be correct, for while the knowledge technology may be grounded in an earlier Industrial Revolution, so evolution has its periods of stagnation, and its periods of fundamental change.[55] We may be entering just such a latter phase now.

The challenge for governments is to respond to this ongoing – and possibly long-term[56] – revolution,[57] and not become victims of it.[58] The more inflexible the state – or the more dogmatic – the greater the risk of failure.[59] Failure by governments to respond fully and effectively to changing paradigms[60] can result in loss of competitive advantage[61] – or even the existence of that state (through the loss of economic viability).[62] This ability to respond is not merely political, social or economic. It is also constitutional. The challenge – or threat – of techno-globalism to sovereign states[63] has profound implications for jurisprudence.[64]

The difficulty with understanding the nature of the information revolution is that we are all part of it – though that is perhaps not a dissimilar difficulty to that presented by evaluating any contemporary political, social or technological change. We do not have the luxury of being an interested (or disinterested) bystander,[65] nor do we enjoy the benefits of hindsight. We are also constrained by our own cultural traditions, which tend to inhibit our appreciation of cross-disciplinary changes. All writing on the constitution – however this was defined – is underpinned by some theoretical perspective, however dimly perceived or narrowly conceived.[66] Legal and constitutional history cannot be left to the lawyers alone, nor to historians.[67] Neither can the analysis of the contemporary constitution by political scientists exclude consideration of its legal and historical, as well as its political, aspects. Constitutional lawyers are concerned particularly with legal validity. They may not be especially interested in the normative standing of the power arrangements that the law validates. None of these approaches are especially sensitive to technology. A multi-disciplinary approach is needed.

4.3 The State

If the constitution is seen as the rules and procedures through which a state is governed, to understand the constitution it is first necessary to consider the nature of the state. As was discussed in Chapter 1, the constitution may be seen to be the result of a formal process of development or adoption, or it may be as a result of evolutionary or revolutionary development (and in many cases a combination of the three). However, although the form and content of the constitution will vary considerably, due to the internal and external influences which have shaped it, including the specific history, politics, culture, geography and so on of the country concerned, the nature of the state itself is perhaps seen more readily as being generic. This is in part because it is a simpler or less multifaceted concept, but also because it is an artificial product of the evolution of international law – though a concept which may have much to commend it in principle. Since the development of the modern nation-state the concept of the state has dominated international law, but it has always been present, in one form or another, since the development of the first city-states, tribal federations and complex social alliances of this nature.[68]

The modern state evolved in Europe in the wake of the fall of the classical world and under the impetus of the crusades against Islamic aggression in Europe and to recover the Holy Land in Palestine.[69] It gained encouragement from the growth of trade and commerce, and from the rediscovery of Roman laws and classical learning, in the years after the collapse of the Eastern Empire centred on Constantinople.[70] Following the advent of the modern nation-state political and legal theory tended to exalt the state as the pinnacle of authority – though this was disputed both by the Church[71] and, at times, by mesne feudal lords, burghers and other communities.

During what might be termed the classical period of statehood – from the Treaty of Westphalia 1648 to the Treaty of Versailles 1919 – the study of politics tendered to centre on the state. But for much of the twentieth century it had focused on political behaviour and policy-making, with governmental decisions explained as a response to societal forces. In part this has been due to a growth in awareness of the limitations of studies based on political events which might themselves be the product of underlying stresses and dynamics. It also suited the increased emphasis in western debate upon countries outside Europe and North America and those countries within their direct and indirect spheres of influence.

This change in emphasis to focus on political behaviour and policy-making can be seen in the growth of behaviouralism, which sought to escape from what has been described as an 'anaemic mixture of law, philosophy, and history'[72] to a more empirical, quantitative, interdisciplinary approach to the study of politics. This was justified on the basis that traditional studies were said to be essentially non-comparative, descriptive, legalistic, and static.[73] It was argued that the state, rather than being a discrete entity whose structure, form and very existence influenced political, social and economic developments, was lacking in autonomy, and largely simply reflected the concerns, ideology and interests of the power players.

Behaviouralism, generally, is an approach which seeks ‘hard data’. Analysis of such mysteries as ‘the state’ did not come readily to it.[74] In an environment in which political behaviour was assessed through such a lens it might be doubted whether the relationship of technology and legal systems – or the constitutional paradigm of a country – would be a likely subject of study.

But the state is not dead. In recent decades state-centred theorists have sought to bring the state back into the forefront of research, arguing that it is more autonomous than society-centred theorists (such as neo-liberals[75]) have suggested. They have argued that the state is indeed an independent player, with interests of its own, independent of those of the leadership of the state. The recent growth of a ‘new institutionalism’ has placed the state at the very centre of political science, ironically at a time when the state has arguably become less involved in society,[76] at least in many countries of the industrialised world, due to policies of economic liberalization.

There are limitations to a conceptual lens which emphasizes the autonomy of the state, just as much as there are in approaches which emphasize the role of the political actors through which the state operates. Both are in danger of underestimating the importance of external influences; for the behaviouralist, the structure and existence of the state, and for the new institutionalist, the political actors, their electorates and personal interests. There are equally limitations to purely legal understandings of the concept of the state.

The traditional understanding of public law (and more especially the more narrowly defined constitutional law) emphasized particular ideas of power that are associated with territory, sovereignty, and law, all concepts about which there is often uncertainty – though some legal systems tend to imply a form of permanence, even akin to Platonic forms.[77] The ideas of state, and state power expressed through law, however remain central to understanding government.[78]

It has been argued, by Morison amongst others, that the nature of public power, and practices of government, have changed so far beyond the public law framework that a new approach is needed. This is because – similar to the behaviouralists approach emphasizing the participants’ individual motivations – government is seen to not be autonomous, nor the monopoly of the ‘formal’ government. Governmentality, which has its origins in the later writings of Michel Foucault[79] and subsequent criticism of his work,[80] has been offered as an important way of understanding how power is arranged in society and how government can be conceptualised.[81]

Government, for Foucault, was not so much the political or administrative structures of the modern state as ‘the way in which the conduct of individuals or of groups might be directed: the government of children, of souls, of communities, of families, of the sick ... To govern, in this sense, is to structure the possible field of action of others’.[82]

In Foucault’s later work he stressed the importance of the active subject as the entity through which and by means of which power is actually exercised. Emphasis is placed on the way in which certain attitudes and behaviours came to be. Foucault observed that 'Political theory has never ceased to be obsessed with the person of the sovereign',[83] in effect, the legitimation of power.

Governmentality is a used to describe centralization and increased government power. This power is not negative. In fact, it produces reality through 'rituals of truth' and it creates a particular style of subjectivity with which one conforms to or resists. Because the individuals are taken into this subjectivity they become part of the normalizing force. According to Foucault, power as a social structure resides in the discourse itself.[84] The rules of the discourse prescribes which arguments can legitimately be used by the participants.[85] Governmentality also includes a growing body of knowledge that presents itself as 'scientific,' and which contributes to the power of governmentality.[86]

The notion of governmentality emphasizes the creation and deployment of a whole range of technologies connecting multiple centres of power within an exercise of government. It avoids, though does not ignore, particular ideas of power associated with territory, sovereignty and law (arguably the greatest single weakness of the traditional – pre-behaviouralist – approach to constitutional law, sovereignty and politics).

Like behaviouralism, governmentality places less emphasis upon the organs of government, and stresses the importance of the active subject as the entity through which and by means of which power is actually exercised beyond traditional state boundaries. This approach adapts itself readily to an environment in which one of the globalizing tendencies – and itself a result of globalization, is the trans-national corporation. Power (not simply political, or legal power, but power more broadly conceived) is diffused.[87] It is influence, rather than control, which is dominant.[88]

The emphasis of Foucault's governmentality, unlike behaviouralism, or new institutionalism, is less upon the state, or the single political entity, than it is upon the discourse. The recognition of the fluidity or multi-directional nature of power relations is one of the strengths of an approach which minimizes the formalism of many of the earlier approaches. This is particularly crucial when we consider that government exists at multiple levels, and that at the level of the state there are also dynamic relations with other states to consider. This latter relationship is formally governed by international law (though it might be observed that even here there is a distinction between public international law, which governs the relations of states with one another, and private international law, or conflict of laws, which is concerned with the laws involved in the settlement of private disputes and relationships[89]).

International law is more fluid and less certain than the domestic legal systems of most if not all states, as is perhaps inevitable for a system which has evolved largely through state practice over a considerable period of years – and which has lacked a truly effective enforcement or sanction system such as was almost indispensable for domestic state legal systems. It is derived from written and unwritten rules, treaties, agreements, and customary law. Custom is general state practice accepted as law. The elements of custom are a generalized repetition of similar acts by competent state authorities and a sentiment that such acts are juridically necessary to maintain and develop international relations.[90] The existence of custom, unlike treaty-law, depends upon general agreement, not deliberate consent.[91] This requires time to develop, and is often uncertain.

The development of public international law, and indeed of law in general, never truly ceases; like all living things, it evolves. There are times when important, indeed profound, changes occur, or milestones are reached – such as the establishment of the League of Nations, or of the Nuremberg and Tokyo war crimes tribunals.[92] These events may be important in themselves, or because of the example which they present for the future – though this latter may not always be perceived at the time as being especially significant. At other times there may appear to be little or no progress, neither improvements nor retrograde changes.[93] But, as Foucault would maintain, formal stasis – if such a thing can be found in international law – does not mean that the discourse has ceased or the power relations unchanging.

Change there may well be, for international law is intensely political and dynamic, as any law must be which is the distillation of the hope, needs and desires of almost two hundred sovereign states.[94] Nor is it immutable by nature, though international laws may evolve more slowly than the domestic laws of some, though not necessarily all, countries.[95] Law itself, as a human artefact, is also inseparable from history and from culture.[96] This is especially true of public international law, which is formed and developed through the interactions of numerous sovereign states, but dominated by concepts derived from Roman law and the laws and practices of European states, principally during the period of European commercial and later colonial expansion.

Throughout the twentieth century, and for much longer, the sovereign state had seemed to be one of the relatively few abiding constants in international law.[97] But the concept of the sovereign state, though one of comparatively ancient origin,[98] has not continued completely unquestioned – nor has it continued unchanged.[99] Its place in the global political and legal system is not absolute, for the sovereign state belongs in a world in which interdependence (whether acknowledged or not) is inescapable.[100] Governmentality would recognize that it is in the discourse, rather than the formal structure (though this informs the discourse), that the real power may be seen.

In the latter years of the twentieth century and the first of the twenty-first century two important developments in particular have had the effect of encouraging the reconsideration of the nature of the sovereign state, and of the limitations upon it. The first was technological in nature, the second may be termed geo-political. Each will be considered in turn.

4.3.1 Global Technological Environment

Technology[101] can have important implications for law, for it can challenge the existing legal norms of any society.[102] We have seen this occurring most recently with respect to developments in the biotechnology field especially.[103] But the advent of the new telecommunications technologies and of the World Wide Web and the Internet[104] in particular has caused some commentators to question the relevance, or even the survival, of the sovereign state. It might seem to be rather surprising that the future of the state, with which we are so familiar and which seems such a permanent feature of the political landscape, should be questioned in this way. The reason, however, is because the Internet's globalizing potential[105] has been seen as potentially weakening, if not destroying, the rational justification for the state. Efficiency, or a form of political Darwinianism,[106] might lead thence to the demise of the inefficient state.

This revolutionary view of the Internet and of the future of the state is not one which is readily acceptable to the realist or the less ideologically-obsessed observer (or possibly even the less technologically perspicacious). Indeed, though it may have been popular in the halcyon days of Internet growth in the 1990s,[107] this radical view of the effect on the state that the Internet is having or is likely to have has since largely fallen out of favour.[108] But it is rather easier to accept that the Internet has caused some practical and possibly also conceptual difficulties for state sovereignty,[109] and may have greater long-term effects – indeed Lessig has written that the battle for the future of the Internet is the most critical battle of our time[110] – whatever the eventual outcome may be. Time alone will tell whether this is so (and if it is, what the shape of the new society will be like), but it is clear that this technological evolution – or revolution[111] – will have an effect upon public international law which is as significant as that it is having upon private international law, and upon the domestic laws of sovereign states.

Public international law is not immune from this influence. Modern state institutions,[112] and the principal western models of state structures themselves, were established or consolidated during the fifteenth to early twentieth century era of European nation-state building.[113] That time also was a revolutionary one in its own way, for it saw the decline of the Middle Ages (itself the product of cultural, social, economic and political change and crisis at the end of the classical period of history) and the growth of the modern era – and much of that political and legal change can be seen as based on technological change.[114] The present technological revolution raises questions about the nature of the state, just as earlier technological, economic, social and political revolutions have done.[115]

Changes in technology which affect states in their relations with one another may be thought to be comparatively rare, but they actually are many and varied. They include all those innovations which enable one state or civilization to impose its will on another (both directly and indirectly), and well as a plethora of less dramatic examples. In order to help us understand the nature of the potential changes these technological revolutions may have in public international law (the relationship of state to state), it is necessary for us to examine the effect the technological environment has had upon law in the past, and its effect today. Whilst to do this comprehensively and systematically would be a major undertaking, and one which would be beyond the scope of this book, the sections which follow do attempt to address a few instances.

4.3.2 Global Geo-Political Environment

Those specific geo-political developments which have also encouraged a re-evaluation of the nature and role of the state have been the recent use of force by great powers and a superpower,[116] in Yugoslavia in the name of humanitarian intervention,[117] and in Iraq on the basis of pre-emptive self-defence,[118] and the attitudes and assumptions which these actions reflect. The Iraq war in particular has served to highlight structural weaknesses in the fabric of the international security framework,[119] since it was widely condemned as illegal, yet little could be done to prevent it, even if this were desirable. But at the same time it is possible to be cautiously optimistic. At the forefront of much of the discourse from the allies in both wars was the perceived need for their actions to be justified in international law.[120] These cases illustrate the dynamic effect of both power projection and technology – of a military sort – upon the relationships between states. Formal political equality may exist, but that is relatively meaningless when the political will exists to ignore or disregard that equality and impose (or attempt to impose) the will of one nation – or a coalition of states – on another.

These recent wars, small though they may have been in historical terms, have served to draw both popular and academic attention to the evolution of, and recent challenges to, the laws of armed conflict – or laws of war as they were commonly known.[121] These laws have long had the effect of imposing limitations upon the freedom of states to levy war without the support of the international community and without 'just' or lawful cause.[122] Just what constituted a just cause (or just war) was never entirely certain, but, like the equally vague concept of the rule of law, it served to impose some limitations on freedom of state action – by operating in a form of Foucaultian discourse among the politicians and rulers who decided national policy. But such limitations on state sovereignty have been challenged by these wars, which were conducted despite lacking clear justification in public international law.

Regretfully, it would appear that the precise legal limits upon the levying of war, perhaps the most ancient and fundamental of a state's responsibilities towards its people,[123] are now more uncertain than they have been for fifty years. Both these wars have also raised important questions about the legal justification for state or international intervention in another state's internal affairs, on humanitarian grounds, or to depose a tyrannical regime.[124]

The geo-political environment is concerned with the strategic balance, and relations between states. This is affected by the law of armed conflict, and other formal legal limitations which are imposed upon state sovereignty. These can be, and often are, challenged by the strategic balance, by wars and by the threat of the use of force by states. It is also affected by technological changes of the more benign – or less obviously malignant – form, such as telecommunications, transportation, agricultural improvements, and so on.

4.3.3 The Global Environment

The late twentieth century and early twenty-first century is an appropriate time to re-evaluate the concept of sovereignty. The sovereign state must evolve, or at least have its nature re-assessed, as its environment changes. The world is very different today to what it was in what may be regarded as the zenith of state sovereignty, in the nineteenth century.[125] The notion that all states are legally equal,[126] whilst perhaps laudable in theory, has also been shown more than once to be subject to important practical qualifications.[127] Nor indeed is the notion of equality of particularly great antiquity.[128] The freedom of action of states can at times be severely restricted, both legally, and practically,[129] by strategic considerations, by international law, and by economic factors. The increasingly pivotal role of international economic law is also having a significant effect.[130]

As a consequence of these developments, and others, the relationship between national law and international law, and the concept of state sovereignty, are arguably more uncertain today than they were one hundred years ago. It is therefore an opportune time for investigation and exploration, albeit one which is narrowly focused, and at times tentative in its conclusions.

4.4 Sovereignty

The heyday of the notion of statehood was perhaps during the late nineteenth century, when states enjoyed almost unfettered independence of action. They were, in general, subject only to the regulation of their diplomatic and military actions, principally by the law of armed conflict (or the law of war).[131] Domestically, nineteenth century social and political theory accorded the state a necessity, functionality and territorialisation which has been described by critics as 'quite illusory'.[132]

However, it would be simplistic to assume that individual states alone determined what international law comprised, or that they were always equally significant. Even a brief look at history tells us that conceptions of world order have by no means always been shaped by the model of sovereign co-equal actors with a territorial basis. It might also be questioned why the concept of state sovereignty reached its apex in the late nineteenth century, at a time when certain European and allied powers were carving up much of the world into formal and informal spheres of influence, in the form of colonies, protectorates,[133] trade concessions, and so on. Rather than epitomising equality of states, this era illustrated the dominance of a relatively small group of economically advanced and sophisticated nations. The less sophisticated peoples – whether they lived in societies which boasted a nation or not – were at the mercy of the technologically advanced and more powerful adversaries.[134] But it is also true that the existence of the concept of the state had a normative effect.

One curious, and instructive, aspect in the history of European colonial expansion in the course of the nineteenth century is that the motivations for establishing colonial empires differed between the participating countries. The United Kingdom was originally motivated, not by political ambition, but by trade – Anglo-Indian law, and later the British Indian Empire, grew from the Mayor's Courts established after 1726 to meet the demands of traders.[135] As her economy grew so it became necessary to find more and further flung markets and sources for raw materials. In contrast, the rather later German colonial empire was established as much to show that Germany was not to be put to shame by the British and French empires as for any pragmatic purpose.[136]

In an earlier period commercial adventure was also a dominant if not the principal motivation for exploration and colonial development. Grants of territory were made to English mariners during Queen Elizabeth's reign, which gave them authority to acquire lands to be governed under the Queen by laws and ordinances 'as near as conveniently might be to the laws of the nation'.[137] There were to be no permanent settlements until Virginia in 1606. Later settlements were to form along the Atlantic coast of North America and throughout the Caribbean and elsewhere, and were to exhibit diverse forms of government. But all were the product of private enterprise, and in all the Crown's sole function was, in the first instance, to confer on the grantees authority to govern lands acquired in its name. This was done through prerogative grants of fiefs to hopeful proprietors, or of charters to companies.[138]

Examples of grants of fiefs, usually based on the model of the County Palatine of Durham, include those to John Cabots 1496, Sir Humphrey Gilbert 1583 (Newfoundland),[139] the Calverts (Newfoundland, then Maryland),[140] Sir Robert Heath 1629 (Carolina – abortively),[141] Sir Ferdinando Gorges 1639 (Maine),[142] the Earl of Clarendon 1663 (Carolinas),[143] James Duke of York 1664 (New York),[144] and William Penn 1680 (Pennsylvania).[145] New Jersey was a proprietary colony till 1702, New Hampshire was a proprietary colony from 1635 to 1679. Georgia was held by trustees from 1732 to 1752.

Elsewhere the model for English colonies was a Crown grant to a chartered company. Early examples included the Virginia Company 1606, the Bermuda Company 1615, the Plymouth Company 1620, and the Massachusetts Bay Company 1628.[146]

There was also a third category, those non-chartered, non-fief territories which were simply settled by subjects of the Crown. These included Connecticut,[147] and Rhode Island.[148] These were comparatively speaking less significant. In all of these cases the primary motivation for colonization was commercial enterprise. Since the risk of investment was borne by the private investors, so some rewards were offered them. The home government could afford to make concessions where the risks were so high, for its own outlay was not significant. Conversely, for a small expense, colonies were being established in previously undeveloped parts of the world, all of which offered economic potential.

In none of these cases were independent sovereign states being established. Indeed, almost by definition this could not have been so. They were subordinate political entities – political because settlers and traders required laws and a means of enforcing it to live safe and productive lives. The arm of the state was not sufficiently long to effectively reach the new colonies – though by the nineteenth century and especially after the advent of steam powered ships – a greater degree of centralization became possible.

The dismemberment of the principal colonial empires after the Second World War (and, in the case of the British Empire, the voluntary emancipation of the main settled colonies from the nineteenth to the mid-twentieth century) has led to the individual sovereign state becoming the normal form of governance. The former hierarchy of states, with a graduation of degrees of independence, has largely passed. Since the ideal – if not the only option for a post-colonial country – was seen to be the sovereign state, this model (evolved in its fullest form during the era of colonial expansion) became the model for the newly-independent countries. Whereas in the early nineteenth century the number of independent countries which conducted relations with one another at a truly international level – the other states, territories, nations and tribes often conducted bi-lateral and even multi-lateral relations, but rarely if ever did so at an international level – was very few, now it is relatively enormous (nearly 200).[149]

The twentieth century, and particularly the second half of that century, saw the growth of international organizations and other bodies now accorded recognition as subjects in international law. With the growth in both the extent and the reach of international agreements, treaties, conventions and codes, the extent to which individual sovereign states retain the final control over their national policies may have diminished.[150] This tendency is becoming more noticeable in the modern commercial environment, and especially in respect of the Internet. The principal of these international bodies was the United Nations, which, in succession to the League of Nations, took a leading role in the post-World War II global security system. This complicated the basic model, which was already shown to be artificial and not actually applicable to much of the world.

While it is possible for organizations and individuals (and in some cases sub-state political entities) to be subjects of international law, states remain the dominant agents in world politics and the dominant actors in international law. This dominance has led some theorists to distinguish 'subjects' of the law from 'objects' of the law, suggesting that although entities other than states may have rights and duties in international law, these rights are conferred upon them by states and, presumably, may be taken away by states.[151] It is possibly more correct now to regard international law as a body of rules that binds states and other agents in world politics in their relations with one another, and that is considered to have the status of law.[152]

Even domestically the sovereignty of the state is greatly limited. Foucault refers to the 'governmentalization of the state', the growth of micro-centres of governance in the course of the twentieth century, after their appearance in the nineteenth century.[153] This of course is arguably not new in any case, since in pre-industrial times state governments were severely restricted in practice, and of necessity much governmental authority was decentralized – even if in theory the state was highly centralized.

Contemporary changes in government in many countries are driven by attempts to 'modernize'. This may be influenced by a developing consumer focus, a desire to improve public sector performance, and by new information and communications technology.[154] The use of information and communications technology (ICT) is a significant aspect of many of the modernization processes that are occurring worldwide.[155] There can be seen to be a general belief that the processes of government can be improved by drawing upon the ability of ICT to store, process and communicate large amounts of data. It also led to the development of the notion of e-government,[156] and even of cyberlaw (for the Internet is the principal ICT). There is a belief, or expectation, that ICT will help transform the accountability, quality, and cost-effectiveness of public services and help to revitalise the relationship between citizens and government through improved consultation and participation in government.

4.5 Conclusion

This Chapter is not concerned with the laws governing the Internet, or genetic engineering, or of the knowledge revolution *per se*.[157] It is not concerned with the social or economic implications of these revolutions – profound though they may be.[158] Rather it is concerned with the effect of technological change upon the structure of government – upon the constitution – and, to a lesser extent, how the structure of governments may in turn have effected technological changes.[159] In effect it is an attempt to identify a link between the societal and economic effects of technology, and the societal and economic influences technology has on constitutions. It is primarily from a constitutional rather than a technological perspective that this issue is approached. From this we may obtain some guidance as to how constitutions might best respond to technological change, and how they might be restructured to best facilitate that change in a way which is for the long-term good.

The Chapter began with a brief examination of the nature of constitutions, and of their relationship with society and technology. It then proceeded to briefly examine several seminal technological eras or changes in the past, in an attempt to identify the effect that these may have had upon government, and the ways in which they were influenced in their development by the nature and form of government. It then looked at several contemporary technological revolutions, with a similar purpose.

The present technological revolution has been described as a reformation, as a series of inter-related revolutions. It may well be that this is so, but perhaps not for the reasons which have been advanced by most commentators. Significant advances in technology – and we have yet to examine the technological revolution to discover whether it is in fact revolutionary (if such identification is possible at this early stage) – do challenge state sovereignty, and even the nature of the state. The state model we have worked with for well over a hundred years is not perhaps as faultless as we have led ourselves to believe. It has hidden a number of – often unpalatable – truths about the nature of the world in which we live. States were not equal; some were much more dominant politically, economically, militarily, legally and culturally; in short, in almost all that went to constitute a state.

Constitutions, in which we may include the overarching structure of international law, recognized the concept of sovereignty – the dominance of one legal system within the one geographical area – yet this has rarely been the norm across the whole world. It recognizes the supremacy of the nation-state, though much of the world comprises states drawn across tribal territories. It recognizes states as equal, though this has never been true except as a polite legal fiction.

Technology has helped to create these paradigms – what Foucault might call the sovereign-state discourse. As a discourse it is the author of its own rules, a self-perpetuating oligarchy of sovereign states. Unfortunately for this nice model, the discourse is maintained, not simply by the states themselves, but by the active subject participants at multiple levels both above and below the state. This does not render the state nugatory, but does mean that the greater the usefulness of a technology the greater the potential risk to the state, either individually (as in the nineteenth century), or collectively (as it has been suggested the Internet is doing now).

Notes

1 'New' is relative. The late twentieth century has seen a range of highly significant technological advances, but some of these may be traced to the Industrial Revolution. In the nineteenth century there were also major societal, and constitutional changes, wrought by technological change; See David Dunstan, *Governing the Metropolis: politics, technology and social change in a Victoria city: Melbourne* (Carlton, 1984). For an African parallel see Jack Goody, *Technology, tradition and the state in Africa* (London, 1980). Generally, see Steven Puro, 'Technology, politics and the new Industrial Revolution', *Public Law Forum*, 4 (1985): 387–98; Thom W. Rudin, 'State involvement in the "new Industrial Revolution"', *Public Law Forum*, 4 (1985): 411–17.

2 See Graciela Chichilnisky, 'The Knowledge Revolution', *Journal of International Trade and Economic Development*, 7 (1998): 39–45.

3 See Charles More, *Understanding the Industrial Revolution* (London, 2000).

4 A quote attributed to English author, courtier, and philosopher Sir Francis Bacon, in 'Religious Meditations, Of Heresies', in *Bacon's essays*, with annotations by Richard Whately (London, 1858, first published 1597).

5 Book burnings in Nazi Germany, and the periodic destruction of literature by Chinese authorities, are examples of the former; Frederick T. Birchall, 'Burning of the Books, May 10, 1933,' in Louis L. Snyder (ed.), *National Socialist Germany: Twelve Years*

that Shook the World (Krieger, 1984), pp. 101–4. As long ago as 213 BC Emperor Shih Huang-ti ordered burned all copies of the first anthology of Chinese poetry compiled by Confucius. On a non-national scale, the Roman Catholic Church sought to maintain doctrinal purity by the use of the list of banned books (*Index Librorum Prohibitorum*), which ran from 1559 to 1966; George Haven Putnam, *The censorship of the Church of Rome and its influence upon the production and distribution of literature* (New York, 1967).

6 Philip Seib, *Beyond the front lines: how the news media cover a world shaped by war* (New York, 2004); David Dadge, *Casualty of war: the Bush administration's assault on a free press* (Amherst, 2004).

7 See Michael Leventhal, 'The Golden Age of Wireless', *Intellectual Property and Technology Law Journal*, 14 (2002): 1.

8 For some of the effects of this, see Masatsugu Tsuji, 'Transformation of the Japanese system towards a network economy', in Emanuele Giovannetti, Mitsuhiro Kagami and Masatsugu Tsuji (eds), *The Internet revolution: a global perspective* (Cambridge, 2003); Ian Tunstall, *Taxation and the Internet* (Pyrmont, 2003); Brian Kahin and Charles Nesson (eds), *Borders in cyberspace: information policy and the global information infrastructure* (Cambridge, 1997); Adam Czarnota, 'A few reflections on Globalization and the constitution of society', *University of New South Wales Law Journal*, 24 (2001): 809–16.

9 Location remains important, but it is virtual location, rather than physical location – there is no necessary connection between an Internet address and a physical location.

10 This might be defined as those processes which tend to create and consolidate a unified world economy, a single ecological system, and a complex network of communications that covers the whole globe, even if it does not penetrate every part of it; William Twining, *Globalization and Legal Theory* (London, 1998), pp. 4–10.

11 And it is also an extremely broad subject of study; Doron M. Kalir, 'Taking Globalization Seriously: Towards General Jurisprudence', *Columbia Journal of Transnational Law*, 39 (2001): 785–821.

12 Particularly in international economic law.

13 All law is prima facie territorial; *American Banana Co v United Fruit Co*, 213 US 347, 357 (1909).

14 The term was coined by novelist William Gibson in 1984 to describe the boundless electronic system of interlinked networks of computers and bulletin boards that provided access to information and interactive communication; *Neuromancer* (New York, 1984). It is also referred to as the Internet, or the World Wide Web (www), whose architecture was designed by Sir Timothy Berners-Lee.

Strictly the Internet, and the World Wide Web, are distinct. Perhaps unlike the Internet itself, which simply grew up, the World Wide Web is a deliberately conceived combination of two computer science ideas. One concerned 'hypertext', that is, the set of related documents filed in any computer which can be cross-referenced, like indexes in books. The Berners-Lee breakthrough was to see that this could apply between computers. He linked this 'hypertext' feature within each computer to the idea of communication between computers, and thus the World Wide Web was born as a practical concept; See John Naughton, *A brief history of the future: the origins of the Internet* (London, 2000).

15 See Georgios Zekos, 'Internet or Electronic Technology: A Threat to State Sovereignty', *Journal of Information, Law and Technology*, 3 (1999), available at <http://elj.warwick.ac.uk/jilt/99-3/zekos.html> (as at 28 November 2003).

16 Kalir, 'Taking Globalization Seriously', 802.

17 'Big Brother' could very well be watching, given the increasing use of video surveillance cameras to combat crime in city streets, and the advent of effective face recognition software; From George Orwell, *Nineteen Eighty-Four, a Novel* (London, 1949), the ubiquitous face of the party leader.

18 See also Walter B. Wriston, *The Twilight of Sovereignty: How the information revolution is transforming our world* (New York, 1992).

19 See E. Donald Elliott, 'The Genome and the law: Should increased genetic knowledge change the law?', *Harvard Journal of Law and Public Policy*, 25 (2001): 61–70; Emily Marden, 'Risk and regulation: U.S. regulatory policy on genetically modified food and agriculture', *Boston College Law Review*, 44 (2003): 733–87; Remigius N. Nwabueze, 'Ethnopharmacology, patents and the politics of plants' genetic resources', *Cardozo Journal of International and Comparative Law*, 11 (2003): 585–632; Organization for Economic Co-operation and Development, *Bio technology and the changing role of government* (Paris, 1988).

20 Genetic engineering may permit scientists to alter the genes of embryos and negate predilections for certain illnesses; See Kathy Hudson, 'The Human Genome Project, DNA Science and the Law: the American Legal System's Response to Breakthroughs in Genetic Science', *American University Law Review*, 51 (2002): 431–45; Simon Young, *Designer evolution: a transhumanist manifesto* (Amherst, 2006).

21 See Denise Stevens, 'Embryonic stem cell research: will President Bush's limitation on federal funding put the United States at a disadvantage? A comparison between United States and international law', *Houston Journal of International Law*, 25 (2003): 623–53.

22 *Frankenstein, or The modern Prometheus*, ed. Marilyn Butler (Oxford, 1998, first published 1818).

23 See David B. Fogel, *Evolutionary computation: toward a new philosophy of machine intelligence* (Hoboken, 2006); Ulrich Furbach, 'Principles of Artificial Intelligence', *Artificial Intelligence*, 145 (2003): 245–52; John McCarthy, 'What is Artificial Intelligence?', at <http://www- formal.stanford.edu/jmc/whatisai/whatisai.html> (as at 20 June 2006); *Ambient intelligence: the evolution of technology, communication and cognition towards the future of human-computer interaction* ed. G. Riva (Amsterdam, 2005).

24 See *Nanoscale science and technology* ed. Robert W Kelsall, Ian W Hamley, and Mark Geoghegan (Chichester, 2005); *Biomedical nanotechnology* ed. Neelina H. Malsch (Boca Raton, 2005); Glenn Harlan Reynolds, 'Environmental Regulation of Nanotechnology: Some Preliminary Observations', *Environmental Law Reports*, 31 (2001): 10681–8.

25 See James Hughes, *Citizen Cyborg: why democratic societies must respond to the redesigned human of the future* (Boulder, 2004); Ralph G. Scurlock (ed.), *History and origins of cryogenics* (Oxford, 1992).

26 See Niva Elkin-Koren, Eli M. Salzberger, *Law, economics and cyberspace: the effects of cyberspace on the economic analysis of law* (Cheltenham, 2004); *E-commerce law:*

national and transnational topics and perspectives ed. Henk Snijders and Stephen Weatherill (The Hague, 2003).

27 See Charles F. De Jager, 'The Development of Regulatory Standards for Gene Therapy in the European Union', *Fordham International Law Journal*, 18 (1995): 1303–39, 1305.

28 See Helen Szoke, 'The nanny state or responsible government', *Journal of Law and Medicine*, 227 (2002): S-1.

29 See Shelly P. Battra, Robert E. Lutz, Ved P. Nanda, David A. Wirth, Daniel Magraw and Gunther Handl, 'International transfer of hazardous technology and substances: caveat emptor or state responsibility? The case of Bhopal, India', *Proceedings of the Seventy-Ninth Annual Meeting of the American Society of International Law* (1985): 303–22.

30 See A.E Safarian and Gilles Y. Bertin (eds), *Multinationals, governments, and international technology transfer* (New York, 1987).

31 See Jack L. Goldsmith and Lawrence Lessig, 'Grounding the Virtual Magistrate', at <http://www.lessig.org/content/articles/works/magistrate.html> (as at 28 November 2003).

32 See, for instance, Noel Cox, 'The extraterritorial enforcement of consumer legislation and the challenge of the internet', *Edinburgh Law Review*, 8(1) (2004): 60–83.

33 At least those of the European model.

34 Philip Cooke, 'Globalization of economic organization and the emergence of regional interstate partnerships', in Colin H. Williams (ed.), *The Political Geography of the New World Order* (London, 1993), pp. 46–58, 47.

35 Max Weber, *The Protestant Ethic and the Spirit of Capitalism*, trans. Talcott Parsons (London, 1992).

36 Steven McGready, 'The Digital Reformation: Total Freedom, Risk, and Responsibility', *Harvard Journal of Law and Technology*, 10 (1996): 148. Even those theorists who dispute Harvey's Marxist accounts of the origins of social and economic acceleration generally accept his observation that 'the history of capitalism has been characterised by a speed-up in the pace of life'; David Harvey, *The Condition of Postmodernity* (London, 1989), p. 240.

37 See Ferdinand Lot, *The end of the ancient world and the beginnings of the Middle Ages* (London, 1953).

38 See Norman Jones, *The English Reformation: religion and cultural adaptation* (Oxford, 2002); Ethan H. Shagan, *Popular politics and the English Reformation* (Cambridge, 2003); Elmore Herbison, *The Christian scholar in the age of the Reformation* (New York, 1956); Lewis W. Spitz, *The Reformation: education and history* (Aldershot, 1997); and Joseph Loewenstein, *The author's due: printing and the prehistory of copyright* (Chicago, 2002) respectively.

39 McGready, 'The Digital Reformation', 139.

40 Ibid.

41 See, for instance, the Universal Declaration of Human Rights, as passed and proclaimed by the General Assembly of the United Nations on the tenth day of December 1948 (Wellington, 1951).

42 See Maria Eduarda Goncalves, 'Technological change, Globalization and the Europeanization of rights', *International Review of Law, Computers and Technology*, 16 (2002): 301–16.

43 Such as raised economic and political expectations in poorer and less democratic countries.

44 See Martin Wolf, 'Will the nation-state survive Globalization?', *Foreign Affairs*,80 (2001): 178–90.

45 See Goncalves, 'Technological change, Globalization and the Europeanization of rights'.

46 The Constitution states that the Union is expressly founded on the values of 'respect for human dignity, freedom, democracy, equality, the rule of law, and respect for human rights ...' in a society in which 'pluralism, non-discrimination, tolerance, justice, solidarity and equality between women and men prevail.' (Article 1-2). It fails to mention Christianity, which is the conceptual basis for these principles, though the preamble does say that the signatories to the Constitution draw inspiration from the 'cultural, religious and humanist inheritance of Europe, from which has developed the universal values of the inviolable and unalienable rights of the human person, freedom, democracy, equality and the rule of law'.

47 L. Ali Khan, *The Extinction of Nation-States: A World without Borders* (The Hague, 1996), p. 1.

48 *De jure belli ac pacis*, ed. F.W. Kelsey (New York, 1964, reprint of 1925 edition).

49 Wolf, for instance, argues that the nation-state is not endangered by globalization. His reasons are that the ability of a society to take advantage of the opportunities offered by international economic integration depends on the quality of public goods; the state normally defines identity; and international governance rests on the ability of individual states to provide and guarantee stability; Wolf, 'Will the nation-state survive Globalization?'.

50 Ibid.

51 The term 'new world order' has been much used in the context of the global security system, but it arguably has greater relevance in the economic sphere, where it is more clearly developing. See Laura Yavitz, 'The WTO and the environment: the Shrimp case that created a new world', *Journal of Natural Resources and Environmental Law*, 16 (2001): 203–55, cf Ernest Easterly, III, 'The rule of law and the new world order', *Southern University Law Review*, 22 (1995): 161–83.

52 James W. Cortada, *Making the Information Society: Experience, Consequences and Possibilities* (Paramus, 2001).

53 Ibid.

54 Lawrence Lessig, *The Future of Ideas: The Fate of the Commons in a Connected World* (New York, 2001).

55 See later sections.

56 It is, of course, impossible to predict what further developments are likely to occur, which makes it necessary that the legal system – and the constitution – is sufficiently flexible so as to allow this development, and yet restrict or prohibit developments which are deemed unsuitable.

57 See Ilene K. Grossman, 'The new Industrial Revolution: meeting the challenge', *Public Law Forum*, 4 (1985): 419–26; Rudin, 'State involvement in the "new Industrial Revolution"'.

58 See Maurice Pearton, *The knowledge state: diplomacy, war, and technology since 1830* (London, 1982).

59 See Bruce Parrott, 'Technology and the Soviet polity: the problem of industrial innovation, 1928 to 1973' (1976) Columbia University PhD thesis; Rensselaer W. Lee, 'The politics of technology in Communist China' (1973) Stanford University PhD thesis.

60 A paradigmatic is a technical concept derived from linguistics and semiotics, used in anthropological theories of meaning, to denote the stable, rule-governed aspect of communication (opposite of syntagmatic, that which flows and moves in time). The concept is often used more loosely about basic premises underlying communication (as grammar underlies language). 'Paradigmatic shifts' should thus be understood as fundamental changes in the premises of communication; Thomas Kuhn, *The Structure of Scientific Revolutions* (Chicago, 1962).

61 For example, see House of Representatives Standing Committee for Long Term Strategies, *Government response: Australia as an information society: grasping new paradigms* (Canberra, c.1992); Nick Moore and Jane Steele, *Information-intensive Britain: an analysis of the policy issues* (London, 1991), where the emphasis of both is upon information technology. See also James Botkin, Dan Dimancescu, Ray Stata and John McClellan, *Global stakes: the future of high technology in America* (Cambridge, c.1982); Thomas L. Friedman, *The Lexus and the Olive Tree* (London, 2000), p. 9.

62 Response does not mean single-issue responses, but refers rather to the matching of constitution and society.

63 See Sylvia Ostry and Richard R. Nelson, *Techno-nationalism and techno-globalism: conflict and cooperation* (Washington, 1995).

64 See Catherine Dauvergne (ed.), *Jurisprudence for an interconnected globe* (Aldershot, 2003); Richard Warren Perry and Bill Maurer (eds), *Globalization under construction: governmentality, law, and identity* (Minneapolis, 2003); Jean Stefancic and Richard Delgado, 'Outsider jurisprudence and the electronic revolution: Will technology help or hinder the cause of law reform?', *Ohio State Law Journal*, 52 (1991): 847–58.

65 Though classical communism would claim that it possesses the tools to achieve this.

66 Martin Partington, 'The Reform of Public Law in Britain,' in Patrick McAuslan and John McEldowney (eds), *Law, Legitimacy and the Constitution: Essays marking the Centenary of Dicey's Law of the Constitution* (London, 1985), pp. 191–211, 192.

67 F.M. Brookfield, *The Constitution in 1985: The Search for Legitimacy* (Auckland, 1985), p. 1.

68 M.I. Finley, *Authority and legitimacy in the classical city-state* (København, 1982); Mason Hammond, *City-State and world state in Greek and Roman political theory until Augustus* (Cambridge, 1951). See also Charles Keith, 'The origins of settlement, agriculture and the city-state in Mesopotamia' (1984) University of Edinburgh PhD thesis.

69 Daniel H. Weiss and Lisa Mahoney (eds), *France and the Holy Land: Frankish culture at the end of the crusades* (Baltimore, 2004).

70 Cecil Stewart, *Byzantine legacy* (London, 1947).

71 See Hyginus Eugene Cardinale, *The Holy See and the international order* (Toronto, 1976); Walter Ullmann, *The growth of papal government in the Middle Ages: a study in the ideological relation of clerical to lay power* (2nd edn, London, 1965).

72 Bernard Susser (ed.), *Approaches to the Study of Politics* (New York, 1992), p. 4.

73 For the criticism of the traditional study of political science, see Roy Macridis, 'Major Characteristics of the Traditional Approach', in Bernard Susser (ed.), *Approaches to the Study of Politics* (New York, 1992), pp. 16–21.

74 Bernard Susser (ed.), *Approaches to the Study of Politics* (New York, 1992) p. 180. As Bogdanor found, it is necessary to range across law, politics and history to understand a historic constitution; Vernon Bogdanor, *The Monarchy and the Constitution* (Oxford, 1995).

75 For definitions of the different perspectives of the State see Shaun Goldfinch, 'The State', in Raymond Miller (ed.), *New Zealand Government and Politics* (Melbourne, 2003), pp. 511–20, 512.

76 See, for example, Jane Kelsey, *Rolling Back the State*: *Privatisation of Power in Aotearoa/New Zealand* (Wellington, 1993).

77 Forms, or ideas, see *The Republic*, eds G.R.F. Ferrari and trans. Tom Griffith (Cambridge, 2000), pp. 476d–80a; R.M. Dancy, *Plato's introduction of forms* (Cambridge, 2004).

78 John Morison, 'Modernising Government and the E-Government Revolution: Technologies of Government and Technologies of Democracy', in Nicholas Bamford and Peter Leyland (eds), *Public Law in a Multilayered Constitution* (Oxford, 2003), pp. 157–88, 157–8.

79 In particular, see Michel Foucault, 'Governmentality', in J.D. Faubion (ed.), *Michel Foucault, Power: The Essential Works* (3 vols, London, 2000), vol. 3; L. Martin, H. Gutman and P. Hutton, (eds), *Technologies of the Self: A Seminar with Michel Foucault* (London, 1998); and P. Rabinow (ed.), *Michel Foucault: Ethics* (London, 1997).

80 See Graham Burchell, Colin Gordon and Peter Miller (eds), *The Foucault Effect: Studies in Governmentality* (1991); A. Barry, T. Osbourne and Nicolas Rose (eds), *Foucault and Political Reason: Liberalism, Neo-Liberalism and Rationalities of Government* (London, 1996); Nicolas Rose, *Powers of Freedom: Reframing Political Thought* (Cambridge, 1999); M. Dean, *Governmentality: Power and Rule in Modern Society* (London, 1999); A. Hunt and G. Wickham, *Foucault and Law: Towards a Sociology of Law and Governance* (London, 1994).

81 Morison, 'Modernising Government and the E-Government Revolution', 158.

82 *The Foucault Effects: Studies in Governmentality*, eds Graham Burchell, Colin Gordon and Peter Miller (London, 1991).

83 Michel Foucault, *Power/Knowledge: Selected Interviews and Other Writings 1972–1977*, ed. Colin Gordon (New York, 1980), p. 121.

84 An authoritative way of describing. Discourses are propagated by specific institutions and divide up the world in specific ways.

85 Michel Foucault, *Dispositive der Macht* (Berlin, 1978); Michel Foucault, 'Politics and the Study of Discourse', in *The Foucault Effects: Studies in Governmentality*, eds Graham Burchell, Colin Gordon and Peter Miller (London, 1991).

86 The 'Governmentality' was introduced in Michel Foucault, *Resume des cours* (Paris, 1989), and illustrated in other articles 'Governmentality', *Ideology and Consciousness*, 6 (Summer 1986): 5–21; 'Omnes et Singulatim: Toward a Criticism of "Political Reason"' in *The Tanner Lectures of Human Values. II* (Salt Lake City, 1981), pp. 223–54; and 'Space, Knowledge and Power', in Paul Rabinow (ed.), *The Foucault Reader* (New York, 1984) pp. 239–56.

87 See particularly, Nicolas Rose, 'Government and Control', *British Journal of Criminology*, 40 (2000): 321–39, 323.

88 See P. Beaumont, C. Lyons and Neil Walker (eds), *Convergence and Divergence in European Public Law* (Oxford, 2002).

89 Sir Peter North and J.J. Fawcett, *Cheshire and North's private international law* (13th edn, London, 1999).

90 *Lotus Case (France v Turkey)* 1927 PCIJ ser A No 10 (Judgment of 7 Sept); *Asylum Case (Colombia v Peru)* 1950 ICJ 266 at 276 (Judgment of 20 Nov); *Delimitation of the Maritime Boundary in the Gulf of Maine Area (Canada v United States)* 1950 ICJ 266 at 299–300 (Judgment of 12 Oct); *Fisheries Case (UK v Norway)* 1951 ICJ 116 (Judgment of 18 Dec); *Military and Paramilitary Activities in and against Nicaragua (Nicaragua v United States)*, 1969 ICJ 3 at 97–98 (Judgment of 27 June). See also *North Sea Continental Shelf Cases (Federal Republic of Germany v Denmark; Federal Republic of Germany v The Netherlands)* 1969 ICJ 3 at 43–45 (Judgment of 20 Feb) in which the International Court of Justice emphasized the importance of *opinio juris* even in the face of inconsistent state practice in *Nicaragua v United States*. *Opinio juris* may be determined from resolutions of international organizations, notably the General Assembly.

91 Gerhard von Glahn, *Law Among Nations: An Introduction to Public International Law* (7th edn, Boston, 1996).

92 See Charles Howard-Ellis, *The origin structure and working of the League of Nations* (Union, 2003); Geoffrey Best, *Nuremberg and after: the continuing history of war crimes and crimes against humanity* (Reading, 1984).

93 What may be perceived initially as a retrograde step may, of course, ultimately prove beneficial for the future development of public international law, by proving an example or lesson for others to learn from.

94 The UN has 191 members; and the United States, for example, recognizes 192 countries – including the Vatican City State, or Holy See, which is not a member of the UN; 'Basics facts about the UN', DPI, 2000, Sales No. E.00.I.21; Fact Sheet, Office of The Geographer and Global Issues, Bureau of Intelligence and Research, United States Department of State, Washington, DC, 7 February 2003. There are a number of other territories which meet most if not all of the requirements for recognition as a sovereign state, such as Taiwan. There are also dozens of dependencies, territories and colonies, many of which are self-governing, and some of which have a significant international profile; see Harvey W. Armstrong and Robert Read, 'Comparing the economic performance of dependent territories and sovereign microstates', *Economic Development and Cultural Change*, 48(2) (2000): 285.

95 Principally through the absence of a single law-making body, the large number of participants involved, the bi-lateral and multi-lateral negotiations, and the gradual evolution of customary law through state practice.

96 Ali Khan, *The Extinction of Nation-States*, p. 1.

97 Though often dated from 1648, the modern state system is very much older. See Benno Teschke, *The myth of 1648: class, geopolitics, and the making of modern international relations* (London, 2003).

98 An international system of sovereign states such as we would recognize today did not exist in mediæval times, which were characterised by a system based on strongly hierarchical and parallel religious or secular concepts of subordination and

dependence; see, for example, Christopher Schreuer, 'The Waning of the Sovereign State: Towards a New Paradigm for International Law', *European Journal of International Law*, 4 (1993): 447–71. Non-European states were not so influential in the development of the international system.

99 As Schreuer has said, '[a] look at history .... tells us that conceptions of world order have by no means always been shaped by the model of sovereign co-equal actors with a territorial basis'; Ibid.

100 One might even say of the state, as did the English poet John Donne of the individual, that 'No man is an island, entire of itself'; 'Meditation XVII', from *Devotions Upon Emergent Occasions* ed Anthony Raspa (Montreal, 1975, first published 1624).

101 Here again 'technology' is defined broadly, as those processes and things people create for the purpose of using them to alter their lifestyle or their surroundings.

102 See, for example, Nasheri Hedieh, 'The Intersection of technology crimes and cyberspace in Europe: The Case of Hungary', *Information and Communications Technology Law*, 12 (2003): 25–48.

103 See Vito; Organization for Economic Co-operation and Development, *Bio technology and the changing role of government* (Paris, 1988); Elliott, 'The Genome and the law'.

104 The architecture of the Internet or World Wide Web was developed by British physicist and computer scientist Sir Timothy Berners-Lee as a project within the European Centre for Nuclear Energy Research (CERN, now the European Laboratory for Particle Physics) in Geneva. Berners-Lee first began working with hypertext in the early 1980s. His implementation of the Web became operational at CERN in 1989, and it quickly spread to universities in the rest of the world through the high-energy physics community of scholars. It is now ubiquitous; World Wide Web Consortium, <http://www.w3.org/People/Berners-Lee/> at 25 January 2004.

105 See Emanuele Giovannetti, Mitsuhiro Kagami and Masatsugu Tsuji (eds), *The Internet revolution: a global perspective* (Cambridge, 2003); Tunstall; Kahin and Nesson.

106 From Darwin's theory of evolution through natural selection – the survival of the fittest; Charles Darwin, *On the origin of species by means of natural selection*, ed. Joseph Carroll (Peterborough, 2003, first published 1859).

107 See David R. Johnson and David G. Post, 'Law and Borders: The Rise of Law in Cyberspace', *Stanford Law Review*, 48 (1996): 1367–402.

108 See Jonathan B. Wolf, 'War games meets the Internet: Chasing 21st century cybercriminals with old laws and little money', *American Journal of Criminal Law*, 28 (2000): 95–117.

109 Remembering that globalization, though perhaps accelerated, is not an unprecedented development; Giovanni Arrighi, 'Globalization, State Sovereignty, and the "Endless Accumulation of Capital"', Paper presented at the Conference on 'States and Sovereignty in the World Economy', University of California, Irvine, 21–23 February 1997.

110 Lessig, *The Future of Ideas*.

111 McGready claims that the advent of the personal computer (PC) and the Internet is causing a reformation rather than a revolution. A revolution changes political systems and governments; the Reformation changed almost every aspect of western European society, including religion, government, scholarship, education, and business. He

argues that the changes being wrought by the knowledge revolution will be as far-reaching as those of the Reformation; McGready, 'The Digital Reformation', 139; See Jones; Shagan.

112 At least those of the European model, non-European models have largely not survived at the level of the sovereign state, though there are some exceptions, particularly in the Middle East, and some hybrid states, such as Samoa.

113 Philip Cooke, 'Globalization of economic organization and the emergence of regional interstate partnerships', in Colin H. Williams (ed.), *The Political Geography of the New World Order* (London, 1993), pp. 46–58, 47.

114 See McGready, 'The Digital Reformation'.

115 For example, Max Weber, *The Protestant Ethic and the Spirit of Capitalism*, links the Protestant Revolution (the Reformation) and the Industrial Revolution, in particular, Calvinism and the rise of entrepreneurial capitalism. Ibid., 138.

116 The collapse of the Soviet block, and the dismemberment of the eastern European Communist empire, have left the United States as the sole superpower. Though it has been predicted that China will one day reach a similar strategic level to that enjoyed alone today by the United States, there are a number of countries whose military, economic or political influence and capabilities qualify them for the lesser, though nonetheless exalted style, of great power. This term, which had been somewhat neglected, has enjoyed a resurgence, though the term major power still seems more prevalent; See David Shambaugh (ed.), *Greater China: the next superpower?* (Oxford, 1995).

117 See Noel Cox, 'Developments in the Laws of War: NATO attacks on Yugoslavia and the use of force to achieve humanitarian objectives', *New Zealand Armed Forces Law Review* (2002): 13–24.

118 See Noel Cox, 'The Consequences for the World Legal Order of the War on Iraq', *New Zealand Armed Forces Law Review* (2003): 11–17.

119 For a view of the inherent weakness in the international security system, see Joseph P. Lorenz, *Peace, power, and the United Nations: a security system for the twenty-first century* (Boulder, 1999).

120 For example, for an attempt to justify the 2003 war against Iraq, see 'War and law: Attorney General statement', *The Times* (London), 17 March 2003.

121 Strictly, the laws of war might be said to cover a narrower field than the laws of armed conflict.

122 See Michael Walzer, *Just and Unjust Wars* (3rd edn, Plymouth, 2000).

123 Whether there is a duty to levy offensive war might be questioned, though sometimes attack is the best form of defence.

124 Both grounds were used, at times, along with self-defence, to justify the United States-led invasion of Iraq in 2003; see Noel Cox, 'The Consequences for the World Legal Order of the War on Iraq'.

125 See Hayward R. Alker, Thomas J. Biersteker and Takashi Inoguchi, 'From Imperial Power Balancing to People's Wars: Searching for Order in the Twentieth Century', in James Der Derian and Michael J. Shapiro (eds), *International/Intertextual Relations: Postmodern Readings of World Politics* (Lexington, 1989), pp. 135–62.

126 Schreuer, 'The Waning of the Sovereign State'.

127 For the origins of state sovereignty, the peace of 1648 was influential, see Leo Gross, 'The Peace of Westphalia, 1648–1948', *American Journal of International Law*, 42 (1948): 20–41. See also Teschke.

128 1648 is also usually given as the decisive date for the transition from the vertical imperial to the horizontal inter-state model; see Richard Falk, 'The Interplay of Westphalia and Charter Conceptions of International Legal Order', in Cyril E. Black and Richard A. Falk (eds), *The Future of the International Legal Order* (2 vols, Princeton, 1969), vol. 1, pp. 32, 43.

129 Not all states follow the same model, either. It was observed (before the collapse of organised Communism) that at least five world orders – Soviet Socialism, Capitalist Power Balancing, Authoritarian Corporatism, Maoist agrarian Communalism and Islamic Transnationalism – could be found within all world regions; Hayward R. Alker, 'Dialectical Foundations of Global Disparities', *International Studies Quarterly*, 25 (1981): 69–98, 81–5.

130 See Joost Pauwelyn, *Conflict of norms in public international law: how WTO law relates to other rules of international law* (Cambridge, 2003); Robert W. Cox, *Production, Power, and World Order: Social Forces in the Making of History* (New York, 1987), p. 107.

131 International law has been called 'the sum of the rules or usages which civilized states have agreed shall be binding upon them in their dealings with one another': *West Rand Central Gold Mining Co v The King* [1905] 2 KB 391 quoting Lord Russell of Killowen in his address at Saratoga in 1876. See also Sir Michael Howard, George J. Andreopoulos and Mark R. Shulman (eds), *The Laws of War: Constraints on Warfare in the Western World* (New Haven, 1994); John Gillingham and J.C. Holt (eds), *War and Government in the Middle Ages* (Cambridge, 1984).

132 Nicolas Rose, *Powers of Freedom*, pp. 17–18.

133 Where the protecting power increases the extent of its responsibility for internal administration, there is a natural, though not an inevitable tendency for protection to be transferred into actual annexation, as was the case with Kenya in 1920. The Protectorate becomes a Crown Colony, and the prerogative, by virtue of which the annexation is made, henceforth takes the place of the Foreign Jurisdiction Act 1890 (53 & 54 Vict c 37) (United Kingdom) as the authority under which the Crown performs the work of government, unless some statutory arrangement otherwise is made.

134 That is not to argue that these peoples were inherently inferior – though such views have been expressed from time to time – but rather that they occupied a different place on what might be called the scale of development.

135 J.D.M. Derrett, 'The Administration of Hindu Law by the British', *Comparative Studies in Society and History*, 4 (1961): 10–52.

136 Arthur J. Knoll and Lewis H. Gann (eds), *Germans in the Tropics: Essays in German Colonial History* (New York, 1987); W.O. Henderson, *Studies in German Colonial History* (Chicago, 1962).

137 H.E. Egerton, *Short History of British Colonial Policy* (London, 1897), p. 17.

138 A.B. Keith, *Constitutional History of the First British Empire* (Oxford, 1930), p. 13.

139 Ibid., p. 37.

140 The latter from 1632. The Lord Proprietor of Maryland lost his political powers in 1691, but regained them in 1715. This was supplanted only in 1776, with the outbreak of the American Revolution. The flag of the State of Maryland comprises a banner of

the arms of the Lords Baltimore, adopted in its present form in 1904. The Lords Baltimore, though barons in England, were earls or counts palatine in Maryland. Clayton Hall, *The Lords Baltimore and the Maryland Palatinate* (Baltimore, 1902).

141 In 1629 the land south of Virginia, which was called Carolina, was granted to Sir Robert Heath. Heath failed to make use of the land.

142 The territory now occupied by the State of Maine was in 1639 granted to Sir Ferdinando Gorges as proprietor. His son did little to develop the region, and in 1658 Massachusetts, itself a proprietary colony to 1684, asserted its jurisdiction over Maine. In 1677 Gorges's grandson sold his rights to the colony and in 1691 it became part of Massachusetts.

143 In 1663 King Charles II granted the Carolina territory to eight proprietors. They divided the territory into North and South Carolina, and established a constitution which included four houses of parliament and three orders of nobility. It was never put fully in operation and was finally abandoned in 1693. The Carolinas did not prove a financial success to most of the proprietors, and in 1728 seven of them sold their grants to the Crown and the period of proprietor government came to an end. In 1744 the eighth proprietor exchanged his grant for a smaller strip of land in North Carolina. This survived until the American Revolution.

144 New York was held by James Duke of York from 1664 till it merged with the Crown in 1685 when he became King James II.

145 Pennsylvania was a proprietary colony from 1681 to 1776.

146 By grants under the Plymouth Company's charter, then under a separate charter 1629; W.A. MacDonald, *Documentary Source Book of American History* (New York, 1908), pp. 23–6.

147 Chartered 1662, lost charter under James II, recovered it under William III.

148 Chartered 1663, lost charter under James II, recovered it under William III. The charter, however, merely confirmed the status quo.

149 The UN has 191 members; and the United States, for example, recognizes 192 countries – including the Vatican City State, or Holy See, which is not a member of the UN; 'Basics facts about the UN', DPI, 2000, Sales No. E.00.I.21; Fact Sheet, Office of The Geographer and Global Issues, Bureau of Intelligence and Research, United States Department of State, Washington, DC, 7 February 2003.

150 Though even in the heyday of state sovereignty, the late nineteenth century, the extent to which any state was truly independent depended much on non-legal factors, such as relative economic strength.

151 Georg Schwarzenberger and E.D. Brown, *A Manual of International Law* (6th edn, Milton, 1976), p. 42.

152 Hedley Bull, *The Anarchical Society: A Study of Order in World Politics* (London, 1977), p. 127; Sir Hersch Lauterpacht, 'The Subjects of the Law of Nations', *Law Quarterly Review*, 63 (1947): 438–60; Dame Rosalyn. Higgins, *The Development of International Law Through the Political Organs of the UN* (London, 1963), p. 1; Philip Jessup, *A Modern Law of Nations* (New York 1968); Jean Gabriel Castel, *International Law: Chiefly as Interpreted and Applied in Canada* (3rd edn, Toronto, 1976), p. 1.

153 Michel Foucault, 'Governmentality', in J.D. Faubion (ed.), *Michel Foucault, Power: The Essential Works* (3 vols, London, 2000), vol. 3, pp. 220–1.

154 Morison, 'Modernising Government and the E-Government Revolution', 168–9.

155 See Cyberspace Policy Research Group, <http://www.cyprg.arizona.edu>, which 'studies diffusion and use of World Wide Web in governments worldwide, particularly in terms of organizational openness and internal effectiveness'.

156 See R. Traunmüller and K. Lenk (eds), *Electronic Government: First International Conference, EGOV 2002, Aix-en-Provence, France, September 2002 Proceedings* (Berlin, 2002); Rachel Silcock, 'What is e-government?', *Parliamentary Affairs* (2001): 88–101; Y Akdeniz, C. Walker and D. Wall, *The Internet, Law and Society* (Harlow, 2000).

157 For each of which there is an ample literature.

158 For a discussion of the nexus between social change and the law, see Alan Watson, *Society and Legal Change* (2nd edn, Philadelphia, 2001). It has also been observed that recent finance scholarship finds that countries with legal systems based on the common law have more developed financial markets than civil-law countries; See Robert G. King and Ross Levine, 'Finance and Growth: Schumpeter Might Be Right', *Quarterly Journal of Economics*, 108 (1993): 717–37. This may be due to the common law's association with limited government; Paul G. Mahoney, 'The Common Law and Economic Growth: Hayek might be right', *Journal of Legal Studies*, 30 (2001): 503–25.

159 There is a considerable body of work on the nexus between constitutions and social and economic change; from the United States' perspective, for example, see John R. Vile, *The Constitutional Amending Process in American Political Thought* (New York, 1992), pp. 137–56; Daniel Lazare, *The Frozen Republic: How the Constitution is Paralysing Democracy* (New York, 1996); David E. Kyvig, *Explicit and Authentic Acts: Amending the United States Constitution* (Lawrence, 1996), pp. 216–314; Richard Kay, 'Constitutional Chrononomy', *Ratio Juris*, 13 (2000): 31–48, 33.

Chapter 5

The Nature of Constitutions and their Relationship with Technology

5.1 Introduction

The scope of this Chapter is the effect of changes in technology upon governments, more particularly, upon constitutions. This proceeds from the previous Chapter, which considered the broader question of the relationship between law (or legal systems) and technology, to the more specific exercise of examining and evaluating the effects of changes in technological paradigms upon constitutions, and the ways in which constitutions have themselves responded to these changing paradigms. By its inherent nature this is partly an historical analysis. The reason for that is that law, as a human artefact, is inseparable from history.[1] Constitutional laws – those which are concerned with the structure and powers of states – are also the product of history,[2] and are especially sensitive to the nuances of cultural, economic and other influences. They are less discrete than most other legal regimes. Indeed, they may be more strictly linked to history than some other laws, because of their need for legitimacy, which is derived in part from continuity and from acquiescence by the populations and communities for which they exist and for and by whom they are applied.[3] But these laws are also influenced by technology,[4] and by economic,[5] as well as by societal change.

We will start by looking at the notion of legitimacy and the state. As we discussed in Chapter 1, government is dependent upon legitimacy in one form or another. Without this it cannot function effectively or efficiently. Technology does not necessarily offer legitimacy, nor does it necessarily change the legitimacy of the state. But it may be a tool in acquiring, preserving, extending or losing that legitimacy.

5.2 Legitimacy and the State

With the dominance of democratic concepts of government[6] it might be thought that if the people believe that a governmental institution is appropriate then it is also legitimate.[7] But this scheme leaves out substantive questions about the justice (or even the role) of the state and the protection it offers the individuals who belong to it.[8] It is generally more usual for commentators to maintain that a state's legitimacy depends upon its upholding certain human rights.[9] This may be seen in the use of such terms as freedom, democracy, rule of law, and tolerance, even in the constitutions of totalitarian dictatorships.[10] Truly democratic states scarcely need to assert such principles (since they comprise the foundations of the constitution, formally or practically), yet they are rarely absent from modern constitutions.[11] But the state is as much an economic as it is a social or legal construct,[12] and it is important for its legitimacy and viability that the constitution remains broadly consistent with economic, and technological, realities.

Economic and technological changes eventually alter constitutions, because they change society, which constitutions reflect to a greater or lesser degree.[13] These changes need not necessarily be in the formal written Constitution, where these exist. It may be – and is indeed more likely to be – in the understanding, operation, or perception of the constitution. It is likely to be in the nature of the fundamental relationship between individuals and the state, between communities or society as a whole and the state, and between state and state. Yet because of their nature they may be only dimly perceived, and then possibly only with the incontestable advantage of hindsight.

Constitutional reform itself may be revolutionary yet preserve apparent formal continuity.[14] Changes need not be revolutionary in a legal sense. Indeed, the formalist approach of Kelsen maintains that if the constitution is changed according to its own provisions then the state and its legal order remain the same.[15] In this view it does not matter how fundamental the changes in the substance of the legal norms may be. If they are performed in conformity with the provisions of the (formal) constitution, continuity of the legal system will not be interrupted.[16] Thus, even though the nature of the relationship between individual and state – or between state and state – may have been profoundly altered, there is no revolutionary change to the constitution.[17] As an illustration, when the former republics of the Soviet Union declared their independence in 1991–92,[18] the provisions and nature of the former Constitution of the Soviet Union (under which the constituent republics apparently enjoyed considerable autonomy) meant that the revolutionary nature of the dismemberment of the union was more real than apparent. Thus the formal structures of the post-Soviet states often closely resembled – at least during the transitional phase – their Soviet forms, yet their actual operation was quite distinct.

Apparent continuity does not mean that there is real continuity. Ross emphasizes the necessary discontinuity of a new constitutional order which has replaced an earlier one.[19] According to Ross the legitimacy of a constitutional order goes beyond the legal system. If the political ideology changes at a time of constitutional change, so the legal continuity is disrupted.[20] In other words, if technology – or any other influence – has resulted in a profound social, political, or economic change, any resulting constitutional change may well be revolutionary in nature.[21] In this model the post-Soviet states were truly revolutionary in nature, since they rejected the social, economic and political model of communism – although their formal constitutional structures survived for a time. But it must be recalled that a constitution is far more than a statement of a formal power structure

– it includes the ways in which that power structure actually operates. Bearing this in mind it may be seen that there are profound constitutional changes occurring even when the formal constitution remains essentially unchanged. This may of course also be observed even in those countries which have not undergone a revolutionary change of political or economic grundnorm. The United States of America is far more centralised politically than it was when it was established a little over two hundred years ago, but the formal constitutional division of responsibilities between the states and the federal government remain largely unaltered.

The importance of this distinction between legitimacy of a continuous legal order (however great the changes in the underlying norms may be), and the discontinuity of a new order, is profound. For, although superficially the constitutional order remains unchanged, yet in one model legitimacy is preserved, in the other it is undermined. It might well be wondered how this could be so, unless the notion of legitimacy is unrelated to any practical social application. Surely, it could be argued, the people of a given country know whether their governing regime is legitimate or not? It shouldn't be a matter for political theorists to advise them, but should rather be an instinctive reaction to the regime which controls the state, the (non-political) apparatus of the state, and the role of the state.

This would again appear to be an illustration of the political discourse of legitimacy being controlled by the academic writers and having comparatively little impact upon the general population. The model of legitimacy envisaged by some of these writers is not always strongly grounded upon sociological and political reality. This may be seen in the development of popular uprisings, mass protests and similar manifestations of popular discontent, however the formal legitimacy of the state may be maintained. Ross would appear to more accurately reflect the political reality, which might be put simply thus: a government, however great its military or bureaucratic stranglehold on a country, cannot survive long if it doesn't have the support or at least the acquiescence of a sizable proportion of the population – though it may lengthen this hold through judicious manipulation of education and communications.

If we wish to understand the relationship between constitution and technology, it is also important to consider the role and purpose of the state – though this has been a fundamental problem of all theories of the state since Aristotle,[22] and doubtless will remain so. Legitimacy of government has its social, political and economic aspects. As Hobbes maintained, government was a product of consensual alliance, and whilst it was generally for the common good, its primary purpose was to further the interests of the individual.[23] These interests are economic, in that the state should be able to ensure that the majority of its people have sufficient resources to live reasonably comfortably. They are also political, in that the population has certain expectations of involvement in decision-making, or at least some degree of consultation over matters which concern them. Social aspects include the element of belonging, a feeling of community with others of the nation-state.

Grady and McGuire have considered the nature of constitutions from an economic perspective. They have concluded that constitutions are not the product of consensual choice, but rather the result of weaker humans banding together to resist forceful appropriations from more dominant humans.[24] This conception may fit one economic model, but it does not necessarily assist us greatly when we consider the constitutional implications of the knowledge revolution. Nor may it be particularly helpful when we consider that government in any modern state – or even any pre-modern state – is more than simply a tribal alliance such as they appear to conceive it to be. That is not to say that this model does not adequately describe the origins of tribal and pre-city government.

The revolutionary potential of the knowledge revolution involves the empowerment of smaller and smaller groups, until one reaches the nadir, the wholly empowered individual. It is possibly true that no true Lockean constitution (where state and society are in a true compact[25]) exists today.[26] However consent – through acquiescence and participation – is found in most governmental systems.[27] It may just be that the level at which consent occurs – and the means of obtaining consent – are in the process of change.

Let us begin with a review of four theories of the origin of the state, courtesy of Grady and McGuire.[28] These are the Hobbes–Buchanan contractarian theory, Karl Wittfogel's hydraulic despotism theory, Robert Carneiro's circumscription theory, and Mancur Olson's stationary bandit theory.[29] We will examine each of these in turn.

Thomas Hobbes famously began his analysis of the state with a consideration of the state of nature. He assumed that before formal governments existed people were reasonably equal in endowments.[30] From this rough equality of mental and physical assets, each had an equal hope of acquiring the same ends, which were scarce. Each depended on their own efforts for his or her livelihood, and those of their family.[31] As a consequence, individuals fell into competition with each other, which resulted in the 'war of every man against every man.'[32] In such a state of being opportunities for production, investment, learning, and exchange were limited, because each individual possessed 'continual fear and danger of violent death.'[33] Life was, or could very easily be, 'nasty, brutish and short.'[34] This created an incentive to seek improvement.

In order to relieve themselves of eternal conflict individuals have an incentive to organize themselves into a commonwealth, which is a hierarchy that 'tie[s] them by fear of punishment to the performance of their covenants and observation of th[e] laws of nature ...'[35] They institute this commonwealth by giving a monarch or an assembly the right to represent them.[36] Government, then, was a product of consensual alliance, and whilst it was generally for the common good, its primary purpose was to further the interests of the individual.[37]

This model, which may be described as a contract theory of government, was especially popular during the seventeenth century, at a time when the tensions of a most-mediæval monarchy and early-modern society come to the fore in England. At a time of dynamic tension it is common to seek for answers in the writings of theorists – rarer perhaps to find the answers there. The importance of the contract theory lay not in its perspicuous author's foresight but rather in its universality and applicability at once to a traditional early modern society and a modern post-industrial state. Whereas in earlier societies the relative immobility of individuals led to a greater sense of community, which would allow the development of commonwealths, modern technological substitutes for the community provide equivalent mechanisms.

The new social and political structures potentially facilitated by advances in information technology offer the possibility of something very much like a constitutional contract,[38] though not necessarily with existing states or forms of states.[39] All existing states may be much more complex constitutional structures than the Hobbesian constitution would appear to suggest, however.

In Grady and McGuire's view,[40] Hobbes and Buchanan[41] have not fully addressed the problem of sovereign appropriation. At least Hobbes assumed that the sovereign would behave benevolently. Nevertheless, with a monopoly of force over a particular geographic area, a sovereign possesses a private incentive to appropriate from his or her subjects.[42] This however is unlikely to happen because the ruler will wish to retain power. When over-reaching occurs, revolution will occasionally restore the balance[43] – though not necessarily rapidly.

The networked economy,[44] by creating a greater mobility of people and assets, reduces the ability of sovereigns to appropriate because their subjects can more easily exit over-reaching regimes.[45] The reduction in transaction costs created by the Internet and by information technology more generally creates the possibility of competing Hobbesian commonwealths, each constituted by customers and dependent upon their continuing loyalty. This view was widely held in the halcyon days of Internet growth in the 1990s,[46] but has since fallen out of favour.[47] But, whilst the Hobbesian state was a social construct, it would appear that its nature – even its existence – was determined by the technological limitations of its makers.

If this is so (and we will shortly proceed to consider the effect of technology on constitutions), fundamental changes in technology may – and perhaps should – result in changes to the constitution itself. If the individual's need for protection, assistance, or supervision, is reduced (or disappears), so the role of the state changes.[48] A specific example of this is the tendency of the Internet, and modern electronic telecommunications in general, to reduce the degree of reliance upon formal contact with governmental agencies – such as educational institutions – for information and knowledge. This both tends to break down the dependence upon and also allow greater interaction with the state – at the user's choice. This may result in a centralization of government agencies, and a gradual decline in the importance of regional, provincial, state and municipal agencies.

The second theory of the state to be considered is that of Karl Wittfogel. In his 1957 book *Oriental Despotism*,[49] Wittfogel argued that despotic governments often arose around rivers, as in ancient Egypt, China, and Mesopotamia. He theorised that the state arose when villages banded together to develop common irrigation projects, which vastly improved the productivity of agriculture.[50] Nevertheless, once the state came into being as a means of developing irrigation, it soon turned its bureaucracy to oppressive purposes.[51] In fact, according to Wittfogel, what he termed an hydraulic state will cease appropriating only when the marginal cost of further administrative control begins to exceed the marginal revenue to those benefiting from state action.[52] This is fundamentally a technology-driven model of the state.[53] While this model might be of particular relevance to more primitive and less sophisticated states than are found today, it nevertheless illustrates the dependence of states on their physical environment.

In an influential article the anthropologist Robert Carneiro theorised that states began in areas of environmental or social circumscription.[54] Carneiro looked at the places where states first arose, areas such as the Nile, Tigris–Euphrates, and Indus valleys in the Old World and the Valley of Mexico and the mountain and coastal valleys of Peru in the New World. He found that all were areas of 'circumscribed agricultural land.'[55] In his words, '[e]ach of them is set off by mountains, seas, or deserts, and these environmental features sharply delimit the area that simple farming peoples could occupy and cultivate.'[56] He contrasted these 'environmentally circumscribed' areas to areas in which states did not arise as early, for instance, the Amazon basin and the eastern woodlands of North America.[57] From this we might conclude that states arose when competition for scarce responses – with no room for expansion – reached a critical level. The necessity of economic survival led to the development of settled states.[58] This may be less obviously a technology-driven state. But even here it was the degree of technological development which determined when this critical level which led to state development would occur.[59] Settled agriculture – as distinct from the hunter-gatherer culture – was a more technologically advanced economic structure,[60] which led to a more advanced constitution.

In the fourth and last of the models of the state considered by Grady and McGuire,[61] Mancur Olson has argued that the state can be likened to a stationary bandit who robs the people within his or her jurisdiction (through taxes and the like) and protects them from roving bandits[62] – competitors. Olson argues that ruled people prefer a stationary bandit to roving bandits because the stationary bandit has an incentive to invest in public goods that increase the people's wealth and therefore the tax revenues that can be extracted from them.[63] This theory is very similar to a more general theory developed independently by Grady and McGuire to explain primate, including human, political structures.[64] In some respects it is an economic model of society, but it is, like Hobbes' model, based on self-interest rather more than physical environment.

The basic idea common to both Grady and McGuire's theory and that of Olson is that the sovereign[65] is effectively the residual claimant of the group he or she (or more usually, it, since the sovereign is likely to be corporate) rules.[66] When the group creates a surplus, the sovereign is in a position to appropriate that surplus.

Olson stressed that the sovereign's position of residual claimant could induce the sovereign to create public goods, such as irrigation projects (to use Wittfogel's example); then, the sovereign could appropriate the surplus from these investments.[67] The sovereign would have a self-interested incentive to keep peace within the group and even to enforce efficient private law because these kinds of legal rules would increase the surplus from group activities and therefore create a greater possibility for sovereign appropriations.[68] The surplus, as in ancient Egypt, was then at the disposal of the state, which might use it to undertake further public works or to feed the population in times of need.[69] The 'surplus' model may be correct – but it was very often the existence of a technological system which enabled this surplus to be achieved in the first place.[70]

Each of these models for the origins of states is, in effect, an attempt to explain not merely why states come into existence, but also why they survive – at least for a time. It is thus an explanation of a principal aspect of the states' legitimacy – that derived from continuity, and (perhaps more importantly), the functional efficiency of the state – what might be called its utility. Without this utility the state ceases to have a reason for existence. Changes in the expectations of its people, through new technologies and greater capabilities – economic, educational and otherwise – place potential pressures upon the legitimacy of the state, as it challenges the underlying reason for the existence of the state.

The state is more than simply a collection of individuals, however powerful; it is a system. This system may be described in accordance with the specific constitution of that state. Whichever model of state is preferred – and it may well be than none are adequate to describe the complex modern state – all are attempts to explain the functional rationale for the existence of the state, and for the particular power structures which they contain. As the physical environment – including human expectations and requirements – which gave rise to the state change so the constitution changes, though this may be less rapid than might be desirable.

5.3 Possible Changes in the Nature of Government and the Global Environment

It is helpful to speculate on the possibility of changes in the nature of government, and of the global environment, as a result of technological – or indeed economic – change. At the level of the individual state government the advent of the most modern and powerful forms of information technology, among both individuals and as tools of the state, has led to what might be called an over-supply of information. More precisely, there is not too much information, but the means of processing and disseminating the information is inadequate.

This prevents the efficient utilization of information at state level and below, though the higher the level arguably the less the efficiency. This is because while a state potentially has access to a vast amount of information its ability to develop policies based on that information is limited. In part this limitation is purely technical. The development of more advanced electronic information processing tools will enable state policy makers to more efficiently utilize the data available. At the level of the individual this is a less serious problem, if only because the individual has less need for an overview such as is needed for policy-making at state level.

Economic pressure on governments at all levels demand a continued emphasis upon efficiency – though this often means choosing the cheapest option (which is not necessarily the most efficient). The mass information media has tended to encourage greater accountability from governments throughout the world, even where democracy is not established. This in term has encouraged the pursuit of efficiency. If efficiency can be achieved through the use of technology, and that technology is available to the governments, then it will be sought. Governments acquired firearms and aeroplanes, radios and ships, because these technological tools rendered the government's control more efficient and more complete.

Efficiency is also achieved by minimizing the number of intermediate steps or stages in a process. This is as applicable to government as it is to any organizational process. The more advanced the system of communication and oversight, the less necessary are subordinates. A country might be divided into fifty states or provinces, originally for purely historical reasons. This division might have been retained for reasons of regional pride, but also because it is more efficient to administer a large country through a decentralised governmental system. But what happens to that system if it is shown that technology offers a more efficient alternative? What if the people can still have a sense of public involvement in the political process through the mass media, and yet instantaneous communications, electronic data processing and record keeping systems, and similar tools enable the central government to have direct oversight of the provinces? This might render the provinces redundant, especially if it were shown that considerable savings would be made by abolishing the regional governments entirely.

There are no examples at present of the provincial, state or regional structure of a country being abolished or significantly reformed due to the advent of modern communications systems, but such reforms are not impossible. The large provinces and states of the Canada and the United States of America are manageable, despite a continuing trend towards complexity in government, because of modern communications systems. Institutional inertia and attachment to historical allegiances, render their absolute abolition unlikely. But the requirements of efficiency (and lately national security), have led to a reduction of the powers and responsibilities of the states of the United States. A similar development in Canada has been partly impeded by the special position of Quebec.

If provincial governments are perhaps more resilient, where does that leave municipal and local authorities? These are more likely to have been subject to repeated reforms over time, and will generally have lesser powers and responsibilities than the states and provinces. Some of their functions might be taken by the states and provinces, but it is unlikely that they will entirely fall victim to technology, whatever the demands for efficiency may be. Local services only be provided by local agencies – and can be dealt with directly by central government. That does not, however, preclude the possibility of provincial and state governments assuming all their functions.

Constitutional change need not be confined to changes in formal constitutional structures. They may include informal changes, or changes in governance. This is particularly apparent with respect to the growth in the use of standards and targets in relation to the provision of government services such as education and health.

But do any of these possible and actual changes actually amount to a change in the nature of government? If we recall from Chapter 1 government may be seen as an institution which carries out the complex process of governing a discrete political entity. Can the nature of government change simply because of technological changes? Evidence from the past suggests that it can, at least to some degree. While the core functions of governments have included defence and foreign policy, the extent to which central governments have concerned themselves with other matters has varied markedly over time, and between country and country. The advent of significant social evils has often necessitated government intervention, however unwilling it may be, but governments have rarely relinquished responsibility once obtained.

But the scope of government's involvement in society, the economy, and people's lives, is also expanded if the tools to do so are available – it does not require altruism or survival to motivate it. The need may be less obvious, than the survival of the state, though it must be discernible. As an example, the passage of the Uniting and Strengthening America by Providing Appropriate Tools Required to Intercept and Obstruct Terrorism (USA Patriot Act) Act of 2001 by the Congress of the United States, in response to a specific incidence of terrorism against the country, has led to a plethora of new technological innovations (primarily surveillance tools, but including data matching and processing systems) which expand the scope of government intervention in daily life. The justification for these measures remains the defence of the country, but the potential of these technologies is disproportionate to what was possible only a few years ago. That does not necessarily mean that it will be utilized for a wider range of purposes than anti-terrorism, but the indications are that they will be (for example in combating drug smuggling, and organized crime). The nature of government may be unchanged, but the degree of interaction that individuals have with it may change. This reflects a change in governance rather than necessarily a change in constitutional structures, though these could follow. For instance, security considerations may lead to the increased use of executive authority at the expense of the legislature.

Technological developments may also have significant effects upon the global environment. However, in the absence of any form of world government the extent to which this affects individual people is likely to remain small. However, just as efficiency can mean that the balance between the nation and the province may alter, so the relationship between nation-state and supra-national entity may alter. Already we see evidence of efficiency being cited as justification for the enactment of the European Union's new constitution. If the Union-level political and administrative bodies are seen by the public to have significant roles to play – through the news media – then the perception may lead to these bodies actually acquiring such powers.

Such evolution – perhaps much slower – may occur at international level. As an example, the December 2004 tsunami which devastated large areas of the coastlines of the Indian Ocean led almost immediately to calls for a regional tsunami-warning system, perhaps to be managed by an agency of the United Nations organization. One of the core roles of government – that of protecting its people – is in danger of being partially usurped by an international organization. Rather than opposing such a move, it was welcomed by the governments concerned, who are well aware than in this matter of technology, efficiency is more important than state sovereignty – at least their short-term responses suggested this.

5.4 The Contextualization of Constitutions and Technology

Technology does not change the essential problems that constitutions seek to address, because these are rooted in the enduring nature of humanity.[71] Not only can technology transform the human environment,[72] but a different environment may substantially modify the constitution. As Burke recognized, the key to sound structures of governance in every age and place is to understand the intersection of humanity's enduring nature with its particular circumstance.[73]

Just as the Reformation, and later the Industrial Revolution, opened up new economic opportunities – and resulted in significant constitutional changes – so the new globally networked economy greatly expands opportunities for exit from the sway of local monopoly, whether sovereign or private.[74] These new 'commonwealths' operate on a radically different economic principle than traditional geographic empires or nation-states. Existing states may be seen as having developed from the Hobbesian model – based as they were on mutual interdependence. This interdependence remains – for no foreseeable technological innovation could make an individual entirely independent.[75] However, dependence is no longer necessarily hierarchical, or community-based.[76] The constitutional structure – and the legal system of which it forms a part – may be unsuited to coping with societal change wrought by this form of changing technology.[77]

All new technologies challenge existing legal concepts.[78] This operates at the micro level, as well as the macro. For instance, copyright law has been seriously affected by the advent of the Internet.[79] Technological changes can also help to produce relatively dramatic changes in economic and social organization in a short span of time.[80]

But constitutions are also affected by changes in technology, for the way in which a state is organized depends upon cultural and historical factors, which include the contemporary technology. For moral as well as economic reasons, sound constitutions aim at promoting exchange and constraining hierarchy.[81] Constitutions are expected to provide stable rules suited to long-term use,[82] and social and economic acceleration makes this more difficult. Constitutions also depend upon technology because the structure of restraints on government most likely to produce justice[83] varies with the technology of the time.[84] A government powerful enough to protect liberty and property may be a government powerful enough to threaten liberty and property.[85] It is a question of balance.

The Lockean constitution was perceived as one which would be unalterable – because it encompassed all that was needed for a sound constitution.[86] This conception of a constitution has been challenged.[87] More importantly, perhaps, social and economic acceleration conflicts with the traditional expectation that constitutional law-makers can be expected to predict future trends with some measure of competence.[88]

Human history shows that at some point significant misalignment between the constitution and the social, economic, and political realities appears. This may cause fundamental departures from existing constitutional arrangements.[89] Constitutions risk becoming out of date, when 'all fixed, fast-frozen relations, with their train of ancient and venerable prejudices and opinions, are swept away, all new-formed ones become antiquated before they can ossify.'[90] Contemporary conditions require constitutions exhibiting enormous flexibility; they now must leave room for a vast and constantly expanding range of novel social and economic experiences, many of which may prove momentous.[91]

5.5 Conclusion

Constitutions are at the mercy of technology as much as is society, and perhaps even more so. They are the formal and informal procedures through which a government is carried on, and as such are the product of various influences, which wax and wane over time. Some are also less important in some countries than in others. But not only is the constitution dependent upon the internal influences of culture, economy, history and so on, it is also the product of the ongoing influence of an international legal, economic and political environment, as well as of the influence of individual states.

One of the most important aspects of this is the need to preserve a role, and a sense of legitimacy. Whatever theoretical model for the origin of the state we may prefer, most – if not all – are premised upon the idea that they exist for a reason (and that reason often being the preservation of the well-being of the individual, the family, or the community). Because the extent to which the state can achieve the objective of advancing this aim may heavily be dependent upon the material resources available to the state, and the relative balance between individual resources and those of the state, so the state is vulnerable to changes in technology which threaten to make the individual, corporate entity, or community more efficient and thus less dependent upon the state.

Notes

1 L. Ali Khan, *The Extinction of Nation-States: A World without Borders* (The Hague, 1996), p. 1.

2 Indeed, a constitutional lawyer must be as much an historian (and political scientist) as he or she is a lawyer, and the reverse holds true also; See Noel Cox, 'The Evolution of the New Zealand Monarchy: The Recognition of an Autochthonous Polity' (2001) University of Auckland PhD thesis.

3 Amongst modern states this is nowhere more apparent than in the United Kingdom, where, until recently, many of its political institutions dated from mediæval times; See 'The Survival of Mediæval Institutions', in A.H. Birch, *The British System of Government* (4th edn, London, 1980).

4 See Tom W. Bell, 'Free speech, strict scrutiny, and self-help: how technology upgrades constitutional jurisprudence', *Minnesota Law Review*, 87 (2003): 743–78; Mark S. Kende, 'Technology's future impact upon state constitutional law: the Montana example', *Montana Law Review*, 64 (2003): 273–94; Deborah Jones Merritt, 'The Constitution in a brave new world: a century of technological change and constitutional law', *Oregon Law Review*, 69 (1990): 1–45.

5 Only systematic empirical research can demonstrate whether social and economic acceleration actually contributes to the amplification of the executive authority long observed by political scientists and legal scholars; See William E. Scheuerman, 'Constitutionalism in an age of speed', *Constitutional Commentary*, 19 (2002): 353–90, 385–6. The reverse may well happen also. The late Saxon legal and fiscal system was comparatively sophisticated, and its efficiency was one of the principal reasons for the strength of the Norman kingdom which was to follow; Noel Cox, 'The Influence of the Common Law and the Decline of the Ecclesiastical Courts of the Church of England', *Rutgers Journal of Law and Religion*, 3 (2001–2002) at <http://www-camlaw.rutgers.edu/publications/law-religion/Cox1.PDF> (as at 28 November 2003).

6 Initially in western liberal democracies, and by extension, particularly through such institutions as the Commonwealth, throughout most of the world; See 'The Harare Commonwealth Declaration, 1991' (Issued by Heads of Government in Harare, Zimbabwe, 20 October 1991) available at <http://www.thecommonwealth.org/gender/htm/commonwealth/about/declares/harare.htm> (as at 6 December 2003).

7 Penelope Brook Cowen, 'Neo Liberalism', in Raymond Miller (ed.), *New Zealand Politics in Transition* (Auckland, 1997), p. 341.

8 This is illustrated by the study of the application of the model to Mummar Qadhafi's Libya; See Saleh Al Namlah, 'Political legitimacy in Libya since 1969' (1992) Syracuse University PhD thesis.

9 See John Rawls, *Political Liberalism* (New York, 1993); Ted Honderich (ed.), *The Oxford Companion to Philosophy* (Oxford, 1995), p. 477; Matthew Swanson, 'The social extract tradition and the question of political legitimacy' (1995) University of Missouri–Columbia PhD thesis.

10 Such as the 1977 Constitution of the Soviet Union; Constitution of the Union of Soviet Socialist Republics, 7 October 1977.

11 The Constitution of the European Union also states that the Union is founded on the values of 'respect for human dignity, freedom, democracy, equality, the rule of law, and respect for human rights …' in a society in which 'pluralism, non-discrimination, tolerance, justice, solidarity and equality between women and men prevail.' (Article 1-2).

12 See, for instance, John Locke; Martyn P. Thompson, *Ideas of contract in English political thought in the age of John Locke* (New York, 1987).

13 See, generally, J. Woodford Howard Jr., 'Constitution and society in comparative perspective', *Judicature*, 71 (1987): 211–15.

14 See Peter Paczolay, 'Constitutional Transition and Legal Continuity', *Connecticut Journal of International Law*, 8 (1993): 559–74; Ralf Dahrendorf, 'Transitions: Politics, Economics, and Liberty', *Washington Quarterly*, 13 (1990): 133–42.

15 Hans Kelsen, *General Theory of Law and State*, trans. Anders Wedberg (Cambridge, 1945), pp. 117–18.

16 Ibid., p. 119.

17 And therefore the knowledge revolution would be economic and social, but not political.

18 Edward W. Walker, *Dissolution: sovereignty and the break-up of the Soviet Union* (Lanham, 2003).

19 See Alf Ross, *On Law and Justice* (London, 1958).

20 Ibid.

21 See, for instance F.M. Brookfield, *Waitangi and indigenous rights: revolution, law, and legitimation* (Auckland, 1999).

22 He maintained that 'all associations are instituted for the purpose of attaining some good'. – *The Politics of Aristotle*, trans. Ernest Barker (London, 1958), p. 1, cited by Hermann Heller, 'The Decline of the Nation State and its Effect on Constitutional and International Economic Law', *Cardozo Law Review*, 18 (1996): 1139.

23 See, generally, works on sixteenth and seventeenth century political economy; Gerald Aylmer, *The struggle for the constitution, 1603–1689: England in the seventeenth century* (4th edn, London, 1975); John Pocock, *The ancient constitution and the feudal law: a study of English historical thought in the seventeenth century* (Cambridge, 1987).

24 Mark F. Grady and Michael T. McGuire, 'The Nature of Constitutions', *Journal of Bioeconomics*, 1 (1999) 227–40.

25 See Martyn P. Thompson, *Ideas of contract in English political thought in the age of John Locke* (New York, 1987).

26 If, that is, it ever did.

27 See Noel Cox, 'The Evolution of the New Zealand Monarchy: The Recognition of an Autochthonous Polity' (2001) University of Auckland PhD thesis, chapter 2.

28 Grady and McGuire, 'The Nature of Constitutions'.

29 Thomas Hobbes, *Leviathan*, ed. Edwin Curley (Indianapolis, 1994, first published 1688); James Buchanan, *The Limits of Liberty: Between anarchy and Leviathan* (Chicago, 1975); Karl A. Wittfogel, *Oriental Despotism: A Comparative Study of Total*

Power (New Haven, 1957); Robert L. Carneiro, 'A Theory of the Origin of the State', *Science*, 169 (1970): 733–8; Mancur Olson, 'Dictatorship, Democracy, and Development', *American Political Science Review*, 87 (1993): 567–76.

30 He wrote that:

Nature hath made men so equal in the faculties of body and mind as that, though there be found one man sometimes manifestly stronger in body or of quicker mind than another, yet when all is reckoned together the difference between man and man is not so considerable as that one man can thereupon claim to himself any benefit to which another may not pretend as well as he.

– Hobbes, p. 74.

31 See J. Desmond Clark, *The common heritage: the significance of hunter-gatherer societies for human evolution* (Canberra, 1990).

32 Hobbes, p. 76. For Hobbes, war did not consist only of actual battles, but also threats of battle ('For War consisteth not in battle only, or the act of fighting, but in a tract of time wherein the will to contend by battle is sufficiently known').

33 Hobbes, p. 76.

34 'No arts; no letters; no society; and which is worst of all, continual fear and danger of violent death; and the life of man, solitary, poor, nasty, brutish, and short'; Hobbes, part 1, ch. xviii.

35 Ibid., p. 106.

36 Ibid., p. 110.

37 See, generally, works on sixteenth and seventeenth century political economy; See Gerald Aylmer, *The struggle for the constitution, 1603–1689: England in the seventeenth century* (4th edn, London, 1975); John Pocock, *The ancient constitution and the feudal law: a study of English historical thought in the seventeenth century* (Cambridge, 1987).

38 For an example, see Ronald M. Peters, Jr., *The Massachusetts constitution of 1780: a social compact* (Amherst, 1978).

39 See, for instance, the arguments of the 'cyberspace'; John Perry Barlow, co-founder of the Electronic Frontier Foundation (EFF), made the seminal statement to this effect:

Governments of the Industrial World, you weary giants of flesh and steel, I come from Cyberspace, the new home of the Mind. On behalf of the future, I ask you of the past to leave us alone. You are not welcome among us. You have no sovereignty where we gather.

– John Perry Barlow, 'A Declaration of the Independence of Cyberspace', at <http://www.eff.org/pub/Publications/John_Perry_Barlow/barlow_0296.declaration> (as at 6 December 2003).

40 Grady and McGuire, 'The Nature of Constitutions'.

41 Buchanan.

42 Grady and McGuire, 'The Nature of Constitutions'.

43 Formerly great theologians of the Church like St Thomas Aquinas (*Summa theologiæ*, ed. John A. Oesterle (Englewood Cliffs, 1964), vol. II–II, Q. xlii, a.2), Francisco Suarez ('Defensio fidei', book VI, ch. iv, p. 15, in *Selections from three works: De legibus, ac deo legislators, 1612, Defensio fidei catholicae, et apostolicae adversus anglicanae sectae errores, 1613, De triplici virtute theologica, fide, spe, et charitate, 1621*, trans. Gladys L. Williams, Ammi Brown and John Waldron (Oxford, 1944)), and Domingo Bañez, O.P. (*De justitia et jure*, Q. lxiv, a. 3), permitted rebellion against oppressive

rulers when the tyranny had become extreme and when no other means of safety were available. This carried to its logical conclusion the doctrine of the Middle Ages that the supreme ruling authority comes from God through the people for the public good. As the people immediately give sovereignty to the ruler, so the people can deprive him of his sovereignty when he has used his power oppressively (mediæval rulers were seldom women).

44 It has been said that a global economy is largely replacing and overwhelming national and regional economies; Louis Henkin, 'That "S." Words: Sovereignty, and Globalization, and Human Rights, Et Cetera', *Ford Law Review*, 68 (1999): 1–14, 5–6.

45 See, for instance, Noel Cox, 'Tax and regulatory avoidance through non-traditional alternatives to tax havens', *New Zealand Journal of Taxation Law and Policy*, 9 (2003): 305–27.

46 See David R. Johnson and David G. Post, 'Law and Borders: The Rise of Law in Cyberspace', *Stanford Law Review*, 48 (1996): 1367–402.

47 See Jonathan B. Wolf, 'War games meets the Internet: Chasing 21st century cybercriminals with old laws and little money', *American Journal of Criminal Law*, 28 (2000): 95–117.

48 The converse is true also. In the course of the Industrial Revolution the scale and complexity of the state grew enormously, in part as a consequence of the technological change, and as a result of the social changes which these wrought. See, for instance, Steven Puro, 'Technology, politics and the new Industrial Revolution', *Public Law Forum*, 4 (1985): 387–98.

49 Wittfogel.

50 He wrote that:

In a landscape characterised by full aridity permanent agriculture becomes possible only if and when coordinated human action transfers a plentiful and accessible water supply from its original location to a potentially fertile soil. When this is done, government-led hydraulic enterprise is identical with the creation of agricultural life. This first and crucial moment may therefore be designated as the 'administrative creation point'.

– Wittfogel, p. 109.

51 Ibid., pp. 126–36.

52 Wittfogel wrote that:

The power of the hydraulic despotism is unchecked ('total'), but it does not operate everywhere. The life of most individuals is far from being completely controlled by the state; and there are many villages and other corporate units that are not totally controlled either.

What keeps despotic power from asserting its authority in spheres of life? Modifying a key formula of classical economics, we may say that the representatives of the hydraulic regime act (or refrain from acting) in response to the law of diminishing administrative returns.

– Ibid., pp. 108–9. In Roman times whole districts were laid waste by the depredation of the tax collectors. See, generally, Jean Andreau, *Banking and business in the Roman world*, trans. Janet Lloyd (Cambridge, 1999).

53 Remembering the definition of technology as processes and things people create for the purpose of using them to alter their lifestyle or their surroundings.

54 Carneiro, 738.

55 Ibid., 734. The degree of circumscription varied considerably.

56 Ibid., 734–5.
57 Ibid., 735. It might be countered that the Amazonian jungle provided a commensurate degree of circumscription – and even the woodlands of North America may have done so.
58 See Anthony Molho, Kurt Raaflaub and Julia Emlen, *City states in classical antiquity and Mediæval Italy* (Ann Arbor, c.1991).
59 The processes used to alter their lifestyles being settled agriculture – including animal husbandry.
60 See Max Weber, *The agrarian sociology of ancient civilizations*, trans. R.I. Frank (London, 1976).
61 Mark F. Grady and Michael T. McGuire, 'A Theory of the Origin of Natural Law', *Journal of Contemporary Legal Issues*, 8 (1997): 87–129.
62 See Olson, 'Dictatorship, Democracy, and Development', 568–70.
63 Ibid., 569.
64 See Grady and McGuire, 'A Theory of the Origin of Natural Law'.
65 Meaning the holder of authority in a state, not necessarily limited to hereditary monarchs of traditional form.
66 The Crown, in British law and practice remains the residual landlord, and entitled to the assets of those who die without any heirs, under the doctrine of *bona vacantia*; Chris Ryan, '"The Crown" and corporate bona vacantia', *Kingston Law Review*, 12 (1982): 75–87.
67 See Olson, 'Dictatorship, Democracy, and Development', 569–71.
68 See Grady and McGuire, 'A Theory of the Origin of Natural Law', 118–20.
69 For Egyptian administration generally, see Klaus Baer, *Rank and title in the Old Kingdom; the structure of the Egyptian administration in the fifth and sixth dynasties* (Chicago, 1960); Naguib Kanawati, *The Egyptian administration in the Old Kingdom: evidence on its economic decline* (Warminster, 1977). See also Joseph G. Manning, *Land and power in Ptolemaic Egypt: the structure of land tenure* (Cambridge, 2003).
70 This may be governmental technology, or human resource management, rather than mechanical technology (though even this latter played a part).
71 See John O. McGinnis, 'The Symbiosis of Constitutionalism and Technology', *Harvard Journal of Law and Public Policy*, 25 (2001): 3–14.
72 Including economic and social environment.
73 Edmund Burke, *Selected Writings and Speeches*, ed. Peter J. Stanlis (Washington, 1997), cited by McGinnis, 'The Symbiosis of Constitutionalism and Technology'.
74 See, for instance, the effect of file-sharing through the Internet has upon the laws of copyright; See Sonia K. Katyal, 'Ending the revolution', *Texas Law Review*, 80 (2002): 1465–86.
75 All mankind is of one author, and is one volume; when one man dies, one chapter is not torn out of the book, but translated into a better language; and every chapter must be so translated ... As therefore the bell that rings to a sermon, calls not upon the preacher only, but upon the congregation to come: so this bell calls us all: but how much more me, who am brought so near the door by this sickness .... No man is an island, entire of itself ... any man's death diminishes me, because I am involved in mankind; and therefore never send to know for whom the bell tolls; it tolls for thee.

– 'Meditation XVII', from John Donne, *Devotions Upon Emergent Occasions* ed Anthony Raspa (Montreal, 1975, first published 1624). This famous meditation of John

Donne's puts forth two essential ideas which are representative of the Renaissance era in which it was written. The first (which is relevant here) is the idea that people are not isolated from one another, but that mankind is interconnected. The second is the vivid awareness of mortality that seems a natural outgrowth of a time when death was the constant companion of life.

76 At least not necessarily upon the physical community.

77 See Thomas G. Hermann, 'Is United States legal system an impediment to scientific progress?', *National Law Journal*, 19 (4 August 1997): C-15. Not all would agree; see the law.com online seminar, 'The Constitution and the Internet', which considered the question 'Can the Constitution Keep Up With the Internet?', at <http://www.law.com/jsp/statearchive.jsp?type=Article&oldid=ZZZRGQ220KC> (as at 6 December 2003).

78 See Nasheri Hedieh, 'The Intersection of technology crimes and cyberspace in Europe: The Case of Hungary', *Information and Communications Technology Law*, 12 (2003): 25–48.

79 See Neil Weinstock Netanel, 'Copyright and a democratic civil society', *Yale Law Journal*, 106 (1996): 283–387; David Friedman, 'Does technology require new law?', *Harvard Journal of Law and Public Policy*, 25 (2001): 71–85.

80 See Manuel Castells, *The Rise of Network Society* (London, 1996); Scheuerman, 'Constitutionalism in an age of speed', 359–60.

81 McGinnis, 'The Symbiosis of Constitutionalism and Technology', 4.

82 Scheuerman, 'Constitutionalism in an age of speed', 360.

83 Or whatever else may be seen as the ultimate aim of a constitution.

84 See McGinnis, 'The Symbiosis of Constitutionalism and Technology'.

85 See Barry Weingast, 'The Economic Role of Political Institutions: Market Preserving Federalism and Economic Development', *Journal of Law Economics and Organization*, 11 (1995): 24–8.

86 See John Locke, 'Fundamental Constitutions for Carolina' in David Wootton (ed.), *Political Writings of John Locke* (London, 1993), p. 232.

87 Scheuerman, 'Constitutionalism in an age of speed', 361.

88 Ibid., 362.

89 Richard Kay, 'Constitutional Chrononomy', *Ratio Juris*, 13 (2000): 31–48, 41.

90 Friedrich Engels to Karl Marx, 'Manifesto of the Communist Party', in Robert C. Tucker, *The Marx–Engels Reader* (New York, 1972), p. 469.

91 Scheuerman, 'Constitutionalism in an age of speed', 365.

Chapter 6

Changes in the Past

6.1 Introduction

This Chapter will briefly examine several historical periods which have each been generally distinguished as containing influential technological changes which have had a significant effect upon the contemporary culture of the age in which they have occurred. The political, social and economic changes which have occurred during these eras may be seen as illustrating the effects which technology has had – or may potentially have had – upon constitutions. These effects have been due to the influence which environment in general has had upon constitutions, and in particular to the influence of technology. To a lesser extent it also looks at the ways in which technological changes may have been influenced in its turn by the nature and form of the constitutional paradigm.

For several reasons this study – which can for reasons of brevity and practicality be little more than cursory or exploratory – is heavily dominated by the European and near eastern civilizations, and (more recently) of those countries which have their cultural origins in these regions. The principal theoretical reason for this is that these regions, and Europe in particular, offer an example of a largely unbroken evolutionary development, and most critically, one for which a detailed recorded history is available. It has not been significantly affected by the advent of external influences such as disrupted the evolution of civilizations elsewhere (for example, in the Americas from the sixteenth century). It is also the centre for many of the most significant developments in technology over the past few thousand years of recorded human history. There are other regions of similar nature – most noticeably that of China – but Europe is the one to which most of the current technological developments can be directly traced, and as such is the appropriate place to begin our discussion.

The first technological change which will be considered is the early development of civilization. Civilizations – of which legal systems and constitutions in particular are major aspects – are, like all living and evolving entities, however simple or complex, the product of their environment. This latter concept must be understood in its widest sense, for many aspects of environment affect the ways in which cultures – and constitutions – develop. Principally the environment with which we are most intimately concerned here is the human environment. This includes the culture, history and prevailing ethos or political nature of the particular society. But the development of civilization may also be heavily influenced by the physical environment in which it is placed – and indeed it is clear that some environments were conducive to the early development of civilization, just as others were not. Just as the Bushmen of southern Africa developed a culture suited to their homeland, in which deserts, semi-deserts and savannahs predominated, so the Indians of the Amazonian basin of South America developed another culture which suited their particular environment.

One of the most influential civilizations which may be categorized as heavily affected by the physical environment in which it developed was that of ancient Egypt. This civilization is not only one of the earliest to evolve, but it is also one for which we may trace a largely complete evolution from the days of the pre-dynastic period to the present time. This was a civilization which was heavily, if not predominately, given shape and form by its physical environment – and most critically – by the means which had to be taken by humanity for the efficient utilization of that environment.

6.2 Egypt

Inundation of the Nile Valley of northern Africa through the annual flooding was eventually to lead to the development of cultivation, and ultimately to a settled civilization, as it encouraged intensive agriculture,[1] and all which developed from that. The precarious nature of the flood – too much and the soil would be washed away, too little and there would be insufficient to ensure a harvest – required strong government, including the use of levies for public works, writing and record-keeping, and of taxation.[2] The waters had to be harnessed, and this had to be done in a timely fashion, or there would be famine and disease in the following season. This harnessing of the productive energy of the river might be undertaken by a single family, or a small community, but only a stable political environment afforded the peace and stability requisite for even that small-scale enterprise to be safely and regularly undertaken. It was more efficient to band together in increasingly large and complex communities, for the good of all, and hence the good of the individual.

In comparatively early times the Nile valley developed what is now classed as the pre-dynastic state (or states) of Egypt. They were states because they were political entities which brought together for a common purpose people of many different families, tribes, villages, and towns. Unity of purpose – in this case the cultivation of the land while the annual inundation provided sufficient water for a crop – required unity of government. The relative simplicity of the requirement produced a relatively simple solution – a single leader. This individual (in all civilizations of this and latter times, with few exceptions until the modern era, styled king) was at once the organizational focus for those public works and private enterprise which were required, as well as the intermediary through which the people might seek the intercession of the many gods with which the creative imagination of the Egyptians peopled the skies. The control of the rains was beyond the direct powers even of the divine Pharaoh (as the leader was styled from early times in Egypt), but he might seek the blessings of the gods through the observance of the proper religious ceremonies.

The Pharaoh also owed his[3] political pre-eminence to his control of the army,[4] which in itself may be seen as mastery of technology having constitutional consequences. Loss of crops due to a failure in the flood (or excessive flooding)[5] could, and sometimes did, lead to political change,[6] despite the Pharaoh's control of the army – though often it was the general of a victorious army who took the throne of a Pharaoh who showed himself incapable of rule through his inability to intercede successfully with the gods. Between the Middle and the New Kingdoms, beginning about 1700 BC (the Second Intermediate Period), a series of unpredictable floods struck the Nile and Egypt, and at least partly as a result of this failure of technology,[7] fragmented Egypt into two kingdoms.[8] The sphere of influence of each Pharaoh was circumscribed by the physical limitations of the ruler's ability to exercise control, the poverty of his treasury, and the parochial nature of the worship of his attendant gods and goddesses. North and south (Lower and Upper Egypt respectively) looked to the Near East and Mediterranean, and to Africa, and developed similar though distinct identities.

Egypt's geopolitics were similar to and yet also very different from those of Mesopotamia.[9] Both cultures had evolved in hot dry river valleys that required irrigation, which in turn required a comparatively advanced and robust form of organization, and a strong government that led in turn to the development of civilization.[10] The Egyptians depended so much on irrigation and the high level of organization and authority needed to maintain it that they considered their rulers, the Pharaohs, gods[11] – though it is true that the rulers of the city states of early Mesopotamia were also ascribed divine status due to their role as intermediaries of the gods (if not actually descended from the gods).

In Egypt the power and effectiveness of these god-kings corresponded directly to the country's prosperity, which itself depended on the floods' regularity and the effectiveness of the irrigation system which was required to take full and efficient advantage of it.[12] The greater the success of the organized irrigation the greater the need for a central organization to maintain the systems necessary to ensure its success. The control of agricultural technology led to a strongly centralized government – and in turn the centralized government fostered intensive agriculture which depended upon the careful use of the available technology, limited though it was.[13] The maintenance of an army for the protection of the country from aggressors, and for the occasional conquest of neighbouring countries, also gave the Pharaoh political power, and assisted in the centralizing of authority in the state – as well as the development of the notion of the state (as distinct from a loose collection of city states – into which Egypt sometimes briefly fell in times of crisis).

It would be unduly simplistic to insist that the irrigation of the Nile river led to the development of the Egyptian monarchy. But it would nevertheless appear true that the technological, and logistical implications of the systematic use of irrigation, the maintenance of a permanent civil bureaucracy for the service of the

Pharaoh and the gods of Egypt, and of the standing army which was necessary for the defence of the Pharaoh, gods and land, were instrumental in the development of the pharaohonic kingdom.

6.3 Rome

While Egypt was an early, and in some respects a rather primitive form of state – primitive in that the dynamics between Pharaoh and people was fairly simple, almost that of overseer and peasant – that of the empire was Rome was, by comparison, highly complex. It also was the product of physical environment, but whereas the environment which formed Egypt's civilization was a comparatively benign but narrowly-confined fertile valley, Rome's empire (like the earlier, but short-lived, empire of Alexander the Great before it) was spread across much of the known world. Thus, at once it offered greater opportunities to the ruler for the enlargement and the exercise of power, but at the same time it required (and inaugurated) a wholly distinct form of government. The development of this government was to tax the mental and physical resources of the empire, and eventually resolve itself (from the time of Diocletian onwards) into a form of decentralized autocracy – prior to the eventual collapse of the empire in the face of mounting internal and external challenges.

The Roman Empire was also dependent upon technology for its political survival, and this also influenced the nature and form of the constitution.[14] For an empire which lacked a clearly defined border, such as Egypt had,[15] communications was essential to government. Initially this was heavily dependent upon the sea – it is not coincidental that the empire developed around the margins of the Mediterranean Sea, nor that the Romans called it the Mare Nostrum, or 'our (Roman) sea'. As McGinnis has noted, one of the most important ways in which technology transforms the environment is by reducing transportation and communication costs.[16] Such reductions made possible new forms of constitutional structures[17] – in the case of Rome – an empire.[18] The advent of roads led to unity, just as unity led to the construction of roads to exploit the new markets and preserve the unity. The saying that 'all roads led to Rome' had a profound meaning in the empire.

Rome depended upon these communications systems for its survival, as the size of the empire meant that military forces had to be moved swiftly wherever necessary to meet a new threat.[19] As the empire expanded into the hinterland of Europe, Asia and North Africa so it became necessary to develop landward communications arteries, both through military necessity, and as the provinces became more settled, administration convenience.

In the Roman world these communications arteries included roads,[20] military networks,[21] and system of civil and military administration – including the legal system.[22] This involved a degree of constitutional centralization,[23] but occasionally this failed.[24] These occasional failures were less serious than might perhaps otherwise have been the case because the next constitutional tier below the imperial government were the provinces, which were run as part of a relatively homogenous imperial system (though the provinces were initially under senatorial governors, this also reflected a significant degree of centralization).[25]

In the later centuries of the empire fiscal, military and population collapse[26] – brought about in part by the increasingly serious invasions from the east – led to the empire being divided, first temporarily and eventually permanently, into east and west.[27] Yet, while the communications systems were operating properly, Rome was able to oversee – if not always aid – provinces many hundreds and even thousands of kilometres from the imperial city.[28] Unfortunately, because the mechanisms through which the empire operated depended greatly upon the army, and particularly because the formal constitutional powers of the emperors' were long disguised (and therefore the management of the imperial succession was often difficult), the army was often to assume a decisive political role.[29] Politico-strategic changes – including an increased emphasis upon the provinces along the eastern borders, meant that a single imperial government was incapable of effectively administering the whole empire.

Communications and transportation technology allowed the Roman empire to be run in a centralized fashion.[30] As utilization of technology declined in effectiveness – partly through over-commitment – decentralization increased.[31] Communications technology of this type made a significant contribution to the form of the imperial Roman imperial constitution and was fostered by a regime built on public works and military technology.

If Egypt may be categorized as showing the development of a simple centralized monarchical government around a single pre-eminent technological requirement, Rome may be seen as the evolution of an artificial state through the requirements of a more complex physical and human environment. Rome became a multi-headed empire because of the failure of communications, but its existence at all was a tribute to the comparatively advanced nature of communications in the ancient world, and to its successful utilization.

6.4 Dark Age and Mediæval Europe

The so-called Dark Ages after the collapse of the Roman empire in the west, and the Middle Ages which followed, were times when the weakness of communications contributed to the division of states, and to feudalism.[32] Feudalism was a political, social, and economic system founded upon the conditions of the time – including technological limitations (especially transportation and communications).[33] Government was limited in scope and breadth by the conditions of the time – and primarily by the limited communications systems. It has been said that the roads of England were not to regain the height of efficiency that they enjoyed in Roman times until the nineteenth century, and this is broadly true also for much of continental Europe. Feudalism, as a constitutional system, relied upon a hierarchical structure of political, social and economic obligations.[34] It might be said to be a type of Lockean constitution, with individuals and communities linked for mutual protection.[35] The limitations of technology meant that the constitutional arrangements were restricted in scope, and decentralization was common in this era – even for a state such as England, which generally lacked the over-mighty baronage more common on the continent of Europe,[36] and which enjoyed an unusually sophisticated centralized fiscal system from late Saxon times.[37] There were of course important influences upon the constitution, and upon society in general, including the gradually increasing rate of literacy, and the consequent spread of new political – and religious – ideas.[38] These were eventually to lead to a profound religious and political revolution – and to technological and constitutional change.

The European Middle Ages might have involved a conceptual world-view markedly different to that of classical Rome, but its environment was in many ways not so dissimilar. The attacks of the Muslims from Arabia replaced the invading Germanic hordes which the later Roman empire had had to face. Feudalism, which had started as a response to the exigencies of the time, became a permanent feature of life in the west, though now imbued with a Christian rationale which changed it considerably from its pagan origins. This was to become especially significant as knowledge of Roman law became more widespread, and Roman notions of property and of state authority were grafted onto the feudal structures.

The definition of feudalism itself is disputed. A wide definition is favoured by French and German historians generally[39] and a narrow definition by historians of the Norman Conquest.[40] The wide definition requires a subject peasantry, widespread use of the service tenements instead of a salary, supremacy of a class of specialized warriors, and ties of obedience and protection which bind man to man. This embraces all mediæval societies between the ninth and twelfth centuries, as its advocates intended. In these terms, late Anglo-Saxon society in England was broadly feudal. Maitland would agree,[41] but not so Stenton, in whose view service must be exactly defined in order to be feudal.[42] This definition is at once legalistic and moralistic, with a strong Christian aspect, but perhaps out of keeping with the context of the time.

A wide definition links the mediæval feudalism more closely with its classical origins. One especially important distinction lay, however, in its juristic nature, one which emphasized legal rights and responsibilities. To some degree at least the most influential technology of the Middle Ages was not the road or aqueduct of the Roman world, but the quill pen and the parchment of the lawyer-cleric. This is seen most clearly in the development of formal feudalism as a political, economic and social system throughout most of western Europe, and elsewhere – including the Latin kingdoms and principalities of the Holy Land, Cyprus, Armenia and other parts of the Near and Middle East.

The nature of feudalism depended upon land ownership, but its defining characteristic was obligation. In the early Carolingian empire the protective relationship set up by one free man over another was called *patrocinium*.[43] One placed oneself in this position by act of commendation.[44] The obligation of serving and respecting the vassal's superior was therefore created,[45] but only so far as compatible with the maintenance of the vassal's status as a free man. In his turn the lord was to aid and support his vassal, in the manner of food and clothing. Although the various obligations became more specialized, this was essentially a formal contractual arrangement.[46]

Feudalism prevented the break-up of the Carolingian state in tenth century France, because although the supremacy of the king was purely theoretical, vassalage remained a real practical bond.[47] Until late in the twelfth century the French king could only exercise power outside the royal domain in a feudal capacity. Monarchical sovereignty was only clearly recognized by a few, and most reliance was placed on the feudal authority of lord-vassal. Feudalism played a similar role in Germany.[48]

The basis of royal power in Germany was not however vassalage,[49] but the surviving organization of the Carolingian state, and the use of the Church until the struggle with the Pope over investiture in the second half of the eleventh century weakened the political role of the Church. Emperor Frederick Barbarossa tried to reform the state on a feudal basis in the second half of the twelfth century, and from the re-grant of the lands of Henry the Lion all imperial grants were of fiefs directly held of the emperor.[50] But this approach did not give the empire the strength it needed, because fiefs which escheated had to be re-granted, effectively preventing the formation of any considerable royal domain.[51] The structure of the Holy Roman Empire – which, for most of its long life was primarily confined to the German-speaking lands – was legalist and theoretical or conceptual, rather than bound by force of arms, or a complex communications system. The notion of the empire as the descendant of the Roman Empire of old, with the added authority of the Church, added strength to what was otherwise a comparatively weak edifice. But the conceptual strength of the empire cannot be underestimated at a time in human history when ideas, and especially those of an esoteric, mystical or metaphysical nature, held considerable sway over the popular mind – and often over those of their leaders too.

One of the principal parts of Europe which never rejoined the revived Roman empire was England. Physically isolated by the English Channel, it enjoyed protection from most invaders, but also was subject to the insularity, emotional and practical, which can arise from the absence of unrestricted and regular contact with other peoples. But England was never immune from political developments on the Continent, both before and after the Norman Conquest of England in 1066. The Norman kings of England were potentially far stronger than their Saxon predecessors. This was in part due to their position as conquerors (and which, in mediæval theory, showed that God had shown them His favour), which left them fully in command of a military, social and political structure.[52] It was also because, with the advent of the formal feudal system of land tenure and its associated social structure, the king became far more the apex of society than he had been to the

Saxons. The relationship of king and subject extended not just to the great tenants-in-chief but to everyone possessed of an interest in land. The eleventh and twelfth century renaissance across Europe, and the accompanying economic expansion also benefited the Normans,[53] in England and elsewhere.

The development of feudalism and the state in England had a number of peculiar features, and was in some respects the converse of what took place in Germany. The pre-Conquest thegnage was similar to vassalage, but royal thegns had allodial land (that is, not held of any lord or superior), not conditional tenure,[54] and true feudalism, in the narrower definition of Stenton, was only introduced by the Normans.

Every estate was held directly or indirectly of the king, and to avoid sub-vassals from being used by tenants-in-chief against the king, an oath of fealty or allegiance was occasionally demanded, as at Salisbury in 1086. By the Salisbury Oath all freemen were bound to swear allegiance directly to the king instead of to the immediate lord from whom they held their lands.[55] This method was used especially to designate the heir and obtain promises of support, as for William Rufus in 1087, and King Henry I in 1100. All those swearing allegiance became liegemen of the king. The obligations of vassals were now fixed in relation to the needs of the royal army. From Henry I onwards the ordinary oath of vassalage included a reservation of fealty to the Crown, and no holder of a normal fief enjoyed powers of jurisdiction or administrative functions comprised in the mediæval concept of *justicia*. The growth in the use of scutage and the replacement of military service by payment made the Crown more independent of the feudal levy.[56] The great census now known as the Doomsday Book aided this process by strengthening the economic independence of the King. Fiscal exemptions, such as were common on the continent – and where they weakened and even impoverished central governments – were rare and comparatively insignificant in England, where a clear and comprehensive inventory showed with precision the true economic – and hence political – fabric of the country.

Feudalism made the king the supreme landowner and invested the relation of king and subject with a contractual character, rights to service and protection. The association of land ownership and the rights of the Crown tended to assimilate the descent of the Crown to the descent of an estate in land, and inevitably increased the hereditary at the expense of the elective character of kingship. The obligation on the king's part however, of providing good government remained. The *Witan* of the Saxon kings gave way to the *Commune Concilium* of the Normans, a body which was much more dominated by the landed interest, because land-ownership was the principal source of wealth and a sign of importance far more to the Norman than to the Saxon.[57]

Had the Norman dynasty lasted, the earliest wave of French settlers might have been assimilated in time without radically affecting the broad lines of indigenous development. But with the death of William's grandson William the Ætheling in the *White Ship*, the Crown went to a count of Boulogne, a member of the House of Blois, and then a count of Anjou. With the sons and descendants of King Henry II the influence of Aquitaine on England is profound.[58] The political development of England became more closely aligned to that on the Continent, and yet subtly different.

The juristic theory of territorial sovereignty, with the king being supreme ruler within the confines of his kingdom, was originally two distinct conceptions. The king owned no superior in temporal matters, and within his kingdom the king was emperor.[59]

The emperor had legal supremacy, or he did not. If the former, theories of the sovereignty of kings were not needed, as they swayed merely *de facto* power. Sovereignty remained essentially *de jure* authority.[60] Bartolus and Baldus led the way towards recognition of a legal sovereignty of kings. The emperor had a genuine *de jure* sovereignty within the *terrae imperii*. Other powers could obtain true sovereignty on a purely *de facto* basis. This was not merely power without legitimacy, but a principled division of authority.[61]

In the later Middle Ages it was believed that England was an independent sovereign monarchy answerable only to God: in mediæval parlance an empire, self-contained and sovereign.[62] The focusing of the Crown's activities almost exclusively on the realm of England after 1216 encouraged such thinking. Sir John Fortescue remarked that 'from of old English kings have reigned independently, and acknowledged no superior on earth in things temporal'. This was a fundamental feature of English monarchy by the fifteenth century, based on precepts of Roman law.[63] They rejected a Holy Roman Empire that had been narrowly German for several centuries, and the temporal authority of the Pope. The French had asserted their own empire for very similar reasons by 1200.

King Henry V especially emphasized his legal status as an emperor in his kingdom. His son Henry VI was occasionally called 'Most Imperial Majesty', and he was the first to wear a new imperial Crown of state: a closed or arched Crown with four curved hoops meeting in the centre above the diadem itself, and surmounted by a cross.[64]

The fact remains, however, that although the mediæval English king always had as one of his principal functions the granting of laws to his subjects, he was never in any way above the law. These kings did not have exclusive legislative authority either, but kings were relatively free from formal and permanent limitations on their powers and freedom of action. When the nobility felt that kings had gone too far they occasionally sought to restrain them. Earthly pressures,[65] including rebellion, were used against kings on six occasions from 1327 to 1485.[66] The feudal theories which were the basis of the right of counsel found in chapter 14 of Magna Carta, were only put forward when feudalism as a method of government was already in decay.[67]

The combination of English and Norman kingship paved the way for an institutional despotism operating through prerogative rights that could only be checked by desperate rebellion and, theoretically, by the application of feudal ideas of mutual duties. These latter ideas provided no sanctions except the renunciation of fealty[68] and, in the last resort, war on the autocratic king.[69]

Monarchy was not the only system of government the twelfth and thirteenth century jurists knew, but it was the only one they treated seriously and extensively. Ruler, nobility, clergy, and people were part of a mediæval constitutionalism, a *societas Christiana* that encompassed all of Christian Europe.[70]

The canonists corporate theory explained the relationship between the head of a *universitas* and its members. In the thirteenth century this led to a new theory of government, based in part on Aristotle's mixed constitution.[71] Aquinas also 'discovered' this system in ancient Israel.[72] At the beginning of the fourteenth century John of Paris combined the corporate theory and Aquinas' mixed constitution, and applied it to the government of the Church.[73]

Kingship conferred a coercive jurisdiction, with the king a dispenser of justice, and repressor of evil. But a king could also be a guide to the end for which the state was ordained. In this, the king disposed of moral authority which could command obedience. Belief in this second attribute of kingship was revived under the influence of Aristotelian teleology.[74] There was philosophical support for monarchy in Aristotle.[75]

King Henry II abandoned the old fiscal system, as well as the *renovatio monetae*, in 1158, and the last *danegeld* was levied in 1162.[76] Nearly the whole of England was organized into shires and hundreds in 1066, and almost all land was assessed in hides and the like, for the purposes of taxation and service. This allowed a uniquely high degree of fiscal mobilisation.[77] In the eleventh century the aristocratic landholding of England twice refashioned. That in the period on either side of Canute's accession weakened the king, whilst that occurring in the two decades after the Battle of Hastings empowered him.[78]

Sub-tenancies were less formal in Saxon times than they were under the feudal system of the Normans, but the patterns of land occupation at the lowest levels changed much less markedly.[79] The barons required the permission of the king to embark on foreign voyages, to build castles, alienate land, marry or arrange the marriage of a child or other dependent. The wide range of economic resources in the hands of the king remained.[80] But the higher nobility were at once the king's main potential enemy and the principal ally of central government. Yet even under William II England was a more centralized country than France, though similarly composed of largely self-governing lordships[81] – though these were rarely formally so, as they were in France.

Because Henry II successfully reversed the tendencies of Stephen's reign, England never developed a formal nobility with powers of life and death over their subjects, and neither did the privileges of noble birth extend equally to all members of a family. There were to be no more hereditary sheriffs, so the nobility did not acquire independence as in France and Germany.[82] The kingship under Henry III was strengthened in no small part by the work of those educated in the newly fashionable civil law.[83]

By 1377 Parliaments were in England an almost annual occurrence, and the monarchy was regularly dependent upon the commons for financial aid, though in theory the king was to continue for a long time to rely upon his own hereditary revenues, perquisites, and large, expensive borrowings. The King was both a beneficiary of the advanced taxation system which he oversaw, and a victim of it. By the time of the 'Good Parliament' of 1376 it had become possible for the commons to organize and launch a far-reaching attack on the conduct and policies of the government, and yet still be allowed to remain in session for more than two months.[84] Richard II tried to revive the personal monarchy which had been on the decline since the last years of his grandfather Edward III.[85] The steady decline in prestige and resources of the monarchy since the end of the fourteenth century brought disaster and decadence in government, and had made civil war not only possible but inevitable.

Fifteenth century England was a limited monarchy, limited by the reliance of the king on laws made by the king in parliament.[86] The king could do no wrong, and his ministers took the blame for decisions even in the fifteenth century.[87] But the extreme weakness of the office of king under Henry VI had gravely jeopardised law and justice, administration, and economic development, and had reduced to a low ebb the position of England on the Continent. It was necessary for the monarchy to be restored, set along more efficient and vigorous lines than Lancaster had achieved. The only alternative was some kind of magnate conciliar government, with all its accompanying corruption, dissension, and administrative anarchy, as found in the time of Henry VI.

The first attempt to wrest actual control of the direction of affairs from the king is found in the Provisions of Oxford, though the council established under it lasted only eighteen months.[88] Henry IV achieved the remedy – by the end of the reign there were no over-mighty subjects left.[89] From 1471 at least, his successor Edward IV had found the solution to the problem of the Crown. He succeeded in reviving and arresting the decline of the kingship and improved markedly the working of government. Henry VII took over the Yorkist monarchy, used its methods and institutions, extended and improved them, and made them efficient.[90] Continual wars led to the need for working arrangements between king and subjects in Parliament.[91] Kings came to rely more and more on their councillors.[92]

Although mediæval and early modern constitutions were to develop in rather different directions in England and elsewhere in Europe, the prevailing technological influence was the evolving body of laws. These were not merely individual laws, but one could speak of 'the law' as an entity in its own right. In much of Europe this was to be heavily influenced by the reception of the laws of ancient Rome, and everywhere they were strongly affected by the laws – and beliefs – of the Church. This technology was of the mind – a knowledge-based technology – but it was one which was to evolve into a technology of matter as the mediæval quest for divine truth came under the influence of a new school of scholarship.

6.5 The Reformation

The Reformation, in contrast to much of the Middle Ages,[93] was a time of significant technological change. In part this was caused by specific inventions such as the printing press,[94] but it was also a result of increased trade with the east,[95] and the importation of new ideas (including from the classical world, and the Islam-dominated Near and Middle East), from as early as time of the first crusade.[96] These developments led to changing perceptions of the role of the state (including the rise in a belief in a social compact between state and individual, or state and community).[97] It also led to an increased awareness of the differences between the peoples of different states of Europe – though the westerners might have been categorized as 'Franks' by the Saracens (another generalization), they were far from homogeneous. It is not clear that these changes were a result of technological changes, or whether the technological changes led to social changes, which in turn led to constitutional changes.[98] Yet the example of the Reformation shows us that even in relatively complex societies constitutions may be effected by technology. Technology itself continued to develop, particularly where constitutions, and societies, were more liberal,[99] and where received wisdom was challenged. As an example, medical science was greatly advanced by the use of dissection, which had been largely proscribed, in most of Europe, for religious reasons throughout the Middle Ages. Arabs, Jews and other non-Christians were however able to engage in such practices and passed much of their knowledge on to Christian physicians in due course.

The invention of the printing press encouraged the circulation of information, which in turn encouraged the development of common politics beyond the immediate community.[100] This spreading of knowledge was to have a major role in German, and somewhat later, Italian re-unification.[101] The modern territorial state was unknown to antiquity and to the Middle Ages, except in those cities which alone saw sufficient division of labour and concentration in a confined area.[102] The Roman empire was a partial example, but even there it remained in many ways a city state to the end, with the relationship between the eternal city and the provinces always uncertain. The advent of the printing press meant that for the first time it was possible to transmit, preserve, and utilize large quantities of information. This was soon used by government bureaucracies, which sought to record as much information as they could – initially often for taxation purposes – but later for other purposes also, as the scope of government – and the complexity of the constitution – grew.[103] While taxation and other records from the ancient near east and elsewhere were at times voluminous, the printing press allowed – and encouraged – record keeping an order of magnitude greater – with profound consequences.

The Reformation did not, of course, affect countries equally, even within Europe, and it was confined to that continent (though its effects were felt further afield). It passed through various stages – including the Counter-Reformation – which also saw a blossoming of constitutional theory,[104] though this was mostly driven by political and religious forces rather than by technological innovation. But it is not a coincidence that the Society of Jesus, one of the leading institutions of the Roman Catholic Church created at least in part as a response to the protestant Reformation, should have the advance of scientific knowledge as one of its aims.[105]

6.6 The Industrial Revolution

At a somewhat later period in the development of European civilization the physical technologies began to evolve at an especially rapid rate. This has been called the Industrial Revolution. It was a time which saw the true advent of mass manufacture, led to greater population size (through the elimination of many diseases and the increased availability of employment for individuals rather than family units as formerly), higher productivity and rapid economic growth.[106] Social theorists tend to agree that the ascent of industrial capitalism in the nineteenth century unleashed a particularly intense period of social and economic acceleration.[107] This led to more taxation revenue for governments, but also to more social and economic problems,[108] and so to enlarged opportunities and requirements for government intervention.[109] This in turn led in turn to greater demands for democracy, such as was manifested by the chartists and the electoral reformers in the United Kingdom during the early nineteenth century.[110] But domestic economic policies in that country at least remained largely laissez-faire, which encouraged further development.[111]

It may well be true that it was economic and social changes, wrought by technological advances, which resulted in constitutional changes during the Industrial Revolution – domestically at least this was possibly so.[112] Technological changes, *per se*, have themselves rarely had a direct influence upon constitutions. But the development of colonial empires by European states in the course of the nineteenth century seems to have been due, in part at least, to the direct effect of technology, more narrowly defined. Naval and military technology enabled colonial powers to built empires in places once beyond their reach.[113] The very needs of those naval forces led to further expansion, as for example, in the building of coaling stations across the globe.[114] Each of these had to be administered, and might in turn become colonies, then self-governing dependencies, and later (depending upon the whim, inclination or weakness of the colonial power) independent, as the need for such stations declined, or the circumstances of the colonial power allowed.

Like the much earlier Roman empire, these new empires relied heavily upon communications. As the empires spread well beyond the narrow confines of Europe – indeed the comparatively long-settled political boundaries and sophisticated societies there rendered the acquisition of new territory difficult, as Napoleon and later Hitler were to find to their cost – so more complex long-distance communications was required. The invention of an effective chronometer, and the invention of longitude, did much to open up the world's oceans in the eighteenth century,[115] and the principal countries of Europe soon took advantage of this. The telegraph,[116] seabed cables, and fast shipping meant that an empire could encompass the globe, and yet be administered – at least without too much difficulty – from the imperial heartland.[117] There was a considerable degree of de-centralization, which was to increase as colonial territories developed more fully.[118] But the oversight of territories changed the nature of domestic political structures – for example, in the British experience, the notion and role of the Crown – considerably.[119]

The Industrial Revolution gave economic power to those countries in which it began – particularly the United Kingdom – but it also gave them technological advantages (especially in respect of communications, mass production, and military and naval force – power projection) which meant that they enjoyed significant political advantages.[120] These resulted in constitutional changes, primarily including a focus on empire, a rapid development in social and educational policies, the scope and reach of government generally, and greater democracy.[121]

6.7 The Constitutional Effects of Technology

Each of the above technological and historical periods was marked by quite different technological, economic, social, political and constitutional features. In some cases, such as in ancient Egypt, the Reformation in Europe, and during the Industrial Revolution, it is comparatively easy to see how technological change seems to have affected society, and therefore the constitution. Even in the Roman empire, and during the Middle Ages, there were signs that this was also occurring. It may be a commonplace that technology changes society and society changes the constitution.

But we can see signs that technology has directly affected the constitution, while perhaps also having social or economic effects. These may perhaps be seen in the way in which Egypt required strongly centralized government and so came into existence as a unified state – and survived the challenges to its continued existence. Rome could not have established a lasting empire except through the development and use of effective communications – nor would the eternal City (Rome) itself have grown to the size which it eventually reached (and therefore its economic and political power) except through the skilful use of technology. The development of colonial empires by the European powers in the nineteenth century was facilitated by the Industrial Revolution, which offered unrivalled opportunities for the efficient deployment of force (through rapid long-distance communications systems), and the mass-production technology which made this possible, and economically affordable.[122]

6.8 Conclusion

Some technological changes have directly affected the constitution, others have not – but it seems that when this has occurred it has been in respect of foreign policy, rather more often than domestic, except in the less complex and sophisticated societies. It would also seem that technology itself develops more rapidly when government requires it (as in Egypt), or where the constitution is sufficiently laissez-faire to allow individual people and groups the freedom and opportunity to develop technology. This may be where the constitution encourages individuality and enquiry, rather than orthodoxy and compliance. It would be overly simplistic to suggest that democracy *per se* encourages the development of technology, for this may also occur under autocratic regimes. But democracy is more usually associated with liberal societies, which would appear to have a tendency to encourage free enquiry. Technological innovation seems to be more easily found where the constitution allows the freedom and opportunity for innovation, and rewards the innovator – at least by protecting him or her from arbitrary confiscation or loss of the proceeds of their invention.

It may be that major changes which have a direct impact on the structure of the constitution will be rare – particularly as the complexity of society increases. However, where a technology – whether a physical technology such as telecommunications, or a technological procedure such as a developed system of private law – has a significant effect on society it may also have constitutional implications. Whether or not these examples give us any guidance to the future we will leave until after considering some contemporary technological revolutions.

Notes

1 See Robert C. Allen, 'Agriculture and the origins of the state in ancient Egypt', *Explorations in Economic History*, 34 (1997): 135–54; Arthur Mirsky, 'Influence of geologic factors on ancient Egyptian civilization', *Journal of Geoscience Education*, 45 (1997): 415.

2 See, generally, David A. Warburton, *State and economy in ancient Egypt: fiscal vocabulary of the New Kingdom* (Göttingen, 1997).

3 Hatchepsut, in the eighteenth dynasty, ruled as a female Pharaoh, not as a queen regnant. Cleopatra, and others of her Macedonian Lagidæ line, were of the post-dynastic Ptolemaic era; See Joyce Tyldesley, *Hatchepsut: the female pharaoh* (London, 1996); Michel Chauveau, *Cleopatra: beyond the myth*, trans. David Lorton (Ithaca, 2002).

4 See Nigel Strudwick, *The administration of Egypt in the Old Kingdom: the highest titles and their holders* (London, 1985).

5 The Egyptians realised quite well that their prosperity and welfare depended on the Nile which provided its people with most of what they needed to survive: fish and wildlife, mud for building materials, a 'highway' for easy transportation, and papyrus for paper. Most importantly, the Nile floods annually from June to October, watering

the ground and replenishing the soil with a rich fertile layer of silt. The Egyptians called their land kmt ('the Black land') after this layer of silt. The real essence of Egypt consisted of a long thin strip of land along the Nile that was never more than a few kilometres wide. Outside of this strip was the 'Red land', the desert.

6 The ten plagues of Egypt could be seen as an example of technology having constitutional effects – Moses and the elders of Israel contended with the priests of Egypt for mastery (Exodus 7–10); See Richard D. Patterson, 'Wonders in the heavens and on the earth: Apocalyptic imagery in the Old Testament', *Journal of the Evangelical Theological Society*, 43 (2000): 385–403.

7 This was not merely a failure of nature, for the annual inundation was merely the first part of a technological process largely controlled by the state.

8 See K.S.B. Ryholt, *The Political Situation in Egypt during the Second Intermediate Period, c.1800–1550 BC* (Copenhagen, 1997).

9 See Gwendolyn Leick, *Mesopotamia: the invention of the city* (London, 2001).

10 See David Warburton, *Egypt and the Near East: politics in the Bronze Age* (Neuchâtel, 2001); Bruce G. Trigger, *Early civilizations: ancient Egypt in context* (Cairo, 1993).

11 See Regine Schulz and Matthias Seidel (eds), *Egypt: the world of the Pharaohs* (Köln, 1998). Whilst the Mesopotamian rulers were also seen as gods, this might be seen as due to the need for the people to have an intermediary with the gods not dwelling on earth. More importantly, each city boasted its own god-king, and there was no comparable unity as found in Egypt; HIH Prince Takahito Mikasa (ed.), 'Monarchies and socio-religious traditions in the ancient Near East: papers read at the 31st International Congress of Human Sciences in Asia and North Africa' (International Congress of Human Sciences in Asia and North Africa, Cairo, 1984).

12 See Allen.

13 Here, technology is largely agricultural, in particular the use of irrigation. Other major civilizations have also depended upon irrigation – or been created by them – as, for example, the Khmer kingdom; See Charles Higham, *The civilization of Angkor* (London, 2001).

14 The law in general was also influenced by economic and social factors; See Jean-Jacques Aubert and Boudewijn Sirks (eds), *Speculum iuris: Roman law as a reflection of social and economic life in antiquity* (Ann Arbor, 2002).

15 Most other civilizations such as the Tigris–Euphrates, and Indus valleys in the Old World and the Valley of Mexico and the mountain and coastal valleys of Peru in the New World also enjoyed defined borders – even if, like Mesopotamia, and the Indus valley, it was a water catchment area. See also Robert L. Carneiro, 'A Theory of the Origin of the State', *Science*, 169 (1970): 733–8, 734.

16 John O. McGinnis, 'The Symbiosis of Constitutionalism and Technology', *Harvard Journal of Law and Public Policy*, 25 (2001): 3–14, 6.

17 Ibid., 6.

18 While not the first empire in Europe – that distinction might go to Alexandria, or to the Minoans (or any of a number of earlier peoples), it was the first viable multinational empire. See Clifford Ando, *Imperial ideology and provincial loyalty in the Roman Empire* (Berkeley, 2000); S.E. Finer, *The history of government from the earliest times* (Oxford, 1997).

19 See Thomas S. Burns, *Barbarians within the gates of Rome: a study of Roman military policy and the barbarians, ca. A.D. 375–425* (Bloomington, 1994).

20 See Raymond Chevallier, *Roman roads*, trans. N.H. Field (Berkeley, 1976).

21 See, for instance, D.J. Woolliscroft, *Roman military signalling* (Stroud, 2001).

22 See Jean-Jacques Aubert and Boudewijn Sirks (eds), *Speculum iuris: Roman law as a reflection of social and economic life in antiquity* (Ann Arbor, 2002). Roman law forms the basis of the civil law system, which is one of the principal legal systems in use today.

23 This was especially so after the evolution of the imperial constitution – such as it was – through the adoption of the eastern model of divine ruler. See J. Rufus Fears, *Princeps a diis electus: the divine election of the emperor as a political concept at Rome* (Rome, 1977).

24 There was, for instance, no satisfactory imperial succession law; See Fears. When the succession was disputed provincial governors, or generals, might contend for the imperial purple. See, for example, in the year of the three emperors; John Grainger, *Nerva and the Roman succession crisis of AD 96–99* (London, 2003).

25 See Andrew Lintott, *Imperium Romanum: politics and administration* (London, 1993). Governors might vie for the purple, but a province would rarely secede for very long.

26 See F.W. Walbank, *The awful revolution: the decline of the Roman Empire in the West* (Liverpool, 1969).

27 See Timothy D. Barnes, *The new empire of Diocletian and Constantine* (Cambridge, 1982).

28 This was at least until the conditions facing the imperial heartlands rendered all contact – and aid – uncertain. See, for instance, Venerable Bede, *Bede's Ecclesiastical history of the English people: a historical commentary*, ed. J.M. Wallace-Hadrill (Oxford, 1988), ch. 13:

To Agitius (Aetius), thrice consul, the Groans of the Britons ... the barbarians drive us to the sea, the sea drives us to the barbarians; between these two means of death we are either killed or drowned. There is no reply.

– from *The Groans of the Britains* (AD 446). By Agitius Gildas presumably meant Aetius. Aetius held his third consulship from 446 to 454.

29 See J.B. Campbell, *The Emperor and the Roman Army, 31 BC–AD 235* (Oxford, 1984); Lukas de Blois, *The Roman army and politics in the first century before Christ* (Amsterdam, 1987).

30 Aqueducts, public granaries, and so on allowed the city of Rome to become a metropolis of at least half a million people; See Gerda de Kleijn, *The Water Supply of Ancient Rome: City Area, Water, and Population* (Amsterdam, 2001); Glenn R. Storey, 'The population of ancient Rome', *Antiquity*, 71 (1997): 966–78.

31 Aqueducts failed, secure food supplies dwindled, people left the cities, causing a decline of the city-state government; See Robert Coates-Stephens, 'The walls and aqueducts of Rome in the early Middle Ages, A.D. 500–1000', *The Journal of Roman Studies*, 88 (1998): 166–78.

32 See Frank M. Stenton, *The first century of English feudalism* (Oxford, 1961); J.M.W. Bean, *The decline of English feudalism, 1215–1540* (Manchester, 1968); Jerome Blum, *The end of the old order in rural Europe* (Princeton, 1978).

33 See, for instance, Ferdinand Lot, *The end of the ancient world and the beginnings of the Middle Ages* (London, 1953); Stenton; J.M.W. Bean, *The decline of English feudalism, 1215–1540* (Manchester, 1968); Blum.

34 See Brian Tierney, *Religion, law, and the growth of constitutional thought, 1150–1650* (Cambridge, 1982); Kenneth Pennington, *The Prince and the Law, 1200–1600: Sovereignty and rights in the Western legal tradition* (Berkeley, 1993); Thomas Ertman, *Birth of the leviathan: building states and regimes in mediæval and early modern Europe* (Cambridge, 1997); Heinrich Mittels, *The state in the middle ages: a comparative constitutional history of feudal Europe*, trans. H.F. Orton (Amsterdam, 1975).

35 See John Hudson, *Land, law, and lordship in Anglo-Norman England* (Oxford, 1994). There were however signs of a more complex form of constitution emerging; See Arthur P. Monahan, *Consent, coercion, and limit: the mediæval origins of parliamentary democracy* (Leiden, 1987).

36 See Jonathan Dewald, *The European nobility, 1400–1800* (Cambridge, 1996). See also Richard Gorski, *The fourteenth-century sheriff: English local administration in the late Middle Ages* (Woodbridge, 2003).

37 See Henry Loyn, *The governance of Anglo-Saxon England, 500–1087* (London, 1984).

38 See Jean Gimpel, *The Mediæval Machine: the industrial revolution of the Middle Ages* (London, 1977); Steven Justice, *Writing and rebellion: England in 1381* (Berkeley, 1994).

39 The wide definition may be taken from Marc Bloch, *Feudal Society* (Chicago 1961).

40 Stenton.

41 Frederic Maitland, *Domesday Book and Beyond – three essays on the early history of England* (New York, 1966, first published 1897).

42 M.T. Clanchy, *England and its Rulers, 1066–1272: Foreign Lordship and National Identity* (London, 1983), p. 83.

43 In Latinized German *mundium* or *mundeburdis*.

44 *Commendatio*.

45 *Dominus*.

46 Francois Ganshof, *Feudalism*, trans. Philip Grierson (London, 1952, first published 1944), pp. 5–8.

47 Commendation, by which men assumed the reciprocal obligations of service and protection, grew out of the needs of the later Roman Empire. While the services owed by a vassal might be domestic, economic, military or all three, where the land he owned was allodial land, the new lord would normally receive the land and grant it back to the new tenant. In this way, the greater part of western Europe passed into the lands of the baronage, and in Germany at least, prepared the way for their political independence as well.

Yet it was in England, where the remaining allodial land passed to the Crown under William the Conqueror, that the central authority grew most at the expense of the baronage, and the reasons must lie in part in the feudal structure which he imposed: G.W. Hinde, D.W. McMorland and P.B.A. Sim, *Land Law* (Wellington, 1978), vol. 1, pp. 7–8. Feudalism, by farming out Crown lands, was necessary to raise revenues, as well as military service: G.C. Cheshire, *Modern Law of Real Property*, ed. E.H. Burn (13th edn, London, 1982), p. 10.

48 Ganshof, pp. 55–6.
49 Although this was common.
50 The imperial princes or *Reichsfürsten*.
51 Ganshof, pp. 145–9.
52 The redistribution of land in 1066 led to an enormous increase in the resources of the Crown, especially in the demesne lands of the king: John Cannon and Ralph Griffiths, *The Oxford Illustrated History of the British Monarchy* (Oxford, 1988), p. 160. The Conqueror allowed all Englishmen who recognised him as king to redeem by money payments the estates which by right of conquest had momentarily passed to him: Cheshire, p. 12.
53 Sir William Anson, *The Law and Custom of the Constitution*, ed. A.B. Keith (5th edn, Oxford 1922; 3rd ed 1907), vol. 2, Part 1, pp. 8–9.
54 Tenure by frankalmoign ('free alms'), which elsewhere was regarded as allodial, was in England after the Conquest regarded as a feudal tenement carrying with it an obligation of prayer.
55 Cheshire, p. 13.
56 Ganshof, pp. 149–51.
57 Anson, *The Law and Custom of the Constitution*, pp. 8–9.
58 Frank Barlow, *The Feudal Kingdom of England, 1042–1216* (2nd edn, London, 1961, first published 1955), p. 108.
59 Walter Ullmann, 'This Realm of England is an Empire', *Journal of Ecclesiastical History*, 30 (1979): 175–203.
60 J.P. Canning, 'Law, sovereignty and corporation theory, 1300–1450' in J.H. Burns (ed.), *The Cambridge History of Mediæval Political Thought c.350–c.1450* (Cambridge, 1988), pp. 465–7.
61 Ibid., pp. 467–71.
62 In 1485 Chief Justice Huse observed that the king was superior to the pope within his realm, and answerable directly to God: YB Hil 1 Hen VII fol. 10 pl. 10. Appeals to the papal courts, which were only abolished by the Ecclesiastical Appeals Act 1532 (24 Hen VIII c 12) and s 4 of the Submission of the Clergy Act 1533 (25 Hen VIII c 19), were prohibited, otherwise than with the royal assent, by the Constitutions of Clarendon 1164. The Ecclesiastical Appeals Act 1532 itself did not expressly confer a *potestas ordinis* (authority for certain purposes which only the possession of holy orders could confer). It was only a *potestas jurisdictionis*, but such a jurisdiction could be pushed far beyond questions of property, of discipline, and of morality.
63 Majesty, the sense of awe-inspiring greatness, in particular, the attribute of divine or sovereign power, was part of the legacy of Rome. The *maiestas* of the Republic or the people of Rome had become that of the emperor, the *maiestas augustalis*. The crime against the majesty of the republic, *crimeri laesae*, became the crime against the emperor, the later *lèse-majesté* or treason. Western emperors were frequently called majesty after the letter of Q. Aurelius Symnachus to Theodosius I. Eastern emperors were styled μεγαλειοτεσ. The Holy Roman emperors were styled 'Majesty' from the time of Louis the Pious.

Kings (such as Henry II of England), popes, cardinals and archbishops were occasionally to enjoy the style. Hugh, Vount of Champagne, was so styled by his own clerks in a letter to the monks of Saint-Remi in 1114, as was Philip the Good, Duke of Burgundy, in a letter from the citizens of Ghent in 1453. Most of these were however instances of a superior being addressed by an inferior, and so did not establish a precedent.

The emperor Charles V allowed the style to King Francis I of France in 1544, though it was qualified by the addition of 'Royal' while Charles styled himself 'Caesarean Majesty'. This technique was adopted generally in subsequent centuries, though not immediately in Spain, whose king was styled 'Majesty' as Charles V was both king and emperor. However, in the eighteenth century the style of qualification used was borrowed from that used by the papacy in addressing sovereigns. Thus the French monarch, styled by the Popes the 'Most Christian King', became 'His Most Christian Majesty'. The Spanish king became 'His Catholic Majesty', while the Portugal was 'His Most Faithful Majesty'.

The Holy Roman Emperor, and his successor the Austrian emperor, was the 'Imperial and Apostolic', the 'Apostolic' coming from the Kingdom of Hungary. In the United Kingdom, the style is 'His (or Her) Britannic Majesty'. 'His Majesty' is usually enough for use within a sovereign's own realms, but may be amplified, in British usage, 'His Most Gracious Majesty', 'His Most Excellent Majesty', or 'His Sacred Majesty', the latter being common in the sixteenth and seventeenth centuries, the others still used occasionally in certain formal instruments.

64 Cannon and Griffiths, p. 203.

65 At great risk to the perpetrators in Heaven and on earth.

66 Cannon and Griffiths, p. 205.

67 Frank Barlow, *The Feudal Kingdom of England*, pp. 112–13.

68 *Diffidatio*.

69 Frank Barlow, *The Feudal Kingdom of England*, p. 113.

70 Kenneth Pennington, 'Law, Legislative authority and theories of government, 1150–1300' in Burns, *The Cambridge History of Mediæval Political Thought c.350–c.1450*, p. 443.

71 A mixture of monarchy, aristocracy, and democracy.

72 St Thomas Aquinas, *Summa theologiæ* (London, 1963), 1.2 q. 1051.

73 John of Paris, *De potestate regia et papali, Johannes Quidort von Paris Über Königliche under päpstliche Gewalt*, ed. F. Bleienstein (Stuttgart, 1969), ch. 19.

74 Jean Dunbabin, 'Government', in Burns, *The Cambridge History of Mediæval Political Thought c.350–c.1450*, pp. 482–3.

75 'Monarchy is the best form of government': Aristotle, *Ethica Nicomachea*, eds R.A. Gauthier and E.J. Brill (Rotterdam, 1972–74), viii, 10, 1160b.

76 James Campbell, *Essays in Anglo-Saxon History* (London, 1986), p. 167.

77 Ibid., pp. 171–2.

78 The dissolution of the monasteries caused a revolution in land ownership comparable with 1066: Cannon and Griffiths, p. 324.

79 Robin Fleming, *Kings and Lords in Conquered England* (Cambridge, 1991), p. 216.

80 This distribution of financial obligations across the entire kingdom allowed a much more efficient royal economy than was available in France or Germany. The ransom for King Richard I was raised 1193–94 by the justiciar using the whole range of feudal and more ancient levies. Levied were a scuttage at 20s, the knights' fee, a tallage on the royal demesne, and a quarter of a man's movable goods and revenues (or a fine instead). More was required, and a *geld* at 2s, the year's crop of wool from the Cistercians and Gilbertines, and the treasure from the churches were taken. All in

fact were fairly apportioned, and reflected the obligation on a vassal to redeem their captive lord: Frank Barlow, *The Feudal Kingdom of England*, p. 389.

81 Ibid., pp. 185–6.

82 M.T. Clanchy, *England and its Rulers*, p. 121.

83 Robin Frame, *The Political Development of the British Isles 1100–1400* (Oxford, 1990), pp. 101–2. From the time of Edward I the influence of the civil law on the development of the common declined. But the legacy of Roman law was still felt in equity. All Chancellors till Wolsey, with one or two exceptions, were clerics as well as statesmen, and consequently learned in canon and civil law rather than the common law. It was therefore to the Roman system that they would naturally turn for a reason, if it could be found, when it was necessary to 'abate the rigour of the common law'. The law merchant (especially that part relating to maritime law) not only had its origin in Roman law, but was developed by civilians in the Admiralty Courts.

As a result of the Renaissance there was a heated controversy over whether there should be a general reception of Roman law. This was fought by scholars, in favour of reception, and the common lawyers, who were opposed. The common lawyers won, but the Church courts survived the Reformation, and preserved their jurisdiction over wills and matrimonial causes. Since they had virtually adopted a civil law procedure, as well as many rules of Roman jurisprudence, advocates in the Church courts were civilians of Doctors' Commons, and could plead only as doctors of the civil law.

After the renaissance, the common law was too mature to be much influenced by external sources, with the exception of the law merchant. Equity was now more inclined to rely on invention, rather than borrow from the principles of the civil law. The law merchant itself is still developing, but is more influenced by the customs of the modern commercial world than by the considered ideas of the Roman world. The same holds true for admiralty law.

84 Stanley Chrimes, *Lancastrians, Yorkists and Henry VII* (2nd edn, London, 1966), p. 4.

85 Ibid., p. 32.

86 Stanley Chrimes, C.D. Ross and RA Griffiths (eds), *Fifteenth-century England 1399–1509* (Manchester, 1972), p. 30.

87 Ibid., p. 32.

88 Cannon and Griffiths, p. 208.

89 Stanley Chrimes, *Lancastrians, Yorkists and Henry VII*, pp. 124–5.

90 Ibid., p. 178.

91 Cannon and Griffiths, p. 211.

92 Ibid., p. 213.

93 There were, of course, many advances at times, especially during the Renaissance of the eleventh and twelfth centuries.

94 See John Man, *The Gutenberg revolution: the story of a genius and an invention that changed the world* (London, 2002). For a slightly later period see David Zaret, *Origins of democratic culture: printing, petitions, and the public sphere in early-modern England* (Princeton, 2000); Alexandra Halasz, *The marketplace of print: pamphlets and the public sphere in early modern England* (Cambridge, 1997).

95 Including with Byzantium, the heart of the eastern empire; See Deno John Geanakoplos, *Constantinople and the West: essays on the late Byzantine (Palaeologan) and Italian Renaissances and the Byzantine and Roman churches*

(Madison, c.1989); Krijnie N. Ciggaar, *Western travellers to Constantinople: the West and Byzantium, 962–1204: cultural and political relations* (Leiden, 1996).

96 See Aziz Suryal Atiya, *Crusade, commerce and culture* (Bloomington, 1962); Vladimir P. Goss and Christine Verzair Bornstein (eds), *The Meeting of two worlds: cultural exchange between East and West during the period of the Crusades* (Kalamazoo, 1986).

97 See David Boucher and Paul Kelly (eds), *The social contract from Hobbes to Rawls* (London, 1994); Patrick Riley, *Will and political legitimacy: a critical exposition of social contract theory in Hobbes, Locke, Rousseau, Kant, and Hegel* (Cambridge, 1982); Martyn P. Thompson, *Ideas of contract in English political thought in the age of John Locke* (New York, 1987).

98 It is probably both working together. The spread of knowledge led to greater awareness, and greater demands. But it is also true that these tools were also utilized by the state, and this subtly changed the ways in which it operated. For instance, the increased administrative efficiency of central government encouraged centralization. See, for example, the decline of the offices of sheriff and coroner; Judith A. Green, *English sheriffs to 1154* (London, 1990); Richard Gorski, *The fourteenth-century sheriff: English local administration in the late Middle Ages* (Woodbridge, 2003); R.F. Hunnisett, *The mediæval coroner* (Cambridge, 1961).

99 As generally in England, and the Protestant parts of Europe.

100 See Joseph Loewenstein, *The author's due: printing and the prehistory of copyright* (Chicago, 2002).

101 McGinnis, 6; Detlev F. Vagts, 'State Succession: The Codifiers View', *Virginia Journal of International Law*, 33 (1993): 275–97.

102 Hermann Heller, 'The Decline of the Nation State and its Effect on Constitutional and International Economic Law', *Cardozo Law Review*, 18 (1996): 1139, 1142.

103 See M.T. Clanchy, *From memory to written record, England 1066–1307* (Oxford, 1993).

104 See Michael A. Mullett, *The Catholic Reformation* (London, 1999); Nicholas S. Davidson, *The Counter-Reformation* (Oxford, 1987).

105 William V. Bangert, *A History of the Society of Jesus* (2nd edn, rev. and updated, St Louis, 1986); Steven Harris, 'Jesuit Ideology and Jesuit Science: Scientific Activity in the Society of Jesus, 1540–1773' (1988) University of Wisconsin – Madison PhD thesis.

106 See Sidney Pollard, *Essays on the industrial revolution in Britain*, ed. Colin Holmes (Aldershot, 2000); Margaret C. Jacob, *Scientific culture and the making of the industrial West* (New York, 1997).

107 William E. Scheuerman, 'Constitutionalism in an age of speed', *Constitutional Commentary*, 19 (2002): 353–90, 357–8. Koselleck highlights key aspects of early modern history, including innovations in transportation and communications inspired by mercantilism, as motivating forces behind much of this development; Reinhart Koselleck, *Zeitschichten* (Frankfurt, 2000), pp. 157–8.

108 See Paul Slack, *The English poor law, 1531–1782* (New York, 1995).

109 See Arthur J. Taylor, *Laissez-faire and state intervention in nineteenth-century Britain* (London, 1972); Sir Norman Chester, *The English administrative system, 1780–1870* (Oxford, 1981). See also Roy MacLeod (ed.), *Government and expertise: specialists, administrators, and professionals, 1860–1919* (Cambridge, 1988);

Bernard S. Silberman, *Cages of reason: the rise of the rational state in France, Japan, the United States, and Great Britain* (Chicago, 1993).

110 See Nancy D. LoPatin, *Political unions, popular politics and the great Reform Act of 1832* (New York, 1999); John Charlton, *The Chartists: the first national workers' movement* (London, 1997).

111 See Arthur J. Taylor, *Laissez-faire and state intervention in nineteenth-century Britain.*

112 Though it could equally be said that it was the social changes which led to constitutional changes – particularly the growth in disparity between those places represented in Parliament, and those which had the largest populations; See John K. Walton, *The Second Reform Act* (London, 1987).

113 See Woodruff D. Smith, *European imperialism in the nineteenth and twentieth centuries* (Chicago, c.1982).

114 For an illustration of these, see Adam Kirkaldy, *British shipping: its history, organization and importance, with a map of main routes and coaling stations and full appendices* (London, 1914).

115 Dava Sobel, *Longitude: the true story of a lone genius who solved the greatest scientific problem of his time* (New York, 1995).

116 See Tom Standage, *The Victorian Internet: the remarkable story of the telegraph and the nineteenth century's online pioneers* (London, 1999).

117 See Alpheus H Snow, *The administration of dependencies: a study of the evolution of the federal empire, with special reference to American colonial problems* (New York, 1902); *Analysis of the system of government throughout the British Empire* (London, 1912); John W. Cell, *British colonial administration in the mid-nineteenth century: the policy-making process* (New Haven, 1970); Cedric Lowe, *The reluctant imperialists: British foreign policy, 1878–1902* (London, 1967).

118 See, for instance, Noel Cox, 'The control of advice to the Crown and the development of executive independence in New Zealand', *New Zealand Armed Forces Law Review*, 13 (2001): 166–89.

119 See George Winterton, 'The evolution of a separate Australian crown', *Monash University Law Review*, 19 (1993): 1–22; Noel Cox, 'The control of advice to the Crown and the development of executive independence in New Zealand'. The office of secretary of state also evolved over time, partly as a consequence of greater emphasis upon external affairs; David Kynaston, *The Secretary of State* (Lavenham, 1978).

120 As exemplified in the era of 'gunboat diplomacy', for instance, Miriam Hood, *Gunboat diplomacy, 1895–1905: great power pressure in Venezuela* (London, 1975).

121 See, for instance, the 1848 revolutions on the European continent; See Rudolf Stadelmann, *Social and political history of the German 1848 revolution*, trans. J.G. Chastain (Athens, 1975).

122 These may be compared with the development of the United States in the nineteenth century, which was accelerated by the construction of the railways, and – somewhat earlier – states and empires such as Zimbabwe, built upon gold-mining; See Innocent Pikirayi, *The Zimbabwe culture: origins and decline of southern Zambezian states* (Walnut Creek, c.2001).

Chapter 7

Changes in the Present

7.1 Introduction

We will now look at several contemporary technological revolutions, in an attempt to identify the effect these are having upon constitutions. Because the current technological revolution is essentially a 'knowledge revolution,' the two examples which will be used are both of this broad type of technology – telecommunications, and the Internet.[1]

Both of these technologies are aspects of the communications revolution. As in earlier eras, communications today are crucial to the development and preservation of civilization and of legal systems. The existence of efficient modes of communications benefits individuals, groups and communities, and governments and societies as political, economic and social entities. The more efficient the communications system the greater the benefit to the community – and the greater the potential implications at a constitutional level.

The Internet is possibly the single most significant technological innovation of the late twentieth century, but its advent was only possible through the development of computer technology, and the extension of this into homes and offices. By including both information technology in general, and the Internet in particular, we will be able to explore the nature of different technologies and their general relationship to legal, social and political economic structures.

7.2 Telecommunications

A contemporary movement toward the deregulation of telecommunications is a worldwide phenomenon, though there is little or no general pattern.[2] This has particularly contributed to a revolution in information technology – but it is also the result of new communications systems offering new potential for use. The revolution in information technology is arguably changing society fundamentally, and will probably continue to do so in the foreseeable future.[3] This is having significant economic and social effects, but it is not yet clear that there are constitutional implications.

The infrastructure of an information society[4] (as any other) will have unique social, economic and political aspects – but it is only with the latter that we are here concerned. Computers and information technology such as telecommunications and management science models for decision-making are commonly used by government agencies in many countries.[5] They affect the relationships between the organs of government, but could also, in Kraemer's view, endanger personal privacy and political elections, and, to a lesser extent, the separation of powers and (American) federalism.[6] The reasons for this lie in the fact that telecommunications lead to faster communications and less need for intermediate levels of government – and therefore an increasingly focus on the centre.

McGinnis argues that the United States constitution, while at the heart of the steady growth of the United States over the last two hundred years, helping it to become an economic superpower by the beginning of the twentieth century, contained within itself the seeds of its own destruction.[7] The drop in transportation costs which were a consequence of the encouragement and facilitation of inter-state commerce undermined the core attachment of citizens to their individual states. The rationale for the existence of intermediary governments was weakened as management – rather than leadership – from the centre became feasible. But these states were seen as a necessary condition for federalism to resist dissolution by interest groups,[8] and to act as a counter-weight to centralization. This tension – between centre and periphery – has been exacerbated by the advent of modern means of telecommunications, though it was always present. In the United States in particular, this has allegedly led to a decline in the enumerated powers – those reserved to the states at the expense of the federal government – through judgments of the United States Supreme Court, principally as a reaction to technological changes.[9] Thus the balance between federal and state powers, which has been characterized as a key to economic success, was changed, in McGinnis' view, because of the advent of telecommunications.[10]

But it may be questioned whether this is an instance of changes in technology causing change in society – which therefore results in changes to the law – or whether it is actually an instance of technology itself directly changing the constitution. The latter would be unusual in a complex, multi-faceted legal system reflecting an equally complex political entity, though it would not necessarily be impossible, if the catalyst were significant enough. Because of the mode of change in McGinnis' model – through the United States Supreme Court's constitutional exegesis[11] – changes in the United States could arguably be more the latter than the former (direct influence). The Supreme Court reacts to specific technical questions which arise because of technological change, and makes direct changes to the informal constitution as a consequence – and in some cases to the formal Constitution as well through its role in constitutional interpretation.

However, it would be unwise to attempt to identify too clearly a distinction between technology changing society, and society changing the constitution, and technology changing the constitution directly. In practice both technology and society are at work simultaneously upon the constitution.[12] It may be, however, that the centralizing tendency of telecommunications, of which McGinnis wrote, is affecting the constitution as directly as is possible in a complex modern pluralist society.

Not all of these changes need be unwelcome. There is some optimism about the use of what has been styled 'e-government' in a wider role of reinvigorating traditional forms of democracy. This can include the use of e-voting – though only limited experiments have yet been made in this field[13] – to steps to strengthen the dialogue between citizen and government. This latter could involve aspects of participatory democracy.[14] But it has been observed that it could potentially lead to 'echo chambers' of our own opinions, magnifying and confirming our inclinations and resulting in a deeply polarised – and individualized – society.[15] Thus participatory democracy, while strengthening the direct links between state and individual, could weaken the broader fabric of community and society.

Internationally as well as domestically developments in information technology are having their effects. The development and operation of international organisations, such as the United Nations, and the World Trade Organization, have been influenced by the ready availability of communications tools, some of which result in the bypassing of pre-existing systems for consultation and decision-making.

Another aspect of the influence that the telecommunications revolution has been having is in the growth of non-governmental organizations and movements. One recent significant instance is the World Summit on Information Society (WSIS). The WSIS was endorsed by United Nations General Assembly Resolution 56/183 (21 December 2001), and was held in two phases under the auspices of the International Telecommunications Union. The first phase of WSIS took place in Geneva in 2003 and hosted by the Government of Switzerland. It addressed a broad range of themes concerning the Information Society and adopted a Declaration of Principles and Plan of Action. The objective of the first phase was to develop and foster a clear statement of political will and to take steps to establish the foundations for an information society for all of humanity. The second phase was held in Tunis in 2005 and hosted by the Government of Tunisia. This concentrated upon the implementation of the plan, and especially the means for bridging the information divide between countries richly-endowed with information technology, and those less well equipped.

Although countries took part in the deliberations of the WSIS, participants included intergovernmental organizations, NGOs and businesses. It did not escape the consequences of being essentially a political process – with the most powerful participants being the representatives of the largest and richest countries – yet it was an international approach to an international challenge, that of the management of information technology in a global environment. States were not neglected, but the proxies were no longer solely the representatives of states. They now included ostensibly – and actually – independent actors.

Information technology primarily involves the control of data. Unlike the special sub-set of the information technology revolution which we call the Internet, information technology in general is concerned with all aspects of the creation, storage, dissemination and analysis of information. It is not ubiquitous, nor is it homogenous. Therefore the influence which it may have upon society, economy and the constitution will not be consistent. Specifically, it may very well be difficult to determine whether a particular technology – for example, personal computers (PC) – have a greater effect in one society than on another. The prevailing level of development, infrastructure and cultural and economic conditions of the society may mean that the PC has much less effect in one society than another. This may be simply due to the greater utilization of the technology in some countries than in others.

Since the impact of information technology is so dependent upon the underlying technological and economic base of the society it is difficult to formulate even general conjectures of the impact of these technologies upon constitutions. The most that can be said is that telecommunications technology offers new opportunities for governments and societies, but that it is uncertain whether the relationship between individual and state, or state and state, will be markedly altered.

7.3 The Internet

The Internet is also not homogeneous, in that the degree of adoption of the technology through which it operates is not found throughout the world in anything which even approximates consistency or equality. Yet by its inherent nature the Internet is ubiquitous and all-embracing – provided the relevant physical infrastructure is provided. Nor is its development necessarily subject primarily to government dictates. For these reasons the Internet and especially the regulation of the Internet is an especially important example in this study.[16]

It has been said that the nature and growing importance of the Internet requires a fundamental re-examination of the constitutional structure within which rule-making takes place.[17] The Internet, or cyberspace, may be seen to have an opposite effect to the centralizing effect of telecommunications (as everyone has access to data everyone can join new communities, leading to a decentralizing effect). Yet Internet-based direct democracy is theoretically possible,[18] as is globalization – the ultimate in centralization. These are clearly more than merely economic or social effects – they strike at the core of the constitution – but it remains to be seen precisely what the constitutional effects of the Internet will be. These will probably vary depending upon the level of Internet exposure, and the relative complexity and rigidity of each country's constitution.[19] The following will seek to explore some of the ramifications of the development of the Internet, in particular the constitutional effects – their effects upon legal systems.

We will begin with a definition of the Internet. The Internet, or 'cyberspace', is an interconnected electronic communications network. It has no physical existence as a whole, though comprised of a large number of individual networks.[20] In essence the Internet exists in a virtual world, rather than in the real, geographical, world.[21] The Internet has no controlling body,[22] although it does have a common language, allowing different operating systems to speak to one another.[23] In essence, it is a facilitator, a means by which computers may be linked, but its effect goes very much further.

As it is in theory simply an enormous communications device, it might be asked why (or indeed whether) the Internet presents particular difficulties for society, economy or constitution. It would appear that these difficulties are because of its global reach into homes, and its universality and immediacy. It is possible, for the first time, for traders to reach consumers directly, without any intermediaries.[24] It might even be possible to bypass national laws altogether. A state created on the Internet – were such a thing possible – would have no corporeal existence, yet it may be no less real for that. Such Internet states could conceivably be used to avoid taxation liability, particularly important in an age of electronic money.[25] Thus the primary problem is the potential threat to the role of the state, and hence to the state itself – both in superseding it but also, more immediately, in its challenge to the regulatory role of the state.

Taking full advantage of the Internet requires an adequate understanding of its potential consequences, and the rigorous adoption of appropriate countermeasures, for example, against serious losses of data confidentiality, system integrity, and resource availability. This is as true for governments as it is for business and individuals. But it remains unclear whether emerging computer and communication technologies introduce fundamental differences with respect to how society and constitutions must respond, or whether there will be merely evolutionary changes. Some commentators see a need for laws that are more clearly enforceable, and in some cases more technology-specific.[26] But this is a law-specific reaction, and is arguably not sufficiently broad. Social scientists are more likely to see many needs that transcend technology and the law.[27]

Certain specific areas of law have undoubtedly already been directly affected – such as information and personal privacy.[28] This has constitutional implications. Even taxation,[29] and government contracting has been affected[30] – the former because it was open to entrepreneurs to argue that they ought not to be subject to taxation for activities which took place in a virtual world[31] – and because of assessment and collection difficulties.

Corporate nationality may have to be rethought as a consequence of the Internet,[32] as well as franchise laws,[33] all of which are based, fundamentally, on state laws. It has also been said that the Internet will be critical for the development of environmental law.[34] Meanwhile, cyber-terrorism[35] remains as a potential threat, one which has been seen increasingly in recent years, as does spamming (the mass dispatch of unsolicited messages), as all those who are even occasional email users will know.[36] Some form of regulation is required, and this causes problems for states, not all of which are able or willing to regulate Internet use. Conceptually more importantly, it is by no means clear that there is a generally accepted regulatory model, or even one which enjoys majority support.

It is clear that, while specific laws are affected, the Internet, because of its scope for development, and its reach, is more than simply a tool, like any other telecommunications tool. It may bring about a new paradigm shift. The metaphor of the Internet as parallel to the American western frontier, a 'place' where government should generally refrain from regulation, has been criticized as misleading people into overestimating the Internet's ability to guarantee freedom and opportunity.[37] An alternative metaphor – that of the feudal society – has been proposed.[38] This metaphor emphasizes the role of law in the development of the Internet – and the mutual interdependence of users. Both may explain some aspects of the Internet, but are possibly incomplete of themselves.

The view which was common during the 1990s, of cyberspace as a place of freedom that cannot be regulated and that is more or less immune to control, has turned out to be far from correct.[39] Lawrence Lessig, who had been seen as one of the proponents of the libertarian view, has detected a trend towards more and more regulation through code under the influence of commerce regulation.[40] This would indicate that significant constitutional effects are less likely to occur. However, the nature of the Internet, and the way in which it was created and operates, give important indications as to possible constitutional consequences.

In Lessig's schema, 'code' is the architecture of the Internet; the software and hardware that make cyberspace what it is. It determines how easy it is to protect personal privacy or how easy it is to censor free speech. It determines whether access to information is general or whether specific information is zoned. It affects who sees what, or who or what is monitored. The architecture of cyberspace can be regulated in a host of ways, ways that one cannot begin to see unless you begin to understand the nature of such code and how it works.

At its highest level the Internet is co-ordinated by the Internet Assigned Numbers Authority (IANA) and a central Internet Registry (IR).[41] However, as might be expected of a system which has no single physical home, the Internet has no controlling body, though the ICANN (Internet Corporation for Assigned Names and Numbers) regulates some aspects of the 'net'. This is the non-profit corporation that was formed to assume responsibility for the Internet Protocol (IP) address space allocation, protocol parameter assignment, domain name system management, and root server system management functions previously performed under United States Government contract by the IANA and other entities.[42]

No one country can alone regulate the Internet effectively, as is seen in the internationalization of ICANN[43] – though it is possible for individual countries to exercise at least partial control of the Internet within their territory.[44] For primarily technological, economic and political reasons, self-regulation by the Internet Service Providers (ISPs) has been proposed as a suitable regulatory system for the Internet.[45] But it may be questioned whether self-regulation of the Internet is sufficient, particularly because of its transnational nature,[46] and because of the need for countries to regulate certain aspects of Internet use. However, there would appear to be some truth in these claims.

From the beginning ICANN attempted to achieve equitable regional representation. But the perception remained that it was dominated by western representatives, particularly those of the United States. Domain name registries remain dominated by companies based in the developed world. ICANN policymaking has also been castigated as having been 'captured' by a coalition dominated by 'IP lawyers, registries in the legacy root, and leading registrars'.

The limits of national control of the Internet were perhaps exaggerated.[47] Principally that is because nations are increasingly acting in concert to deal with the borderless nature of cyberspace by creating both relatively uniform laws across jurisdictions, and agreements for international co-operation in surveillance and investigation.[48] A country has no choice but to promote vigorously the introduction of new technology in order to maintain and increase its international competitiveness[49] – and this may mean the adoption of international norms – such as the United Nations Commission on International Trade Law (UNCITRAL), in the drafting of which it may have had comparatively little influence.[50] Increasingly, private non-state parties are regulating cyberspace.[51] The resulting uncertainty has led some to argue that law should recognize a separate jurisdiction, or even a separate sovereignty, for the Internet.[52]

Although the Internet might be a threat to sovereign authority, the Internet may also allow new opportunities for an increase in surveillance[53] and authority[54] – or for an increase in public participation in government. In addition to this globalizing effect, Grady argues that the Internet is affecting liberty.[55] He asserts that the traditional view has been pessimistic about information technology's probable effect on liberty.[56] His view is that the new networks, spawned by the Internet and other information technology, are hopeful developments.[57] Essentially, these break down constitutional, governmental and administrative barriers. This is a libertarian's dream world.

As well as possibly leading to increased liberty,[58] the Internet may potentially also improve the quality of development in less developed countries, through increased political participation and communication.[59] Kalir has also noted the trend towards democratization in the 1990s,[60] though whether it can be said to be seen as a defining phenomenon of globalization[61] may perhaps be doubted. Globalization itself can also be a tool against corruption.[62] Certainly greater exposure through improved communications, and increased expectations brought about by globalization, have raised awareness of different political, social and economic norms.

Sunstein has argued that, by increasing the possibility of community, the Internet has undermined the American republic.[63] In his view, the printing press helped create modern nationalism, as books and newspapers came to be written in the vernacular, encouraging a conception of a shared community among groups of people who would never actually meet. His concern is that through the Internet we may choose to find only 'echo chambers' of our own opinions, magnifying and confirming our inclinations and resulting in a deeply polarised society.[64] This is Grady's liberty carried to an extreme.[65] It has been countered with the obvious but important critique that cyberspace in fact also functions in exactly the opposite way – it allows us to discover the new, to learn about the unfamiliar, and to begin to understand one another.[66] What may be different about the Internet is not its function, but its breadth and scope. It is truly global,[67] or as global as anything can be in a largely heterogeneous world.

It should come as no surprise then that an emerging international law dimension of the Internet has been identified.[68] The reach of the Internet is global, and therefore its legal implications are global. If the Internet is to continue to function effectively it will be necessary to strengthen the architecture or code through which it operates,[69] but international law is also a means for preventing this from being captured by powerful private vested interests or by countries more advanced in computer technology.[70]

There is evidence that this latter may be already happening. The 2003 draft free-trade agreement between the United States and Singapore included a requirement that both countries participate in the ICANN Government Advisory Committee, the group that manages the Internet's domain name system. This involved adopting policies similar to ones created by ICANN,[71] which is a United States-based incorporation, subject to United States laws.[72] The United States' response to disputes over domain names (the Anticybersquatting Consumer Protection Act (ACPA)[73]) permits a trademark owner to seek cancellation or transfer of the domain name itself, thereby expanding the scope of the ACPA to encompass disputes with little direct connection to the United States.[74] It is perhaps inevitable that the United States should be in this position, given its dominant Internet presence. However, it is clearly unsatisfactory to have one country, however benign it might appear to be, dictating terms to others.

One possible solution is to draw from current economic regulation examples. The World Trade Organization (WTO) governance arrangements have traditionally reflected the interests of producers channelled through government trade negotiators. Abbott has argued that the producer-driven governance model is not suited to the highly integrated international society of the twenty-first century. He argues that the WTO governance structure should be adapted to account for more diverse interests, including those of marginalized developing countries, non-governmental organizations (NGOs), and individuals.[75] This view has also been advanced by McGinnis,[76] who envisages the prospect of international federalism through the WTO and other global economic organization.[77] But he also foresees such international federalism collapsing for much the same reason that he saw United States federalism decline – a tendency to centralization at the expense of the states.[78]

Both Lessig[79] and Vaidhyanathan[80] are concerned about the future of creativity in an increasingly regulated world in which knowledge is increasing turned into property, leading them to conclude that the world is faced with a crucial choice regarding the future of the Internet. This is not a choice which is cast along ideological or political lines, but rather a choice between old and new conceptions of legal regulation, property, and creativity.[81] This raises constitutional issues – concerns about the role of the state in the economy and society. Nor can we be sure whether regulation of the Internet is impeding commerce, or aiding it.[82] The Napster case has been seen as a symbol heavy with political overtones about the future of the relationship between innovation and law in a high technology world.[83] This case involved an online music service which utilized peer-to-peer file-sharing – which facilitated the exchange of music files in breach of copyright laws. Although the original service was closed down by court order decentralized file-sharing, which is much more difficult to regulate, has survived. This case illustrated more than any other the challenge to regulation which the Internet brings. Traditional copyright laws could be enforced – at a cost – but there was often a technical means of avoiding liability.

We can see a range of tensions, between countries, and within countries, including between states where there is a federal constitution. It is not yet clear what the long-term effects of the Internet will be, but so far we see a tendency to centralization (including usurpation of regulation by federal government),[84] and increased international co-operation (as for UNCITRAL). This latter example is particularly apparent in the field of international commerce.

7.3.1 The Internet and Commerce

The Internet is having a particularly important impact upon commerce, especially business-to-consumer commerce.[85] It is altering the nature of global trade in ways of which we can only guess at. But the analogy between the rise of a separate law of cyberspace and the Law Merchant – the international legal rules and procedures which regulated commerce for centuries – has been observed.[86] This analogy may give us some guidance to the possible legal and broader constitutional implications of the Internet.

Commerce has rarely if ever been exclusively national. Throughout the course of human history the practical realities of international trade meant that much business was conducted at a distance, often overseas, with only limited opportunities for face-to-face contact between merchants.[87] Many transactions were conducted by agents, whilst many relied upon correspondence. In Europe, and those countries which derived their legal traditions from that continent, each form of trade was regulated by rules of private international law, including the custom and usages of the merchants, what became known as the Law Merchant, or *lex mercatoria*.[88] Gerard de Malynes regarded Law Merchant as customary law approved by the authority of all kingdoms and not as law established by the sovereignty of any prince.[89] It was the 'law of all nations.'[90] It was thus a form of international law. Certain elements of the modern commercial law grew out of the Law Merchant,[91] which indeed continues to develop today as customary private international law.[92] Custom is general state practice accepted as law.[93] The elements of custom are a generalized repetition of similar acts by competent state authorities and a sentiment that such acts are juridically necessary to maintain and develop international relations.[94]

The Law Merchant evolved over a relatively long period of time, so that no particular country or era could be said to have had an excessive influence on its development.[95] The process was largely evolutionary and, in so far as it was not imposed by a single sovereign state, was democratic.[96] It was largely created by the merchants themselves,[97] though subject to alteration by individual states.[98] This latter process became more pronounced – particularly during the eighteenth and nineteenth centuries[99] – but the Law Merchant remained and still remains a supra-national law.[100] It may be that the same will be said of the Internet also, when its definitive history is written.[101]

The almost instantaneous global reach of the Internet and the potentially adverse affects of the Internet on countries – particularly in economic and social terms – combine to ensure that governments have responded to the challenge of this emerging technology. But they have not responded consistently.

Unlike the *lex mercatoria*, which developed over an extended period of time, just as customary international law has traditionally developed,[102] the growth of the Internet may not permit the international community the luxury of time to develop customary rules. For this reason states may have little choice but to defer to the views of the majority, or the stronger economic blocks, whatever implications that may have for the longer-term future of state sovereignty, and for domestic laws.[103]

The approaches of states vary, as might be expected. In its broad approach to the Internet the United States has chosen to rely on self-regulation[104] rather than direct regulation. This is subject to increasingly important exceptions, however, such as with respect to Internet pornography,[105] and where national security concerns prevail.[106] The latter is of increasing importance, especially in Europe and North America. The Federal Trade Commission (FTC) has also been seeking a more active role with regard to spammers.[107] An alternative approach to that of self-regulation is a balance of self-regulation and direct regulation, as has been advocated by the European Union.[108] A third option would be direct regulation, which also has support, as for instance in China.[109] Thus far there has been little sign of a global consensus developing as to the appropriate form of Internet regulation, domestic, trans-national, or international, or a combination of one or more of these. This presents major problems, in particular for the consumer of goods and services sold via the Internet. It also prevents the adoption of consistent approaches to cyber-crime jurisdiction, for instance.

The international aspect of the Internet also has implications for constitutions. Legislation is no longer overwhelmingly domestic in origin, even though it may still be enacted by domestic legislative bodies,[110] due to an increasing number of treaties and conventions. Some legislative provisions have been made to accommodate this new grundnorm of the globalization of electronic commerce.[111] If commerce is now seen to be primarily international in nature, the role of domestic law is restricted. The limitations of paper-based evidential requirements when faced with the requirements of modern electronic communications are a case in point. The United Nations Commission on International Trade Law (UNCITRAL) Model Law on Electronic Commerce provides that an electronic signature may be legally effective as a manual signature, but does not define an electronic signature.[112] Thus although international treaties or conventions may give some guidance, it remains for the domestic legislature to provide the detail.

As an example, the Electronic Transactions Act 2000 (NZ) is based on work carried out by the New Zealand Law Commission, and closely follows both the Model Law on Electronic Commerce prepared by UNCITRAL in 1996 and the Australian Electronic Transactions Act 1999 (Cth) – the latter heavily influenced by UNCITRAL.[113] The purpose of the Electronic Transactions Act is to facilitate the use of electronic technology. It does this by reducing uncertainty regarding the legal effect of electronic communications, and allows certain paper-based legal requirements to be met by using functionally equivalent electronic technology.[114]

The Act is predicated upon the idea that the principles applicable to the making of a contract by electronic means should be no different to the principles applicable to contracts formed orally or in writing on paper. Indeed, the decided cases appear to have accepted that proposition as self-evident.[115] These principles may vary from country to country, as for instance in the concept of consideration, though there are certain points upon which all jurisdictions agree.

It is these common elements which form the basis for the United Nations Commission on International Trade (UNCITRAL) Model Law on Electronic Commerce. Under article 7 of the Model Law, the elements of the functional equivalent to a signature are the need:

1. To identify the person and to indicate that person's approval of the information contained in the data message; and
2. For the method to be as reliable as was appropriate for the purpose for which the message was generated or communicated.[116]

Article 7 only applies where a signature is a requirement of law in the relevant jurisdiction. Where a signature is not required by law then the normal rules in relation to proving an agreement apply. These general rules allow some flexibility to domestic law. But they also impose some common standards.

Whilst it is not unusual for domestic laws to be influenced by international developments, it is perhaps true that New Zealand – and most other countries – had little choice but to adopt the UNCITRAL model, and alter its domestic laws accordingly.[117] The nature of electronic commerce has some important differences from traditional trade, not least of which is its speed and universality, and general lack of physical evidence. This former attribute means that the electronic age poses particular problems for municipal legal systems, and for the states which created them.

Although there was always an important international law element, all law was – and is – *prima facie* territorial in nature.[118] But many international laws were recognized by national legal systems, just as the laws of war involved both domestic and international elements.[119] In the English experience, which was to largely shape the laws of the common law world, these international laws were recognized by the law, albeit often at the instigation of Parliament.[120] Although the substantive law and procedures of the common law world broadly reflected the international character of trade, it was also influenced by the insular tendencies of domestic law.[121] This was scarcely surprising since it was administered in national courts, imbued with the approach of a national legal system.[122] Sometimes the domestic influences prevailed, and the law was but little affected by international developments.[123] At other times international developments had a great influence on domestic laws.[124] In part this depended upon the contemporary strength of the individual nation-state, or upon its size and international influence.[125]

The advent of modern electronic trade conducted through the Internet, and the consequent challenges to territorial borders, combined with the growth in regional free-trade alliances, has meant that there is an increased emphasis upon the international aspects of law.[126] But though the number of international treaties and conventions has increased,[127] this is only partly a consequence of technological change. Globalization, for political and economic reasons, continues to have widespread effects on law. Nor is the Internet, as a challenge to the legal system, a novel phenomenon.[128] Domestic legal systems have faced before the challenge of accommodating other legal traditions and technological changes.[129] What may be different now is the extent to which the changes which this new technology brings are being decided at international and supranational level, and this has important implications for national sovereignty and independence.[130] Indeed, it has been said that the view that the nation-state alone should monopolize international affairs in an increasingly inadequate proposition.[131]

The literature on the jurisdictional challenges of e-commerce is voluminous, and is largely focussed on private law aspects of this issue, namely whose courts and whose laws will apply in relation to private disputes arising out of e-commerce.[132] These rules are those of private international law, or the rules of conflict of laws. The fundamental question, in any legal dispute, is in which country's legal system will the dispute be resolved? This is the forum question, and concerns the jurisdiction.[133] Secondly, whose law will apply to the transaction? This is the choice of law question – the proper or applicable law.[134] Thirdly, there is the question of the recognition and enforcement of judgements.[135] In the absence of evidence that foreign law applies, courts have traditionally applied the substantive and procedural rules of the forum.[136] In theory the Internet should not change this.

These rules have developed over time, and have been influenced by international conventions, such as the Hague,[137] Brussels and Lugano (for the European Union),[138] and Rome Conventions.[139] But each country has its own conflict of laws rules,[140] and there is no effective or established customary international law that regulates personal jurisdiction[141] – despite the failed attempt to introduce a Hague Convention on International Jurisdiction and Foreign Judgments in Civil and Commercial Matters.[142] The position in New Zealand is that the courts will have jurisdiction if documents initiating proceedings may properly be served on that court.[143] The United States position is that even if a foreign court passes a judgment or direction against a legal entity of a particular country say Country A, then that judgment or direction would not be applicable automatically to country A's legal entity or citizen.[144] Since 1995 there has been a great increase in the amount of cyberspace litigation, especially in the United States. Some courts have simply applied traditional jurisdictional rules,[145] while others have tried to devise new tests to accommodate the peculiarity of the medium.[146] This has caused uncertainty and difficulties for courts. But the precise nature of cyber-law remains uncertain. Is it primarily national law, or a mixture of national and international? Or is it (as some have suggested) altogether different?[147]

These are important questions, for the effective enforcement of consumer laws will only be possible if these can be answered, as there are limitations to what can be achieved through international co-operation alone. If enforcement remains purely (or perhaps, more accurately, principally) national, this itself presents difficulties, though not fundamentally different to those presented by traditional international trade.[148] However, the number of international contracts being made has greatly increased over time, and the proportion of these business-to-customer has increased at an even greater rate.[149] This has brought with it difficulties for national regulators and enforcement agencies, to whom their nationals turn when presented with a consumer grievance. The response from the regulators is varied, but that from the courts has generally been to apply national consumer laws over Internet contracts, wherever possible.[150] This presents important conflict of laws questions. For how may a consumer obtain legal redress against an Internet-based trader except by complex litigation through national courts? Consumer laws by their nature should be consumer-friendly, and should enable consumers to have recourse through national courts. Indeed, conflict of laws principles do allow laws to be applied extraterritorially.

Historically, there has been a legislative presumption against the extra-territorial application of public law statutes, as a matter of statutory interpretation.[151] This is based on a historical concern not to infringe on the sovereignty of other states (or provinces) by purporting to regulate conduct that occurs wholly within the boundaries of another jurisdiction.[152] Customary international law however permits a nation to apply its law to extraterritorial behaviour with substantial local effect,[153] as well as the extraterritorial conduct of its citizens or domiciliary.[154]

The United States Federal Trade Commission (FTC) acts against fraudulent and deceptive foreign e-businesses that harm United States consumers.[155] The FTC Act gives the FTC authority over acts 'in or affecting commerce' and defines 'commerce' to include 'commerce with foreign nations.'[156] The Act also gives the FTC specific authority to investigate practices that 'may affect the foreign trade of the United States.'[157]

United States' anti-trust laws provide a broad base for assertion of jurisdiction, which permit jurisdiction over foreign activities that have 'a direct, substantial, and reasonably foreseeable effect' on commerce in the United States.[158] However, extraterritorial enforcement by the United States often generates a perception abroad of a sort of 'United States' imperialism.'[159] This is particularly so where the effects are profound.[160] The extraterritorial application of the United States' antitrust laws caused considerable disquiet in other countries:

> Where a transnational antitrust issue is really a manifestation of a policy conflict between governments, it should be recognized that there may be no applicable international law to resolve the conflict. In such cases, resolution should be sought through the normal methods of consultation and negotiation. For one government to seek to resolve the conflict in its favour by invoking its national law before its domestic tribunals is not the rule of law but an application, in judicial guise, of the principle that economic might is right.[161]

Other countries have of course also applied their laws extraterritorially from time to time.[162] But the larger the economy the greater the influence, and perhaps, the greater the resentment of smaller economies. The political power of the country is also relevant. In *Libman*,[163] the Supreme Court of Canada ruled that it is sufficient that there be a 'real and substantial link' between the proscribed conduct and the jurisdiction seeking to apply and enforce its law.[164] Clearly, the 'real and substantial link' test for the proper assertion of prescriptive jurisdiction will often result in more than one, and perhaps many, jurisdictions being capable of properly asserting authority over conduct that has effects in more than one jurisdiction. It is this fact that suggests the need for clearer prescriptive jurisdictional rules,[165] especially for consumer laws. This is a constitutional dilemma, one which strikes at the heart of the nation-state.

Appropriately, when we are considering developments of supra-national laws, it is the European Union, the first successful supra-national state (embryonic though it remains in many respects) in modern times,[166] which has led the way. The European Union has been active in developing rules relating to jurisdictional issues in the context of e-commerce.[167] Undoubtedly this is facilitated by the existence of a treaty-based regime integral to the development of the Single Market, a regime that, perforce, has long provided for resolution of jurisdictional matters.[168] The primary instruments in the civil or private law context in this regard have been the Brussels Convention on Jurisdiction and the Enforcement of Judgments in Civil and Commercial Matters, which deal with jurisdiction to adjudicate matters as well as with the enforcement of extra-territorial judgments, and the Rome Convention on the Law Applicable to Contractual Obligations.[169] The latter determines which state's substantive law shall be applied in cross-border disputes.[170] The Brussels 2 Regulation is now also applicable.[171] But none of these have direct application to consumer laws.

Most private international law rules and principles are evolving, and may be traced some distance into the past. There is nothing new about courts being called upon to decide which court will have jurisdiction, which law will apply, or how judgment will be enforced. But these questions are rendered more difficult by the virtual nature of the Internet. Complex litigation – or arbitration – may be possible in business-to-business transactions involving millions of dollars, but are impracticable for business-to-consumer transactions and smaller commercial contracts. If governments fail to resolve this they fail in their prime function – and risk obsolescence.

Legal systems have developed rules for regulating disputes. But nineteenth and twentieth century conflict of laws principles do not satisfy the requirements of most modern consumer laws. These require immediate, simple, low-cost remedies.

For the most part the Internet is international, and its users are not adequately served by existing laws with respect to conflict of laws.[172] The efficacy of the concept of 'closest and most real connection'[173] is also reduced, in that no part of the world is any more directly affected than any other by events on the web, as information is available simultaneously to anyone with a connection to the Internet.[174] In the field of protection of intellectual property rights the same is also probably true.[175]

The difficulty facing national jurisdictions is partly one of enforcement,[176] which has led to other forms of regulation, including (but not limited to) transnational, international, institutional, sectoral and private.[177] There are an increasing number of examples of private control or self-regulatory control, sometimes involving codes.[178] Unfortunately these disparate approaches exasperate the already marked divisions.[179] Nor are there signs that international co-operation will be practical outside narrow legal fields such as copyright and operations against cyber-crime.[180] It is only possible in these narrow fields because of political will, and the relatively technical – rather than broader economic or political – nature of the issues.

To date, most efforts to address this deficiency have concentrated on increased international co-operation. Some of this is web-based, such as the econsumer.gov website, which tracks consumer complaints from a number of countries.[181] This co-operation often results in some degree of *de facto* self-regulation of the Internet. The Organization for Economic Co-operation and Development has issued guidelines calling on the organization's 30 member states – which include the United States, Japan, Germany and the United Kingdom – to cooperate in the fight against international fraud.[182] This clearly alludes to the problem of unsolicited commercial e-mail. The Internet may not be outside the law, but the application and enforcement of laws remain difficult. Ultimately, a new legal regime may emerge, one which responds to the difficulty of regulating a technology which has either insufficient, or conversely, too many laws.[183]

Whether in principle the Internet can, or should be, subject to international law (or efficiently regulated by such a system) is a question the answer to which could be as important as the adoption of the Law of Oléron[184] – which established the law of the sea, or the resolution of the Thirty Years War at the Treaty of Westphalia[185] – which inaugurated the modern concept of state sovereignty. Perhaps the response of governments to the age of electronic communications cannot be limited to the piecemeal adoption of laws in response to individual problems.

The Internet and the advent of almost instantaneous communications have had, and will continue to have, major effects upon international trade law. In particular, evidential rules founded on former paper-based procedures have not proven to be flexible enough to accommodate the advent of the Internet and contracts made in cyberspace.[186] Just as the Law Merchant evolved to accommodate contracts negotiated between parties who were physically apart, so cyberspace law must do so for the electronic age.

Traditionally, the formation of legal norms for conducting trade was by states, subject to certain principles accepted by the international community. But this has proven inadequate for the control of electronic commerce, because this can be said to be truly international, having no truly physical presence. The new environment has necessitated an increased degree of international co-ordination, if not co-operation. Unlike the evolutionary development of the *lex mercatoria*, the advent of electronic communications has resulted in the enforced adoption of international norms, such as the UNCITRAL Model Law on Electronic Commerce.[187]

This poses a threat to state sovereignty. It is no longer possible for the nation-state to be the sole, or even prime, regulator of economic norms. Decisions respecting the forms of law will be made not at the national level, but internationally. These will be made by political blocks such as the European Union and the United Nations, and, in some instances, by non-governmental organizations. The result could be the evolution of an international cyberspace law. But there are wider implications for national legal systems which cannot be ignored. Failure to protect and encourage international trade could well result in states being bypassed economically in favour of those which are more active in using the new avenues for the passage of tangible and intangible trade commodities and information.

7.3.2 The Internet and the State

A prediction made some years ago that the Internet would change international law because it would erode the dominance of the traditional sovereign state[188] has not become reality yet.[189] But the Internet is potentially a threat to state sovereignty,[190] and therefore has profound constitutional implications. The dominance of the nation-state, itself largely the product of the technological, economic and political conditions of the sixteenth to nineteenth centuries, is susceptible to a new technological paradigm.

Partly because of the international – and unregulated (or self-regulating) nature of the Internet, there has been a tendency to claim that the changes we observe in notions of sovereignty, the state, jurisdiction, and law in general are caused by the Internet.[191] It has been said that the very nature and growing importance of the net calls for a fundamental re-examination of the institutional structure within which rule-making takes place.[192] But this is a relatively extreme view. As has been observed by various writers, globalization of commerce is not a new phenomenon.[193] Nor would it necessarily be valid to assign to the one cause a range of paradigm changes in society, economics and governance.[194] Our existing international law is predicated largely on the existence of the sovereign state. The notions of sovereignty and statehood were once among the most important aspects of public international law. But it is not based solely upon this. We may however ask whether the Internet, as one of the newest and most potent technological innovations, threatens this dominance.

As Hall has noted, primarily international law governs the relations of independent states, but 'to a limited extent ... it may also govern the relations of certain communities of analogous character.'[195] Nor is he alone, similar views being expressed by other writers.[196] Lawrence also wrote that the subjects of international law are sovereign states, 'and those other political bodies which, though lacking many of the attributes of sovereign states, possess some to such an extent as to make them real, but imperfect, international persons.'[197] Whereas these scholars tended to define subjects of international law as states and certain unusual exceptions, there are others who go further in opening up the realm of reasonable subjects of the law of nations[198] – possibly to include the Internet.

The advent of the sovereign cyberspace is as far away as it ever was, but it remains true however that our existing international laws are predicated on the existence of the sovereign state. Its heyday was perhaps in the late nineteenth century, when sovereign states enjoyed almost unfettered independence of action.[199] International law has been called 'the sum of the rules or usages which civilized states have agreed shall be binding upon them in their dealings with one another.'[200] But the norms of international law, even in the nineteenth century, which saw the acme of the concept of the sovereign nation-state, recognized multiple sources of authority.[201]

Many modern philosophers of law (not to mention political scientists) have concluded that using largely nineteenth century concepts of sovereignty as a benchmark of what political authority should be seen as being either teleological at best or wrong at worst.[202] We are now questioning the place of the sovereign state, not because we necessarily wish to abolish it, but because we must question their place. The Internet and globalization have raised questions about the place of the state, when it is possible to communicate in real time with people across the globe, without regard to place of residence, and to conduct business with them.[203]

What, then, is the place of the state? As discussed in Chapter 5.2 the economic role of the state is based on self-interest or self-preservation. But this led to the development of states which possessed a rationale and a role of their own. To some extent they existed for their own sake. This became clearer in the development of the modern nation-state, but its origins were also apparent in early modern states, and especially with respect to sovereignty.

The traditional juristic theory of territorial sovereignty, with the King being supreme ruler within the confines of his kingdom, originated as two distinct concepts. The King acknowledged no superior in temporal matters, and within his kingdom the King was emperor.[204] If the Holy Roman Emperor had legal supremacy within the *terrae imperii*, the confines of the empire, theories of the sovereignty of kings were not needed, for they had merely *de facto* power.[205] In Roman law it was originally considered that the emperor's power had been bestowed upon him by the people,[206] but when Rome became a Christian state his power was regarded as coming from God.[207] In the United States God also had been recognized as the source of governmental authority, although it is commonly thought in a republican or democratic government 'all power is inherent in the people.'[208] The focus of authority was both a consequence, and an imperative, of the economic model of the state.

Sovereignty remained essentially *de jure* authority.[209] Emperor Frederick I Barbarossa saw the advantages of Roman law and legal science for his ambitions and his inception of absolutism.[210] This led to the growth of royal absolutism, and eventually to the emergence of opposition to this, throughout Europe.[211] This was not merely power without legitimacy.[212] Mediæval jurists cared not whether the emperor had jurisdiction and authority over kings and princes, but focused on his power to usurp the rights of his subjects. Whether this power was *de facto* or *de jure* was unimportant.[213]

But in the course of the nineteenth century the notion of state sovereignty prevailed,[214] and after World War One, the nation-state.[215] This was reinforced by de-colonisation after World War Two.[216] A counter-movement is now underway. The Internet, as a transnational system of communications, has shown signs of developing a distinct legal form.[217] But the Law Merchant evolved, as did other forms of international customary law, through usage and practice. It did not require a central authority, and nor was it inconsistent with sovereignty, *de facto* or *de jure* – and it developed over a considerable period of time.[218]

Even if a sovereign cyberspace is unlikely to develop as some have predicted, it may be that there is scope for the creation of novel forms of new states,[219] but such scope appears to be restricted. Statehood has hitherto been the necessary precondition of tax haven status. For only a state is able to impose – and repeal – taxation and regulatory laws.[220]

Traditionally only a state was regarded as an international person, capable of having rights and duties under international law.[221] That entities other than states might be the subjects of international law is even today not a universally accepted idea,[222] and exactly which entities do have this status is an even more controversial topic. Whereas scholars such as Hall and Lawrence tended to define subjects of international law as states and certain unusual exceptions, there are others who went further in opening up the realm of reasonable subjects of the law of nations. Notable among them was Lauterpacht. In his view:[223]

> International practice shows that persons and bodies other than states are often made subjects of international rights and duties, that such developments are not inconsistent with the structure of international law and that in each particular case the question whether a person or a body is a subject of international law must be answered in a pragmatic manner by reference to actual experience and to the reason of the law as

> distinguished from the preconceived notion as to who can be the subjects of international law.

Indeed, it has since been observed that 'a look at history, however, tells us that conceptions of world order have by no means always been shaped by the model of sovereign co-equal actors with a territorial basis.'[224] The recognition of non-state entities has indeed become more pronounced since the 1960s.[225]

The status of organizations in international law is less controversial than the assumption of rights and duties by individuals or groups of individuals. In 1949, the International Court of Justice recognized the United Nations Organization as an international person,[226] marking an important stage in the process whereby an ever-increasing number of modern international organizations are recognized as having personality in international law. That is not, however, the same thing as saying that such an organization is a state, or that its legal personality and rights and duties are the same as those of a state.[227]

There are now many organizations operating on an international plane. Whilst many such organizations, such as the European Union and the United Nations Organization, receive ambassadors from member countries, the Sovereign Military Order of Malta almost alone among international organizations claims the right to send representatives to other states for the purpose of carrying on diplomatic negotiations,[228] as well as to receive representatives from other states for the same purpose.[229] Most importantly, the Sovereign Military Order of Malta claims, and is sometimes acknowledged by states, to be a sovereign state in its own right.[230] This status has been claimed since at least the fourteenth century, well before international law began to accord legal personality to international organizations.[231] But the Order is not unique in such claims. Its own parent body, the Holy See, has for long been regarded as sovereign, apparently even when the papacy was without territorial possessions.[232] Territorial possessions gave both the Holy See and the Sovereign Military Order of Malta their status as sovereign states, but the loss of territory did not necessarily extinguish that status.[233]

The twentieth century, and particularly the second half of that century, saw the growth of international organizations and other bodies now accorded recognition as subjects in international law. With the growth in both the extent and the reach of international agreements, treaties, conventions and codes, the extent to which individual sovereign states retain the final control over their national policies may have diminished.[234] This tendency is becoming more noticeable in the modern commercial environment, and especially in respect of the Internet. The development of the Internet has presented new opportunities for those keen to escape the shackles of government. As yet, however, only states and international organizations that have been recognized as analogous are exempt from taxation by other states.[235]

The principal actor in international law is the state. If one cannot find a state whose fiscal and regulatory policies accord exactly with one's requirements, the option remains of creating one's own 'ideal' state. Most of the attempts to create new states have been in oceanic or marine situations. The freedom and isolation of the open seas inhibit the control exercised by established powers, and encourage the formation of alternative political societies.[236] Menefee has identified four principal categories of territory that have been so used:

1. the appropriation of apparently unclaimed islets (for example, Mead's State in the Spratly Islands);[237]
2. the promulgation of sovereignty over reefs or low-tide elevations (for example, Grand and Triumph reefs);[238]
3. the creation of states in shallow waters by dumping or other means (for example, Abalonia);[239] and
4. the creation of states on totally artificial structures (for example, Sealand).[240]

Each of these categories presents particular difficulties for the would-be state-builder, whether that person be motivated by notions of unbridled free enterprise or libertarianism, or by pure eccentricity.[241]

But to be a state, a territory must have a permanent population,[242] it must have a defined territory,[243] it must have a government, and it must have the capacity to enter into diplomatic relations.[244] No other entity could be regarded as a state, whatever its *de facto* power. This definition remains politically important, though additional factors have increased in relevance and importance.

Although the formal application of the Montevideo Convention is confined to Latin America, it is regarded as declaratory of customary international law.[245] The Arbitration Commission of the European Conference on Yugoslavia, in Opinion No 1, declared that:

> The State is commonly defined as a community which consists of a territory and a population subject to an organised political authority.[246]

No other entity could be regarded as a sovereign state, whatever its *de facto* power. But this does not mean that sovereign states alone enjoy a monopoly of power or authority.[247] As the concept of state sovereignty declined,[248] so notions of racial sovereignty have grown. The idea that a given population group is, or ought to be, sovereign within a larger country is not confined to any one country, such as New Zealand.[249] Yet, sovereign states have clung tenaciously to their rights, rights which have become more precious as they become rarer.[250]

Even if a territory meets the Montevideo criteria, it will not necessarily be recognized by the international community. An old debate, between declaratory and constitutive theorists, centred on the role of recognition in transforming communities into states. Declaratory theorists asserted that recognition by existing states merely acknowledged that a community possessed the empirical attributes of a state – territory, population, a government, and the capacity to engage in international relations. Under this view, the function of recognition was merely to acknowledge that the state has come into existence and to signal a willingness to enter into diplomatic relations with the new state. Constitutive theorists, by contrast, considered recognition necessary to the creation of a new state. They further believed that recognition was a matter within the discretion of the recognizing state to extend or withhold. The effect of the constitutive view is to hold a community's right to statehood hostage to the discretion of existing states.[251]

Grant considers the declaratory theory to be the better view, but he argues that neither view accurately describes the emergence of new states. Recent state practice renders the debate between declaratory and constitutive theory all the more inadequate. Some scholars have amended existing constitutive and declaratory theories by proposing additional requirements that communities must fulfil before becoming states, such as democratic governance or respect for minority rights. These additional rules, which have yet to gain widespread acceptance, pose additional difficulties in that they threaten to enlarge the scope of state discretion with respect to recognition. Grant contends that the alternative is to focus on the process that governs recognition rather than the substance of statehood.[252] A non-territorial state is perhaps possible.[253]

However far-fetched this possibility may be, we must reconsider the balance of international and domestic law. The jurisdiction of national courts is based upon the domestic laws of individual countries.[254] Similarly, the legislative jurisdiction of a state is limited to its territory.[255] The advent of cyberspace has not meant the decline of domestic law. But it has 'pushed the boundaries' of such laws.[256] Border controls on the Internet are not impossible to develop and implement.[257] Many governments already regulate cyberspace.[258] It may be that the most effective means to achieve this is to regulate the architecture of cyberspace.[259] But for the most part the Internet is international; nor are its users adequately served by existing laws with respect to conflict of laws.[260] The efficacy of the private international law concept of the 'closest and most real connection'[261] is also reduced, in that no part of the world is any more directly affected than any other by events on the web, as information is available simultaneously to anyone with a connection to the Internet.[262] Global computer-based communications cut across territorial borders,[263] creating a new realm of human activity and undermining the feasibility[264] – and legitimacy[265] – of applying laws based on geographic boundaries.[266] Furthermore, the Internet threatens traditional political institutions and perhaps even the very concept of sovereignty itself.[267] As Zekos has written, the real jurisdictional novelty of cyberspace is that it will give rise to more frequent circumstances in which effects are felt in multiple territories at once.[268] Traditional international legal rules on jurisdiction do not fit the Internet context, nor do they facilitate cooperation on international regulation.

The legal right of countries to control the Internet is undoubted,[269] but the practical difficulties involved have been considerable. It may be that the most effective means to achieve this is to regulate the architecture of cyberspace[270] – but this is international. Perhaps more importantly, the advent of the Internet has encouraged debate as to the proper form of regulation of international trade. Should it be through separate legal systems generally conforming to certain norms, or should there be some form of international regulation? However, the speed of globalization through the Internet means that the development of customary international law may not be sufficient to meet the needs of the new media – leaving international agreement or unilateral action as alternatives.

The notions of sovereignty and statehood are principally political concepts, rather than merely legal principles.[271] With the growth in both the (horizontal) extent and (vertical) reach of international agreements, treaties, conventions and codes, national independence is becoming less dominant. This tendency is becoming more noticeable in the modern commercial environment, and especially the Internet. For if electronic communication is (almost) instantaneous and global, who should regulate it and define its rules? Should it be subject to national regulation within some normative system – as the Law Merchant – or should it be recognized as a uniquely international system which requires international control?[272]

Further, the Internet itself threatens traditional political institutions and perhaps even the concept of sovereignty itself.[273] Traditional international legal rules on jurisdiction do not fit the Internet context, nor do they facilitate international co-operation on international regulation.

If sovereignty means the 'final authority within a given territory',[274] then the contemporary growth of internationalization, especially that brought about by the Internet, must have serious implications for state sovereignty.[275] Whilst the *lex mercatoria* impinged upon domestic sovereignty, in so far as this had developed in the early days of the Law Merchant, it did so to a limited extent. Perhaps more importantly, the Law Merchant evolved slowly, and did not impose an expectation of compliance upon any country.[276] It was, and is, a form of customary law. The existence of custom, unlike treaty-law, depends upon general agreement, not deliberate consent.[277] This requires time to develop, and is often uncertain. The Internet presents immediate problems, though not such as cannot be resolved through recourse to traditional legal principles and mechanisms. At present there is no reason to conclude that the Internet is in any sense a source of authority in its own right.[278] However, it has greatly accelerated the globalization process, particularly with respect to trade, and as a consequence reduced the extent to which economic regulation remains in the hands of individual states. As a result of this the development of supra-states,[279] such as the European Union, is encouraged. This is a profoundly constitutional effect – and not one which relies on changes in society but is itself advancing ahead of social change – a case of capture by technology.

7.4 Conclusion

The benefit of hindsight is not available to those to attempt to derive large generalizations, or principles, from the observation of contemporary events of which they are observers. The current revolution in information technology, and more specifically the development of the Internet, are having significant economic and social effects – particularly in those countries which already had a high level of economic development. But whereas the effects of information technology on society, legal systems, and constitutions may be understood as being slight, if identifiable at all (except in such highly specific instances such as electronic voting), that of the Internet may be more direct, and more profound.

The challenge of the Internet is that this technology is not one which is readily amenable to regulation by states – though this is certainly possible. Crucially, the nature of the technology itself invites globalization, for only in outward expansion is the tool efficiently utilized. Unlike earlier technologies, this outward thrust has implications at once on the domestic economic, social and political balance, and between nations, and truly globally. It is possible to discount national origins, and conduct business between business and consumer. Such innovations can scarcely fail to challenge the nature of global business, economic regulation, and the relationship between states.

Notes

1 Biotechnology and genetics are similar, but there the effects may be more social and ethical than constitutional.

2 See David Lazer and Viktor Mayer-Schonberger, 'Governing networks: telecommunication deregulation in Europe and the United States', *Brooklyn Journal of International Law*, 27 (2002): 819–51.

3 See Nasheri Hedieh, 'The Intersection of technology crimes and cyberspace in Europe: The Case of Hungary', *Information and Communications Technology Law*, 12 (2003): 25–48.

4 See Bahaa El-Hadidy and Esther E. Horne (eds), *The infrastructure of an information society: proceedings of the First International Information Conference in Egypt, Cairo, 13–15 December, 1982* (Amsterdam, 1982).

5 See Kenneth L. Kraemer, 'Computers and the Constitution: A Helpful, Harmful or Harmless Relationship?', *Public Administration Review*, 47 (1987): 93–105.

6 Ibid.

7 John O. McGinnis, 'The Symbiosis of Constitutionalism and Technology', *Harvard Journal of Law and Public Policy*, 25 (2001): 3–14, 6–7.

8 Ibid., 7. See also John O. McGinnis, 'The Original Constitution and Our Origins', *Harvard Journal of Law and Public Policy*, 19 (1995): 251–61, 253.

9 McGinnis, 'The Symbiosis of Constitutionalism and Technology', 8. Note that this reform is through judicial interpretation rather than constitutional amendment.

10 Ibid.

11 For which see Nickolai G. Levin, 'Constitutional statutory synthesis', *Alabama Law Review*, 54 (2003): 1281–373.

12 Though the balance may vary over time, and from place to place.

13 S. Coleman (ed.), *2001: Cyber Space Odyssey: The Internet in the United Kingdom Election* (London, 2001); Electoral Commission, *Modernising Elections: a*

Strategic Evaluation of the 2002 Electoral Pilot Schemes (2002) at <http://www.electoralcommission.org.uk/publications.htm#anchor1>.

14 Jay G. Blumler and Stephen Coleman, *Realising Democracy Online: A Civic Commons in Cyberspace* (March 2001), available at <http://www.edemocracy.gov.uk/library/papers/Realising_Democracy_Online.pdf>.

15 Cass R. Sunstein, *Republic.com* (Princeton, 2001).

16 It may be accepted that regulation of some form is necessary, if only to protect consumers; See Jessica Bagner, Vanessa Kaye Watson and K Brooke Welch, 'Internet auction fraud targeted by FTC, state and local law enforcement officials', *Intellectual Property and Technology Law Journal*, 15 (2003): 22.

17 See David R. Johnson and David G. Post, 'And How Shall the Net be Governed? A Meditation on the Relative Virtues of Decentralised, Emergent Law', draft paper at Cyberspace Law Institute Papers on Cyberspace Law, available at <http://www.cli.org/emdraft.html> (as at 28 November 2003).

18 See Bruce E. Cain, 'The Internet in the (dis)service of democracy?', *Loyola of Los Angeles Law Review*, 34 (2001): 1005–21.

19 There is a tendency to look only at examples from one's own country.

20 The result being a conceptual confusion: see Jack L. Goldsmith and Lawrence Lessig, 'Grounding the Virtual Magistrate', at <http://www.lessig.org/content/articles/works/magistrate.html> (as at 28 November 2003).

21 See Georgios Zekos, 'Internet or Electronic Technology: A Threat to State Sovereignty', *Journal of Information, Law and Technology*, 3 (1999), available at <http://elj.warwick.ac.uk/jilt/99-3/zekos.html> (as at 28 November 2003); David G. Post and David R. Johnson, '"Chaos Prevailing on Every Continent": Towards a New Theory of Decentralised Decision-Making in Complex Systems', Social Science Research Network Electronic Library (14 June 1999), available at <http://papers.ssrn.com/sol3/delivery.cfm/99032613.pdf?abstractid=157692> (as at 1 December 2003). See also Dan L. Burk, 'Federalism in Cyberspace', *Connecticut Law Review*, 28 (1996): 1095–127; Joel R. Reidenberg, 'Governing Networks and Rule-Making in Cyberspace', in Brian Kahin and Charles Nesson (eds), *Borders in Cyberspace* (Cambridge: 1997), pp. 84, 85–7.

22 Though the Internet Corporation for Assigned Names and Numbers (ICANN) regulates some aspects of the net. This is the non-profit corporation that was formed to assume responsibility for the Internet Protocol (IP) address space allocation, protocol parameter assignment, domain name system management, and root server system management functions previously performed under United States Government contract by Internet Assigned Numbers Authority (IANA) and other entities. That no single country can regulate the Internet is seen in the internationalization of ICANN. See for instance, James S. Fishkin, 'Deliberate Polling As a Model for ICANN Membership', study paper from the Berkman Centre for Internet and Society at Harvard Law School, available at <http://www.cyber.law.harvard.edu/rcs/fish.html> (as at 28 November 2003).

23 The Internet is a system for linking existing computer networks, rather than a separate system in its own right. At its highest level coordinated by the Internet Assigned Numbers Authority (IANA) and a central Internet Registry (IR); See Johnson and Post, 'And How Shall the Net be Governed?'.

24 The Internet service providers (ISPs), who provide access to the Internet, are intermediaries, though the consumer is largely unaware of their existence, as they operate behind the scenes.

25 See Stephen Bill and Arthur Kerrigan, 'Practical application of European Value Added Tax to E-Commerce', *Georgia Law Review*, 38 (2003): 71–83; Noel Cox, 'Tax and regulatory avoidance through non-traditional alternatives to tax havens', *New Zealand Journal of Taxation Law and Policy*, 9 (2003): 305–27.

26 Current problems of enforcement may be such that piecemeal approach is necessary; see Noel Cox, 'The regulation of cyberspace and the loss of national sovereignty', *Information and Communications Technology Law*, 11 (2002): 241–53.

27 See also Peter G. Neumann, 'Technology, laws, and society', *Association for Computing Machinery. Communications of the ACM*, 37 (1994): 138.

28 See Paul M. Schwartz, 'Internet privacy and the State', *Connecticut Law Review*, 32 (2000): 815–59; Jae-Young Kim, 'Deregulation reconsidered: Protecting Internet speech in the United States, Germany, and Japan', *Communications and the Law*, 24 (2002): 53–75.

29 See Reuven S. Avi-Yonah, 'Globalization, Tax Competition, and the Fiscal Crisis of the Welfare State', *Harvard Law Review*, 113 (2000): 1573–676; Cox, 'Tax and regulatory avoidance through non-traditional alternatives to tax havens'; R. Palan, 'Tax Havens and the Commercialisation of State Sovereignty', *International Organization*, 56 (2002): 151–76; Edward A. Morse, 'State taxation of Internet commerce: something new under the sun?', *Creighton Law Review*, 30 (1997): 1113–67; Richard Jones and Subhajit Basu, 'Taxation of electronic commerce: A developing problem', *International Review of Law, Computers and Technology*, 16 (2002): 35–52. See also Anthony van Fossen, 'Financial frauds and pseudo-states in the Pacific Islands', *Crime, Law and Social Change*, 37 (2002): 357–78.

30 See Dan McLennan, 'The online revolution in government contracting', *Law Institute Journal*, 76 (2002): 78–81.

31 See Cox, 'Tax and regulatory avoidance through non-traditional alternatives to tax havens'.

32 See Linda A. Mabry, 'Multinational corporations and United States technology policy: rethinking the concept of corporate nationality', *Georgetown Law Journal*, 87 (1999): 563–673.

33 See Lane Fisher and Cheryl L. Mullin, 'Franchise laws in the age of electronic communication', *Franchise Law Journal*, 19 (1999): 47–51.

34 See Jocelyn C. Adkins, 'The Internet: a critical technology for the state of environmental law', *Villanova Environmental Law Journal*, 8 (1997): 341–57.

35 See Renee M. Fishman, Kara Josephberg, Jane Linn, Jane Pollack and Jena Victoriano, 'Threat of international cyberterrorism on the rise', *Intellectual Property and Technology Law Journal*, 14 (2002): 23.

36 'Spam,' unsolicited email messages, constitutes a growing proportion of messages received; See Jonathan Krim, 'Spam's Cost To Business Escalates', *The Washington Post*, 13 March 2003, available at <http://www.washingtonpost.com/ac2/wp-dyn/A17754-2003Mar12> (as at 10 December 2003).

37 See Alfred C. Yen, 'Western frontier or feudal society?: Metaphors and Perceptions of cyberspace', *Berkeley Technology Law Journal*, 17 (2002): 1207–63.

38 Ibid.; Peter Drahos and John Braithwaite, *Information feudalism: who owns the knowledge economy?* (New York, 2003).
39 Lawrence Lessig, *Code and other Laws of Cyberspace* (New York, 1999) p. 5.
40 Ibid., p. 61 onwards.
41 See Post and Johnson, 'Chaos Prevailing on Every Continent'.
42 See Kim G. von Arx, 'ICANN – Now and then: ICANN's Reform and its problems', *Duke Law and Technology Review* (2003) 7.
43 See, for instance, Fishkin, 'Deliberate Polling As a Model for ICANN Membership'.
44 See Jack Linchuan Qiu, 'Virtual Censorship in China: Keeping the Gate between the Cyberspaces', *International Journal of Communications Law and Policy*, 4 (1999–2000): 1–25; C. Elliott, 'The Internet – A New World without frontiers', *New Zealand Law Journal* (1998): 405–7.
45 These have limitations, such as being bound by national boundaries (they regulate behaviour of participants coming from a particular territory), lacking in efficient sanctions, public accountability and actual monitoring and reviewing systems; See Joseph A. Cannataci and Jeanne Pia Mifsud Bonnici, 'Can self-regulation satisfy the transnational requisite of successful Internet regulation?', *International Review of Law, Computers and Technology*, 17 (2003): 51–61.
46 Ibid.
47 See Jack L. Goldsmith, 'Against Cyberanarchy', *University of Chicago Law Review*, 65 (1998): 1199–250.
48 See A.B. Overby, 'Will cyberlaw be uniform?: an introduction to the UNCITRAL Model law on Electronic Commerce', *Tulane Journal of International and Comparative Law*, 7 (1999): 219–310; Graham Greenleaf, 'An Endnote on Regulating Cyberspace: Architecture vs Law?', *University of New South Wales Law Journal*, 21 (1998): 593–622.
49 Cf Shirley Serafini, and Michel Andrieu, *The Information Revolution and its Implications for Canada* (Ottawa, 1981), p. 96.
50 See Kara Josephberg, Jane Pollack, Jenna Victoriano and Oriyan Gitig, 'Singapore free trade agreement addresses domain names', *Intellectual Property and Technology Law Journal*, 15 (2003): 20.
51 See Paul Schiff Berman, 'Cyberspace and the State Action Debate: The Cultural Value of Applying Constitutional Norms to "Private" Regulation', *University of Colorado Law Review*, 71 (2000): 1265–6.
52 See Goldsmith and Lessig, 'Grounding the Virtual Magistrate'. At the very least, that it should self-regulate; David R. Johnson and David G. Post, 'Law and Borders: The Rise of Law in Cyberspace', *Stanford Law Review*, 48 (1996): 1367–402.
53 See Greenleaf, 'An Endnote on Regulating Cyberspace: Architecture vs Law?'.
54 See, for instance, Qiu, 'Virtual Censorship in China'.
55 Mark F. Grady, 'The state and the networked economy', *Harvard Journal of Law and Public Policy*, 25 (2001): 15–29.
56 He cites the novels *1984* (George Orwell, London, 1949), and *Brave New World* (Aldous Huxley, London, 1932). Pessimism is not, of course, limited to predictions concerning the Internet – an informal pre-millennial survey of world leaders and Nobel laureates garnered generally pessimistic predictions across a range of fields; See Leonard M. Salter, 'Predictions for the Next Millennium', *Orange County Lawyer*, 42 (2000): 16–22.

57 Grady, 'The state and the networked economy'.

58 Ibid.

59 See William J. Stover, *Information technology in the Third World: Can I.T. lead to humane national development?* (Boulder, 1984).

60 Doron M. Kalir, 'Taking Globalization Seriously: Towards General Jurisprudence', *Columbia Journal of Transnational Law*, 39 (2001): 785–821, 816.

61 Ibid., 816.

62 Africa is the only continent none of whose states have joined the conventions against international bribery, and very few African states have national laws attempting to fill the gap. The Internet and other new technologies are developing as parallel, mostly non-governmental tools against corruption. Unlike transnational and most national laws, their impact has already been clearly visible in Africa and they offer at least the possibility of substantial interference with corruption in the short to medium term; See Peter W. Schroth and Preeti Sharma, 'Transnational law and technology as potential forces against corruption in Africa', *Management Decision*, 41 (2003): 296–303.

63 Sunstein, *Republic.com*.

64 Ibid.

65 Grady, 'The state and the networked economy'.

66 See Anupam Chander, 'Whose Republic?', *University of Chicago Law Review*, 69 (2002): 1479–500.

67 See 'Global Internet Statistics', Global Reach, available at <http://www.glreach.com/globstats/> (as at 10 December 2003).

68 See Franz C. Mayer, 'The Internet and Public International Law – Worlds Apart?', *European Journal of International Law*, 12 (2001): 617–22; Ruth Wedgwood, 'The Internet and Public International Law: Cyber-Nations', *Kentucky Law Journal*, 88 (2000): 957–65; Klaus W. Grewlich, *Governance in 'Cyberspace' – Access and Public Interest in Global Telecommunications* (The Hague, 1999); Makoto Ibusuki (ed.), *Transnational Cyberspace Law* (Oxford, 2000).

69 In particular, see Lessig, *Code and other Laws of Cyberspace* (For Lessig the 'code' of cyberspace means its architectural combination of software and hardware. For him this was its most significant body of law, one which transcended the strictures of ordinary law).

70 Mayer, 'The Internet and Public International Law', 621–2. Contemporary international law envisions a pluralist world in which communities may preserve their cultural and religious diversity; L. Ali Khan, *The Extinction of Nation-States: A World without Borders* (The Hague, 1996), p. 3.

71 The Internet Corporation for Assigned Names and Numbers (ICANN) regulates some aspects of the net. This is the non-profit corporation that was formed to assume responsibility for the Internet Protocol (IP) address space allocation, protocol parameter assignment, domain name system management, and root server system management functions previously performed under United States Government contract by Internet Assigned Numbers Authority (IANA) and other entities. That no single country can regulate the Internet is seen in the internationalization of ICANN. See for instance, Fishkin, 'Deliberate Polling As a Model for ICANN Membership'.

72 See Kara Josephberg, Jane Pollack, Jenna Victoriano and Oriyan Gitig, 'Singapore free trade agreement addresses domain names'.

73 In § 1000(a)(9) of Pub. L. No. 106-113 (Nov. 29, 1999), and published as title III, § 3001 et seq., in Appendix I of that law.

74 See Catherine T. Struve and R. Polk Wagner, 'Realspace sovereigns in cyberspace: Problems with the Anticybersquatting Consumer Protection Act', *Berkeley Technology Law Journal*, 17 (2002): 989–1041.

75 See Frederick M. Abbott, 'Distributed governance at the WTO–WIPO: An evolving model for open-architecture integrated governance', *Journal of International Economic Law*, 3 (2000): 63.

76 McGinnis, 'The Symbiosis of Constitutionalism and Technology', 9; John O. McGinnis and Mark L. Movsesian, 'The World Trade Constitution', *Harvard Law Review*, 114 (2000): 511–605, 514–15.

77 McGinnis, 'The Symbiosis of Constitutionalism and Technology', 9–10.

78 Ibid., 10. However, due to the much greater complexity of world federalism, this process would be much slower than the American prototype; McGinnis and Movsesian, 'The World Trade Constitution', 543–4.

79 Lawrence Lessig, *The Future of Ideas: The Fate of the Commons in a Connected World* (New York, 2001).

80 Siva Vaidhyanathan, *Copyright and copywrongs: The rise of intellectual property and how it threatens creativity* (New York, 2001).

81 See Sonia K. Katyal, 'Ending the revolution', *Texas Law Review*, 80 (2002): 1465–86.

82 See John C. Williams, 'The role of the United States government in encouraging technological innovation', *Canada–United States Law Journal*, 15 (1989): 219–28; Robert G. Blackburn, 'The role of the Canadian government in encouraging innovations', *Canada–United States Law Journal*, 15 (1989): 229–36. For a more specific example, see Derek E. Empie, 'The dormant Internet: are state regulators of motor vehicle sales by manufacturers on the Information Superhighway obstructing interstate and Internet commerce?', *Georgia State University Law Review*, 18 (2002): 827–57.

83 See Katyal, 'Ending the revolution'.

84 McGinnis, 'The Symbiosis of Constitutionalism and Technology', 8.

85 'B2C.' It greatly increases the scope for international trade by private persons, with the resulting regulatory problems, particularly difficulties of dispute resolution, and enforcement.

86 See I. Trotter Hardy, 'The Proper Legal Regime for "Cyberspace"', *University of Pittsburgh Law Review*, 55 (1994): 993–1055, 1020; Cox, 'The regulation of cyberspace and the loss of national sovereignty'.

87 This remained true in more recent times; See Michael B. Miller, 'The business trip: Maritime networks in the twentieth century', *Business History Review*, 77 (2003): 1–32.

88 See Leon Trakman, *The Law Merchant – The Evolution of Commercial Law* (Littleton, 1983).

89 See Gerard de Malynes, *Consuetudo vel Lex Mercatoria, or the Ancient Law Merchant* (London, 1622, facsimile Amsterdam, 1979).

90 *Luke v Lyde* (1759) 2 Burr 882; 97 ER 614, per Lord Mansfield, CJ.

91 See Trakman, *The Law Merchant*; Bruce Benson, 'The Spontaneous Evolution of Commercial Law', *Southern Economic Journal*, 55 (1989): 644–61, 646–7.

92 See Klaus Peter Berger, *The Creeping Codification of Lex Mercatoria* (The Hague, 1999).

93 *Lotus Case (France v Turkey)* 1927 PCIJ ser A No 10 (Judgment of 7 September), *Asylum Case (Colombia v Peru)* 1950 ICJ 266 at 276 (Judgment of 20 November), *Delimitation of the Maritime Boundary in the Gulf of Maine Area (Canada v United States)* 1950 ICJ 266 at 299–300 (Judgment of 12 October), *Fisheries Case (UK v Norway)* 1951 ICJ 116 (Judgment of 18 December), *North Sea Continental Shelf Cases (Federal Republic of Germany v Denmark; Federal Republic of Germany v The Netherlands)* 1969 ICJ 3 at 43–45 (Judgment of 20 February), and *Military and Paramilitary Activities in and against Nicaragua (Nicaragua v United States)*, 1969 ICJ 3 at 97–98 (Judgment of 27 June).

94 *North Sea Continental Shelf Cases (Federal Republic of Germany v Denmark; Federal Republic of Germany v The Netherlands)* 1969 ICJ 3 at 44–45 (Judgment of 20 February). The International Court of Justice emphasized the importance of *opinio juris* even in the face of inconsistent state practice in *Military and Paramilitary Activities in and against Nicaragua (Nicaragua v United States)* Merits 1986 ICJ 14 (Judgment of 27 June). *Opinio juris* may be determined from resolutions of international organizations, notably the General Assembly.

95 See Oliver Volckart and Antje Mangels, 'Are the roots of the modern lex mercatoria really mediæval?', *Southern Economic Journal*, 65 (1999): 427–50.

96 'Mercocratic' would perhaps be a more accurate term.

97 See Trakman, *The Law Merchant*.

98 *The Antelope* (1825) 10 Wheat 66, per Marshall CJ.

99 See S. Todd Lowry, 'Lord Mansfield and the Law Merchant: Law and Economics in the Eighteenth Century', *Journal of Economic Issues*, 7 (1973): 605–22.

100 See Robert D. Cooter, 'Structural adjudication and the new law merchant: A model of decentralised law', *International Review of Law and Economics*, 12 (1994): 215–31.

101 If such a thing ever comes to pass.

102 See W.P. Heere and J.P.S. Offerhaus, *International Law in Historical Perspective* (The Hague, 1998).

103 See, for instance, the situation of Singapore, in its negotiations with the United States; Kara Josephberg, Jane Pollack, Jenna Victoriano and Oriyan Gitig, 'Singapore free trade agreement addresses domain names'.

104 See The White House, 'A Framework for Global Electronic Commerce' (1997), at <http://www.technology.gov/digeconomy/framewrk.htm> (as at 28 November 2003).

105 See Children's Online Protection Act, 1998, Pub. L. No. 105-277, Div C, tit. 13, ch 1302(6) available at <http://www.cdt.org/legislation/105th/speech/copa.html> (as at 28 November 2003). States may even resort to the use of force in cyberspace; Dimitrios Delibasis, 'The right to use force in cyberspace: Defining the rules of engagement', *Feature*, 11(3) (2002): 255–68.

106 See, for instance, the United States Patriot Act of 2001, Public Law 107-56.

107 The FTC uses the unsolicited emails stored in its database to pursue law enforcement actions against people who send deceptive spam email; See 'You've Got Spam: How to "Can" Unwanted Email', <http://www3.ftc.gov/bcp/conline/pubs/online/inbox.htm> (as at 1 December 2003). The FTC enters Internet, telemarketing, identity theft and other fraud-related complaints into 'Consumer Sentinel' at <http://www.consumer.gov/sentinel/> (as at 1 December 2003), a secure, online

database available to hundreds of civil and criminal law enforcement agencies in the United States and abroad.

108 Common Position Adopted by the Council with a View to the Adoption of a Directive of the European Parliament and the Council on Certain Legal Aspects of Information Society Services, in Particular Electronic Commerce, in the Internal Market 14263/1/99 REV (February 28, 2000) ('Electronic Commerce Directive'). See now 'Electronic Commerce' Directive 2000/31/EC OJ 2000 L178/1.

109 See Qiu, 'Virtual Censorship in China'; Renee M. Fishman, Kara Josephberg, Jane Linn, Jane Pollack and Jena Victoriano, 'China issues rules on content enforcement', *Intellectual Property and Technology Law Journal*, 14(10) (2002): 24. China has regulated access to the Internet through centralized filtered servers, and by requiring filters for in-state Internet service providers and end-users; Timothy Wu, 'Cyberspace Sovereignty? – The Internet and the International System', *Harvard Journal of Law and Technology*, 10 (1997): 647, 652–4.

110 Unless, of course, they have relinquished legislative authority, in part or whole, as have members of the European Union. See Trevor C. Hartley, *Constitutional Problems of the European Union* (Oxford, 1999).

111 In Kelsen's philosophy of law, a grundnorm is the basic, fundamental postulate, which justifies all principles and rules of the legal system and which all inferior rules of the system may be deduced; See Michael Hayback, 'Carl Schmitt and Hans Kelsen in the crisis of Democracy between World Wars I and II' (1990) Universitaet Salzburg DrIur thesis.

112 Art 7.

113 See J.D. Gregory, 'The authentication of digital records', *EDI Law Review: Legal Aspects of Paperless Communication*, 6 (1999): 47–63; J.D. Gregory, 'Solving legal issues in electronic commerce', *Canadian Business Law Journal*, 32 (1999): 84–131.

114 Explanatory Note to Electronic Transactions Bill (New Zealand).

115 *Databank Systems Ltd v Commissioner of Inland Revenue* [1990] 3 NZLR 385 (PC); *Corinthian Pharmaceutical Systems Inc v Lederle Laboratories*, 724 F Supp 605 (1989); *Electronic Commerce Part One* (Wellington, 1998), para. 52.

116 *Electronic Commerce Part One* (Wellington, 1998), paras 316–20, 344–5.

117 See also Singapore; See Kara Josephberg, Jane Pollack, Jenna Victoriano and Oriyan Gitig, 'Singapore free trade agreement addresses domain names'.

118 *American Banana Co v United Fruit Co*, 213 US 347, 357 (1909). Recognizing the problems of extraterritorial enforcement, the United States Supreme Court has held that 'legislation of Congress, unless a contrary intent appears, is merely to apply only within the territorial jurisdiction of the United States.' *EEOC v Arabian American Oil Co*, 499 US 244, 248 (1991), citing *Foley Bros Inc v Filardo*, 336 US 281, 285 (1949). Although Congress 'has the authority to enforce its laws beyond [United States] boundaries,' this principle 'serves to protect against unintended clashes between our laws and those of other nations, which could result in international discord.' *EEOC*, 499 US at 248, citing *McCulloch v Sociedad Nacional de Marineros de Honduras*, 372 US 10, 20–2 (1963).

119 See Adam Roberts and Richard Guellf (eds), *Laws of War* (Oxford, 2000); Geoffrey Best, *Humanity in Warfare: The Modern History of the International Law of Armed Conflict* (New York, 1980).

120 As with the Statute of the Staple 1352–3 (27 Edw III stat 2).

121 See Cox, 'The regulation of cyberspace and the loss of national sovereignty'.

122 See Johnson, and Post, 'Law and Borders'.

123 As in the commercial law of England from the late nineteenth century to the late twentieth century; see Alan Harding, *A Social History of English Law* (Harmondsworth, 1966).

124 Particularly from within the same legal tradition, see, for example, Jerome Elkind (ed.), *The impact of American law on English and Commonwealth law: A book of essays* (St Paul, 1978).

125 See Roderick Floud, and Donald McCloskey, *The Economic History of Britain since 1700* (2nd edn, Cambridge, 1994).

126 For one small aspect of this see Ben Boer, 'The Globalization of Environmental Law: The Role of the United Nations', *Melbourne University Law Review*, 20 (1995): 101–25.

127 See for example, J. Clift, 'The UNCITRAL Model Law and electronic equivalents to traditional bills of lading', *Journal of the Section on Business Law of the International Bar Association*, 27 (1999): 311–17; S. Eiselen, 'Electronic commerce and the United Nations Convention on Contracts for the International Sale of Goods (CISG) 1980', *EDI Law Review: Legal Aspects of Paperless Communication*, 6 (1999): 21–46.

128 Jack L. Goldsmith, 'Regulation of the Internet: Three Persistent Fallacies', *Chicago–Kent Law Review*, 73 (1998): 1119–31.

129 See Goldsmith for a criticism of the 'regulation sceptics', who (using descriptive and normative claims) assert that the Internet is fundamentally different to earlier situations, and requires unique means of regulation; Goldsmith, 'Against Cyberanarchy'.

130 See, for example, Cox, 'The regulation of cyberspace and the loss of national sovereignty'.

131 Louis Henkin, 'That "S." Word: Sovereignty, and Globalization, and Human Rights, Et Cetera', *Ford Law Review*, 68 (1999): 1–14, 6–7.

132 See Roger Tassé and Maxime Faille, 'Online Consumer Protection in Canada: The Problem of Regulatory Jurisdiction', *Internet and E-Commerce Law in Canada*, 2 (2000–01): 41–8; Ronald de Bruin, *Consumer trust in electronic commerce: time for best practice* (The Hague, 2002); Goldsmith, 'Regulation of the Internet'; Tapio Puurunen, 'The Legislative Jurisdiction of States over Transactions in International Electronic Commerce', *John Marshall Journal of Computer and Information Law*, 18 (2000): 689–754.

133 See Franco Ferrari, '"Forum shopping" despite international uniform contract law conventions', *International and Comparative Law Quarterly*, 51 (2002): 689–707; Ralph U. Whitten, 'United States conflict-of-laws doctrine and forum shopping, international and domestic (revisited)', *Texas International Law Journal*, 37 (2002): 559–89.

134 Substantive foreign law will apply, generally, where the parties have included a choice of law provision in a contract; where under the forum's own laws status is determined under the laws of the place of birth or marriage; in tort, where *lex loci delicti* applies; and in the enforcement of foreign judgments (assuming that the application of foreign law does not offend public order); See Ogilvy Renault, 'Jurisdiction and the Internet: Are the traditional rules enough?' paper prepared by the Uniform Law Conference of

Canada (1998), available at <http://www.law.ualberta.ca/alri/ulc/current/ejurisd.htm> (as at 1 December 2003), n7.

135 In New Zealand this is governed by the Reciprocal Enforcement of Judgments Act 1934 (New Zealand). This has been applied to Orders in Council that have been made in respect of the following countries and states: Australia (SR 1987/22), Australian Capital Territory (SR 1955/108), Basutoland (Lesotho) (SR 1940/88), Bechuanaland (Botswana) (SR 1940/88), Belgium (SR 1938/177), Cameroons (SR 1957/43), Ceylon (Sri Lanka) (SR 1958/23), Fiji (SR 1940/88), France (SR 1938/176), Gilbert and Ellice Islands (Kiribati) (SR 1940/88), Hong Kong (SR 1957/263), India (SR 1957/219), Malaya (Malaysia) (SR 1951/12), New South Wales (SR 1940/88), Nigeria (SR 1957/43), Norfolk Island (SR 1940/88), North Borneo (Sabah) (SR 1954/5), Northern Territory of Australia (SR 1957/264), Pakistan (SR 1958/117), Papua New Guinea (SR 1956/79), Queensland (SR 1940/88), Sarawak (SR 1951/12), Singapore (SR 1951/12), Solomon Islands (Tuvalu) (SR 1940/88), South Australia (SR 1940/88), Swaziland (SR 1940/88), Tasmania (SR 1940/306), Tonga (SR 1988/215), Victoria (SR 1940/88), Western Australia (SR 1940/88), and Western Samoa (SR 1971/124).

136 See Franco Ferrari, '"Forum shopping" despite international uniform contract law conventions'; Ralph U. Whitten, 'United States conflict-of-laws doctrine and forum shopping, international and domestic (revisited)', *Texas International Law Journal*, 37 (2002): 559–89.

137 Convention on the Law Applicable to Contracts for the International Sale of Goods, The Hague Convention, 15 June 1955.

138 Convention on Jurisdiction and the Enforcement of Judgments in Civil and Commercial matters, Brussels, 27 September 1968; Convention on Jurisdiction and the Enforcement of Judgments in Civil and Commercial matters, Lugano, 16 September 1988.

139 Convention on the law applicable to contractual obligations, Rome, 19 June 1980.

140 *Electronic Commerce Part Two: A Basic Legal Framework* (Wellington, 1999), paras 12–21.

141 Friedrich Juenger, 'Judicial Jurisdiction in the United States and in the European Communities: A Comparison', *Michigan Law Review*, 82 (1984): 1195, 1211.

142 See, the 'Report on the Second Meeting of the Informal Working Group on the Judgments Project', 6–9 January 2003 (February 2003). This failed largely due to United States opposition, grounded in concerns that it would hinder the development of the Internet.

143 *Cockburn v Kinzie Industries Inc* (1998) 1 PRNZ 243, 246 per Hardie Boys J (HC); *Biddulph v Wyeth Australia Pty Ltd* [1994] 3 NZLR 49.

144 *Yahoo! Inc v La Ligue contre Le Racisme et L'Antisemitisme*, 145 F Supp 2d 1168; 169 F Supp 2d 1181 (2001); Andreas Manolopoulos, 'Raising "Cyber-Borders": The Interaction Between Law and Technology', *International Journal of Law and Information Technology*, 11 (2003): 40–58.

145 Such as *Bensusan Restaurant Corp. v. King*, 40 USPQ (2d) 1519 (SDNY), confirmed by United States Court of Appeals (2d cir) 10 September 1997.

146 See Ogilvy Renault, 'Jurisdiction and the Internet: Are the traditional rules enough?', paper prepared by the Uniform Law Conference of Canada (1998), available at <http://www.law.ualberta.ca/alri/ulc/current/ejurisd.htm> (as at 1 December 2003).

147 See Goldsmith and Lessig, 'Grounding the Virtual Magistrate'.

148 See Richard M. Bird, 'Taxation and e-commerce', *Canadian Business Law Journal*, 38 (2003): 466–71.

149 See Udaykiran Vallamsetty, Krishna Kant and Prasant Mohapatra, 'Characterization of E-Commerce Traffic', *Electronic Commerce Research*, 3 (2003): 167–92.

150 This is also effected by the relevant national laws and international conventions – see, for example, Peter Stone, 'Internet consumer contracts and European private international law', *Information and Communications Technology Law*, 9 (2000): 5–15.

151 Though there are important exceptions, including in the consumer law field. For example, the Fair Trading Act 1986 (New Zealand) states, in s 3, that 'This Act extends to the engaging in conduct outside New Zealand by any person resident or carrying on business in New Zealand to the extent that such conduct relates to the supply of goods or services, or the granting of interests in land, within New Zealand.'

152 See Tassé and Faille, 'Online Consumer Protection in Canada'. See also *Buchanan v Rucker* (1808) 9 East 192; 103 ER 546, 547: 'Can the Island of Tobago pass a law to bind the rights of the whole world?'

153 *The Case of the* 'SS Lotus', 1927 PCIJ (ser A) No 10, 18-25.

154 *Blackmer v United States*, 284 US 421, 436 (1932); *United States v Rech*, 780 F 2d 1541, 1543 n 2 (11th cir, 1986).

155 See Roscoe B. Starek III and Lynda M. Rozell, 'The Federal Trade Commission's commitment to on-line consumer protection', *The John Marshall Journal of Computer and Information Law*, 15 (1997): 679–702.

156 Federal Trade Commission Act, 15 USC § 41–44, ss 5, 6.

157 See Jodie Bernstein, Director, Bureau of Consumer Protection, US Federal Trade Commission, 'Fighting Internet Fraud: A Global Effort', *Economic Perspectives, An Electronic Journal of the United States Department of State*, 5 (May 2000), available at <http://usinfo.state.gov/journals/ites/0500/ijee/ftc2.htm> (as at 1 December 2003).

158 From the Sherman Anti-trust Act (1890) Title 15 USC §§ 1–7; Federal Trade Commission Act (1914) Title 15 USC §§ 41–51.

159 See Robert Pitofsky, 'Competition Policy in a Global Economy – Today And Tomorrow', The European Institute's Eighth Annual Transatlantic Seminar on Trade and Investment Washington, D.C., USA, 4 November 1998, available at <http://www.techlawjournal.com/atr/81104ftc.htm> (as at 1 December 2003).

160 As, for example, in *Hartford Fire Insurance Co v California*, 509 US 764 (1993) (where United Kingdom re-insurers were compelled to adhere to the United States regulatory regime).

161 See J.S. Stanford, 'The Application of the Sherman Act to Conduct Outside the United States: A View from Abroad', *Cornell International Law Journal*, 11 (1978): 195. See also Joseph P. Griffin, 'Foreign Governmental Reactions to United States Assertion of Extraterritorial Jurisdiction', *George Mason Law Review*, 6 (1998): 505.

162 As for example, the High Court of Australia found in *Dow Jones & Company Inc v Gutnick* (2002) 194 ALR 433.

163 *R v Libman* [1985] 2 SCR 178.

164 Ibid.

165 See Tassé and Faille, 'Online Consumer Protection in Canada'.

166 Though it may be questioned whether it is premature to categorise it as successful. Earlier empires, such as Rome, may also be regarded as successful supranational states.

167 For instance, see Peter Stone, 'Internet consumer contracts and European private international law', *Information and Communications Technology Law*, 9 (2000): 5–15.

168 See K.P.E. Lasok, *The European Court of Justice: practice and procedure* (2nd edn, London, 1994).

169 Convention on the law applicable to contractual obligations, Rome, 19 June 1980.

170 Convention on Jurisdiction and the Enforcement of Judgments in Civil and Commercial matters, Brussels, 27 September 1968; Convention on the law applicable to contractual obligations, Rome, 19 June 1980.

171 The Council of the European Union regulation (EC) N° 1348/2000 of 29 May 2000 on the service in the Member States of judicial and extrajudicial documents in civil or commercial matters. This came into force March 2002.

172 Though not necessarily because of any profound difference between cyberspace and territorial space, but rather because of the complexity of cyberspace; See Goldsmith, 'Against Cyberanarchy'.

173 *McConnell Dowell Constructors Ltd v Lloyd's Syndicate 396* [1988] 2 NZLR 257 (CA); Lawrence Collins (ed.), *Dicey and Morris on the Conflict of Laws* (13th edn, London, 2000), ch. 32.

174 See Johnson, and Post, 'Law and Borders'. It can of course be argued that a webpage can be 'directed' at certain countries.

175 See Dan L. Burk, 'Muddy Rules for Cyberspace', *Cardozo Law Review*, 21 (1998–99): 121–79.

176 It also has constitutional implications if states relinquish enforcement to other bodies or countries.

177 See, for example, Lessig, *Code and other laws of cyberspace*; Christopher Marsden, *Regulating the Global Information Society* (London, 2000).

178 See Cannataci and Mifsud Bonnici, 'Can self-regulation satisfy the transnational requisite of successful Internet regulation?'; Philip J. Weiser, 'Internet governance, standard setting, and self-regulation', *Northern Kentucky Law Review*, 28 (2001): 822–46.

179 Such as between the United States and the European Union.

180 The WIPO, Council of Europe convention, respectively; World Intellectual Property Organization Copyright Treaty, adopted in Geneva on 20 December, 1996; Convention on Cybercrime, Budapest, 23 November 2001 (ETS No 185). See also Jonathan B. Wolf, 'War games meets the Internet: Chasing 21st century cybercriminals with old laws and little money', *American Journal of Criminal Law*, 28 (2000): 95–117.

181 <http://www.econsumer.gov/> (as at 1 December 2003). As yet, such tools are only partly successful, due to incomplete coverage and limited knowledge of their existence among consumers.

182 'OECD Guidelines for Protecting Consumers from Fraudulent and Deceptive Commercial Practices Across Borders', 11 June 2003 (Paris, 2003).

183 Too many, if this is seen as primarily a jurisdictional problem in traditional conflict of laws terms.

184 According to tradition, these were adopted in Castile by King Alphonso X in the thirteenth century, derived from the code founded in the republic of Rhodes and adopted by the Romans and other maritime powers of the Mediterranean, and were introduced into England by King Richard I. Originally they were connected with wine shipments from France, but afterwards took on a wider significance; Sir William Blackstone, *Commentaries on the Law of England* (New York, 1983, first published 1765–69), Bk 1, ch, 13.

185 1648. See Benno Teschke, *The myth of 1648: class, geopolitics, and the making of modern international relations* (London, 2003).

186 See Gregory P. Joseph, 'Internet and email evidence', *The Computer and Internet Lawyer*, 19 (2002): 17–22.

187 In the United States, the Digital Millennium Copyright Act (1998), Pub L No 105-304, 112 Stat 2860, 2905, in New Zealand, the Electronic Transactions Act 2000 (New Zealand).

188 See Henry H. Perritt, 'The Internet is Changing International Law', *Chicago–Kent Law Review*, 73 (1998): 997–1054.

189 Mayer, 'The Internet and Public International Law', 621. It might perhaps be helpful to remember the short story 'Dial F for Frankenstein', by the distinguished writer Sir Arthur C. Clarke. This concerned the formation of a worldwide telephone network (in many ways equivalent to the Internet). Unfortunately for humankind, the network becomes self-aware, and decidedly malignant; published in *The Wind from the Sun: stories of the space age* (London, 1962).

190 See Post and Johnson, 'Chaos Prevailing on Every Continent'. See also Burk, 'Federalism in Cyberspace'; Reidenberg, 'Governing Networks and Rule-Making in Cyberspace', pp. 84, 85–7.

191 It has been said that the very nature and growing importance of the Internet requires a fundamental re-examination of the institutional structure within which rulemaking takes place: see Johnson and Post, 'And How Shall the Net be Governed?'; Anne Wells Branscomb, 'Jurisdictional Quandaries for Global Networks', in Linda M. Harasim (ed.), *Global Networks: Computers and International Communication* (Cambridge, 1993).

192 See Post and Johnson, 'Chaos Prevailing on Every Continent'.

193 The analogy between the rise of a separate law of cyberspace and the Law Merchant has been observed: see I. Trotter Hardy, 'The Proper Legal Regime for "Cyberspace"', *University of Pittsburgh Law Review*, 55 (1994): 993–1055, 1020; Cox, 'The regulation of cyberspace and the loss of national sovereignty'.

194 As was seen in the Middle Ages, for example.

195 William E. Hall, *A Treatise on International Law*, ed. A. Pearce Higgins (8th edn, Oxford, 1924).

196 See George Schwarzenberger, *A Manual of International Law* (1st edn, London, 1947); Wolfgang Friedmann, *The Changing Structure of International Law* (New York, 1964).

197 See T.J. Lawrence, *The Principles of International Law* (7th edn, London, 1924).

198 See Sir Hersch Lauterpacht, 'The Subjects of the Law of Nations', *Law Quarterly Review*, 63 (1947): 438–60, 444.

199 See W. Ross Johnston, *Sovereignty and protection: a study of British jurisdictional imperialism in the late nineteenth century* (Durham, 1973).

200 *West Rand Central Gold Mining Co v. The King* [1905] 2 KB 391 quoting Lord Russell of Killowen in his address at Saratoga in 1876. See also Sir Michael Howard, George J. Andreopoulos and Mark R. Shulman (eds), *The Laws of War – Constraints on Warfare in the Western World* (New Haven, 1994); J. Gillingham and J.C. Holt (eds), *War and Government in the Middle Ages* (Cambridge, 1984).

201 See Maurice H. Keen, *The Laws of War in the Late Middle Ages* (London, 1965). International law has been called 'the sum of the rules or usages which civilized states have agreed shall be binding upon them in their dealings with one another'; *West Rand Central Gold Mining Co v The King* [1905] 2 KB 391. Standard histories of the laws of war include Roberts and Guellf; Best.

202 Kenneth Pennington, *The Prince and the Law, 1200–1600: Sovereignty and rights in the Western legal tradition* (Berkeley, 1993), p. 121.

203 It also encourages the use of the English language, though there are signs that this dominance of English may be declining. See 'Global Internet Statistics', Global Reach, available at <http://www.glreach.com/globstats/> (as at 10 December 2003) (35% of users in 2003 spoke English as their native language, and 65% were non-English – of which the largest group was the 12% who spoke Chinese).

204 See Walter Ullmann, 'This Realm of England is an Empire', *Journal of Ecclesiastical History*, 30 (1979): 175–203.

205 A similar argument was made for the Pope's legal supremacy; See Hyginus Eugene Cardinale, *The Holy See and the international order* (Toronto, 1976); Walter Ullmann, *The growth of papal government in the Middle Ages: a study in the ideological relation of clerical to lay power* (2nd edn, London, 1965).

206 'SPQR' (*Senatus Populusque Romae*) – for the Senate and People of Rome, was a was a kind of 'motto' of the Roman Republic, but which never passed entirely out of use until the later years of the empire.

207 See David Potter, *Prophets and Emperors: Human and Divine Authority from Augustus to Theodosius* (Cambridge, 1994).

208 This is reflected in the words of the pledge of allegiance to the flag of the United States – 'one nation under God' – adopted 1954 when President Dwight D. Eisenhower approved adding the words 'under God' to the existing pledge, despite the constitutional separation of church and State in the United States (in the First Amendment of the United States Constitution: 'Congress shall make no law respecting an establishment of religion, or prohibiting the free exercise thereof.').

209 J.P. Canning, 'Law, sovereignty and corporation theory, 1300–1450', in J.H. Burns (ed.), *The Cambridge History of Mediæval Political Thought c.350–c.1450* (Cambridge, 1988), pp. 465–7.

210 Harold J. Berman, *Law and Revolution: The Formation of the Western Legal Tradition* (Cambridge, 1983), ch. 14.

211 Pennington, *The Prince and the Law, 1200–1600*, p. 12.

212 Canning, 'Law, sovereignty and corporation theory, 1300–1450'.

213 Pennington, *The Prince and the Law, 1200–1600*, p. 30.

214 See Johnston, *Sovereignty and protection.*

215 See Montserrat Guibernau, *Nationalisms: the nation-state and nationalism in the twentieth century* (Cambridge, 1996).

216 See Robert Carr, *Black nationalism in the new world: reading the African American and West Indian experience* (Durham, 2002).

217 Though a separate jurisdiction for cyberspace has been rejected by the courts; *New Zealand Post v Leng* [1999] 3 NZLR 219, 226 per Williams J.

218 See Cooter, 'Structural adjudication and the new law merchant'.

219 For the recognition of new states see C. Hillgruber, 'The Admission of New States to the International Community', *European Journal of International Law*, 9 (1998): 491–509; T. Grant, *The Recognition of States: Law and Practice in Debate and Evolution* (Westport, 1999). The European practice of recognizing new States in Eastern Europe and in the former Soviet Union in 1991–1992 was based on the guidelines adopted by the European Commission Member States on 16 December 1991. The list of criteria lays down the conditions that had to be fulfilled before the Community was prepared to recognize the new States, and thus to agree to their admission to the community of States and to the international community. It has been claimed that the conditions listed in the guidelines are merely the criteria for the establishment of diplomatic relations – something which is in the political discretion of the States in any case – and not requirements for Statehood in the sense of international law; See M. Weller, 'The International Response to the Dissolution of the Socialist Federal Republic of Yugoslavia', *American Journal of International Law*, 86 (1992): 569, 588, 604. See also S. Talmon, 'Recognition of Governments: An Analysis of the New British Policy and Practice', *British Yearbook of International Law*, 58 (1992): 231–97, 250–1; *Montevideo Convention on the Rights and Duties of States*, 26 December 1933, 49 Stat 3097; USA Treaty Series 881, entered into force 26 December 1934, in Manley Ottmer Hudson (ed.), *International Legislation* (6 vols, Washington, 1931–50), vol. 6, p. 620; Ian Brownlie, *Principles of Public International Law* (5th edn, New York, 1998), ch. 5. Although the application of the Convention is confined to Latin America, it is regarded as declaratory of customary international law. See also *Island of Palmas Arbitration Case* (1928) No xix (2) Reports of International Arbitral Awards 829; (1928) 22 *American Journal of International Law* 986; 4 *Arbitration Decisions* 3.

220 See Cox, 'Tax and regulatory avoidance through non-traditional alternatives to tax havens'.

221 The assumptions of international lawyers about the near-exclusive role of States seem to be largely shared by international relations theory. See K. Abbott, 'Modern International Relations Theory: A Prospectus for International Lawyers', *Journal of International Law*, 14 (1989): 335–411.

222 See S. Charnovitz, 'Opening the WTO to Non-Governmental Interests' (2000) 24 *Fordham International Law Journal* 173; Legal Affairs Committee of the Parliamentary Assembly of the Council of Europe, *Legal Status of International Non-Governmental Organizations in Europe*, ed D. Smith (Legal Affairs Committee of the Parliamentary Assembly of the Council of Europe, Brussels, 1986); 'International Status, privileges and immunities of international organizations, their officials, experts, etc' in *Analytical Guide to the Practice of the International*, available at <http://www.un.org/law/ilc/guide/gfra.htm> (as at 1 December 2003). See also *European Convention on the Recognition of the Legal Personality of International Non-Governmental Organizations*, 24 April 1986, ETS 124, entered into force 1 January 1991.

223 Sir Hersch Lauterpacht, 'The Subjects of the Law of Nations'. See also C. Schreuer, 'The Waning of the Sovereign State: Towards A New Paradigm for International

Law?' (1993) 4 *European Journal of International Law* 447, available at <http://www.ejil.org/journal/Vol4/No4/art1.html> (as at 1 December 2003).

224 See C. Schreuer, 'The Waning of the Sovereign State: Towards a New Paradigm for International Law', *European Journal of International Law*, 4 (1993): 447–71.

225 See ibid.; M. Koskenniemi, 'The Future of Statehood', *Harvard International Law Journal*, 32 (1991): 397; N. MacCormick, 'Beyond the Sovereign States', *Modern Law Review*, 56 (1993): 1.

226 *Reparation for Injuries Suffered in the Service of the UN* (1949) 4 ICJR 179.

227 '[The UN] is a subject of international law and capable of possessing international rights and duties, and ... it has capacity to maintain its rights by bringing international claims'; see *Reparation for Injuries Suffered in the Service of the UN* (1949) 4 ICJR 179, pp. 178, 179.

228 The Holy See is in a similar position, though the existence of the Vatican City complicates the situation. It is important to realize that it is the Holy See which is recognized by the United Nations, and not Vatican City State (which fulfils the fuller requirements for State sovereignty). In United Nations documents, the term 'Holy See' is used except in texts concerning the International Telecommunications Union and the Universal Postal Union, where the term 'Vatican City State' is used. States do not entertain diplomatic relations with Vatican City State, but with the Holy See. The term 'Holy See' refers to the supreme authority of the Church, the Pope as Bishop of Rome and head of the College of Cardinals. It is the central government of the Roman Catholic Church: See Archbishop R. Martino, 'A Short History of the Holy See's Diplomacy', available at <http://www.holyseemission.org/short_history.html> (as at 1 December 2003).

229 The Order was also involved in the Geneva Conventions, and is a member of the International Red Cross. The European Communities also accredit some ambassadors. Both the Order of Malta and the International Red Cross have had permanent observer status at the United Nations since 1994. For a list of permanent members, non-member States with permanent observer missions at UN headquarters, and entities with a standing invitation to participate as observers in the sessions and work of the General Assembly and maintaining permanent offices at headquarters, see <http://www.un.org/Overview/missions.htm#nperm> (as at 1 December 2003).

230 For example, San Marino acknowledged the Order as a sovereign State in a treaty of amity in 1935; See A. Astraudo, 'Saint-marin et l'Ordre de Malta', *La Revue Diplomatique*, (1935): 7.

231 Though the canon law of the Church accorded recognition to certain organizations.

232 The best statement of this position – though dated – is that of J. Hatschek, *An Outline of International Law*, trans. C. Manning (London, 1930), p. 56, cited in D.P. O'Connell, *International Law* (2nd edn, London, 1970), pp. 85–6; Archbishop R. Martino, 'A Short History of the Holy See's Diplomacy', available at <http://www.holyseemission.org/short_history.html> (as at 1 December 2003).

233 Many countries (the United States and most Western European countries) did not recognize the incorporation of the Baltic States into the USSR in 1940, at least initially: United States Mission to the United Nations, see 'The United States reaffirms recognition of independence of Estonia, Latvia and Lithuania', 29 July 1983, available at <http://web-static.vm.ee/static/failid/182/President_Reagan_statement.pdf> (as at 1 December 2003); cf G. Marston, 'The British Acquisition of the Nicobar Islands,

1869: A Possible Example of Abandonment of Territorial Sovereignty', *British Yearbook of International Law*, 69 (1998) 245.

234 Though even in the heyday of State sovereignty, the late nineteenth century, the extent to which any State was truly independent depended much on non-legal factors, such as relative economic strength.

235 See Cox, 'Tax and regulatory avoidance through non-traditional alternatives to tax havens'.

236 See S.P. Menefee, 'Republics of the Reefs: Nation-Building on the Continental Shelf and in the World's Oceans', *California Western International Law Journal*, 25 (1994): 81–111.

237 See Cox, 'Tax and regulatory avoidance through non-traditional alternatives to tax havens'.

238 See L. Horn, 'To Be or Not to Be: The Republic of Minerva – Nation-founding by Individuals', *Columbia Journal of Transnational Law*, 12 (1973): 520; Menefee, 'Republics of the Reefs: Nation-Building on the Continental Shelf and in the World's Oceans'.

239 See Menefee, 'Republics of the Reefs: Nation-Building on the Continental Shelf and in the World's Oceans'.

240 See N. Papadakis, *The International Legal Regime of Artificial Islands* (Leiden, 1977); Menefee, 'Republics of the Reefs: Nation-Building on the Continental Shelf and in the World's Oceans', 82.

241 See Cox, 'Tax and regulatory avoidance through non-traditional alternatives to tax havens'.

242 See the judgment of the International Court of Justice in the *Western Sahara*, Advisory Opinion, International Court of Justice Reports 12, 63–65 (1975); 59 ILR 30, 80–82.

243 Which may however be very small, or even of varying extent: *United States v Ray*, 281 F Supp 876 (SD Fla 1965); *Atlantis Development Corporation v United States*, 379 F 2d 818 (5th Cir 1967); *United States v Ray*, 294 F Supp 532 (SD Fla 1969); and *United States v Ray*, 423 F 2d 16 (5th Cir 1970); *Chierici and Rosa v Ministry of the Merchant Navy and Harbour Office of Rimini*, 71 ILR 258 (14 November 1969) partial English translation and fact summary (citing (1975) 1 *Italian Yearbook of International Law* 265 (Council of State); *In re Duchy of Sealand* (1978) 80 ILR 683 (Administrative Court of Cologne), cf <http://www.sealandgov.com> (as at 1 December 2003).

244 This was expressly outlined in the *Montevideo Convention on the Rights and Duties of States*, 26 December 1933, 49 Stat 3097; USA Treaty Series 881, entered into force on 26 December 1934, in Hudson, vol. 6, p. 620; available at <http://www.yale.edu/lawweb/avalon/intdip/interam/intam03.htm> (as at 1 December 2003). Although the formal application of the Convention is confined to Latin America, it is regarded as declaratory of customary international law. The Arbitration Commission of the European Conference on Yugoslavia, in Opinion No 1, declared that: 'The state is commonly defined as a community which consists of a territory and a population subject to an organised political authority'. (See 92 ILR 162, 165). On the Arbitration Commission generally, see M. Craven, 'The EC Arbitration Commission on Yugoslavia', *British Yearbook of International Law*, 66 (1995): 333.

245 The Montevideo Convention on the Rights and Duties of States, signed 26 December 1933; Hudson, vol. 6, p. 620.

246 92 International Law Reports 162, 165. On the Arbitration Commission generally see Craven, 'The EC Arbitration Commission on Yugoslavia'.

247 See Cox, 'Tax and regulatory avoidance through non-traditional alternatives to tax havens'.

248 In some countries it has also declined as a concept in domestic law, with an increased justiciability and limits upon sovereign immunity. See Maurice Sunkin and Sebastian Payne, *The Nature of the Crown: A Legal and Political Analysis* (Oxford, 1999).

249 For comparative purposes, see Richard Conley, 'Sovereignty or the Status Quo? The 1998 pre-referendum debate in Quebec', *Journal of Commonwealth and Comparative Politics*, 35 (1997): 67–92; Paul Howe, 'Nationality and Sovereignty Support in Quebec', *Canadian Journal of Political Science*, 31 (1998): 31–60.

250 For the impact of electronic commerce generally, see C.C. Nicoll, 'Electronic Commerce: a New Zealand perspective', *EDI Law Review: Legal Aspects of Paperless Communication*, 6 (1999): 5–20.

251 See Hillgruber, 'The Admission of New States to the International Community'.

252 Grant, *The Recognition of States*. The European practice of recognizing new States in Eastern Europe and in the former Soviet Union in 1991–1992 was based on the guidelines adopted by the European Commission Member States on 16 December 1991 (see *International Legal Materials*, 31 (1992): 1486). The list of criteria lays down the conditions that had to be fulfilled before the Community was prepared to recognize the new States, and thus to agree to their admission to the community of States and to the international community. It has been claimed that the conditions listed in the guidelines are merely the criteria for the establishment of diplomatic relations – something which is in the political discretion of the States in any case – and not requirements for Statehood in the sense of international law; See Weller, 'The International Response to the Dissolution of the Socialist Federal Republic of Yugoslavia', 588, 604. See also Talmon, 'Recognition of Governments: An Analysis of the New British Policy and Practice', 250–1.

253 See Cox, 'Tax and regulatory avoidance through non-traditional alternatives to tax havens'.

254 See Johnson, and Post, 'Law and Borders'.

255 See Brownlie, *Principles of Public International Law*, p. 301; Sir Robert Jennings and Sir Arthur Watts (eds), *Oppenheim's International Law* (9th edn, London, 1992), vol. 1, p. 456; F.A. Mann, 'The Doctrine of Jurisdiction in International Law', *Recueil des Cours*, 111 (1964): 9, 10–3; F.A. Mann, 'The Doctrine of Jurisdiction in International Law Revisited After Twenty Years', *Recueil des Cours*, 186 (1984): 9, 20.

256 See, for example, Puurunen, 'The Legislative Jurisdiction of States over Transactions in International Electronic Commerce'.

257 *United States v Montoya de Hernandez*, 473 US 531. See also Branscomb, 'Jurisdictional Quandaries for Global Networks', pp. 83, 103.

258 See 'Framework for Global Electronic Commerce', available at <http://www.ecommerce.gov/> (as at 1 December 2003); 'Management of Internet', available at <http://www.ntia.doc.gov/> (as at 1 December 2003). Their legal right to do so is undoubted: *United States v Smith*, 680 F 2d 255 (1st Cir Mass 1982). See also President's Working Group on Unlawful Conduct on the Internet, 'The Electronic

Frontier: The Challenge of Unlawful Conduct Involving the Use of the Internet' (March 2000), available at <http://www.usdoj.gov/criminal/cybercrime/unlawful.htm> (as at 1 December 2003).

259 See Greenleaf, 'An Endnote on Regulating Cyberspace: Architecture vs Law?'.

260 The efficacy of the concept of 'closest and most real connection' (*McConnell Dowell Constructors Ltd v Lloyd's Syndicate 396* [1988] 2 NZLR 257 (CA)) is also reduced, in that no part of the world is any more directly affected than any other by events on the web, as information is available simultaneously to anyone with a connection to the Internet; Johnson, and Post, 'Law and Borders'. Nor, in terms of the protection of intellectual property rights: Burk, 'Muddy Rules for Cyberspace'.

261 *McConnell Dowell Constructors Ltd v Lloyd's Syndicate 396* [1988] 2 NZLR 257 (CA).

262 See Johnson, and Post, 'Law and Borders'.

263 Location remains important, but it is virtual location, rather than physical location. There is no necessary connection between an Internet address and a physical location. For a general description of the Domain Naming System, see D.L. Burk, 'Trademarks Along the Infobahn: A First Look at the Emerging Law of Cybermarks', *University of Richmond Journal of Law and Technology*, 1 (1995): 1.

264 Something which may be related to the relative length of the virtual border: see Johnson, and Post, 'Law and Borders'.

265 With the dominance of democratic concepts of government, it might be thought that if the people believe that an institution is appropriate, then it is legitimate: See Penelope Brook Cowen, 'Neo Liberalism', in Raymond Miller (ed.), *New Zealand Politics in Transition* (Auckland, 1997), p. 341. But this scheme leaves out of account substantive questions about the justice of the State and the protection it offers the individuals who belong to it. This point is illustrated by the study of the application of the model to Mummar Qadhafi's Libya: Saleh Al Namlah, 'Political Legitimacy in Libya Since 1969' (1992) Syracuse University PhD thesis. It is generally more usual to maintain that a State's legitimacy depends upon its upholding certain human rights: John Rawls, *Political Liberalism* (New York, 1993); Ted Honderich (ed.), *The Oxford Companion to Philosophy* (Oxford, 1995), p. 477 'Legitimacy'; M. Swanson, 'The Social Extract Tradition and the Question of Political Legitimacy' (1995) University of Missouri–Columbia PhD thesis 1995.

266 See Johnson, and Post, 'Law and Borders'.

267 See W. Lash, 'The Decline of the Nation State in International Trade and Development', *Cardozo Law Review* (1996–97): 1001; B. Sanford and Michael J. Lorenger, 'Teaching an Old Dog New Tricks', *Connecticut Law Review*, 28 (1995–96): 1137–70, 1143; Dan L Burk, 'Patents in Cyberspace: Territoriality and Infringement on Global Computer Networks', *Tulane Law Review*, 68 (1993–94): 1–67; W.B. Wriston, *The Twilight of Sovereignty* (New York, 1992) (examining the challenges to sovereignty posed by the information revolution).

268 See Zekos, 'Internet or Electronic Technology'.

269 *United States v Smith*, 680 F 2d 255 (1st Cir. Mass 1982). See also President's Working Group on Unlawful Conduct on the Internet, 'The Electronic Frontier: The Challenge of Unlawful Conduct Involving the Use of the Internet' (March 2000), available at <http://www.usdoj.gov/criminal/cybercrime/unlawful.htm> (as at 1 December 2003).

270 See Greenleaf, 'An Endnote on Regulating Cyberspace: Architecture vs Law?'.

271 See Stephen Krasner, 'Sovereignty: an institutional perspective', *Comparative Political Studies*, 21 (1988): 66–94.

272 See Zekos, 'Internet or Electronic Technology'.

273 See Lash, 'The Decline of the Nation State in International Trade and Development'; Sanford and Lorenger, 'Teaching an Old Dog New Tricks'; Burk, 'Patents in Cyberspace.

274 See F. Hinsley, *Sovereignty* (2nd edn, Cambridge, 1996); Krasner, 'Sovereignty'.

275 See Cox, 'The regulation of cyberspace and the loss of national sovereignty'.

276 See Trakman, *The Law Merchant.*

277 See Gerhard von Glahn, *Law Among Nations: An Introduction to Public International Law* (7th edn, Boston, 1996).

278 Though it has been argued that it should be; See Johnson, and Post, 'Law and Borders'; Johnson and Post, 'And How Shall the Net be Governed?'. Geist, Reidenberg, and others have rejected this notion; See, for example, Reidenberg, 'Governing Networks and Rule-Making in Cyberspace'; Joel R. Reidenberg, 'Lex Informatica: The Formulation of Information Policy Rules Through Technology', *Texas Law Review*, 76 (1998): 553–94.

279 A supra-state, not a super-state, because it is not a state but rather a political entity linking existing states.

Chapter 8

Technological Challenges to Law, Property and Ethics

8.1 Introduction

Technological innovations such as the Internet also offer opportunities for global communications which present some challenges to the state. But the Internet is, in principle at least, little more than a new means of communications, though it may be considerably more effective than previous systems (and indeed its 'newness' might be questioned also) – and with greater potential for growth. But constitutions are concerned with more than merely the regulation of information, and with the interchange of knowledge; they also reflect, to a greater or lesser degree, notions of property and an ethical or moral dimension. Certain new technologies present particularly significant challenges to these underlying conceptual perspectives.

Technological advances in fields other than the Internet challenge the boundaries of law, science, public policy, and ethics.[1] Biological research, and in particular genetic research, is especially significant in this respect. Embryonic stem cell research[2] and therapeutic cloning,[3] challenge perceptions of personality and society.[4] Genetic engineering[5] also has serious implications for the medical and health insurance field,[6] since illness and diseases could potentially be significantly reduced in frequency or severity by human genetic engineering. In this Chapter we shall consider some of the legal implications of the ethical and property aspects of some modern technology, using genetic engineering as an example. We will then consider the constitutional implications of this.

Perhaps to an even greater extent than with the Internet, for genetic engineering the questions of the existence and nature of controls on the technology are of paramount importance. This involves decisions about what may be done and what may not be done which are culturally-grounded. As was discussed in Chapter 2.3, where technological opportunities exist for businesses to make new products, or enlarge their businesses, these opportunities will be seized. But governments respond to these in various ways, depending upon the political, social and ethical complexion and complexity of the state – and this may well (and indeed invariably does) change radically over time.

8.2 The Advent of Modern Genetic Engineering

Fundamental changes in technology necessitate, or cause, significant changes in legal systems. The protection accorded intellectual property is as important as the restrictions on certain types of work, for they protect the investment which is required to undertake further research and development work. The formal structure however appears largely unchanged – and it is only in its scale that a fundamental change is apparent.

Genetic engineering for agricultural purposes has major implications – not least of which in that it is promoted as a solution to ongoing food production problems in the Third World.[7] Biotechnicians have altered plants and animals for improved nutritional value. They have produced potatoes with more starch[8] and pigs with an increased protein-to-fat ratio.[9] Researchers are also attempting to produce larger, faster growing, and more productive agricultural animals that require less feed.[10] Biotechnicians are already altering plants to withstand pests and disease, and those that fix their own nitrogen and resist drought and cold.[11] The first genetically-altered whole food-product to appear on supermarket shelves was a tomato that spoiled less quickly than unaltered tomatoes.[12] These developments raise hopes for an increase in the world's food supply and a decrease in the use of chemicals in agriculture.[13] Each of these potential developments – agricultural and human – also involves considerable investment and potentially large profits for businesses.

Biotechnology itself is an old technology. The use of living organisms to make bread, wine, and cheese is a longstanding human practice. Humanity has 'genetically-engineered' plants and animals, including humans, by selective breeding for desirable characteristics for thousands of years.[14] From the time people first began cultivating and harvesting cereal grains, plants and their products have been a necessary component of the material foundations upon which human societies are formed.[15]

However, because seeds are not easily commodified, until the latter part of the twentieth century the genetics of most major crop plants have been regarded as common heritage, and comparatively little private investment has been made in plant and crop improvement.[16] That is not to say there were not laws concerning intellectual property in plants and animals, but their scope and application was limited.[17] The high-technology genetic engineering revolution – as distinct from breeding and cultivation – began at least by 1952 with the discovery by James Watson and Sir Francis Crick of the structure of the deoxyribonucleic acid (DNA) molecule – the molecule that contains our genetic information.[18] But the pace of the revolution has accelerated most rapidly in the last ten years.[19] The search for new pharmaceutical, biotechnological or agricultural applications has led to a growing interest both from the public and from the private sector in genetic resources.[20]

The biotechnological revolution of the 1980s and 1990s enabled scientists to isolate the genetic materials of living organisms and induce precise modifications so that organisms manifest and carry desired genetic traits.[21] Biotechnology is beginning to revolutionise agriculture by developing genetically superior plants and animals[22] (though there have been at least as many spectacular failures as successes) and therefore will have profound long-term economic consequences. It is also offered as a solution to difficult environmental problems and challenges.[23]

It is sometimes suggested that the new biotechnologies[24] are not radical departures from these historical practices. One defender of biotechnology claimed that 'centuries of selective breeding have altered domestic animals far more than the next several decades of transgenic modifications are expected to alter them.'[25] Another of biotechnology's defenders argued that nature routinely reshuffles genetic material by combining genes in new ways during sexual reproduction, by altering genes through mutations, and by transferring foreign genes into already existing organisms.[26]

While it is probable that the differing attitudes to genetic engineering reflect different ethical, moral and religious attitudes, some opinions may be too extreme to receive widespread support. However, unlike the Internet, which might be said to be relatively amoral (though aspects of its use may be immoral – not necessarily through any inherent fault on the part of the system), genetic engineering has been perceived as being much more sensitive. Issues of morality and immortality, and broader ethical considerations, arise. This is scarcely surprising, since it involves the use and manipulation of living tissue, animal and vegetable – potentially including human.

While no state is (generally speaking) immoral, few are entirely amoral. This is reflected in their laws. Some element of morality underpins the legal system. Law is not law if it lacks the power to bind, to compel, and to punish. While it would not be correct to define law simply as compulsion or coercion, it is also an error to define law without recognizing that coercion is basic to it. To separate power from law is to deny it the status of law.[27] Power itself is partly a religious concept, and the god or gods of any system of thought have been the sources of power for that system.[28] The sovereign or ruler has a religious significance in part because of his power. Indeed, Christians had always – at least from the fourth century – considered the state a divine institution, recognizing and promoting the Christian religion at the centre of its moral identity.[29] When the democratic state gains power, it too arrogates to itself religious claims and prerogatives. Power is jealously guarded in the state,[30] and any division of powers in the state, designed to limit its power and prevent its concentration, is bitterly contested.[31] It is not a coincidence that the conflict between church and state reached a climax in Europe in the sixteenth century, at a time when the modern state began to succeed in its claims to a monopoly of allegiance.[32] This had serious implications for law reflected today in the on-going debate over genetic engineering.

The law, both criminal and civil, claims to be able to speak about morality and immorality generally. Where it gets its authority to do this and how it settles the moral principles which it enforces, are vital questions. Undoubtedly, as a matter of history in the west, it derives both partly from Christian teaching.[33] But the secular law can no longer rely on doctrine in which citizens are entitled to disbelieve, and even the law of the church is not immune from this destabilizing influence.[34] It is necessary therefore to look for some other source of authority.[35]

The law of western civilization has been Christian law, but its faith is increasingly humanist. But in a society where the church has ceased to be (or never was) the church of the people, but rather a voluntary association, questions of the morality or ethnical acceptability of actions become increasingly difficult. Thus the law is unlikely to 'speak with one voice' with respect to genetic engineering, given its inherent nature and potential scope.

Commentators suggested that the changes in the planet resulting from the creation, use, and release of biotechnical products could dwarf the changes that have resulted from the use of petrochemical products.[36] The World Resources Institute, for instance, sees genetic material as the 'oil of the Information Age.'[37] Whichever view is correct, a new legal regime has evolved, to respond to what is a paradigmatic change in technology. Partly this is because of ethical, moral and religious concerns, but economic factors have also been important, for example concerns that previous laws meant that developed countries were advantaged over Third World countries which were the source of much of the raw genetic material.[38] Knowledge alone becomes valuable, as the building blocks of organisms have economic value. Therefore business seizes the opportunity offered – and laws respond to this by allocating and protecting intellectual property rights.

Just as the underlying basis of genetic engineering is subject to controversy, so its utilization is fraught with difficulties. Not least of these is the question of the control of the information, the raw materials, and the products of genetic engineering.

In recent years, advances in biotechnology have allowed for increased commodification of seeds not only by relying on utility patent protection for bioengineered varieties, but also by taking a new route to commodification – through biotechnical processes that, among other things, render seeds sterile or insert easily recognizable 'marker' genes that identify plants' DNA strains as the intellectual property of various biotech firms.[39] It thus becomes possible to identify crops as the intellectual property of a particular company or individual. The translation of these innovations into the international realm of global trade and property protection has been awkward and at times controversial.[40] Genetic engineering has business, ethical, religious, and legal ramifications.[41] Thus as the investment increases so does the demand for legal protection of the associated intellectual property rights.

Business-wise, biotechnology has stimulated the creation and growth of small (and some medium and large) businesses, generated new jobs, and encouraged agricultural and industrial innovation.[42] It is one of the most research-intensive and innovative industries in the scientific fields.[43] But it is also carefully regulated by law – and there are detailed limits on the types of research which may be conducted, and the commercial exploitation of genetically modified organisms. So far as it is able business funds genetic research, because of its potential returns.

But little research would occur – beyond the most fundamental – if no protection was accorded the results of the research. Basic research is rarely undertaken by private enterprise without some expectation of a return.

Since the 1970s much attention has been paid to the patentability of biotechnology.[44] In the United States, the patent system played a critical role in the growth of the biotechnology industry. In the 1990s biotechnology grew into a US$13 billion industry, and the number of biotechnology patent applications exceeded 14,000 annually.[45] Similar levels of growth continue to be maintained. Patent protection is vital to the biotechnology industry, particularly because small biotechnology companies invest enormous sums of money in research and development. Often, intellectual property is the only product that a young company can show its potential investors; and patents are ideally suited to protect technology-based intellectual property.[46]

Proponents of biotechnology patenting suggest that the new biotechnology patents, or 'biopatents,' are minor and logical extensions from past practice, not radical revisions.[47] Thus they rely upon the pre-existing legal processes, such as intellectual property laws – specifically patent laws.

Genetic engineering is not, of course, limited to the vegetable kingdom. Harvard University received the first patent on animal life. Its patent was for a mouse genetically altered to be susceptible to breast cancer.[48] As the project's major sponsor Du Pont possessed commercial rights and the chemical company sold the patented research animals.[49] It is in the animal kingdom that the legal response may have been most significant, because of the ethical issues which it raises. But human genetics is increasingly the cause for popular concern. This is because of the ethical, moral and religious issues which the manipulation of human organisms raise, and because of the commercialisation or commodification of these organisms.

In the 1990s, J. Craig Venter, a biologist at the National Institutes of Health (NIH), in Bethesda, Maryland, proposed the wholesale patenting of human gene fragments. Venter's laboratory, using automated machines, had sequenced random fragments of cDNA, called an 'expressed sequence tag,' or EST,[50] derived from part of the brain.[51] Each was unique and served to identify the gene of which it was a part.[52] In June 1991, Venter and NIH filed for patents on 315 ESTs and the human genes from which they came.[53] The NIH could produce EST sequences so quickly that it planned to file patent applications for 1,000 of them a month.[54]

This wholesale patenting of EST sequences – rather than whole genes – did not pass without opposition. A number of patent experts insisted that ESTs were not patentable.[55] This was on the relatively narrow ground that NIH had failed to show sufficient legal grounds. More fundamentally Venter's initiative also provoked denunciations from scientists concerned that EST patents, if issued, would restrict research by others on human genes. The Association of Biotechnology Companies in Washington, DC, which represented 280 companies and institutions, endorsed EST patenting by NIH so long as it did not favour any one company over another.[56] But concerns were expressed by the wider biotechnology industry. In addition, many of the opponents of EST patenting were concerned at the prospect that the government – through the NIH – would own those patents.[57] The control of these patents would thus fall into the hands of the US Government, rather than remain in the hands of private enterprise, a matter of some concern to those concerned about the ethical use of technology – though it might be argued that this would be safer than relying on private enterprise, driven as it is by the need to make a financial profit.

This was also a matter of concern for governments, and was not left entirely to industry. There was opposition to NIH's EST patents from the Governments and scientific communities of a number of countries, who feared that the patents would confer competitive advantage on the US biotechnology industry, and seriously harm their own fledgling industries.[58] The French Academy of Sciences condemned 'any measure which, answering purely to a logic of industrial competition, strove to obtain the legal property of genetic information data, without even having taken care to characterise the genes considered.'[59] Similar concern was expressed in Italy and Japan.

In contrast to this position the United Kingdom chose to follow the US lead. Alan Howarth, the then Minister of Science, announced in March 1992 that the Medical Research Council would also seek complementary DNA (cDNA) patents.[60] Howarth explained that 'a decision ... not to seek patents when researchers funded by public bodies in other countries have or may do so could place the United Kingdom at a relative disadvantage.'[61] Private business and research laboratories conducted much of the research in the United States, but the public institutions conducted most of the research in the United Kingdom and elsewhere.

The immediate cause for concern ended almost as suddenly as it had begun. In August 1992 the United States Patent Office rejected the Venter/NIH claims, calling them 'vague, indefinite, misdescriptive, inaccurate and incomprehensible.'[62] The patent experts who had insisted that ESTs were not patentable because NIH had failed to show sufficient legal grounds were proven at least partly right. But the broader question of the potential for a monopoly on patents required for further fundamental genetic research remained unanswered.[63]

The question of patenting biological inventions was reconsidered by the European Parliament in 1997.[64] In the following year it approved a directive on biotechnology designed to encourage patents while adopting explicit ethical restrictions – for the first time anywhere – on what can be patented.[65] The directive prohibits patents on human parts, human embryos, and the products of human cloning.[66] The rationale here is that biotechnology patents must safeguard the dignity and integrity of the person. The directive also prohibits patents on animals if what they suffer by being modified exceeds the benefits that the modification would yield.[67]

One of the most important on-going jurisprudential debates has been the proper balance between the protection of intellectual property and the encouragement of innovation. This is particularly pronounced in the high technology field, such as genetic engineering. Not only do researchers and developers potentially acquire monopolies, but the owners of the genetic source material may not gain any benefits. They may even, like the horticulturalists, find themselves paying royalties to the developers for planting crops which they thought they owned. This was especially sensitive when ethical factors were introduced.

Meanwhile basic and applied research continues, as there was no doubt that, though genetic research is expensive, great potential exists for long-term profit – provided the investment is legally protected.

The Human Genome Project (HGP), funded by the United States Government, was projected to be completed in fifteen years at a cost of US$3 billion.[68] The purpose of the HGP is to decipher the human genome, which is the master control program of human biological life.[69] With knowledge gained from the HGP, diagnostic tests for genetic defects are now available,[70] and it is hoped that cures for diseases caused by these genetic defects will follow.[71] This project proceeded despite uncertainties regarding patents, as the work itself would not produce patentable outputs – but would rather facilitate genetic work.

The difficulty for patenting the 'codes of life' – and their potential risk – led to government intervention, and new laws. Indeed, for human DNA, some people question whether there should be any property rights at all.[72] Such a position would seriously inhibit privately-funded research, since little or no protection would be accorded to its findings.

For more than two centuries intellectual property laws have sought – often successfully, but more often than not unsuccessfully – to keep abreast with rapid technological change. The biotechnology revolution is not unique, but already has posed significant new problems for intellectual property laws – including patent laws – and especially in balancing the interests of scientists, investors and those from whom valuable genetic material is obtained.

It has been said that intellectual property law is designed to advance knowledge and to stimulate innovation for the benefit of society.[73] To encourage this goal, a patent confers upon an inventor a government-backed limited monopoly.[74] This balances the need to stimulate the dissemination of knowledge, and the encouragement of the development of ideas, by allowing the inventor to profit from his or her invention. But the details of patent laws vary from country to country.

Australia and the United Kingdom, as well as most other countries (the United States being a notable exception), adopt the 'first-to-file' principle of patent law. This means that the person entitled to the patent is the first to file the application, even if he or she was not also the first person to have conceived the invention. The date at which the invention is assessed for both novelty and inventive step ('priority date') is the date on which the application was filed.[75] The principle of national treatment under the Paris Convention for the Protection of Industrial Property[76] establishes the date of first filing in a member country as the priority date for subsequent filings in other states, provided that these occur within 12 months from the original filing.[77] The effect was to encourage developers to file patents as soon as possible, but it also potentially discouraged fundamental research, the economic benefits of which – if any – might be lost simply through delayed filing. In this respect biotechnology laws may have limited the potential for further research and development.[78]

Existing intellectual property protection laws have been modified, and the only major legal shift has been with respect to human gene research. Research is now allowed, but with restrictions.[79] For agricultural research political issues have caused even more difficulties, because in addition to ethical concerns there are differences between regions, a north-south divide, and so on.

It has been argued that there is a clear need for an international regulation on genetic engineering,[80] because the lack of clear legislation has been creating uncertainty in terms of safety and international trade; has been making it more difficult to perceive when a country is violating the principle of state responsibility, just because its obligations under international law are not clear;[81] makes it more difficult for a country to observe its duty to assess environmental impacts, just because scientific findings are not absolutely conclusive in this matter, creating the possibility of discussion under World Trade Organization/General Agreement on Tariffs and Trade (WTO/GATT) (such as the Monarch Butterfly Case[82]); on the other hand makes it more difficult to identify when a country is violating its obligation not to cause environmental harm. Further, the lack of specific international legislation has been causing the impairment of commerce, and one of the consequences here may be the limitation on research and development of new biotechnology products; and has been creating a tension between international trade law and international environmental law.

At the present time, intellectual property law is the mechanism that determines international protection and control over biotechnology innovations in plant varieties – and human and animal genetic material – and the genetic resources that form the basis for those innovations.[83] The intellectual property paradigm that is utilized employs western definitions of property in order to provide a framework in which to allocate rights. This has resulted in serious distributive problems including western-specific ideas about property, authorship, and individual creative inventors.

Due to the failure of the legal system to adapt itself to changed agricultural technology the cost – or rather loss of benefit – to the indigenous peoples who possessed many of the raw materials has been great. The benefits – such as there have been – have often been to the major companies which already had sufficient market penetration to effectively introduce their new products.[84]

At a practical and normative level the issues thus raised converge on eligibility, and on whether modern biotechnology, however conceived, is a suitable subject matter for patent protection, or whether it is truly beyond the normative and doctrinal capacities of the patent system as that system currently exists.[85] This has been important at an international level, but nationally patent laws have been used by companies to protect their intellectual property – and to enhance its value. Yet without this the western companies – who do most of the research – could be discouraged.

As the laws stands, it advantages existing established companies. One example of this is through sector capture.[86] For instance, Monsanto's 'private property' in specific seed genomes, possessing genetically engineered characteristics such as drought and insect resistance, has been supplanting traditional agricultural understandings of seeds. This has accordingly changed farmers from seed saving 'proprietors' into mere licensees of a patented agricultural technology.[87] The sector capture was obvious: when a farmer bought high-yield hybrid seed, the seeds from that crop wouldn't duplicate the high yield, so the farmer had to return to the seed company the next season if he or she wanted continued high yields.[88] The 2001 Canadian *Schmeiser* case ('canola'[89]) is similar.[90]

These types of arrangements were of economic benefit to established suppliers, but may have a restrictive effect on others. The apparent economic failure in the genetically engineered crop market has been said to be because of asymmetry and the economic phenomena known as the 'lemon problem'.[91] Environmental and biological controversies have not helped either.[92]

There is perhaps still scope for the small research firm. Generally, however, it must be said that the response of business to the advent of genetic engineering has been cautious, because of the high regulatory risks and high costs, and uncertain benefits. The major legal determinant seems to be protection of ideas as intellectual property. The companies work around the restrictions – but only if their ideas are safeguarded. So far this has largely been through traditional intellectual property laws. Care must also be taken to ensure that there is a proper balance between protection of intellectual property – including that of indigenous peoples – and the common pool of human knowledge (the so-called 'global commons'), both issues for exploration at greater length than the constraints of this book will allow. Restrictions on certain types of research, and safeguards against the escape of organisms, seem less significant. In this case the paradigm shift is yet to come.

In the case of genetic engineering, business took advantage of pre-existing legal mechanisms – predominantly patent laws – in order to safeguard their investments. They also utilized licensing to achieve market capture – as in the Monsanto example. Both of these are relatively traditional uses of legal systems. However, where the difference lies is in the scale of the utilization of these mechanisms, and of the indirect effects – such as for indigenous peoples' property rights.

8.3 Conclusion

The changes to the legal regime governing genetic engineering – and particularly human genetics – have been influenced as much by political and ethical considerations as by economic considerations. The failure of the agricultural sector, in particular, to achieve the high returns which had been predicted also emphasize the need for caution in dealing with high risk, high return technologies where the legal protection is relatively undeveloped.

The protection of the economies of less developed countries and the prevention of the creation of cartels and monopolies are particularly important. Existing legal mechanisms are ill-matched to the conditions. It is possible for one basic genetic building block, patented as an invention might be, to form the basis for an extensive range of new products – each of which being the property of the developer. Governments are reminded of the ethical, moral and even religious context in which they operate. Just as we saw in the last Chapter how technological pressures affect constitutional developments and the external relations of states, so internally technology has a significant normative effect. This highlights the contextualization of constitutions, which are not purely utilitarian. The underlying philosophical basis remains important, though its nature may be uncertain.

Notes

1 Christine Vito, 'State biotechnology oversight: the juncture of technology, law, and public policy', *Maine Law Review*, 45 (1993): 329–83; Organization for Economic Co-operation and Development, *Bio technology and the changing role of government* (Paris, 1988); Robert Blank, *The political implications of human genetic technology* (Boulder, 1981); Donald Elliott, 'The Genome and the law: Should increased genetic knowledge change the law?', *Harvard Journal of Law and Public Policy*, 25 (2001): 61–70.

2 The United States National Institutes of Health define a stem cell as 'a cell from the embryo, foetus, or adult that has, under certain conditions, the ability to reproduce itself for long periods or, in the case of adult stem cells, throughout the life of the organism'; National Institutes of Health, US Department of Health and Human Services, *Stem Cells: Scientific Progress and Future Research Directions* ES-2 (Washington, 2001).

3 The term therapeutic cloning refers to cloning embryos for use in medical research and therapy. Synonyms include research cloning, cloning for biomedical research, somatic-cell nuclear transfer (or transplantation), and simply cloning (though, without further clarification, this last term may imply reproductive cloning). Paul Root Wolpe and Glenn McGee, '"Expert Bioethics" as Professional Discourse: The Case of Stem Cells', in Suzanne Holland, Karen Lebacqz and Laurie Zoloth (eds), *The Human Embryonic Stem Cell Debate: Science, Ethics, and Public Policy* (Cambridge, 2001), pp. 185, 188.

4 Janet L. Dolgin, 'Embryonic discourse: Abortion, stem cells, and cloning', *Florida State University Law Review*, 31 (2003): 101–62.

5 Christopher Cates, 'Property in Human Tissues: History, Society and Possible Implementations', *Appeal: Review of Current Law and Law Reform*, 4 (1998): 32–43.

6 Roberta M. Berry, 'The Human Genome Project and the End of Insurance', *Florida Journal of Law and Public Policy*, 7 (1996): 205–56; Jennifer S. Geetter, 'Coding for Change: The Power of the Human Genome to Transform the American Health Insurance System', *American Journal of Law and Medicine*, 28 (2001): 1–76.

7 See Gregory Rose, 'International law of sustainable agriculture in the 21st century: The International Treaty on Plant Genetic Resources for Food and Agriculture', *Georgetown International Environmental Law Review*, 15 (2003): 583–632.

8 See David M. Stark et al, 'Regulation of the Amount of Starch in Plant Tissues by ADP Glucose Pyrophosphorylase', *Science*, 258 (1992): 287–92.

9 Henry J. Miller, 'Patenting Animals', *Issues of Science and Technology* (1988–89): 24.

10 Experiments are also under way to make chickens and pigs with flesh more suitable for microwaving. See Kathleen Hart, 'Making Mythical Monsters', *The Progressive* (March 1990): 22.

11 William K. Stevens, 'Bioengineering Points to Better Rice Plant', *New York Times*, 6 February 1990, at C1.

12 For a description of Calgene Inc.'s Flavr Savr tomato, see 'Union of Concerned Scientists, FDA Approves the Calgene Tomato, No Labelling Required', *The Gene Exchange* (June 1994): 1.

13 See Sheldon Krimsky, *Biotechnics and society: The rise of industrial genetics* (Westport, 1991), pp. 44, 88–9; William K. Stevens, 'Bioengineering Points to Better Rice Plant', *New York Times*, 6 February 1990, at C1.

14 See Andrew Goudie, *The Human impact on the natural environment* (4th edn, Oxford, 1990), pp. 15–20.

15 See Jack Ralph Kloppenburg, Jr., *First the seed: The political economy of plant biotechnology 1492–2000* (Cambridge, 1988), p. 1; Sheldon Krimsky and Roger P. Wrubel, *Agricultural biotechnology and the environment* (Urbana, 1996), p. 9; H. Garrison Wilkes, 'Plant Genetic Resources over Ten Thousand Years: From a Handful of Seed to the Crop-Specific Mega-Gene Banks', in Jack R. Kloppenburg, Jr. (ed.), *Seeds and Sovereignty: The use and control of plant genetic resources* (Durham, 1988), pp. 67, 68.

16 See, generally, Kloppenburg, Jr., *First the seed.*

17 See, for example, Plant Variety Protection Act, 7 USC § 2402 (2003) (1970) (United States) (typically, its purpose is to 'encourage the development of novel varieties of sexually reproduced plants' by providing their owners with exclusive marketing rights of them in the United States. The requirements of protection are that the variety be uniform, stable, and distinct from all other varieties); Plant Variety Rights Act 1987 (New Zealand); Plant Varieties (Proprietary Rights) Act 1980 (Ireland); Plant Variety Act 1997 (United Kingdom).

18 It is a long linear polymer found in the nucleus of a cell and formed from nucleotides and shaped like a double helix; associated with the transmission of genetic information.

19 Jennifer S. Geetter, 'Coding for Change'; James Watson and Sir Francis Crick, 'Genetical Implications of the Structure of Deoxyribonucleic Acid', *Nature*, 171 (1953): 964–7.

20 J. Straus, 'Biodiversity and Intellectual Property', *AIPPI Yearbook*, 9 (1998): 99–128, 100: 'Genetic resources have become an issue of high priority to scientists, industry, politicians and even the public at large ... they form a warehouse of enormous use potentials for plant and animal breeding, food, chemical and environmental industries, pharmaceuticals and medicine'.

21 W. French Anderson, 'Human Gene Therapy', *Science*, 256 (1992): 808–13, 810; see also Stephen A. Duzan, 'The 1992 Biotechnology Agenda: A Message for Candidates Bush and Clinton', *Healthspan*, 9 (1992): 12–15.

22 Approximately 25 per cent of all the corn and 40 per cent of the soybeans that are grown in the United States are genetically modified. See Melinda Kimble, et al, 'Press Briefing of the United States Delegation to the Sixth Meeting of the Working Group on Biosafety

Convention on Biological Diversity', 18 February 1999, cited in Jasemine Chambers, 'Patent eligibility of biotechnological inventions in the United States, Europe, and Japan: How much patent policy is public policy?', *George Washington International Law Review*, 34 (2002): 223–46, 237 n 4.

23 See Duzan, 'The 1992 Biotechnology Agenda'.

24 For a description of these technologies, see Office of Technology Assessment, Congress of the United States, *New developments in biotechnology: Ownership of human tissues and cells – Special Report* (Washington, 1987).

25 Reid G. Adler, 'Controlling the Applications of Biotechnology: A Critical Analysis of the Proposed Moratorium on Animal Patenting', *Harvard Journal of Law and Technology*, (1988): 1–62, 20, n. 126.

26 See Lisa J. Raines, 'The Mouse That Roared: Patent Protection for Genetically Engineered Animals Makes Legal, Moral, and Economic Sense', *Issues of Science and Technology* (1988): 65, 67.

27 Norman Doe, 'Non-Legal rules and the courts: enforceability' (1987) 9 *Liverpool Law Review* 173–88; R. Baldwin and J. Houghton, 'Circular Arguments: The Status and Legitimacy of Administrative Rules' (1986) *Public Law* 239.

28 i.e. Emile Durkheim, *Elementary Forms of Religious Life* trans. Carol Cosman (Oxford, 2001).

29 Edward Norman, 'Authority in the Anglican Communion' (Ecclesiastical Law Society Lecture given during the Lambeth Conference 1998, transcribed by the Society of Archbishop Justus 1998). Even before Christianity was established as the official state religion, the church taught that Christians owed allegiance to the state: Luke 20.25 ('And he said unto them, Render therefore unto Caesar the things which be Caesar's, and unto God the things which be God's'); Mark 12.17; Matthew 22.21.

30 Whether the State is post-Christian is another question; compare Sir Ivor Richardson, *Religion and the Law* (Wellington, 1962), p. 61 and Rex Ahdar, 'New Zealand and the Idea of a Christian State', in Rex Ahdar and John Stenhouse (eds), *God and Government* (Dunedin, 2000), pp. 59–76.

31 Rousas John Rushdoony, *The Institutes of Biblical Law* (Los Angeles, 1973), pp. 58–59.

32 This conflict dates from the original linkage of Church and State under Constantine the Great, and has parallels in the state-sponsored paganism of (particularly) imperial Rome; Alan Watson, *The state, law, and religion* (Athens, 1992).

33 Matthew 28.18: 'All authority hath been given unto me in heaven and on earth'. This is then delegated to the church (John 20.21) 'As the Father hath sent me, even so send I you'.

34 See Norman, 'Authority in the Anglican Communion'.

35 Patrick Lord Devlin, *The Enforcement of Morals* (London, 1959), p. 9. See, for example, changes in the marriage laws.

36 Jeremy Rifkin, 'Creating the Efficient Gene', in Michael Ruse (ed.), *Philosophy of Biology* (Albany, 1989), pp. 222, 223.

37 See Jack Kloppenburg, 'No Hunting: Scientific Poaching and Global Biodiversity', *Z Magazine* (1990): 104–8.

38 See Kim JoDene Donat, 'Engineering Akerlof lemons: Information asymmetry, externalities, and market intervention in the genetically modified food market', *Minnesota Journal of Global Trade*, 12 (2003): 417–59. However, there is some room for optimism; see Mark Hannig, 'An examination of the possibility to secure intellectual

property rights for plant genetic resources developed by indigenous peoples of the NAFTA states: Domestic legislation under the International Convention for Protection of New Plant Varieties', *Arizona Journal of International and Comparative Law*, 13 (1996): 175–252.

39 See Michael Pollan, 'Playing God in the Garden', *New York Times*, 25 October 1998 § 6 (magazine), at 44.

40 See Charles McManis, 'The Interface Between International Intellectual Property and Environmental Protection: Biodiversity and Biotechnology', *Washington University Law Quarterly*, 76 (1998): 255–79, 255–6.

41 Daniel J. Kevles and Ari Berkowitz, 'The gene patenting controversy: A convergence of law, economic interests and ethics', *Brooklyn Law Review*, 67 (2001): 233–48.

42 President Clinton proclaimed January 2000 'National Biotechnology Month'. See Proclamation No. 7269 (2001) 3 CFR 19, 19.

43 Duzan, 'The 1992 Biotechnology Agenda'.

44 Justine Pila, 'Bound Futures: Patent law and modern biotechnology', *Boston University Journal of Science and Technology Law*, 9 (2003): 326–78, 326.

45 See Jenna Greene, 'He's Not Just Monkeying Around', *Legal Times*, 16 August 1999, at 16, 20.

46 Chambers, 'Patent eligibility of biotechnological inventions in the United States, Europe, and Japan', 224.

47 See Raines, 'The Mouse That Roared: Patent Protection for Genetically Engineered Animals Makes Legal, Moral, and Economic Sense', 65–6.

48 The 'oncomouse', as it is known, was developed by Harvard researchers Philip Leder and Timothy Stewart. See Sheldon Krimsky, *Biotechnics and society: The rise of industrial genetics* (Westport, 1991), pp. 44–5; Daniel J. Kevles, 'Diamond v. Chakrabarty and Beyond: The Political Economy of Patenting Life', in Arnold Thackray (ed.), *Private Science: Biotechnology and the Rise of the Molecular Sciences* (Philadelphia, 1998), pp. 65, 65–79.

49 See Elizabeth Corcoran, 'A Tiny Mouse Came Forth', *Scientific American* (1989) 73.

50 Ibid.

51 Mark D. Adams et al, 'Complementary DNA Sequencing: Expressed Sequence Tags and Human Genome Project', *Science*, 252 (1991): 1651–6; Christopher Anderson, 'United States Patent Application Stirs Up Gene Hunters', *Nature*, 353 (1991): 485–6.

52 Ibid.

53 Craig Venter and Mark Adams, 'Sequences', USPTO No. 07/716,831, at 235–6 (applied 20 June 1991).

54 Ibid.

55 See Leslie Roberts, 'Genome Patent Fight Erupts', *Science*, 254 (1991): 184–6, 185.

56 Rebecca S. Eisenberg, 'Genes, Patents, and Product Development', *Science*, 257 (1992): 903–8; ABC Statement on NIH Patent Filing for the Human Genome Patent, *Biotechnology Law Report* (July–August 1992): 408–10.

57 Ibid.

58 Norton D. Zinder, 'Patenting cDNA 1993: Efforts and Happenings', *Gene*, 135 (1993): 295–8.

59 Academy of Sciences, *The Patentability of the Genome* (Paris, 1995).

60 Anna Maria Gillis, 'The Patent Question of the Year', *BioScience*, 42 (1992): 336–40, 336–9. CDNA, or complementary DNA is single-stranded DNA that is complementary

to messenger RNA or DNA that has been synthesized from messenger RNA by reverse transcriptase.

61 Ibid., 336–9.

62 Leslie Roberts, 'NIH Gene Patents, Round Two', *Science*, 255 (1992): 912–13; James Martinell, USPTO, Art Unit 1805, Examiner's Action on Venter et al, Patent Application No. 07/807,195, 20 August 1992, *Biotechnology Law Report* (September–October 1992): 578–96.

63 Henrique Freire de Oliveira Souza, 'Genetically Modified Plants: A Need for International Regulation', *Annual Survey of International and Comparative Law*, 6 (2000): 129–74; Gilbert L. Carey, 'The resurgence of states' rights creates new risk to intellectual property', *Albany Law Journal of Science and Technology*, 11 (2000): 123–52.

64 Nigel Williams, 'European Parliament Backs New Biopatent Guidelines', *Science*, 277 (1997): 472; Alison Abbott, 'EuroVote Lifts Block on Biotech Patents ... But Parliament Wants Closer Scrutiny', *Nature*, 388 (1997): 314–15.

65 Alison Abbott, 'Transgenic Patents a Step Closer in Europe', *Nature* 390 (1997): 429; Alison Abbott, 'Europe's Life Patent Moratorium May Go', *Nature*, 393 (1998): 200.

66 European Community, Directive 98/44/EC of the European Parliament and of the Council of 6 July 1998, On the Legal Protection of Biotechnological Inventions, 213 *Official Journal of the European Communities*, 13–21 (1998).

67 For example, a mouse genetically engineered to suffer physically from birth would not be patentable if the modification did not lead to greater medical understanding, therapies, or cures.

68 The HGP was formally undertaken as a federal program in 1991 with an initial funding of approximately US$135 million. Daniel Kevles, 'Out of Eugenics: The Historical Politics of the Human Genome', in Daniel J. Kevles and Leroy Hood (eds), *The Code of Codes, Scientific and social issues in the human genome project* (Harvard, 1992), pp. 3, 36. The target date for completion was 2005; Victor A. McKusick, 'The Human Genome Project: Plans, Status, and Applications in Biology and Medicine', in George J. Annas and Sherman Elias (eds), *Gene Mapping: Using law and ethics as guides* (New York, 1992), p. 18.

69 The human genome consists of 46 chromosomes located in the nucleus of every somatic human cell. Kevles, 'Out of Eugenics', pp. 3, 16. McKusick, 'The Human Genome Project', pp. 18, 26; see also Horace F. Judson, 'A History of the Science and Technology Behind Gene Mapping and Sequencing', in Daniel J. Kevles and Leroy Hood (eds), *The Code of Codes, Scientific and social issues in the human genome project* (Harvard, 1992), pp. 37, 38.

70 See Gina Kolata, 'Tests to Assess Risks for Cancer Raising Questions', *New York Times*, 27 March 1995, at A1; see also 'A Genetic Vulnerability to Carcinogens', *Science News*, 149 (1996): 188; 'Epilepsy Gene Identified', *Science News*, 149 (1996): 221; Kathleen Fackelmann, 'Forecasting Alzheimer's Disease', *Science News*, 149 (1996): 312, 313.

71 As Leroy Hood concludes: 'I believe that we will learn more about human development and pathology in the next twenty-five years than we have in the past two thousand.' Leroy Hood, 'Biology and Medicine in the Twenty-First Century', in Daniel J. Kevles and Leroy Hood (eds), *The Code of Codes, Scientific and social issues in the human*

genome project (Harvard, 1992), pp. 136, 163; see also C. Thomas Caskey, 'Molecular Medicine; A Spin-Off from the Helix', *JAMA*, 269 (1993): 1986–92.

72 Peter J. Gardner, 'United States Intellectual Property Law and the Biotech Challenge: Searching for an elusive balance', *Vermont Bar Journal*, 29 (2003): 24.

73 Linda R. Cohen and Roger G. Noll, 'Intellectual Property, Antitrust and the New Economy', *University of Pittsburgh Law Review*, 62 (2001): 453–73.

74 Lawrence M. Sung, 'Collegiality and Collaboration in the Age of Exclusivity' (2000) 3 *DePaul Journal of Health Care Law* 411, 412–13. See also Cohen and Noll, 'Intellectual Property, Antitrust and the New Economy'.

75 Patents Act 1990, (Commonwealth), s. 43; Patents Act 1977, (United Kingdom), s 5.

76 10 March 1883, as revised.

77 Paris Convention, Art. 4A-C.

78 Colleen Chien, 'Cheap drugs at what price to innovation: Does the compulsory licensing of pharmaceuticals hurt innovation?', *Berkeley Technology Law Journal*, 18 (2003): 853–908; Pila, 'Bound futures'.

79 The type of concerns commonly expressed may be seen to echo the underlying message in Mary Wollstonecraft Shelley's, *Frankenstein*, ed. M.K. Joseph (New York, 1980).

80 de Oliveira Souza, 'Genetically Modified Plants', 172.

81 For example some actions or measures taken by an isolated state in order to protect its environment or the health of its population may violate some other international agreement.

82 Prepared Statement of Ambassador David L. Aaron Under Secretary for International Trade, United States Department of Commerce, 15 June 1999, <www.ogc.Doc.gov/ogc/legreg/testmon/106f/aaron0615.htm> (as at 23 December 2003).

83 Lara E. Ewens, 'Seed Wars: Biotechnology, Intellectual Property, and the Quest for High Yield Seeds', *Boston College International and Comparative Law Review*, 23 (2000): 285–310; Keith Aoki, 'Weeds, seeds and deeds: Recent skirmishes in the seed wars', *Cardozo Journal of International and Comparative Law*, 11 (2003): 247–331.

84 For more on this question see Johanna Gibson, *Community resources: intellectual* ***property,*** *international trade and protection of traditional knowledge* (Aldershot, 2005).

85 Pila, 'Bound Futures', 344.

86 In the information technology field Microsoft was found liable for similar conduct, on a sufficiently large scale to account for a breach of anti-trust law; Samuel Noah Weinstein, 'United States v. Microsoft Corp', *Berkeley Technology Law Journal*, 17 (2002): 273.

87 Aoki, 'Weeds, seeds and deeds', 254. Given the deeply ingrained, millennia-old tradition of seed saving, it is understandable that Monsanto has continued to have problems with farmers that don't comply with Monsanto's licence terms; See *Monsanto Canada, Inc. v. Schmeiser*, T-1593-98 (29 March, 2001) [2001] FTC 256, available at <http://decisions.fct-cf.gc.ca/fct/2001/2001fct256.html> (as at 23 December 2003); see also Percy Schmeiser's website, 'Monsanto v. Schmeiser', at <http://www.percyschmeiser.org> (as at 23 December 2003).

88 The early 1990s saw the advent of patented seed technology systems, such as Monsanto's Roundup Ready™ crops, that possessed a patented genetic sequence making them resistant to Monsanto's broad band herbicide Roundup; Aoki, 'Weeds, seeds and deeds', 303.

89 'Canola' (*Brassica napus*) is also known as rape seed, a name which has been superseded in commercial use due to its unfortunate connotations.

90 Aoki, 'Weeds, seeds and deeds', 330.

91 George A. Akerlof, 'The Market for "Lemons": Quality Uncertainty and the Market Mechanism', *Quarterly Journal of Economics*, 84 (1970): 488–500, 489–92; Donat, 'Engineering Akerlof lemons', 441–3.

92 Ibid., 439–40.

Chapter 9

Lessons for the Future

9.1 Introduction

We have considered several examples of the effects which technological innovations and changes have had upon legal systems and upon constitutions in the past, and those which they may be having today. Technology has influenced both the nature and the form of the state, and the reverse is also true. Every few centuries there has been a seminal shift in the balance of society, technology, and constitution. Those countries which were unable to adjust to these changes, or which were not directly affected by them, generally suffered a relative decline in power balance.[1] Conversely those that made the adjustment prospered.[2] This could perhaps indicate that a state must harness technology, rather than be harnessed by it, in order to succeed – which raises questions about the interrelationship of private enterprise and capital, and the state.

Each of the technological and historical periods we considered was marked by quite different technological, economic, social, political and constitutional features. In some cases, such as that of ancient Egypt, the Reformation, and during the Industrial Revolution, it may be comparatively easy to see how technological change affected society, and therefore the constitution. Even in the course of the Roman empire – which was not, of course, homogeneous – and during the Middle Ages, there were signs that this was also occurring. That technology changes society, and society changes the constitution, may be a commonplace. But we can see signs that technology has directly affected the constitution, while also having social or economic effects.

Some technological changes have directly affected the constitution, others have not. Significant changes which have a direct impact on the structure of the constitution may be rare, but it may be that we are facing one now. The difference between technological changes in the past and those now is a matter of pace rather than essential nature. The changes are so rapid – particularly the Internet and the move to globalization – that it is scarcely possible for a state to resist it. This has an effect upon the relationship of states, and the ways in which domestic laws are made.

Not only has, to use the United States example, the balance between federal and state powers changed – in McGinnis' view because of the advent of telecommunications[3] – but the Internet is potentially capable of undermining state identity and cohesion.[4] This is due to the availability of the Internet to millions of ordinary citizens.

But at a different level, that of international trade, the division between states has also been weakened. Traditionally, the formation of legal norms for conducting trade was by states, subject to certain customary principles accepted by the international community. But this has proven inadequate for the control of electronic commerce, because this can be said to be truly international, having no physical presence, and the development has been too swift to allow for the evaluation of customary norms.

The new environment has necessitated an increased degree of international co-ordination, if not co-operation. Unlike the evolutionary development of the *lex mercatoria*, the advent of electronic communications has resulted in the adoption of international norms, such as the UNCITRAL Model Law on Electronic Commerce.

This does pose a threat to state sovereignty. It is no longer possible for the nation-state to be the sole, or even prime, regulator of economic norms. Decisions respecting the forms of law will be made not at the national level, but internationally. These will be made by political blocks, and, in some instances, by non-governmental organizations. There are wider implications for national legal systems which cannot be ignored.

A prediction made some years ago that the Internet would change international law because it would erode the dominance of the traditional sovereign state[5] has not become reality yet. But it is potentially a threat to state sovereignty,[6] and therefore of profound constitutional implications. The knowledge revolution is likely to be as revolutionary in effect as was the Reformation. But this may well be over a much longer period of time than some might have expected, and it is likely to be in the international field rather than the domestic. The prime determinant of statehood is war – the laws of war (now called those of armed conflict) are still important, and they have not been subjected to the same degree of globalization.[7] The security of the state – as perceived by state authorities – will continue to determine policy.[8]

It would appear that modern high technology does affect the constitution, but mostly indirectly. Its most significant effect is in the international sphere and this is particularly important given the globalizing effect of current technological developments. But the moral and ethical context cannot be underestimated also, and this varies from country to country.

It has been suggested by Scheuerman that we should see constitutions as expressive of a broadly-defined set of abstract moral principles, along the lines proposed by Dworkin.[9] These may be challenged by changing social norms, brought about by the Internet and by globalization in general, or by other technological changes. The case of the United States Constitution suggests that rigidity in formal amendment procedures[10] might be compensated for by flexibility within constitutional exegesis.[11] For Justice Cardozo observed that 'nothing is stable. Nothing absolute. All is fluid and changeable. We are back with Heraclites.'[12] This situation, for him, defied formalistic modes of constitutional exegesis. He believed that judges therefore should adopt a 'more plastic, more malleable' reading of the United States Constitution in order to guarantee its relevance to the changing exigencies of the times.[13] This approach is likely to be satisfactory to respond to the domestic influences of technological change. But in the international – or trans-national – effects of technological change that approach may not be sufficient.

Slaughter argues that the state is not disappearing but is rather disaggregating into its separate functionally distinct parts.[14] These elements are networking with their counterparts abroad, creating a network of relations that constitute a new trans-governmental order. Bureaucracies which can respond to the networking logic of the new technologies and the exercise of fragmented sovereign powers and functions gives them scope to co-ordinate and regulate activities, allowing cross-border links, and addressing global problems and situations.[15]

From the earliest times, through the Middle Ages, the Reformation, and to the present, technology has affected the constitution indirectly, through its effects upon society and economy. Yet, there have been significant technologies which have proven to be of great importance in shaping the nature of the constitution. Whether this was by fostering a centralized system of government, or the opposite, the effect must be seen as more than merely indirect. Success came to those states which were able to respond most quickly to the changing environment in which it found itself. Sometimes – as in the Industrial Revolution – this meant taking a more active role than hitherto. Failure to act resulted in economic stagnation.[16]

With the present technological revolution bringing about globalization at an unparalleled rate it would appear to be essential for states to take the initiative, rather than merely respond to what others have done. The potential changes are such that the revolution may be seen as paradigmatic. Failure to act will render states subservient to changes beyond their control. The difficulty is in determining what changes are needed. Constitutional reforms which accelerate the process for the enactment of international agreements, and the removal of any which inhibit the extraterritorial jurisdiction of national courts, might be worthwhile.

9.2 Global Governance as a Result of Technology

Recent initiatives for greater global governance may well be a result of technology itself. For instance new forms of regulation involving the Basel Group of Bankers have come about to a large extent because the exponential acceleration of technology enables security and financial transactions to develop in particular ways. In effect the availability of technology influenced the direction of regulation, specifically towards greater globalization.

The Basel Committee was established in 1974. Member countries were represented by their central bank and also by the authority with formal responsibility for the prudential supervision of banking business where this was not the central bank. The Committee did not possess any formal supranational supervisory authority, and its conclusions do not, and were never intended to, have legal force. One important objective of the Committee's work was to close perceived gaps in international supervisory coverage in pursuit of two basic principles. These were that no foreign banking establishment should escape supervision and that supervision should be adequate. To achieve this, the Committee has issued a long series of documents since 1975.

In 1988 the first Basel Accord was seen as a breakthrough in regulation. For the first time, regulators from a number of countries had set a truly global standard for capital adequacy in relation to banking operations. This initial Accord, however, only explicitly covered credit risk. It required international banks from the G10[17] countries to hold minimum total capital equal to 8 per cent of risk-adjusted[18] assets, with at least half of this met by Tier 1 capital (equity capital and disclosed reserves). Tier 2 capital (other hybrid debt/capital instruments) could also be used in the calculation.

In 1996 an amendment to the Accord introduced Tier 3 capital to cover market risk exposures and the main objective of the amendment was that it 'allowed banks to use their own internal models to determine the required capital charge for market risk'.

In June 2004, the Basel Committee published the document 'International Convergence of Capital Measurement and Capital Standards, a Revised Framework' (widely known as Basel II). While this may be seen as a continuation of a progressive series of regulatory development, it was also a departure in that regulation now depended heavily upon technology. Compliance involved heavy compliance costs – largely because of the requirement for new technology and procedures.[19]

The United Kingdom financial industry regulator the Financial Services Authority (FSA) set out new guidelines for banking industry compliance with the credit risk requirements of the Basel II accord. The FSA issued its proposals in 2004 in a consultation paper on the key aspects of United Kingdom implementation of the European Union's Capital Requirements Directive (CRD), which was closely linked to Basel II. A key aspect of this was massive changes to internal processes and information technology systems to enable banks to profile and monitor credit risk exposure when the Basel II accord became effective in 2007.[20] Not only does such compliance involve considerable costs, but it increased the degree to which the banking and financial sectors were globalized – and reduced their national diversity. The availability of technology meant that the means for achieving this were at hand. The efficiency it offered was attractive at once to the Basel Committee and to central banks.

Further global initiatives have resulted from the globalization of risk based on technology. These have included the spread of nuclear risk, biological weapons, and the destruction of ecological systems.

Various theorists have sought to bring some order to the apparently chaotic state of globalization. One of these attempts is that of Hardt and Negri,[21] written in the context of the collapse of communism as an operating economic (and political) system. They argued that the modern era of inter-capitalist nation-state rivalries, uneven development of core and periphery countries, and the struggle between proletariat and bourgeoisie is being supplanted by 'Empire'. This new historical stage they define as the globalization of world space, where boundless flows of capital, labour and information transcend the older imperial order. In their revisionist Marxist worldview Empire is a result of a shift from modern to imperial sovereignty. For them the problem of sovereignty is central to the formation of modernity.

In an influential reflection on the relationship between the decline of the nation state and the future of the concept of citizen, Agamben considered what he identified as the fundamental issues of contemporary creativity. He identified these firstly as how to represent humanity in its 'bare life', stripped of, and unable to rely on the structures of citizenship. Secondly, how might we imagine the new kinds of communities that could incorporate such beings.[22]

In *Homo Sacer* (named after the Roman law concept of the sacred criminal who might not be condemned for his offence, yet might be killed by any citizen), Agamben traced throughout the history of Western political thought a limit-concept that he identifies as the fundamental element of sovereign power. Agamben examined Carl Schmitt's theory of sovereignty. The paradox of sovereignty for Agamben is that the sovereign sphere is structured by the logic of *homo sacer* such that 'the life caught in the sovereign ban is the life that is originarily sacred – that is, that may be killed but not sacrificed – and in this sense, the production of bare life is the originary activity of sovereignty.'[23] On Agamben's account, the operation of sovereignty abandons individuals whenever they are placed outside the law and in so doing, exposes and threatens them to a sphere where there is no possibility of appeal.[24]

Poggi, who published his leading text on *The Development of the Modern State* in 1978,[25] did not expressly consider globalization. Poggi's focus on law making and enforcing institutions is however integral to today's discussions regarding human rights and the states' exercise of power. According to Poggi, law can be regarded as positive and absolute, but the very nature of law is to protect the rights of some individuals against the interests of others. Therefore, the lawmakers have very specific agendas and an in-depth study of laws and their intents are necessary in order to answer how governments maintain power. The state, according to Poggi, has developed in such a way that it must take into account the demands of its citizens. It is the people, which over time have had more interest in the government, not just for selfish or economic purposes, but for an interest in society's general well being. In this model it is a liberal democratic state. The state/society line is perhaps displaced by an even greater world/global citizens model in which the challenges that Poggi addresses as facing the modern state are now magnified.

Held maintains that a globalization of technology does not mean a globalization of culture.[26] Nor does it mean the end of states, but rather new forms of power. He believes that the current era of globalization is characterized by 'the appearance of a territorial policy, leadership that combines the local with the global, the deterritorialization of decision making, the development of international law, the appearance of new labour relations and the trans-nationalization of politics.[27]

Each of these models or attempts to explain the globalizing effects of technology, or the development of the world political and economic system in the post-modern era suffers from one or more weaknesses. Hardt and Negri, while concerned with the growth of what they classify as Empire, fail to explore the real possibilities and dangers of political reality and take measure of the lessons of history – they are 'inhumanly abstract'.[28] The difficulty which this presents it that there is possibly insufficient connection with real events, and the discourse which they identify as crucial to history may have less effect than their model would suggest. But they may well be on stronger ground when they identify the problem of sovereignty as central to the formation of modernity.

The problem with Agamben's work, especially within the context of Internet theory, is that he takes an uncritical position on the work of Carl Schmitt without examining the object of Schmitt's own critical regard, the liberal economists of the Austro-Hungarian Empire. Thus, like Hardt and Negri there is insufficient connection between theory and reality. In Agamben's case the difficulty lies particularly in the utilization of a model – that of Austria-Hungary – in which subjectivist liberal economics dominated. This basic assumption of subjectivism is inconsistent with the assumptions of the Enlightenment. There is no room for universal Cartesian continuity; discontinuities are assumed. There is no objective reality to be projected onto Locke's *tabula rasa*; we are all making what passes as reality up as we go along. There is no progress towards a predetermined end. There is no destiny. There can be no final solution because there will always be problems, and each problem is unique. They saw political institutions such as the nation-state, or democratic processes as strategies developed incrementally to reduce the phenomenally high costs of multi-lateral exchange. The same goes for financial systems, money itself acts to reduce transactions costs. It is a mistake to assume that there is any continuity between the various solutions that we have constructed and put to use over the last three hundred or so years.

Carl Schmitt's theory of sovereignty and the nation-state is also a product of Enlightenment thinking. Power comes down from the top. It is the sovereign's duty to decide on where the distinction between friend and enemy is to be made; the subject's duty is to obey. But Schmitt's nation-state cannot be reconciled with the liberalism of the Austrian School because where the nation-state is a construction of Enlightenment assumptions of objectivity, Austrian School economic liberalism was looking for solutions to the problems of the multi-national Austro-Hungarian Empire which drove it towards globalization through strategies of arbitrage and the hedging of risk.

9.3 Conclusion

We have seen from earlier examples that technology may compel and direct constitutional change. But these constitutions may also themselves to hostage to the legal paradigm in which they are placed. While this may be simply that of the neo-liberal western market economy, it may also include such complex systems as the global financial market-place. In the case of the regulation of banking by the Basel Committee system, the availability of technology, as much as the expectation of objective equality of standards, compelled compliance. In the neo-Marxian models, such as that of Hardt and Negri, the paradigm is a global, or at least regional, economic and political hegemony. But whether this can be seen as truly reflective of a disparate 'system' remains uncertain.

If we look at the example of the collapse of communism as an economic and political system in eastern Europe, we also see the limitations of utilizing a theoretical model to describe the action of business, or any other 'free' actors.

If there are any lessons which might be derived from these and earlier examples, it would be that the complexity of society renders theoretical models of limited value – though their value appears to be enhanced when the attempt to consider all aspects of society, such as in the Marxist theory, however much this model may have failed in practice to describe the true economic system is utilized.

This book is an exploration of the relationship between technology and legal systems, specifically the ways in which technology and constitutions interact, but also the relationship between technology and the legal environment, or what may be styled the legal system.

In the first Chapter of this book we considered the relationship of law and government. It was postulated that government is both a product of society, history and environment, but is also instrumental in determining the form and direction of laws, of creating its own self-limiting discourse. Law both constrains and encourages developments both of technology and of other social and economic change, but is itself also a product of its environment. Society influences law, for law is but a reflection of the society of which it is a product. Specifically this includes the constitutional discourse in which it is set. Using the example of a fluid, non-entrenched constitution, we explored the ways in which the political, historical and social environment have determined the development of the constitution, and how the constitution itself in term influenced the development of politics and society.

This fluidity extends to the relationship between society and legal systems. This was explored in the specific context of how business responds to changes in legal systems, whether wrought by technological changes, or otherwise. It was shown that this response varies depending on the pre-existing state of the economy and of the legal system. Where there is a less well developed private sector, and where the economy tightly controlled, the ending of control also offers opportunities. But here the outcome will be influenced by the weakness of the private sector.

Technology is simply a process, or tool, through which mankind alters its environment. It may be complex or it may be simple. The consequences of the existence of the technology, and of its use, will be correspondingly great or small. But it will often be difficult to identify any clear instance of technology directly affecting legal systems. That is not, however, to suggest that this never occurs. As we saw in the course of the book there are many instances where profound changes have occurred, primarily as the result of the development and the utilization of a new technology, or the new use of an old technology.

The core of the book is the study of the effect of technological change upon the structure of government – upon the constitution – and, to a lesser extent, how the structure of governments may in turn have effected technological changes. In effect it was an attempt to identify a link between the societal and economic effects of technology, and the societal and economic influences technology has on constitutions. It was primarily from a constitutional rather than a technological perspective that this issue was approached.

The key historical examples, from Egypt, the Renaissance, the Industrial Revolution and so on served to illustrate the contemporary interdependence of law and technology, not merely at the technical and specific level, but (most importantly) at the state level. This influence is not, of course, limited to the national constitutional arrangements. Significant advances in technology challenge state sovereignty, and even the nature of the state. The state model we have worked with for well over a hundred years hid a number of truths about the nature of the world in which we live.

Technology has helped to create these paradigms – what Foucault might call the sovereign-state discourse. As a discourse it is the author of its own rules, a self-perpetuating oligarchy of sovereign states. Unfortunately for this model the discourse is maintained, not simply by the states themselves, but by the active subject participants at multiple levels both above and below the state. This does not render the state nugatory, but does mean that the greater the usefulness of a technology the greater the potential risk to the state, either individually, or collectively.

Constitutions are at the mercy of technology as much as is society in general, and perhaps even more so. They are the formal and informal procedures through which government is carried on, and as such are the product of various influences, which wax and wane over time. Some are also less important in some countries than in others. But not only is the constitution dependent upon the internal influences of culture, economy, history and so on, it is also the product of the ongoing influence of an international legal, economic and political environment, as well as of the influence of individual states.

One of the most important aspects of this is the need to preserve a role, and a sense of legitimacy. Whatever theoretical model for the origin of the state we may prefer, most – if not all – are premised upon the idea that they exist for a reason. Because the extent to which the state can achieve the objective of advancing this aim may heavily be dependent upon the material resources available to the state, and the relative balance between individual resources and those of the state, so the state is vulnerable to changes in technology which threaten to make the individual, corporate entity, or community more efficient and thus less dependent upon the state.

Some technological changes have directly affected the constitution, others have not – but it seems that when this has occurred it has been in respect of foreign policy, rather more often than domestic, except in the less complex and sophisticated societies. It would also seem that technology itself develops more rapidly when government requires it, or where the constitution is sufficiently laissez-faire to allow individual people and groups the freedom and opportunity to development technology. This may be where the constitution encourages individuality and enquiry, rather than orthodoxy and compliance. It would be overly simplistic to suggest that democracy *per se* encourages the development of technology, for this may also occur under autocratic regimes. But democracy is more usually associated with liberal societies, which tend to encourage free enquiry. Technological innovation is more easily found where the constitution allows the freedom and opportunity for innovation, and rewards the innovator – at least by protecting him or her from arbitrary confiscation or loss of the proceeds of their invention.

It may be that seminal changes which have a direct impact of the structure of the constitution will be rare. However, where a technology has a significant effect on society it may also have constitutional implications. The benefit of hindsight is not available to those who attempt to derive large generalizations, or principles, from the observation of contemporary events of which they are observers. The current revolution in information technology, and more specifically the development of the Internet, are having significant economic and social effects – particularly in those countries which already had a high level of economic development. But whereas the effects of information technology on society, legal systems, and constitutions may be understood as being slight, if identifiable at all, that of the Internet may be more direct, and more profound.

The challenge of the Internet is that this technology is not one which is readily amenable to regulation by states. Crucially, the nature of the technology itself invites globalization, for only in outward expansion is the tool efficiently utilized. Unlike earlier technologies, this outward thrust has implications at once on the domestic economic, social and political balance, and between nations, and truly globally. It is possible to discount national origins, and conduct business between business and consumer. Such innovations can scarcely fail to challenge the nature of global business, economic regulation, and the relationship between states.

Technology is not immune from the influence of the legal system in which it is found, any more than the legal system is uninfluenced by contemporary technological systems. The greater the sophistication of the technology the more complex the constitutional model, in the broadest sense, is likely to be. Equally, a sophisticated and nuanced constitutional system is more likely to engender a complex technology. It is however evident that generalizations, here as elsewhere, are fraught with risk. The greater the complexity of the environment the greater this is true, even where theoretical modelling attempts to minimize variables. This does not however necessarily make all attempts at modelling futile or destined to failure.

The changes to the legal regime governing genetic engineering have been influenced more by political and ethical considerations than by economic considerations. The failure of the agricultural sector, in particular, to achieve the high returns which had been predicted also emphasize the need for caution in dealing with high risk, high return technologies where the legal protection is relatively undeveloped.

If there is any single tentative conclusion to which we might end, it would be that, complex as the relationship between law and technology is, at the constitutional level at least it may be possible to identify certain common themes. One of these is that the constitutional arrangements of a country are as much hostage to the technology of a country as they are to its history and social culture.

Notes

1 For example, Egypt during the Second Intermediate Period.

2 As did the United Kingdom during the Industrial Revolution.

3 See John O. McGinnis, 'The Symbiosis of Constitutionalism and Technology', *Harvard Journal of Law and Public Policy*, 25 (2001): 3–14, 6.

4 Cass R. Sunstein, *Republic.com* (Princeton, 2001).

5 See Henry H. Perritt, 'The Internet is Changing International Law', *Chicago–Kent Law Review*, 73 (1998): 997–1054.

6 See Georgios Zekos, 'Internet or Electronic Technology: A Threat to State Sovereignty', *Journal of Information, Law and Technology*, 3 (1999), available at <http://elj.warwick.ac.uk/jilt/99-3/zekos.html> (as at 28 November 2003); David G. Post and David R. Johnson, '"Chaos Prevailing on Every Continent": Towards a New Theory of Decentralised Decision-Making in Complex Systems', Social Science Research Network Electronic Library (14 June 1999), available at <http://papers.ssrn.com/sol3/delivery.cfm/99032613.pdf?abstractid=157692> (as at 1 December 2003). See also Dan L. Burk, 'Federalism in Cyberspace', *Connecticut Law Review*, 28 (1996): 1095–1127; Joel R. Reidenberg, 'Governing Networks and Rule-Making in Cyberspace', in Brian Kahin and Charles Nesson (eds), *Borders in Cyberspace* (Cambridge, 1997), pp. 84, 85–7.

7 Though there have been major advances in the course of the latter part of the nineteenth century and the twentieth century – influenced not a little by technology (the threat of chemical, biological, and nuclear weapons, for example); See Adam Roberts and Richard Guellf (eds), *Laws of War* (Oxford, 2000); Geoffrey Best, *Humanity in Warfare: The Modern History of the International Law of Armed Conflict* (New York, 1980).

8 See, for instance, the United States Patriot Act of 2001, Public Law 107–56.

9 William E. Scheuerman, 'Constitutionalism in an age of speed', *Constitutional Commentary*, 19 (2002): 353–90, 366.

10 The United States Constitution contains a system of amendment now widely seen as one of the most slow-going in the world; James L. Sundquist, *Constitutional Reform and Effective Government* (Washington, 1992), p. 17; Donald S. Lutz, 'Toward a Theory of Constitutional Amendment', in Sanford Levinson (ed.), *Responding to Imperfection* (Princeton, 1995), p. 237. For amendment processes generally, see Keith G. Banting and Richard Simeon (eds), *Redesigning the state: the politics of constitutional change* (Toronto, 1985).

11 James Bryce, *Constitutions* (London, 1901), pp. 72–3.

12 Benjamin N. Cardozo, *The Nature of the Judicial Process* (New Haven, 1921), p. 28. Heraclitus said that nothing is stable, that permanence is an illusion conceived by man, and that strife 'is the justice of the world ...'; Eduard Zeller, *Outlines of the History of Greek Philosophy*, trans. L.R. Palmer (13th rev edn, London, 1948), p. 46.

13 Cardozo, p. 161.

14 A. Slaughter, 'The Real New World Order', *Foreign Affairs*, 76 (1997): 183–97.

15 Lawrence Tshuma, 'Hierarchies and Government versus Networks and Governance: Competing Regulatory Paradigms in Global Economic Regulation', Law, Social Justice and Global Development (1999) <http://elj.warwick.ac.uk/global/issue/2000-1/tshuma.html> (as at 22 January 2005).

16 For instance, in the Iberian countries, in which the Reformation was less profound then elsewhere, partly because constitutional rigidity led to restrictions in the development and adoption of technology – and a general educational backwardness – for many years; See Richard L. Kagan, *Students and society in early modern Spain* (Baltimore, 1974).

17 The Group of 10 is in fact a group of 11 nations: Canada, Belgium, France, Germany, Italy, Japan, the Netherlands, Sweden, Switzerland, the United Kingdom and the United States.

18 The calculation for risk adjusting assets involves taking both on and off balance sheet items and assigning them to risk categories which would weight them (by factors of 0%, 20%, 50% and 100%) according to the perceived risk of the asset.

19 'Banks face heavy IT bill over Basel II', *Financial Times*, 27 January 2005.

20 Andy McCue, 'Banks get new Basel II compliance guidelines', *Silicon.com*, 28 January 2005.

21 Hardt, Michael and Antonio Negri, *Empire* (Cambridge, 2000).

22 Giorgio Agamben, 'We refugees', trans. Michael Roche, available at <http://www.egs.edu/faculty/agamben/agamben-we-refugees.html> (as at 11 February 2005).

23 Giorgio Agamben, *Homo Sacer: Sovereign Power and Bare Life*, trans. D. Heller-Roazen (Stanford, 1998), p. 83.

24 Ibid., p. 29.

25 Gianfranco Poggi, *The Development of the Modern State: A Sociological Introduction* (London, 1978).

26 David Held, *Political Theory and the Modern State* (Cambridge, 1989)

27 David Held, 'Globalization: an empirical evaluation and an analytic interpretation', speech at the Barcelona Forum, 2004.

28 'Buchbesprechung Brian C. Anderson on Hardt and Negri's "Empire"', available at <http://www.politische-geographie.de/empire.htm> (as at 11 February 2005).

Bibliography

Abbott, Alison, 'Europe's Life Patent Moratorium May Go', *Nature*, 393 (1998): 200

———, 'EuroVote Lifts Block on Biotech Patents ... But Parliament Wants Closer Scrutiny', *Nature*, 388 (1997): 314–15

———, 'Transgenic Patents a Step Closer in Europe', *Nature* 390 (1997): 429

Abbott, Frederick M., 'Distributed governance at the WTO–WIPO: An evolving model for open–architecture integrated governance', *Journal of International Economic Law*, 3 (2000): 63

Abbott, K., 'Modern International Relations Theory: A Prospectus for International Lawyers', *Journal of International Law*, 14 (1989): 335–411

Academy of Sciences, *The Patentability of the Genome* (Academy of Sciences, Paris, 1995) Paris Bilingual Report No. 32

Ackerman, Bruce, *We the People* (Cambridge: Harvard University Press, 1991)

Adams, Mark D. et al, 'Complementary DNA Sequencing: Expressed Sequence Tags and Human Genome Project', *Science*, 252 (1991): 1651–6

Adkins, Jocelyn C., 'The Internet: a critical technology for the state of environmental law', *Villanova Environmental Law Journal*, 8 (1997): 341–57

Adler, Reid G., 'Controlling the Applications of Biotechnology: A Critical Analysis of the Proposed Moratorium on Animal Patenting', *Harvard Journal of Law and Technology*, (1988): 1–62

Agamben, Giorgio, *Homo Sacer: Sovereign Power and Bare Life*, trans. D. Heller-Roazen (Stanford: Stanford University Press, 1998)

Ahrens, Judith D. and Gerardo A. Esquer, 'Internet's potential as a global information infrastructure: A case study and assessment', *Journal of Global Information Management*, 1 (1993): 18–27

Akdeniz, Y., C. Walker and D. Wall, *The Internet, Law and Society* (Harlow: Longman, 2000)

Akerlof, George A., 'The Market for "Lemons": Quality Uncertainty and the Market Mechanism', *Quarterly Journal of Economics*, 84 (1970): 488–500

Alderson, Stanley, *Yea or nay?: referenda in the United Kingdom* (London: Cassell, 1975)

Alker, Hayward R., 'Dialectical Foundations of Global Disparities', *International Studies Quarterly*, 25 (1981): 69–98

———, Thomas J. Biersteker and Takashi Inoguchi, 'From Imperial Power Balancing to People's Wars: Searching for Order in the Twentieth Century', in James Der Derian and Michael J. Shapiro (eds), *International/Intertextual*

Relations: Postmodern Readings of World Politics (Lexington: D.C. Heath, 1989)

Allen Consulting Group, *Economic perspectives on copyright law: research paper* (Strawberry Hills: Centre for Copyright Studies, 2003)

Allen, Robert C., 'Agriculture and the origins of the state in ancient Egypt', *Explorations in Economic History*, 34 (1997): 135–54

Anderson, W. French, 'Human Gene Therapy', *Science*, 256 (1992): 808–13

Anderson, Christopher, 'NIH Drops Bid For Gene Patents', *Science*, 263 (1994): 909–10

———, 'United States Patent Application Stirs Up Gene Hunters', *Nature*, 353 (1991): 485–6

Ando, Clifford, *Imperial ideology and provincial loyalty in the Roman Empire* (Berkeley: University of California Press, 2000)

Andreau, Jean, *Banking and business in the Roman world*, trans. Janet Lloyd (Cambridge: Cambridge University Press, 1999)

Anonymous of Rouen, *Die Texte des Normannischen Anonymous*, ed. K Pellens (Stuttgart: Franz Steiner Verlag, 1966)

Anson, Sir William, *The Law and Custom of the Constitution*, ed. A.B. Keith (5th edn, Oxford: Clarendon Press, 1922, 3rd edn, 1907)

Aoki, Keith, 'Weeds, seeds and deeds: Recent skirmishes in the seed wars', *Cardozo Journal of International and Comparative Law*, 11 (2003): 247–331

Aquinas, St Thomas, *Summa theologiæ*, ed. John A. Oesterle (Englewood Cliffs: Prentice-Hall, 1964)

Arendt, Hannah, 'What was authority', in Carl Friedrich (ed.), *Authority* (Cambridge: Harvard University Press, 1958)

Aristotle, *Ethica Nicomachea*, eds R.A. Gauthier and E.J. Brill (Rotterdam: Brouwer, 1972–74)

———, *The Politics of Aristotle*, trans. Ernest Barker (London: Oxford University Press, 1958)

Armstrong, Harvey W. and Robert Read, 'Comparing the economic performance of dependent territories and sovereign microstates', *Economic Development and Cultural Change*, 48(2) (2000): 285

Arnold, Guy, *World government by stealth: the future of the United Nations* (New York: St Martin's Press, 1997)

von Arx, Kim G., 'ICANN – Now and then: ICANN's Reform and its problems', *Duke Law and Technology Review* (2003) 7

Astraudo, A., 'Saint-marin et l'Ordre de Malta', *La Revue Diplomatique*, (1935): 7

Atiya, Aziz Suryal, *Crusade, commerce and culture* (Bloomington: Indiana University Press, 1962)

Attenborough, F.L. (ed.), *Laws of the earliest English kings* (Cambridge: Cambridge University Press, 1922)

Aubert, Jean-Jacques and Boudewijn Sirks (eds), *Speculum iuris: Roman law as a reflection of social and economic life in antiquity* (Ann Arbor: University of Michigan Press, 2002)

Avi-Yonah, Reuven S., 'Globalization, Tax Competition, and the Fiscal Crisis of the Welfare State', *Harvard Law Review*, 113 (2000): 1573–676

Awatere, Dona, *Maori Sovereignty* (Auckland: Broadsheet, 1984)

Aylmer, Gerald, *The struggle for the constitution, 1603–1689: England in the seventeenth century* (4th edn, London: Blandford, 1975)

Bacon, Sir Francis, 'Religious Meditations, Of Heresies', in *Bacon's essays* with annotations by Richard Whately (London: J.W. Parker, 1858, first published 1597)

Baer, Klaus, *Rank and title in the Old Kingdom; the structure of the Egyptian administration in the fifth and sixth dynasties* (Chicago: University of Chicago Press, 1960)

Bagner, Jessica, Vanessa Kaye Watson and K. Brooke Welch, 'Internet auction fraud targeted by FTC, state and local law enforcement officials', *Intellectual Property and Technology Law Journal*, 15 (2003): 22

Baker, Sir John, 'English Law and the Renaissance', *Cambridge Law Journal* (1985) 46

Bangert William V., *A History of the Society of Jesus* (2nd edn, rev. and updated, St. Louis: Institute of Jesuit Sources, 1986)

Banting, Keith G. and Richard Simeon (eds), *Redesigning the state: the politics of constitutional change* (Toronto: University of Toronto Press, 1985)

Barker, Sir Ernest, *Reflections on Government* (London: Oxford University Press, 1942)

Barker, Rodney, *Political Legitimacy and the state* (Oxford: Clarendon Press, 1990)

Barlow, Frank, *The Feudal Kingdom of England, 1042–1216* (2nd edn, London: Longmans, 1961, first published 1955)

——————, *William Rufus* (London: Methuen, 1983)

Barnes, Timothy D., *The new empire of Diocletian and Constantine* (Cambridge: Harvard University Press, 1982)

Barrow, G.W.S., *Feudal Britain: The Completion of the Mediæval Kingdoms, 1066–1314* (London: Edward Arnold, 1956)

Barry, A., T. Osbourne and Nicolas Rose (eds), *Foucault and Political Reason: Liberalism, Neo-Liberalism and Rationalities of Government* (London: UCL Press, 1996)

Bartlett, Joseph W., *Venture capital: law, business strategies, investment planning* (New York: J. Wiley, 1988)

Battra, Shelly P., Robert E. Lutz, Ved P. Nanda, David A. Wirth, Daniel Magraw and Gunther Handl, 'International transfer of hazardous technology and substances: caveat emptor or state responsibility? The case of Bhopal, India', *Proceedings of the Seventy-Ninth Annual Meeting of the American Society of International Law* (1985): 303–22

Bean, J.M.W., *The decline of English feudalism, 1215–1540* (Manchester: Manchester University Press, 1968)

Beaumont, P., C. Lyons and Neil Walker (eds), *Convergence and Divergence in European Public Law* (Oxford: Hart, 2002)

Bede, Venerable, *Bede's Ecclesiastical history of the English people: a historical commentary*, ed. J.M. Wallace-Hadrill (Oxford: Clarendon Press, 1988)

Bell, Tom W., 'Free speech, strict scrutiny, and self-help: how technology upgrades constitutional jurisprudence', *Minnesota Law Review*, 87 (2003): 743–78

Bennet, Robert, *King Charle's Trial Iustified* (London: R.A., 1649)

Benson, Bruce, 'The Spontaneous Evolution of Commercial Law', *Southern Economic Journal*, 55 (1989): 644–61

Bercuson, David and Barry Cooper, 'From Constitutional Monarchy to Quasi Republic', in Janet Ajzenstat (ed.), *Canadian Constitutionalism, 1791–1991* (Ottawa: Canadian Study of Parliament Group, 1992)

Berger, Carl (ed.), *Imperialism and Nationalism, 1884–1914: A Conflict in Canadian Thought* (Toronto: Copp Clark, 1969)

Berger, Klaus Peter, *The Creeping Codification of Lex Mercatoria* (The Hague: Kluwer Law International, 1999)

Berman, Harold J., *Law and Revolution: The Formation of the Western Legal Tradition* (Cambridge: Harvard University Press, 1983)

Berman, Paul Schiff, 'Cyberspace and the state Action Debate: The Cultural Value of Applying Constitutional Norms to "Private" Regulation', *University of Colorado Law Review*, 71 (2000): 1265–6

Bernstein, Jodie, Director, Bureau of Consumer Protection, US Federal Trade Commission, 'Fighting Internet Fraud: A Global Effort', *Economic Perspectives, An Electronic Journal of the United States Department of State*, 5 (May 2000), available at <http://usinfo.state.gov/journals/ites/0500/ijee/ftc2.htm> (as at 1 December 2003)

Berry, Roberta M., 'The Human Genome Project and the End of Insurance', *Florida Journal of Law and Public Policy*, 7 (1996): 205–56

Best, Geoffrey, *Humanity in Warfare: The Modern History of the International Law of Armed Conflict* (New York: Columbia University Press, 1980)

Bierstedt, Robert, 'Legitimacy', in Julian Gould and William Kolb (eds), *A Dictionary of the Social Sciences* (London: Tavistock Publications, 1964)

Bill, Stephen and Arthur Kerrigan, 'Practical application of European Value Added Tax to E-Commerce', *Georgia Law Review*, 38 (2003): 71–83

Birch, Anthony, *The British System of Government* (4th edn, London: George Allen and Unwin, 1980, 9th edn, London: Routledge, 1993)

Birchall, Frederick T., 'Burning of the Books, May 10, 1933', in Louis L. Snyder (ed.), *National Socialist Germany: Twelve Years that Shook the World* (Malabor: Krieger, 1984)

Bird, M., Richard, 'Taxation and e-commerce', *Canadian Business Law Journal*, 38 (2003): 466–71

Biryukov, Alexander, 'The Doctrine of Dualism of Private Law in the Context of Recent Codifications of Civil Law: Ukrainian Perspectives', *Annual Survey of International and Comparative Law*, 8 (2002): 53–4

Black, Bernard S. and Anna S. Tarassova, 'Institutional reform in transition: A case study of Russia', *Supreme Court Economic Review*, 10 (1993): 211–78

Blackburn, Robert G., 'The role of the Canadian government in encouraging innovations', *Canada–United States Law Journal*, 15 (1989): 229–36

Blackstone, Sir William, *Commentaries on the Laws of England*, ed. E. Christian (New York: Garland Publishing, 1978)

Blank, Robert H., *The political implications of human genetic technology* (Boulder: Westview Press, 1981)

Bloch, Marc, *Feudal Society* (Chicago: University of Chicago Press, 1961)

Blum, Jerome, *The end of the old order in rural Europe* (Princeton: Princeton University Press, 1978)

Bodin, Jean, *Les Six Livres de la République* ('*The Six bookes of a Commonwealth*'), trans. M.J. Tooley (Oxford: Blackwell, 1955)

Boer, Ben, 'The Globalization of Environmental Law: The Role of the United Nations', *Melbourne University Law Review*, 20 (1995): 101–25

Bogdanor, Vernon, 'Britain and Europe', in R. Holme and Michael Elliott (eds), *1688–1988 Time for a New Constitution* (London: Macmillan, 1988)

——————, *The Monarchy and the Constitution* (Oxford: Clarendon Press, 1995)

Booth, Rev'd Ken, 'A Pakeha Perspective on Te Tino Rangatiratanga', in J. Crawford (ed.), *Church and State: Te Tino Rangatiratanga* (Auckland: College of St John the Evangelist, 1998)

Boston, Jonathan, Stephen Levine, Elizabeth McLeay, Nigel Roberts and Hannah Schmidt, 'Caretaker governments and the evolution of caretaker conventions in New Zealand', *Victoria University of Wellington Law Review*, 28 (1998): 629

Botkin, James, Dan Dimancescu, Ray Stata and John McClellan, *Global stakes: the future of high technology in America* (Cambridge: Ballinger Publishing Co., c.1982)

Boucher, David and Paul Kelly (eds), *The social contract from Hobbes to Rawls* (London: Routledge, 1994)

Bowman, James E., 'Symposium Genetics and the Law: the Ethical, Legal and Social Implications of Genetic Technology and Biomedical Ethics: The Road to Eugenics', *University of Chicago Law School Roundtable*, 3 (1996): 491

Bracton, Henry de, *On the Laws and Customs of England* ('*Henri de Bracton de Legibus et Consuetudis Angliæ*'), ed. G.E. Woodbine; trans. S.E. Thorne (Cambridge: Belknap Harvard: 1968)

Branscomb, Anne Wells, 'Jurisdictional Quandaries for Global Networks', in Linda M. Harasim (ed.), *Global Networks: Computers and Informational Communication* (Cambridge: MIT Press, 1993)

Braun, Christopher K., 'Alternative rhythms in law and economics: the Posner–Malloy dialectic', *The Legal Studies Forum*, 15 (1991): 153–65

Brinton, Clarence, *From many one: the process of political integration, the problem of world government* (Cambridge: Harvard University Pres, 1948)

Brookfield, F.M., 'Parliamentary Supremacy and Constitutional Entrenchment', *Otago Law Review*, 5 (1984): 603

———, *The Constitution in 1985: The Search for Legitimacy* (Auckland: University of Auckland Press, 1985)

———, 'The Monarchy and the Constitution today', *New Zealand Law Journal* (1992): 438

———, *Waitangi and Indigenous Rights: Revolution, Law and Legitimation* (Auckland: University of Auckland Press, 1999)

Brown, Andrew and Anthony Grant, *The law of intellectual property in New Zealand: an exposition of the New Zealand law relating to trade marks, passing off, copyright, registered designs, patents, trade secrets and the Fair Trading Act 1986* (Wellington: Butterworths, 1989)

Brownlie, Ian, *Principles of Public International Law* (5th edn, New York: Clarendon Press, 1998)

Bryce, James, *Constitutions* (London: Oxford University Press, 1901)

Buchanan, James, *The Limits of Liberty: Between anarchy and Leviathan* (Chicago: University of Chicago Press, 1975)

Bull, Hedley, *The Anarchical Society: A Study of Order in World Politics* (London: Macmillan, 1977)

Burk, Dan L., 'Federalism in Cyberspace', *Connecticut Law Review*, 28 (1996): 1095–127

———, 'Muddy Rules for Cyberspace', *Cardozo Law Review*, 21 (1998–99): 121–79

———, 'Trademarks Along the Infobahn: A First Look at the Emerging Law of Cybermarks', *University of Richmond Journal of Law and Technology*, 1 (1995): 1

———, 'Patents in Cyberspace: Territoriality and Infringement on Global Computer Networks', *Tulane Law Review*, 68 (1993–94): 1–67

Burke, Edmund, *Selected Writings and Speeches,* ed. Peter J. Stanlis (Washington: Regnery Publications, 1997)

Burns, Thomas S., *Barbarians within the gates of Rome: a study of Roman military policy and the barbarians, ca. AD375–425* (Bloomington: Indiana University Press, 1994)

Cain, Bruce E., 'The Internet in the (dis)service of democracy?', *Loyola of Los Angeles Law Review*, 34 (2001): 1005–21

Campbell, J.B., *The Emperor and the Roman Army, 31 BC–AD 235* (Oxford: Clarendon Press, 1984)

Campbell, James, *Essays in Anglo-Saxon History* (London: Hambledon Press, 1986)

Campos, Nauro and Fabrizzio Coricelli, 'Growth in Transition: What We Know, What We Don't, and What We Should', *Journal of Economic Literature*, 40 (2002): 793–836

Cannataci, Joseph A. and Jeanne Pia Mifsud Bonnici, 'Can self-regulation satisfy the transnational requisite of successful Internet regulation?', *International Review of Law, Computers and Technology*, 17 (2003): 51–61

Canning, J.P., 'Law, sovereignty and corporation theory, 1300–1450', in J.H. Burns (ed.), *The Cambridge History of Mediæval Political Thought c.350–c.1450* (Cambridge: Cambridge University Press, 1988)

Cannon, John and Ralph Griffiths, *The Oxford Illustrated History of the British Monarchy* (Oxford: Oxford University Press, 1988)

Cardinale, Hyginus Eugene, *The Holy See and the international order* (Toronto: Macmillan of Canada, 1976)

Cardozo, Benjamin N., *The Nature of the Judicial Process* (New Haven: Yale University Press, 1921)

Carey, Gilbert L., 'The resurgence of states' rights creates new risk to intellectual property', *Albany Law Journal of Science and Technology*, 11 (2000): 123–52

Carlyle, Sir Robert and A.J. Carlyle, *A History of Mediæval Political Theory in the West* (Edinburgh: Blackwood, 1928–36)

Carneiro, Robert L., 'A Theory of the Origin of the State', *Science*, 169 (1970): 733–8

Carr, Robert, *Black nationalism in the new world: reading the African American and West Indian experience* (Durham: Duke University Press, 2002)

Carter, F.W. and David Turnock (eds), *Environmental problems in Eastern Europe* (London: Routledge, 1993)

Caskey, C. Thomas, 'Molecular Medicine; A Spin-Off from the Helix', *JAMA*, 269 (1993): 1986–92

Castel, Jean Gabriel, *International Law: Chiefly as Interpreted and Applied in Canada* (3rd edn, Toronto: University of Toronto Press, 1976)

Castells, Manuel, *The Rise of Network Society* (London: Blackwell, 1996, 2nd edn, 2000)

Cates, Christopher, 'Property in Human Tissues: History, Society and Possible Implementations', *Appeal: Review of Current Law and Law Reform*, 4 (1998): 32–43

Cell, John W., *British colonial administration in the mid-nineteenth century: the policy-making process* (New Haven: Yale University Press, 1970)

Chambers, Jasemine, 'Patent eligibility of biotechnological inventions in the United States, Europe, and Japan: How much patent policy is public policy?', *George Washington International Law Review*, 34 (2002): 223–46

Chander, Anupam, 'Whose Republic?', *University of Chicago Law Review*, 69 (2002): 1479–1500

Charlton, John, *The Chartists: the first national workers' movement* (London: Pluto Press, 1997)

Charnovitz, S., 'Opening the WTO to Non-Governmental Interests', *Fordham International Law Journal*, 24 (2000): 173

Chauveau, Michel, *Cleopatra: beyond the myth*, trans. David Lorton (Ithaca: Cornell University Press, 2002)

Cheshire, G.C., *Modern Law of Real Property*, ed. E.H. Burn (13th edn, London: Butterworths, 1982)

Chester, Sir Norman: *The English administrative system, 1780–1870* (Oxford: Clarendon Press, 1981)

Chevallier, Raymond, *Roman roads*, trans. N.H. Field (Berkeley: University of California Press, 1976)

Chichilnisky, Graciela, 'The Knowledge Revolution', *Journal of International Trade and Economic Development*, 7 (1998): 39–45

Chien, Colleen, 'Cheap drugs at what price to innovation: Does the compulsory licensing of pharmaceuticals hurt innovation?', *Berkeley Technology Law Journal*, 18 (2003): 853–908

Chrimes, Stanley and A.L. Brown, *Select Documents of English Constitutional History 1307–1485* (London: A. and C. Black, 1961)

Chrimes, Stanley, C.D. Ross and R.A. Griffiths (eds), *Fifteenth-century England 1399–1509* (Manchester: Manchester University Press, 1972)

Chrimes, Stanley, *Lancastrians, Yorkists and Henry VII* (2nd edn, London: Macmillan and Co., 1966)

Christie, I.R., *Wars and Revolutions*: *Britain, 1760–1815* (Cambridge: Edward Arnold, 1982)

Ciggaar, Krijnie N., *Western travellers to Constantinople: the West and Byzantium, 962–1204: cultural and political relations* (Leiden: E.J. Brill, 1996)

Clanchy, M.T., *England and its Rulers, 1066–1272: Foreign Lordship and National Identity* (London: Fontana, 1983)

——————, *From memory to written record, England 1066–1307* (Oxford: Blackwell, 1993)

Clark, Bruce, *Native liberty, Crown Supremacy – the Existing Aboriginal Right of Self-Government in Canada* (Montreal: McGill-Queen's University Press, 1990)

Clark, J. Desmond, *The common heritage: the significance of hunter-gatherer societies for human evolution* (Canberra: Australian National University, 1990)

Clarke, Sir Arthur C., *The Wind from the Sun: stories of the space age* (London: Corgi, 1962)

Clift, J., 'The UNCITRAL Model Law and electronic equivalents to traditional bills of lading', *Journal of the Section on Business Law of the International Bar Association*, 27 (1999): 311–17

Coates-Stephens, Robert, 'The walls and aqueducts of Rome in the early Middle Ages, A.D. 500–1000', *The Journal of Roman Studies*, 88 (1998): 166–78

Cobbett, William (ed.), *The Parliamentary History of England* (12 vols, London: Nelson, 1806–20)

Cohen, David, 'Thinking about the State', *Osgoode Hall Law Journal*, 24 (1986): 379–409

Cohen, Linda R. and Roger G. Noll, 'Intellectual Property, Antitrust and the New Economy', *University of Pittsburgh Law Review*, 62 (2001): 453–73

Coleman, S. (ed.), *2001: Cyber Space Odyssey: The Internet in the UK Election* (London: Hansard Society, 2001)

Collins, Lawrence (ed.), *Dicey and Morris on the Conflict of Laws* (13th edn, London: Sweet and Maxwell, 2000)

Collins, Randall, *Weberian Sociological Theory* (Cambridge: Cambridge University Press, 1986)

Conley, Richard, 'Sovereignty or the Status Quo? The 1998 pre-referendum debate in Quebec', *Journal of Commonwealth and Comparative Politics*, 35 (1997): 67–92

Cooke, Philip, 'Globalization of economic organization and the emergence of regional interstate partnerships', in Colin H. Williams (ed.), *The Political Geography of the New World Order* (London: Belhaven Press, 1993)

Cooter, Robert D., 'Structural adjudication and the new law merchant: A model of decentralised law', *International Review of Law and Economics*, 12 (1994): 215–31

Corbett, Sir William, '"The Crown" as representing the State', *Commonwealth Law Review*, 1 (1903): 23

Corcoran, Elizabeth, 'A Tiny Mouse Came Forth', *Scientific American* (1989) 73

Cortada, James W., *Making the Information Society: Experience, Consequences and Possibilities* (Paramus: Prentice Hall, 2001)

Cowen, Penelope Brook, 'Neo Liberalism', in Raymond Miller (ed.), *New Zealand Politics in Transition* (Auckland: Oxford University Press, 1997)

Cox, Noel, 'Developments in the Laws of War: NATO attacks on Yugoslavia and the use of force to achieve humanitarian objectives', *New Zealand Armed Forces Law Review* (2002): 13–24

——————, 'Tax and regulatory avoidance through non-traditional alternatives to tax havens', *New Zealand Journal of Taxation Law and Policy*, 9 (2003): 305–27

——————, 'The Consequences for the World Legal Order of the War on Iraq', *New Zealand Armed Forces Law Review* (2003): 11–17

——————, 'The control of advice to the Crown and the development of executive independence in New Zealand', *New Zealand Armed Forces Law Review*, 13 (2001): 166–89

——————, 'The extraterritorial enforcement of consumer legislation and the challenge of the internet', *Edinburgh Law Review*, 8 (2004): 60–83

——————, 'The Law of Succession to the Crown in New Zealand', *Waikato Law Review*, 7 (1999): 49–72

——————, 'The regulation of cyberspace and the loss of national sovereignty', *Information and Communications Technology Law*, 11 (2002): 241–53

——————, 'The Theory of Sovereignty and the Importance of the Crown in the Realms of The Queen', *Oxford University Commonwealth Law Journal*, 2 (2002): 237–55

Cox, Robert W., *Production, Power, and World Order: Social Forces in the Making of History* (New York: Columbia University Press, 1987)

Craven, M., 'The EC Arbitration Commission on Yugoslavia', *British Yearbook of International Law*, 66 (1995): 333

Czarnota, Adam, 'A few reflections on Globalization and the constitution of society', *University of New South Wales Law Journal*, 24 (2001): 809–16

Dadge, David, *Casualty of war: the Bush administration's assault on a free press* (Amherst: Prometheus Books, 2004)

Dahrendorf, Ralf, 'Transitions: Politics, Economics, and Liberty', *Washington Quarterly*, 13 (1990): 133–42

Dallago, Bruno, Gianmaria Ajani and Bruno Grancelli (eds), *Privatisation and entrepreneurship in post-socialist countries: economy, law, and society* (New York: St Martin's, 1992)

Dancy, R.M., *Plato's introduction of forms* (Cambridge: Cambridge University Press, 2004)

Darwin, Charles, *On the origin of species by means of natural selection*, ed. Joseph Carroll (Peterborough: Broadview Press, 2003, first published 1859)

Dauvergne, Catherine (ed.), *Jurisprudence for an interconnected globe* (Aldershot: Ashgate, c.2003)

Davidson, Nicholas S., *The Counter-Reformation* (Oxford: Blackwell, 1987)

de Blois, Lukas, *The Roman army and politics in the first century before Christ* (Amsterdam: J.C. Gieben, 1987)

de Bruin, Ronald, *Consumer trust in electronic commerce: time for best practice* (The Hague: Kluwer Law International, 2002)

De Jager, Charles F., 'The Development of Regulatory Standards for Gene Therapy in the European Union', *Fordham International Law Journal*, 18 (1995): 1303–39

de Malynes, Gerard, *Consuetudo vel Lex Mercatoria, or the Ancient Law Merchant* (London: Adam Islip, 1622, facsimile Amsterdam: Theatrum Orbis, 1979)

de Oliveira Souza, Henrique Freire, 'Genetically Modified Plants: A Need for International Regulation', *Annual Survey of International and Comparative Law*, 6 (2000): 129–74

Dean, M., *Governmentality: Power and Rule in Modern Society* (London: Sage, 1999)

Dearlove, John, 'Bringing the State Back In', *Political Studies* (1989) 521–39

Delibasis, Dimitrios, 'The right to use force in cyberspace: Defining the rules of engagement', *Feature*, 11(3) (2002): 255–68

DeNoce, Kevin G., 'Internet privacy jurisdiction begins to develop; courts and legislators address e-mail confidentiality and other New Age constitutional issues', *The National Law Journal*, 19 (1997): B11

Derrett, J.D.M., 'The Administration of Hindu Law by the British', *Comparative Studies in Society and History*, 4 (1961): 10–52

Dewald, Jonathan, *The European nobility, 1400–1800* (Cambridge: Cambridge University Press, 1996)

Dicey, Albert, *Introduction to the Study of the Law of the Constitution* introduction and appendix by E.C.S. Wade (10th edn, London: Macmillan, 1959)

Dickinson, H.T., 'The Eighteenth-Century Debate on the "Glorious Revolution"', *History*, 61 (1976): 28–45

————, 'The Eighteenth-Century Debate on the Sovereignty of Parliament', *Transactions of the Royal Historical Society (5th Series)*, 26 (1976): 189–210

Dixon, Chandra, 'Marxism', in Raymond Miller (ed.), *New Zealand Politics in Transition* (Auckland: Oxford University Press, 1997)

Dixon, Sir Owen, 'The Law and the Constitution', *Law Quarterly Review*, 51 (1935): 590

Djilianova, Dora, 'To be or not to be: What went right in the Bulgarian foreign Investment climate after 1997', *Thomas Jefferson Law Review*, 25 (2002): 223

Dobek, Mariusz Mark, *The Political logic of privatisation* (Westport: Praeger, 1993)

Dolgin, Janet L., 'Embryonic discourse: Abortion, stem cells, and cloning', *Florida State University Law Review*, 31 (2003): 101–62

Donat, Kim JoDene, 'Engineering Akerlof lemons: Information asymmetry, externalities, and market intervention in the genetically modified food market', *Minnesota Journal of Global Trade*, 12 (2003): 417–59

Donne, John, *Devotions Upon Emergent Occasions*, ed. Anthony Raspa (Montreal: McGill-Queen's University Press, 1975 first published 1624)

Drahos, Peter and John Braithwaite, *Global Business Regulation* (Cambridge: Cambridge University Press, 2000)

————, *Information Feudalism – Who owns the Knowledge Economy?* (New York: New Press, 2003)

Driesen, David M., *The economic dynamics of environmental law* (Cambridge: MIT Press, 2003)

Du Plessis, Rosemary, 'Women, Feminism and the State', in Brian Roper and Chris Rudd (eds), *The Political Economy of New Zealand* (Auckland: Oxford University Press, 1997)

Dunbabin, Jean, 'Government', in J.H. Burns (ed.), *The Cambridge History of Mediæval Political Thought c.350–c.1450* (Cambridge: Cambridge University Press, 1988)

Dunn, John, 'The concept of trust in the politics of John Locke', in R. Rorty (ed.), *Philosophy in History* (Cambridge: Cambridge University Press, 1984)

————, *The Political Thought of John Locke: An historical account of the Two Treatises of Government* (London: Cambridge University Press, 1969)

Dunstan, David, *Governing the Metropolis: politics, technology and social change in a Victoria city: Melbourne* (Carlton: Melbourne University Press, 1984)

Duzan, Stephen A., 'The 1992 Biotechnology Agenda: A Message for Candidates Bush and Clinton', *Healthspan*, 9 (1992): 12–15

Dyson, Kenneth and Kevin Featherstone, *The road to Maastricht: negotiating Economic and Monetary Union* (Oxford: Oxford University Press, 1999)

Easterly, Ernest, III, 'The rule of law and the new world order', *Southern University Law Review*, 22 (1995): 161–83

Eaton, Howard O., *Federation: the coming structure of world government* (Norman: University of Oklahoma Press, 1944)

Egerton, H.E., *Short History of British Colonial Policy* (London: Methuen, 1897)

Eiselen, S., 'Electronic commerce and the United Nations Convention on Contracts for the International Sale of Goods (CISG) 1980', *EDI Law Review: Legal Aspects of Paperless Communication*, 6 (1999): 21–46

Eisenberg, Rebecca S., 'Genes, Patents, and Product Development', *Science*, 257 (1992): 903–8

Elkind, Jerome (ed.), *The impact of American law on English and Commonwealth law: A book of essays* (St Paul: West Publishing Co., 1978)

Elliott, C., 'The Internet – A New World without frontiers', *New Zealand Law Journal* (1998): 405–7

Elliott, E. Donald, 'The Genome and the law: Should increased genetic knowledge change the law?', *Harvard Journal of Law and Public Policy*, 25 (2001): 61–70

Elton, Sir Geoffrey, *Reform and Reformation, 1509–1558* (London: Edward Arnold, 1979)

Empie, Derek E., 'The dormant Internet: are state regulators of motor vehicle sales by manufacturers on the Information Superhighway obstructing interstate and Internet commerce?', *Georgia State University Law Review*, 18 (2002): 827–57

English Historical Documents 1327–1485, ed. A.R. Myers (London: Eyre and Spottiswoode, 1969), vol. 4

Ertman, Thomas, *Birth of the leviathan: building states and regimes in mediæval and early modern Europe* (Cambridge: Cambridge University Press, 1997)

Ewens, Lara E., 'Seed Wars: Biotechnology, Intellectual Property, and the Quest for High Yield Seeds', *Boston College International and Comparative Law Review*, 23 (2000): 285–310

Fackelmann, Kathleen, 'Forecasting Alzheimer's Disease', *Science News*, 149 (1996) 312

Falk, Richard, 'The Interplay of Westphalia and Charter Conceptions of International Legal Order', in Cyril E. Black and Richard A. Falk (eds), *The Future of the International Legal Order* (Princeton: Princeton University Press, 1969)

Fears, J. Rufus, *Princeps a diis electus: the divine election of the emperor as a political concept at Rome* (Rome: American Academy in Rome, 1977)

Ferrari, Franco, '"Forum shopping" despite international uniform contract law conventions', *International and Comparative Law Quarterly*, 51 (2002): 689–707

Ficsor, Mihály, *The law of copyright and the Internet: the 1996 WIPO treaties, their interpretation and implementation* (Oxford: Oxford University Press, 2002)

Figgis, J.N., *The theory of the Divine Right of Kings* (2nd edn, Cambridge: Cambridge University Press, 1914)

Filmer, Sir Robert, *Patriarcha and other writings*, ed. J.P. Sommerville (London: Cambridge University Press, 1991)

Finer, S.E., *The history of government from the earliest times* (Oxford: Oxford University Press, 1997)

Finley, M.I., *Authority and legitimacy in the classical city-state* (København: Munksgaard, 1982)

Firth, Alison (ed.), *The prehistory and development of intellectual property systems* (London: Sweet and Maxwell, 1997)

Fisher, Lane and Cheryl L. Mullin, 'Franchise laws in the age of electronic communication', *Franchise Law Journal*, 19 (1999): 47–51

Fishman, Renee M., Kara Josephberg, Jane Linn, Jane Pollack and Jena Victoriano, 'Threat of international cyberterrorism on the rise', *Intellectual Property and Technology Law Journal*, 14 (2002): 23

————, 'China issues rules on content enforcement', *Intellectual Property and Technology Law Journal*, 14(10) (2002): 24

Fleming, Robin, *Kings and Lords in Conquered England* (Cambridge: Cambridge University Press, 1991)

Floud, Roderick and Donald McCloskey, *The Economic History of Britain since 1700* (2nd edn, Cambridge: Cambridge University Press, 1994)

Foley, Michael, *The Silence of Constitutions: Gaps, 'Abeyances' and Political Temperament in the Maintenance of Government* (London: Routledge, 1989)

Fortescue, Sir John, *In Praise of the laws of England (De Laudibus Legum Angliæ)*, ed. Stanley Chrimes (Cambridge: Cambridge University Press, 1942)

————, *The Governance of England*, notes by Charles Plummer (Westport: Hyperion Press, 1979)

van Fossen, Anthony, 'Financial frauds and pseudo-states in the Pacific Islands', *Crime, Law and Social Change*, 37 (2002): 357–78

Foucault, Michel, *Dispositive der Macht* (Berlin: Merve Verlag, 1978)

————, 'Governmentality', in J.D. Faubion (ed.), *Michel Foucault, Power: The Essential Works* (London: Allen Lane Penguin Press, 2000)

————, 'Governmentality', *Ideology and Consciousness*, 6 (Summer 1986): 5–21

————, 'Omnes et Singulatim: Toward a Criticism of "Political Reason"', in *The Tanner Lectures of Human Values. II* (Salt Lake City: University of Utah Press/Cambridge University Press, 1981)

————, *Power/Knowledge: Selected Interviews and Other Writings 1972–1977*, ed. C. Gordon (New York: Pantheon, 1980)

————, *Resume des cours* (Paris: conferencs, essais et lecons du college de France/Julliard, 1989) 1980–1982

————, 'Space, Knowledge and Power', in Paul Rabinow (ed.), *The Foucault Reader* (New York: Pantheon Books, 1984)

————, *The Foucault Effects: Studies in Governmentality*, eds Graham Burchell, Colin Gordon and Peter Miller (London: Harvester Wheatsheaf, 1991)

Fox, Michael R., 'Nuclear regulation: the untold story; poor management? Yes, but lay the blame on too much regulation', *Public Utilities Fortnightly*, 133 (1994): 37–41

Frame, Robin, *The Political Development of the British Isles 1100–1400* (Oxford: Oxford University Press, 1990)

Friedman, David, 'Does technology require new law?', *Harvard Journal of Law and Public Policy*, 25 (2001): 71–85

Friedman, Thomas L., *The Lexus and the Olive Tree* (London: HarperCollins, 2000)

Friedmann, Wolfgang, *The Changing Structure of International Law* (New York: Columbia University Press, 1964)

Furbach, Ulrich, 'Principles of Artificial Intelligence', *Artificial Intelligence*, 145 (2003): 245–52

Ganshof, Francois, *Feudalism*, trans. Philip Grierson (London: Longman, 1952, first published 1944)

Gardner, Peter J., 'United States Intellectual Property Law and the Biotech Challenge: Searching for an elusive balance', *Vermont Bar Journal*, 29 (2003): 24

Geanakoplos, Deno John, *Constantinople and the West: essays on the late Byzantine (Palaeologan) and Italian Renaissances and the Byzantine and Roman churches* (Madison: University of Wisconsin Press, c.1989)

Geetter, Jennifer S., 'Coding for Change: The Power of the Human Genome to Transform the American Health Insurance System', *American Journal of Law and Medicine*, 28 (2001): 1–76

Gibney, Mark, 'Decommunization: Human Rights Lessons from the Past and Present, and Prospects for the Future', *Denver International Law and Policy*, 23 (1994): 87–133

Gibson, William, *Neuromancer* (New York: Ace Books, 1984)

Giles of Rome, *De regimine principum* (Rome: 1556, completed 1270s or 1280s)

Gillingham, John and J.C. Holt (eds), *War and Government in the Middle Ages* (Cambridge: Boydell Press, 1984)

Gillis, Anna Maria, 'The Patent Question of the Year', *BioScience*, 42 (1992): 336–40

Gimpel, Jean, *The Mediæval Machine: the industrial revolution of the Middle Ages* (London: Book Club Associates, 1977)

von Glahn, Gerhard, *Law Among Nations: An Introduction to Public International Law* (7th edn, Boston: Allyn and Bacon, 1996)

Gluckman, M., *Politics law and ritual in tribal society* (Oxford: Oxford University Press, 1977)

Goldenman, Gretta et al (eds), *Environmental liability and privatisation in Central and Eastern Europe* (London: Graham and Trotman, 1994)

Goldfinch, Shaun, 'The State', in Raymond Miller (ed.), *New Zealand Government and Politics* (Melbourne: Oxford University Press, 2001)

Goldsmith, Jack L., 'Against Cyberanarchy', *University of Chicago Law Review*, 65 (1998): 1199–250

——————, 'Regulation of the Internet: Three Persistent Fallacies', *Chicago–Kent Law Review*, 73 (1998): 1119–31

Goldwin, Robert A., 'Locke's state of nature in political society', *Western Political Quarterly*, 31 (1976): 126–35

Gomez, Ivette P., 'Beyond the neighbourhood drugstore: United States regulation of online prescription drug sales by foreign businesses', *Rutgers Computer and Technology Law Journal*, 28 (2002): 431–62

Goncalves, Maria Eduarda, 'Technological change, Globalization and the Europeanization of rights', *International Review of Law, Computers and Technology*, 16 (2002): 301–16

Goody, Jack, *Technology, tradition and the state in Africa* (London: Hutchinson, 1980)

Gorski, Richard, *The fourteenth-century sheriff: English local administration in the late Middle Ages* (Woodbridge: Boydell Press, 2003)

Goss, Vladimir P. and Christine Verzair Bornstein (eds), *The Meeting of two worlds: cultural exchange between East and West during the period of the Crusades* (Kalamazoo: Mediæval Institute Publications, Western Michigan University, 1986)

Goudie, Andrew, *The Human impact on the natural environment* (4th edn, Oxford: Blackwell, 1990)

Grady, Mark F. and Michael T. McGuire, 'A Theory of the Origin of Natural Law', *Journal of Contemporary Legal Issues*, 8 (1997): 87–129

——————, 'The Nature of Constitutions', *Journal of Bioeconomics*, 1 (1999) 227–40

Grady, Mark F., 'The state and the networked economy', *Harvard Journal of Law and Public Policy*, 25 (2001): 15–29

Grainger, John, *Nerva and the Roman succession crisis of AD 96–99* (London: Routledge, 2003)

Grant, T., *The Recognition of States: Law and Practice in Debate and Evolution* (Westport: Praeger, 1999)

Gratian of Bologna, *Concordia discordantium canonum* (or *Decretum magistri Gratiani*) in A. Friedberg (ed.), *Corpus Iuris Canonici* (2 vols, Leipzig: Tauchnitz, 1879–81)

Green, Judith A., *English sheriffs to 1154* (London: HMSO, 1990)

Greenleaf, Graham, 'An Endnote on Regulating Cyberspace: Architecture vs Law?', *University of New South Wales Law Journal*, 21 (1998): 593–622

Gregory, J.D., 'Solving legal issues in electronic commerce', *Canadian Business Law Journal*, 32 (1999): 84–131

——————, 'The authentication of digital records', *EDI Law Review: Legal Aspects of Paperless Communication*, 6 (1999): 47–63

Grewlich, Klaus W., *Governance in 'Cyberspace' – Access and Public Interest in Global Telecommunications* (The Hague: Kluwer Law International, 1999)

Griffin, Joseph P., 'Foreign Governmental Reactions to United States Assertion of Extraterritorial Jurisdiction', *George Mason Law Review*, 6 (1998): 505

Gross, Leo, 'The Peace of Westphalia, 1648–1948', *American Journal of International Law*, 42 (1948): 20–41

Grossman, Ilene K., 'The new Industrial Revolution: meeting the challenge', *Public Law Forum*, 4 (1985): 419–26

Grotius, Hugo, *De jure belli ac pacis*, ed. F.W. Kelsey (reprint of 1925 edn, New York: Oceana, 1964)

Guibernau, Montserrat, *Nationalisms: the nation-state and nationalism in the twentieth century* (Cambridge: Polity Press, 1996)

El-Hadidy, Bahaa and Esther E. Horne (eds), *The infrastructure of an information society: proceedings of the First International Information Conference in Egypt, Cairo: 13–15 December, 1982* (Amsterdam: Egyptian Society for Information Technology/American Society for Information Science, 1982)

Halasz, Alexandra, *The marketplace of print: pamphlets and the public sphere in early modern England* (Cambridge: Cambridge University Press, 1997)

Hall, Clayton, *The Lords Baltimore and the Maryland Palatinate* (Baltimore: J. Murphy and Co., 1902)

Hall, John, *The Grounds and Reasons of Monarchy* prefixed to *The Political Works of James Harrington*, ed. J.G.A. Pocock (Cambridge: Cambridge University Press, 1977)

Hall, William E., *A Treatise on International Law*, ed. A. Pearce Higgins (8th edn, Oxford: Clarendon Press, 1924)

Hammond, Mason, *City-State and world state in Greek and Roman political theory until Augustus* (Cambridge: Harvard University Press, 1951)

Hanham, H.J., *The Nineteenth Century Constitution, 1815–1914* (Cambridge: Cambridge University Press, 1969)

Hannig, Mark, 'An examination of the possibility to secure intellectual property rights for plant genetic resources developed by indigenous peoples of the NAFTA states: Domestic legislation under the International Convention for Protection of New Plant Varieties', *Arizona Journal of International and Comparative Law*, 13 (1996): 175–252

Hardie, Frank, *The Political Influence of Queen Victoria, 1861–1901* (London: Oxford University Press, 1935)

Hardin, I. and N. Lewis, *The Noble Lie: The British Constitution and the Role of Law* (London: Hutchinson, 1987)

Harding, Alan, *A Social History of English Law* (Harmondsworth: Penguin Books, 1966)

Hardt, Michael and Antonio Negri, *Empire* (Cambridge: Harvard University Press, 2000)

Hardy, Trotter, 'The Proper Legal Regime for "Cyberspace"', *University of Pittsburgh Law Review*, 55 (1994): 993–1055

Harlow: Carol, 'Power from the People?', in Patrick McAuslan and John McEldowney (eds), *Law, Legitimacy and the Constitution: Essays marking the*

Centenary of Dicey's Law of the Constitution (London: Sweet and Maxwell, 1985)

Harris, Bruce, 'Law-making powers of the New Zealand General Assembly', *Otago Law Review*, 5 (1984): 565

————, 'The "Third Source" of Authority for Government Action', *Law Quarterly Review*, 109 (1992): 626–51

Harrison, Roger, *Diagnosing organizational culture: trainer's manual* (San Diego: Pfeiffer, 1993)

Hart, Kathleen, 'Making Mythical Monsters', *The Progressive* (March 1990): 22

Hartley, Trevor C., *Constitutional Problems of the European Union* (Oxford: Hart Publishing, 1999)

Harvey, David, *The Condition of Postmodernity* (London: Blackwell, 1989)

Hatschek, J., *An Outline of International Law*, trans. C. Manning (London: Bell and Sons, 1930)

Hearn, William, *The Government of England: Its Structure and its Development* (London: Longmans, Green, Reader and Dyer, 1867)

Hedieh, Nasheri, 'The Intersection of technology crimes and cyberspace in Europe: The Case of Hungary', *Information and Communications Technology Law*, 12 (2003): 25–48

Heere, W.P. and J.P.S. Offerhaus, *International Law in Historical Perspective* (The Hague: Martinus Nijhoff Publishers, 1998)

Held, David, *Political Theory and the Modern State* (Cambridge: Polity Press, 1989)

Heller, Hermann, 'The Decline of the Nation State and its Effect on Constitutional and International Economic Law', *Cardozo Law Review*, 18 (1996): 1139

van Hemel, Annemoon and Niki van der Wielen (eds), *Privatisation/desetatisation and culture. Conference reader for the Circle Round Table 1997* (Amsterdam: Boekman Foundation/Twente University, 1997)

Henderson, W.O., *Studies in German Colonial History* (Chicago: Quadrangle Books, 1962)

Henkin, Louis, 'That "S" Word: Sovereignty, and Globalization, and Human Rights, Et Cetera', *Ford Law Review*, 68 (1999): 1–14

Herbison, Elmore, *The Christian scholar in the age of the Reformation* (New York: Scribners, 1956)

Hermann, Thomas G., 'Is United States legal system an impediment to scientific progress?', *National Law Journal*, 19 (4 August 1997): C-15

Heuston, Robert, *Essays in Constitutional Law* (2nd edn, London: Stevens and Son, 1964)

Higgins, Dame Rosalyn, *The Development of International Law Through the Political Organs of the UN* (London: Oxford University Press, 1963)

Higham, Charles, *The civilization of Angkor* (London: Weidenfeld and Nicolson, 2001)

Hillgruber, C., 'The Admission of New States to the International Community', *European Journal of International Law*, 9 (1998): 491–509

Hinde, G.W., D.W. McMorland and P.B.A. Sim, *Land Law* (Wellington: Butterworths, 1978)

Hinsley, F., *Sovereignty* (2nd edn, Cambridge: Cambridge University Press, 1986)

Hobbes, Thomas, *Leviathan*, ed. Edwin Curley (Indianapolis: Hackett Publishing Co., 1994, first published 1688)

Hogg, P.W., *Constitutional Law of Canada* (3rd edn, Scarborough, Ontario: Carswell, 1992)

——————, *Liability of the Crown in Australia, New Zealand and the United Kingdom* (Sydney: The Law Book Co., 1971)

Holton, R.J., *Cities, capitalism, and civilization* (London: Allen and Unwin, 1986)

Honderich, Ted (ed.), *The Oxford Companion to Philosophy* (Oxford: Oxford University Press, 1995)

Hood, Leroy, 'Biology and Medicine in the Twenty-First Century', in Daniel J. Kevles and Leroy Hood (eds), *The Code of Codes, Scientific and social issues in the human genome project* (Harvard: Harvard University Press, 1992)

Hood, Miriam, *Gunboat diplomacy, 1895–1905: great power pressure in Venezuela* (London: Allen and Unwin, 1975)

Horn, Lawrence A., 'To Be or Not to Be: The Republic of Minerva – Nation-founding by Individuals', *Columbia Journal of Transnational Law*, 12 (1973): 520

Hornby, Susan and Zoë Clarke (eds), *Challenge and change in the information society* (London: Facet, 2003)

Hovenkamp, Herbert, 'Technology, politics, and regulated monopoly: an American historical perspective', *Texas Law Review*, 62 (1984): 1263–312

Howard, J. Woodford, Jr., 'Constitution and society in comparative perspective', *Judicature*, 71 (1987): 211–15

Howard, Sir Michael, George J. Andreopoulos and Mark R. Shulman (eds), *The Laws of War: Constraints on Warfare in the Western World* (New Haven: Yale University Press, 1994)

Howard-Ellis, Charles, *The origin, structure and working of the League of Nations* (Union: The Lawbook Exchange, 2003)

Howe, Paul, 'Nationality and Sovereignty Support in Quebec', *Canadian Journal of Political Science*, 31 (1998): 31–60

Hudson, John, *Land, law, and lordship in Anglo-Norman England* (Oxford: Clarendon Press, 1994)

Hudson, Kathy, 'The Human Genome Project, DNA Science and the Law: the American Legal System's Response to Breakthroughs in Genetic Science', *American University Law Review*, 51 (2002): 431–45

Hudson, Manley O. (ed.), *International Legislation* (Washington: Carnegie Endowment for International Peace, 1931–50)

Hunnisett, R.F., *The mediæval coroner* (Cambridge: Cambridge University Press, 1961)

Hunt, A. and G. Wickham, *Foucault and Law: Towards a Sociology of Law and Governance* (London: Pluto Press, 1994)

Huxley, Aldous, *Brave New World* (London: Chatto and Windus, 1932)

Ibusuki, Makoto (ed.), *Transnational Cyberspace Law* (Oxford: Hart, 2000)

International Labour Organization, *World Labour Report* (London: International Labour Organization, 1995)

Jackson, Moana, 'Maori Law', in Ramari Young (ed.), *Mana Tiriti: The Art of Protest and Partnership* (Wellington: Haeata Project Waitangi/City Art Gallery/Daphne Brasell Associates Press, 1991)

Jacob, Margaret C., *Scientific culture and the making of the industrial West* (New York: Oxford University Press, 1997)

Jacobs, Joseph, *The Republican Crown: Lawyers and the Making of the State in Twentieth Century Britain* (Aldershot: Dartmouth, 1996)

James I, HM King, *Basilikon Doron* (Menston: Scolar Press, 1969, first published 1599)

James, Colin (ed.), *Building the Constitution* (Wellington: Victoria University of Wellington Institute of Policy Studies, 2000)

Jennings, Sir Robert and Sir Arthur Watts (eds), *Oppenheim's International Law* (9th edn, London: Longman, 1992)

Jessup, Philip, *A Modern Law of Nations* (New York: Macmillan, 1968)

John of Paris, *De potestate regia et papali, Johannes Quidort von Paris Über Königliche under päpstliche Gewalt*, ed. F. Bleienstein (Stuttgart: Klett, 1969)

Johnson, David R. and David G. Post, 'Law and Borders: The Rise of Law in Cyberspace', *Stanford Law Review*, 48 (1996): 1367–402

Johnston, W. Ross, *Sovereignty and protection: a study of British jurisdictional imperialism in the late nineteenth century* (Durham: Duke University Commonwealth Studies Centre, Duke University Press, 1973)

Jones, Norman: *The English Reformation: religion and cultural adaptation* (Oxford: Blackwell, 2002)

Jones, Richard and Subhajit Basu, 'Taxation of electronic commerce: A developing problem', *International Review of Law, Computers and Technology*, 16 (2002): 35–52

Joseph, Gregory P., 'Internet and email evidence', *The Computer and Internet Lawyer*, 19 (2002): 17–22

Joseph, Philip, *Constitutional and Administrative Law in New Zealand* (Sydney: The Law Book Co., 1993)

——————, 'Crown as a legal concept (I)', *New Zealand Law Journal* (1993): 126

——————, 'Suspending Statutes Without Parliament's Consent', *New Zealand Universities Law Review*, 14 (1991): 282

——————, 'The Crown as a legal concept (II)', *New Zealand Law Journal* (1993): 179

Josephberg, Kara, Jane Pollack, Jenna Victoriano and Oriyan Gitig, 'Singapore free trade agreement addresses domain names', *Intellectual Property and Technology Law Journal*, 15 (2003): 20

Judson, Horace F., 'A History of the Science and Technology Behind Gene Mapping and Sequencing', in Daniel J. Kevles and Leroy Hood (eds), *The Code of Codes, Scientific and social issues in the human genome project* (Harvard: Harvard University Press, 1992)

Juenger, Friedrich, 'Judicial Jurisdiction in the United States and in the European Communities: A Comparison', *Michigan Law Review*, 82 (1984): 1195

Justice, Steven, *Writing and rebellion: England in 1381* (Berkeley: University of California Press, 1994)

Kagan, Richard L., *Students and society in early modern Spain* (Baltimore: Johns Hopkins University Press, 1974)

Kahin, Brian and Charles Nesson (eds), *Borders in cyberspace: information policy and the global information infrastructure* (Cambridge: MIT Press, 1997)

Kalir, Doron M., 'Taking Globalization Seriously: Towards General Jurisprudence', *Columbia Journal of Transnational Law*, 39 (2001): 785–821

Kanawati, Naguib, *The Egyptian administration in the Old Kingdom: evidence on its economic decline* (Warminster: Aris and Phillips, 1977)

Kantorowicz, Ernst, 'Kingship under the impact of scientific jurisprudence', in Marshall Clagett et al (eds), *Twelfth century Europe* (Madison: University of Wisconsin Press, 1961)

——————, *The King's Two Bodies: A Study in Mediæval Political Theology* (Princeton: Princeton University Press, 1957)

Katyal, Sonia K., 'Ending the revolution', *Texas Law Review*, 80 (2002): 1465–86

Kay, Richard, 'Constitutional Chrononomy', *Ratio Juris*, 13 (2000): 31–48

Keen, Maurice H., *The Laws of War in the Late Middle Ages* (London: Routledge and Kegan Paul, 1965)

Keith, A.B., *Constitutional History of the First British Empire* (Oxford: Clarendon Press, 1930)

Kelsen, Hans, *General Theory of Law and State*, trans. Anders Wedberg (Cambridge: Harvard University Press, 1945)

Kelsey, Jane, 'Legal Imperialism and the Colonization of Aotearoa', in Paul Spoonley et al (eds), *Tauiwi: Racism and Ethnicity in New Zealand* (Palmerston North: Dunmore Press, 1984)

——————, 'Restructuring the Nation', in Peter Fitzpatrick (ed.), *Nationalism, Racism and the Rule of Law* (Aldershot: Dartmouth, 1995)

——————, *Rolling Back the State: Privatisation of Power in Aotearoa/New Zealand* (Wellington: Bridget Williams Books, 1993)

Kende, Mark S., 'Technology's future impact upon state constitutional law: the Montana example', *Montana Law Review*, 64 (2003): 273–94

Kevles, Daniel J. and Ari Berkowitz, 'The gene patenting controversy: A convergence of law, economic interests and ethics', *Brooklyn Law Review*, 67 (2001): 233–48

Kevles, Daniel J., 'Diamond v. Chakrabarty and Beyond: The Political Economy of Patenting Life', in Arnold Thackray (ed.), *Private Science: Biotechnology and the Rise of the Molecular Sciences* (Philadelphia: University of Pennsylvania Press, 1998)

——————, 'Out of Eugenics: The Historical Politics of the Human Genome', in Daniel J. Kevles and Leroy Hood (eds), *The Code of Codes, Scientific and social issues in the human genome project* (Harvard: Harvard University Press, 1992)

Khan, L. Ali, *The Extinction of Nation-States: A World without Borders* (The Hague: Kluwer Law International, 1996)

Kim, Jae-Young, 'Deregulation reconsidered: Protecting Internet speech in the United States, Germany, and Japan', *Communications and the Law*, 24 (2002): 53–75

King, Robert G. and Ross Levine, 'Finance and Growth: Schumpeter Might Be Right', *Quarterly Journal of Economics*, 108 (1993): 717–37

Kirkaldy, Adam, *British shipping: its history, organization and importance, with a map of main routes and coaling stations and full appendices* (London: K. Paul, Trench and Trubner, 1914)

Kirkwood, Genevieve and Michael Purdue, 'High technology; role and status of central government policy', *Journal of Planning and Environmental Law* (1988): 111–8

Kleijn, Gerda de, *The Water Supply of Ancient Rome: City Area, Water, and Population* (Amsterdam: Gieben, 2001)

Klep, Paul and Eddy Van Cauwenberghe (eds), *Entrepreneurship and the transformation of the economy (10th–20th centuries): essays in honour of Herman Van der Wee* (Leuven: Leuven University Press, 1994)

Kloppenburg, Jack Ralph, Jr., *First the seed: The political economy of plant biotechnology 1492–2000* (Cambridge: Cambridge University Press, 1988)

——————, 'No Hunting: Scientific Poaching and Global Biodiversity', *Z Magazine* (1990): 104–8

Knoll, Arthur J. and Lewis H. Gann (eds), *Germans in the Tropics: Essays in German Colonial History* (New York: Greenwood Press, 1987)

Komesar, Neil, 'Taking Institutions seriously', *University of Chicago Law Review*, 51 (1984): 366

Kornberg, Allan and Harold Clarke, *Citizens and Community – Political Support in a Representative Democracy* (Cambridge: Cambridge University Press, 1992)

Koselleck, Reinhart, *Zeitschichten* (Frankfurt: Suhrkamp Verlap, 2000)

Koskenniemi, M., 'The Future of Statehood', *Harvard International Law Journal*, 32 (1991): 397

Kraemer, Kenneth L., 'Computers and the Constitution: A Helpful, Harmful or Harmless Relationship?', *Public Administration Review*, 47 (1987): 93–105

Krasner, Stephen, 'Sovereignty: an institutional perspective', *Comparative Political Studies*, 21 (1988): 66–94

Krimsky, Sheldon and Roger P. Wrubel, *Agricultural biotechnology and the environment* (Urbana: University of Illinois Press, 1996)

Krimsky, Sheldon, *Biotechnics and society: The rise of industrial genetics* (Westport: Praeger, 1991)

Krygier, Martin and Adam Czarnota (eds), *The Rule of Law After Communism: Problems and Prospects in East-Central Europe* (Brookfield: Ashgate, 1998)

Kuhn, Thomas, *The Structure of Scientific Revolutions* (Chicago: University of Chicago Press, 1962)

Kuran, Timur, 'The Islamic Commercial Crisis: Institutional Roots of Economic Underdevelopment in the Middle East', *The Journal of Economic History*, 63 (2003): 414–46

Kynaston, David, *The Secretary of State* (Lavenham: Dalton, 1978)

Kyvig, David E., *Explicit and Authentic Acts: Amending the United States Constitution* (Lawrence: University of Kansas Press, 1996)

La Nauze, J.A., *The Making of the Australian Constitution* (Melbourne: Melbourne University Press, 1972)

Lander, J.R., *The Limitations of English Monarchy in the Later Middle Ages* (Toronto: University of Toronto Press, 1989)

Lash, W., 'The Decline of the Nation State in International Trade and Development', *Cardozo Law Review* (1996–97): 1001

Laski, Harold, *Authority in the Modern State* (New Haven: Yale University Press, 1919)

——————, 'The Responsibility of the State in England', *Harvard Law Review*, 32 (1919): 447–72

——————, 'The Theory of Popular Sovereignty', *Harvard Law Review*, 17 (1919): 201–15

Lasok, K.P.E., *The European Court of Justice: practice and procedure* (2nd edn, London: Butterworths, 1994)

Lassalle, Ferdinand, 'Uber Verfassungswesen', in E. Bernstein (ed.), *Gesammelte Reden und Schriften* (Berlin: P. Cassirer, 1919)

Lauterpacht, Sir Elihu, 'Sovereignty – Myth or Reality?', *International Affairs*, 73 (1997): 137–50

Lauterpacht, Sir Hersch, 'The Subjects of the Law of Nations', *Law Quarterly Review*, 63 (1947): 438–60

Law Commission of New Zealand, *Electronic Commerce Part One* (Wellington: Law Commission of New Zealand, 1998)

Law Commission of New Zealand, *Electronic Commerce Part Two: A Basic Legal Framework* (Wellington: Law Commission of New Zealand, 1999)

——————, *Liability for loss resulting from the development, supply or use of genetically modified organisms* (Wellington: Law Commission of New Zealand, 2002)

Law Reform Commission of British Columbia, *Legal Position of the Crown* (Vancouver: The Law Reform Commission of British Columbia, 1972)

Law Reform Commission of Canada, *The Legal Status of the Federal Administration* (Ottawa: Law Reform Commission of Canada, 1985)

Lawrence, T.J., *The Principles of International Law* (7th edn, London: Macmillan, 1925)

Lazare, Daniel, *The Frozen Republic: How the Constitution is Paralysing Democracy* (New York: Harcourt Brace and Co., 1996)

Lazer, David and Viktor Mayer-Schonberger, 'Governing networks: telecommunication deregulation in Europe and the United States', *Brooklyn Journal of International Law*, 27 (2002): 819–51

Legal Affairs Committee of the Parliamentary Assembly of the Council of Europe, *Legal Status of International Non-Governmental Organizations in Europe*, ed. D. Smith (Brussels: Legal Affairs Committee of the Parliamentary Assembly of the Council of Europe, 1986)

Leick, Gwendolyn, *Mesopotamia: the invention of the city* (London: Allen Lane, 2001)

Lessig, Lawrence, *Code and other Laws of Cyberspace* (New York: Basic Books, 1999)

————, *The Future of Ideas: The Fate of the Commons in a Connected World* (New York: Random House, 2001)

Leventhal, Michael, 'The Golden Age of Wireless', *Intellectual Property and Technology Law Journal*, 14 (2002): 1

Levin, Nickolai G., 'Constitutional statutory synthesis', *Alabama Law Review*, 54 (2003): 1281–373

Levy-Ullmann, Henri, *The English Legal Tradition: Its Sources and History*, trans. M Mitchell rev and ed. Frederick Goadly (London: Macmillan, 1935)

Lintott, Andrew, *Imperium Romanum: politics and administration* (London: Routledge, 1993)

Lipset, Seymour Martin, *Political Man*: *The Social Bases of Politics* (New York: Doubleday, Garden City, 1960)

Little, Gavin, 'Scotland and Parliamentary Sovereignty', *Legal Studies*, 24(4) (2004): 540–67

Locke, John, 'Fundamental Constitutions for Carolina', in David Wootton (ed.), *Political Writings of John Locke* (London: Penguin, 1993)

————, *Two Treatises of Government*, ed. Peter Laslett (Cambridge: Cambridge University Press, 1988)

Locke, Robert R., *The end of the practical man: entrepreneurship and higher education in Germany, France, and Great Britain, 1880–1940* (Greenwich: Jai Press, 1984)

Loewenstein, Joseph, *The author's due: printing and the prehistory of copyright* (Chicago: University of Chicago Press, 2002)

von Loon, Richard and Michael Whittington, *The Canadian Political System*: *Environment, Structure and Process* (3rd edn, Toronto: McGraw-Hill Ryerson, 1981)

LoPatin, Nancy D., *Political unions, popular politics and the great Reform Act of 1832* (New York: St Martin's Press, 1999)

Lorenz, Joseph P., *Peace, power, and the United Nations: a security system for the twenty-first century* (Boulder: Westview Press, 1999)

Lot, Ferdinand, *The end of the ancient world and the beginnings of the Middle Ages* (London: Routledge and Kegan Paul, 1953)

Lowe, Cedric, *The reluctant imperialists: British foreign policy, 1878–1902* (London: Routledge and Kegan Paul, 1967)

Lowry, S. Todd, 'Lord Mansfield and the Law Merchant: Law and Economics in the Eighteenth Century', *Journal of Economic Issues*, 7 (1973): 605–22

Loyn, Henry, *The governance of Anglo-Saxon England, 500–1087* (London: Edward Arnold, 1984)

Lucy, R., *The Australian Form of Government* (Melbourne: Macmillan, 1985)

Lutz, Donald S., 'Toward a Theory of Constitutional Amendment', in Sanford Levinson (ed.), *Responding to Imperfection* (Princeton: Princeton University Press, 1995)

Mabry, Linda A., 'Multinational corporations and United States technology policy: rethinking the concept of corporate nationality', *Georgetown Law Journal*, 87 (1999): 563–673

MacCormick, N., 'Beyond the Sovereign States', *Modern Law Review*, 56 (1993): 1

MacDonald, W.A., *Documentary Source Book of American History* (New York: Macmillan, 1908)

McGinnis, John O., 'The Original Constitution and Our Origins', *Harvard Journal of Law and Public Policy*, 19 (1995): 251–61

——————, 'The Symbiosis of Constitutionalism and Technology', *Harvard Journal of Law and Public Policy*, 25 (2001): 3–14

McGinnis, John O. and Mark L. Movsesian, 'The World Trade Constitution', *Harvard Law Review*, 114 (2000): 511–605

McGready, Steven, 'The Digital Reformation: Total Freedom, Risk, and Responsibility', *Harvard Journal of Law and Technology*, 10 (1996): 137–48

Machiavelli, Niccolo, *The Prince*, eds Quentin Skinner and Russell Price (Cambridge: Cambridge University Press, 1988)

McHugh, P.G., 'Constitutional Myths and the Treaty of Waitangi', *New Zealand Law Journal* (1991): 316–20

——————, 'Constitutional Theory and Maori Claims', in Sir Hugh Kawharu (ed.), *Waitangi: Maori and Pakeha Perspectives of the Treaty of Waitangi* (Auckland: Oxford University Press, 1989)

McKusick, Victor A., 'The Human Genome Project: Plans, Status, and Applications in Biology and Medicine', in George J. Annas and Sherman Elias (eds), *Gene Mapping: Using law and ethics as guides* (New York: Oxford University Press, 1992)

McLennan, Dan, 'The online revolution in government contracting', *Law Institute Journal*, 76 (2002): 78–81

MacLeod, Roy (ed.), *Government and expertise: specialists, administrators, and professionals, 1860–1919* (Cambridge: Cambridge University Press, 1988)

McManis, Charles, 'The Interface Between International Intellectual Property and Environmental Protection: Biodiversity and Biotechnology', *Washington University Law Quarterly*, 76 (1998): 255–79

Macridis, Roy, 'Major Characteristics of the Traditional Approach', in Bernard Susser (ed.), *Approaches to the Study of Politics* (New York: Macmillan Publishing, 1992)

Mahoney, Paul G., 'The Common Law and Economic Growth: Hayek might be right', *Journal of Legal Studies*, 30 (2001): 503–25

Maine, Sir Henry Sumner, *Early Law and Custom* (London: John Murray, 1890)

Maitland, Frederic and Sir Frederick Pollock, *History of English Law before the Times of Edward I* (2nd edn, Cambridge: Cambridge University Press, 1895)

Maitland, Frederic 'The Crown as a Corporation', *Law Quarterly Review*, 17 (1901): 131–46

——————, *Domesday Book and Beyond – three essays on the early history of England* (New York: Norton, 1966, first published 1897)

Mallory, J.R., 'The Appointment of the Governor General', *Canadian Journal of Economics and Political Science* (1960): 96

Man, John, *The Gutenberg revolution: the story of a genius and an invention that changed the world* (London: Review, 2002)

Mann, F.A., 'The Doctrine of Jurisdiction in International Law Revisited After Twenty Years', *Recueil des Cours*, 186 (1984): 9

——————, 'The Doctrine of Jurisdiction in International Law', *Recueil des Cours*, 111 (1964): 9

Manning, Joseph G., *Land and power in Ptolemaic Egypt: the structure of land tenure* (Cambridge: Cambridge University Press, 2003)

Manolopoulos, Andreas, 'Raising "Cyber-Borders": The Interaction Between Law and Technology', *International Journal of Law and Information Technology*, 11 (2003): 40–58

Marden, Emily, 'Risk and regulation: U.S. regulatory policy on genetically modified food and agriculture', *Boston College Law Review*, 44 (2003): 733–87

Marsden, Christopher, *Regulating the Global Information Society* (London: Routledge, 2000)

Marston, G., 'The British Acquisition of the Nicobar Islands, 1869: A Possible Example of Abandonment of Territorial Sovereignty', *British Yearbook of International Law*, 69 (1998) 245

Martin, L., H. Gutman and P. Hutton, (eds), *Technologies of the Self: A Seminar with Michel Foucault* (London: Tavistock, 1998)

Marx, Karl, *Das Kapital: Kritik der politischen Ökonomie* (*Capital: A Critique of Political Economy*), ed. Frederick Engels (New York: International Publishers, 1967)

Mathieson, DL, 'Does the Crown have Human Powers?', *New Zealand Universities Law Review*, 15 (1992): 117–42

Matthews, J., 'Power Shift', *Foreign Affairs*, 76 (1997): 50–71

Maurice, Pearton, *The knowledge state: diplomacy, war, and technology since 1830* (London: Burnett Books, 1982)

Mayer, Franz C., 'The Internet and Public International Law – Worlds Apart?', *European Journal of International Law*, 12 (2001): 617–22

Menefee, S.P., 'Republics of the Reefs: Nation-Building on the Continental Shelf and in the World's Oceans', *California Western International Law Journal*, 25 (1994): 81–111

Merelmen, Richard, 'Learning and Legitimacy', *American Political Science Review*, 60 (1966): 548–61

Merritt, Deborah Jones, 'The Constitution in a brave new world: a century of technological change and constitutional law', *Oregon Law Review*, 69 (1990): 1–45

Mikasa, HIH Prince Takahito (ed.), 'Monarchies and socio-religious traditions in the ancient Near East: papers read at the 31st International Congress of Human Sciences in Asia and North Africa' (Cairo: International Congress of Human Sciences in Asia and North Africa, 1984)

Miller, Chris (ed.), *Planning and environmental protection: a review of law and policy* (Oxford: Hart, 2001)

Miller, Henry J., 'Patenting Animals', *Issues of Science and Technology* (1988–89): 24

Miller, Michael B., 'The business trip: Maritime networks in the twentieth century', *Business History Review*, 77 (2003): 1–32

Miller, Raymond, *New Zealand Government and Politics* (3rd edn, Melbourne: Oxford University Press, 2003)

Mirsky, Arthur, 'Influence of geologic factors on ancient Egyptian civilization', *Journal of Geoscience Education*, 45 (1997): 415

Mittels, Heinrich, *The state in the middle ages: a comparative constitutional history of feudal Europe* trans. H.F. Orton (Amsterdam: North-Holland Publishing Co., 1975)

Molho, Anthony, Kurt Raaflaub and Julia Emlen, *City states in classical antiquity and Mediæval Italy* (Ann Arbor: University of Michigan Press, c.1991)

Moloney, Pat, 'Neo-Liberalism: A Pluralist Critique', in Raymond Miller (ed.), *New Zealand Government and Politics* (2nd edn, Melbourne: Oxford University Press, 2001)

———, 'Pluralist Theories of the State', in Raymond Miller (ed.), *New Zealand Politics in Transition* (Auckland: Oxford University Press, 1997)

Monahan, Arthur P., *Consent, coercion, and limit: the mediæval origins of parliamentary democracy* (Leiden: Brill, 1987)

Montesquieu, Charles de Secondat Baron de, 'The Spirit of the Laws', in Arend Lijphart (ed.), *Parliamentary versus Presidential Government* (Oxford: Oxford University Press, 1992)

Moore, Nick and Jane Steele, *Information-intensive Britain: an analysis of the policy issues* (London: Policy Studies Institute, 1991)

Moore, Sir William, 'Law and Government', *Commonwealth Law Review*, 3 (1905): 205

——————, 'Liability for the Acts of Public Servants', *Law Quarterly Review*, 23 (1907): 112

Moorhouse, Geoffrey, *The diplomats: the Foreign Office today* (London: Jonathan Cape, 1977)

More, Charles, *Understanding the Industrial Revolution* (London: Routledge, 2000)

Morison, John, 'Modernising Government and the E-Government Revolution: Technologies of Government and Technologies of Democracy', in Nicholas Bamford and Peter Leyland (eds), *Public Law in a Multilayered Constitution* (Oxford: Hart Publishing, 2003)

Morrow, John, 'Neo-Liberalism', in Raymond Miller (ed.), *New Zealand Government and Politics* (2nd edn, Melbourne: Oxford University Press, 2001)

Morse, Edward A., 'State taxation of Internet commerce: something new under the sun?', *Creighton Law Review*, 30 (1997): 1113–67

Mozley and Whiteley's Law Dictionary, ed. E.R. Hardy Ivamy (10th edn, London: Butterworths, 1988)

Mulgan, Richard, 'A pluralist analysis of the New Zealand State', in Brian Roper and Chris Rudd (eds), *State and Economy in New Zealand* (Auckland: Oxford University Press, 1993)

——————, 'Can the Treaty of Waitangi provide a constitutional basis for New Zealand's political future?', *Political Science*, 41 (1989): 51–68

——————, *Democracy and Power in New Zealand: A study of New Zealand politics* (2nd edn, Auckland: Oxford University Press, 1989)

Mullett, Michael A., *The Catholic Reformation* (London: Routledge, 1999)

Munro, C., 'Laws and conventions distinguished', *Law Quarterly Review*, 91 (1975): 218–35

Muschter, G., 'Kunstlerforderung in der Bundesrepublik Deutschland', in R. Strachwitz and S. Toepler (eds), *Kulturforderung: Mehr als Sponsoring* (Wiesbaden: Gabler, 1993)

National Institutes of Health, US Department of Health and Human Services, *Stem Cells: Scientific Progress and Future Research Directions* ES-2 (Washington: National Institutes of Health, 2001)

Naughton, John, *A brief history of the future: the origins of the Internet* (London: Phoenix, 2000)

Nelson, Janet L., 'Kingship and empire', in J.H. Burns (ed.), *The Cambridge History of Mediæval Political Thought c.350–c.1450* (Cambridge: Cambridge University Press, 1988)

Nenner, Howard, *The Right to be King – The Succession to the Crown of England, 1603–1714* (London: Macmillan, 1995)

Netanel, Neil Weinstock, 'Copyright and a democratic civil society', *Yale Law Journal*, 106 (1996): 283–387

Neumann, Peter G., 'Technology, laws, and society', *Association for Computing Machinery. Communications of the ACM*, 37 (1994): 138

Nicoll, C.C., 'Electronic Commerce: a New Zealand perspective', *EDI Law Review: Legal Aspects of Paperless Communication*, 6 (1999): 5–20

Noll, R.G. and B.M. Owen, 'The Anticompetitive Use of Regulation: *United States v. AT&T*', in J.E. Kwoka and L.J. White (eds), *The Antitrust Revolution* (Glenview: Scott, Foresman and Co., 1989)

Norris, Pippa, *Digital Divide: Civic Engagement, Information Poverty, and the Internet Worldwide* (New York: Cambridge University Press, 2001)

North, Sir Peter and J.J. Fawcett, *Cheshire and North's private international law* (13th edn, London: Butterworths, 1999)

Novotny, O., 'Key issues in the transformation of culture in the post-socialist countries: With particular reference to the Slovak Republic', *European Journal of Cultural Policy*, 1 (1995): 217–23

Nwabueze, Remigius N., 'Ethnopharmacology, patents and the politics of plants' genetic resources', *Cardozo Journal of International and Comparative Law*, 11 (2003): 585–632

O'Connell, D.P., *International Law* (2nd edn, London: Stevens, 1970)

Office of Technology Assessment, Congress of the United States, *New developments in biotechnology: Ownership of human tissues and cells – Special Report* (Washington: Office of Technology Assessment, 1987) pub. no. OTA-BA-337

Olson, Mancur, 'Dictatorship, Democracy, and Development', *American Political Science Review*, 87 (1993): 567–76

Oresme, Nicole, *Le Livre des Politiques d'Aristote*, eds Albert D. Menut *Transactions of the American Philosophical Society*, 60 (1970): 1–380

Organization for Economic Co-operation and Development, *Bio technology and the changing role of government* (Paris, Organization for Economic Co-operation and Development, 1988)

Orwell, George, *Nineteen Eighty-Four, a Novel* (London: Secker and Warburg, 1949)

Ostry, Sylvia and Richard R. Nelson, *Techno-nationalism and techno-Globalism: conflict and cooperation* (Washington: Brookings Institution, c.1995)

Overby, A.B., 'Will cyberlaw be uniform?: an introduction to the UNCITRAL Model law on Electronic Commerce', *Tulane Journal of International and Comparative Law*, 7 (1999): 219–310

Paczolay, Peter, 'Constitutional Transition and Legal Continuity', *Connecticut Journal of International Law*, 8 (1993): 559–74

Palan, R., 'Tax Havens and the Commercialisation of State Sovereignty', *International Organization*, 56 (2002): 151–76

Papadakis, N., *The International Legal Regime of Artificial Islands* (Leiden: Sijthoff, 1977)

Partington, Martin, 'The Reform of Public Law in Britain', in Patrick McAuslan and John McEldowney (eds), *Law, Legitimacy and the Constitution: Essays marking the Centenary of Dicey's Law of the Constitution* (London: Sweet and Maxwell, 1985)

Passerin d'Entrèves, A., *The Notion of the State: An Introduction to Political Theory* (Oxford: Clarendon Press, 1967)

Patterson, Richard D., 'Wonders in the heavens and on the earth: Apocalyptic imagery in the Old Testament', *Journal of the Evangelical Theological Society*, 43 (2000): 385–403

Pauwelyn, Joost, *Conflict of norms in public international law: how WTO law relates to other rules of international law* (Cambridge: Cambridge University Press, 2003)

Pearson, Hilary and Clifford Miller, *Commercial exploitation of intellectual property* (London: Blackstone, 1990)

Pecock, Reginald, *Donet*, ed. Elsie Vaughan Hitchcock (London: Early English Text Society, 1921, repr 1971) EETS OS 156

Pennington, Kenneth, 'Law, Legislative authority and theories of government, 1150–1300', in J.H. Burns (ed.), *The Cambridge History of Mediæval Political Thought c.350–c.1450* (Cambridge: Cambridge University Press, 1988)

——————, *The Prince and the Law, 1200–1600: Sovereignty and rights in the Western legal tradition* (Berkeley: University of California Press, 1993)

Perelman, Michael, *Classical political economy: primitive accumulation and the social division of labour* (Totowa: Rowman and Allanheld, 1984)

Perritt, Henry H., 'The Internet is Changing International Law', *Chicago–Kent Law Review*, 73 (1998): 997–1054

Perry, Paul and Alan Webster, *New Zealand Politics at the Turn of the Millennium: Attitudes and Values about Politics and Government* (Auckland: Alpha Publications, 1999)

Perry, Richard Warren and Bill Maurer (eds), *Globalization under construction: governmentality, law, and identity* (Minneapolis: University of Minnesota Press, c.2003)

Peters, Ronald M., Jr., *The Massachusetts constitution of 1780: a social compact* (Amherst: University of Massachusetts Press, 1978)

Peterson, D.J., *Troubled lands: the legacy of Soviet environmental destruction* (Boulder: Westview Press, 1993)

Phillips, Jock, 'The Constitution and Independent Nationhood', in Colin James (ed.), *Building the Constitution* (Wellington: Victoria University of Wellington Institute of Policy Studies, 2000): 69–76

Philpott, Daniel, 'Sovereignty', *Journal of International Affairs*, 48 (1995): 353–68

Pikirayi, Innocent, *The Zimbabwe culture: origins and decline of southern Zambezian states* (Walnut Creek: AltaMira Press, c.2001)

Pila, Justine, 'Bound Futures: Patent law and modern biotechnology', *Boston University Journal of Science and Technology Law*, 9 (2003): 326–78

Plato, *The Republic*, ed. G.R.F. Ferrari trans. Tom Griffith (Cambridge: Cambridge University Press, 2000)

Pocock, John G.A., *The Ancient Constitution and the Feudal Law; A Study of English Historical Thought in the Seventeenth Century* (2nd edn, Cambridge: Cambridge University Press, 1987)

——————, *The ancient constitution and the feudal law: a study of English historical thought in the seventeenth century* (Cambridge: Cambridge University Press, 1987)

Poggi, Gianfranco, *The Development of the Modern State: A Sociological Introduction* (London: Hutchinson, 1978)

Pollard, Sidney, *Essays on the industrial revolution in Britain*, ed. Colin Holmes (Aldershot: Ashgate, 2000)

Post, David G. and David R. Johnson, '"Chaos Prevailing on Every Continent": Towards a New Theory of Decentralised Decision-Making in Complex Systems', Social Science Research Network Electronic Library (14 June 1999), available at <http://papers.ssrn.com/sol3/delivery.cfm/99032613.pdf?abstractid=157692> (as at 1 December 2003)

Postle, H.T., 'Commonwealth and Crown', *Australian Law Journal*, 3 (1929): 109

Potter, David, *Prophets and Emperors: Human and Divine Authority from Augustus to Theodosius* (Cambridge: Harvard University Press, 1994)

Puro, Steven, 'Technology, politics and the new Industrial Revolution', *Public Law Forum*, 4 (1985): 387–98

Putnam, George Haven, *The censorship of the Church of Rome and its influence upon the production and distribution of literature* (New York: B. Blom, 1967)

Puurunen, Tapio, 'The Legislative Jurisdiction of States over Transactions in International Electronic Commerce', *John Marshall Journal of Computer and Information Law*, 18 (2000): 689–754

Qiu, Jack Linchuan, 'Virtual Censorship in China: Keeping the Gate between the Cyberspaces', *International Journal of Communications Law and Policy*, 4 (1999–2000): 1–25

Rabinow, P. (ed.), *Michel Foucault: Ethics* (London: Penguin, 1997)

Raines, Lisa J., 'The Mouse That Roared: Patent Protection for Genetically Engineered Animals Makes Legal, Moral, and Economic Sense', *Issues of Science and Technology* (1988): 65

Rawls, John, *Political Liberalism* (New York: Columbia University Press, 1993)

Rege, Vinod, 'Economies in transition and developing countries: prospects for greater co-operation in trade and economic fields', *Journal of World Trade (Law-Economics-Public Policy)*, 27 (1993): 83–115

Reidenberg, Joel R., 'Governing Networks and Rule-Making in Cyberspace', in Brian Kahin and Charles Nesson (eds), *Borders in Cyberspace* (Cambridge: MIT Press, 1997)

——————, 'Governing Networks and Rule-making in Cyberspace', *Emory Law Journal*, 45 (1996): 911–30

——————, 'Lex Informatica: The Formulation of Information Policy Rules Through Technology', *Texas Law Review*, 76 (1998): 553–94

Reinicke, W.H., 'Global Public Policy', *Foreign Affairs* (1997): 127–38

Reynolds, Glenn Harlan, 'Environmental Regulation of Nanotechnology: Some Preliminary Observations', *Environmental Law Reports*, 31 (2001): 10681–8

Reynolds, Susan, 'Law and Community in Western Christendom', *American Journal of Legal History* (1981): 206

Richardson, Martin (ed.), *Globalization and international trade liberalisation: continuity and change* (Cheltenham: Edward Elgar, 2000)

Rifkin, Jeremy, 'Creating the Efficient Gene', in Michael Ruse (ed.), *Philosophy of Biology* (Albany: State University of New York Press, 1989)

Riley, Patrick, *Will and political legitimacy: a critical exposition of social contract theory in Hobbes, Locke, Rousseau, Kant, and Hegel* (Cambridge: Harvard University Press, 1982)

Roberts, Adam and Richard Guellf (eds), *Laws of War* (Oxford: Oxford University Press, 2000)

Roberts, Leslie, 'Genome Patent Fight Erupts', *Science*, 254 (1991): 184–6

——————, 'NIH Gene Patents, Round Two', *Science*, 255 (1992): 912–13

Robertson, A.J., *Laws of the Kings of England* (Cambridge: Cambridge University Press, 1925)

Rose, Gregory, 'International law of sustainable agriculture in the 21st century: The International Treaty on Plant Genetic Resources for Food and Agriculture', *Georgetown International Environmental Law Review*, 15 (2003): 583–632

Rose, Kenneth, *Kings, Queens and Courtiers: Intimate Portraits of the Royal House of Windsor from its foundation to the Present Day* (London: Weidenfeld and Nicolson, 1985)

Rose, Nicolas, 'Government and Control', *British Journal of Criminology*, 40 (2000): 321–39

——————, *Powers of Freedom: Reframing Political Thought* (Cambridge: Cambridge University Press, 1999)

Ross, Alf, *On Law and Justice* (London: Stevens, 1958)

Rouseau, Jean-Jacques, *The Social Contract and other later political writings*, ed. and trans. Victor Goureatres (Cambridge: Cambridge University Press, 1997)

Royal Commission on the Electoral System, *Report of the Royal Commission on the Electoral System 'Towards a better democracy'* (Wellington: Government Printer, 1986)

Rudin, Thom W., 'State involvement in the "new Industrial Revolution"', *Public Law Forum*, 4 (1985): 411–17

Rushdoony, Rousas John, *The Institutes of Biblical Law* (Philadelphia: Presbyterian and Reformed Publishing, 1973)

Russell, Bertrand Earl, *Towards world government* (London: New Commonwealth, 1947)

Russell, Peter, *Constitutional Odyssey: Can Canadians become a Sovereign People*? (Toronto: University of Toronto Press, 1992)

Ryan, Chris, '"The Crown" and corporate bona vacantia', *Kingston Law Review*, 12 (1982): 75–87

Ryholt, K.S.B., *The Political Situation in Egypt during the Second Intermediate Period, c.1800–1550 BC* (Copenhagen: The Carsten Niebuhr Institute of Near Eastern Studies, 1997)

Safarian, A.E. and Gilles Y. Bertin (eds), *Multinationals, governments, and international technology transfer* (New York: St Martins, 1987)

Salter, Leonard M., 'Predictions for the Next Millennium', *Orange County Lawyer*, 42 (2000): 16–22

Sanford, B. and Michael J. Lorenger, 'Teaching an Old Dog New Tricks', *Connecticut Law Review*, 28 (1995–96): 1137–70

Sarcević, P. *Privatisation in Central and Eastern Europe* (London: Graham and Trotman, 1992)

Schaar, John, 'Legitimacy in the Modern State', in William Connolly (ed.), *Legitimacy and the State* (Oxford: Blackwell Basil, 1984)

——————, 'Legitimacy in the Modern State', in William Connolly (ed.), *Legitimacy and the State* (Oxford: Blackwell Basil, 1984)

Scheuerman, William E., 'Constitutionalism in an age of speed', *Constitutional Commentary*, 19 (2002): 353–90

Schreuer, Christopher, 'The Waning of the Sovereign State: Towards a New Paradigm for International Law', *European Journal of International Law*, 4 (1993): 447–71

Schroth, Peter W. and Preeti Sharma, 'Transnational law and technology as potential forces against corruption in Africa', *Management Decision*, 41 (2003): 296–303

Schultz, Cynthia B. and Tamara Raye Crockett, 'Economic development, democratization, and environmental protection in Eastern Europe', *Boston College Environmental Affairs Law Review*, 18 (1990): 53–84

Schulz, Regine and Matthias Seidel (eds), *Egypt: the world of the Pharaohs* (Köln: Könemann, 1998)

Schuster, J.M., 'Deconstructing a Tower of Babel: Privatisation, decentralisation and devolution as ideas in good currency in cultural policy', *Voluntas*, 8 (1997): 261–82

Schwartz, Paul M., 'Internet privacy and the State', *Connecticut Law Review*, 32 (2000): 815–59

Schwarzenberger, Georg and E.D. Brown, *A Manual of International Law* (6th edn, Milton: Professional Books, 1976)

Schwarzenberger, Georg, *A Manual of International Law* (1st edn, London: Stevens and Sons, 1947)

Scott, Jonathan, *Algernon Sidney and the Restoration Crisis, 1677–1683* (Cambridge: Cambridge University Press, 1991)

Seib, Philip, *Beyond the front lines: how the news media cover a world shaped by war* (New York: Palgrave Macmillan, 2004)

Serafini, Shirley and Michel Andrieu, *The Information Revolution and its Implications for Canada* (Ottawa: Minister of Supply and Services, 1981)

Shagan, Ethan H., *Popular politics and the English Reformation* (Cambridge: Cambridge University Press, 2003)

Shambaugh, David (ed.), *Greater China: the next superpower?* (Oxford: Oxford University Press, 1995)

Shapiro, Michael H., 'Thinking about biomedical advances: The role of ethics and law: On the possibility of "progress", in managing biomedical technologies: Markets, lotteries, and rational standards in organ transplantation', *Capital University Law Review*, 31 (2003): 13–127

Sharp, Andrew (ed.), *Leap into the dark: the changing role of the state in New Zealand since 1984* (Auckland: Auckland University Press, 1994)

——————, 'Constitution', in Raymond Miller (ed.), *New Zealand Government and Politics* (2nd edn, Melbourne: Oxford University Press, 2001)

——————, *Justice and the Maori: the philosophy and practice of Maori claims in New Zealand since the 1970s* (2nd edn, Auckland: Oxford University Press, 1997)

Sharpe, Kevin, *The Personal Rule of Charles I* (New Haven: Yale University Press, 1992)

Shelley, Mary Wollstonecraft, *Frankenstein, or The modern Prometheus*, ed. Marilyn Butler (Oxford: Oxford University Press, 1998, first published 1818)

Siedel, George J., *Using the Law to Gain Competitive Advantage* (San Francisco: Wiley, 2002)

Silberman, Bernard S., *Cages of reason: the rise of the rational state in France, Japan, the United States, and Great Britain* (Chicago: University of Chicago Press, 1993)

Silcock, Rachel, 'What is e-government?', *Parliamentary Affairs* (2001): 88–101

Silver, Lee M., *Remaking Eden: How Genetic Engineering and Cloning will Transform the American Family* (New York: Avon Books, 1998)

Simpson, Alan (ed.), *Constitutional Implications of MMP* (Wellington: School of Political Science and International Relations, Victoria University of Wellington: 1998)

Skinner, Quentin, 'Conquest and Consent: Thomas Hobbes and the Engagement Controversy', in G.E. Aylmer (ed.), *The Interregnum – The Quest for Settlement, 1640–1660* (Hamden: Archon Books, 1972)

Skocpol, Theda, *States and Social Revolution* (Cambridge: Cambridge University Press, 1979)

Slack, Paul, *The English poor law, 1531–1782* (New York: Economic History Society/ Cambridge University Press, 1995)

Slaughter, A., 'The Real New World Order', *Foreign Affairs*, 76 (1997): 183–197

Smart, P.St.J. 'Revolution, Constitution and the Commonwealth: Grenada', *International and Comparative Law Quarterly*, 35 (1986): 950

Smith, David E., 'Bagehot, the Crown, and the Canadian Constitution', *Canadian Journal of Political Science*, 28 (1995): 619–37

——————, 'Empire, Crown and Canadian Federalism', *Canadian Journal of Political Science*, 24 (1991): 451–73

——————, *The Invisible Crown*: *The First Principle of Canadian Government* (Toronto: University of Toronto Press, 1995)

——————, *The Republican Option in Canada, Past and Present* (Toronto: University of Toronto Press, 1999)

Smith, Sir Thomas, 'Pretensions of English Law as "Imperial Law"', in *The Laws of Scotland* (Edinburgh: Law Society of Scotland/Butterworths, 1987)

Smith, Woodruff D., *European imperialism in the nineteenth and twentieth centuries* (Chicago: Nelson Hall, c.1982)

Snow, Alpheus H., *The administration of dependencies: a study of the evolution of the federal empire, with special reference to American colonial problems* (New York: G.P. Putnam's and Sons, 1902)

Sobel, Dava, *Longitude: the true story of a lone genius who solved the greatest scientific problem of his time* (New York: Walker, 1995)

Spitz, Lewis W., *The Reformation: education and history* (Aldershot: Variorum, 1997)

Stadelmann, Rudolf, *Social and political history of the German 1848 revolution* trans. J.G. Chastain (Athens: Ohio University Press, 1975)

Standage, Tom, *The Victorian Internet: the remarkable story of the telegraph and the nineteenth century's online pioneers* (London: Phoenix, 1999)

Stanford, J.S., 'The Application of the Sherman Act to Conduct Outside the United States: A View from Abroad', *Cornell International Law Journal*, 11 (1978): 195

Starek, Roscoe B., III and Lynda M. Rozell, 'The Federal Trade Commission's commitment to on-line consumer protection', *The John Marshall Journal of Computer and Information Law*, 15 (1997): 679–702

Stark, David M. et al, 'Regulation of the Amount of Starch in Plant Tissues by ADP Glucose Pyrophosphorylase', *Science*, 258 (1992): 287–92

Stefancic, Jean and Richard Delgado, 'Outsider jurisprudence and the electronic revolution: Will technology help or hinder the cause of law reform?', *Ohio State Law Journal*, 52 (1991): 847–58

Stenton, Frank M., *The first century of English feudalism* (Oxford: Clarendon Press, 1961)

Stern, Nicholas, *Transition: Private Sector Development and the Role of Financial Institutions* (London: European Bank for Reconstruction and Development, 1994) Working paper no 13. XY/N-1

Stevens, Denise, 'Embryonic stem cell research: will President Bush's limitation on federal funding put the United States at a disadvantage? A comparison between United States and international law', *Houston Journal of International Law*, 25 (2003): 623–53

Stewart, Cecil, *Byzantine legacy* (London: Allen and Unwin, 1947)

Stock, Gregory, *Redesigning Humans, Our Inevitable Genetic Future* (Boston: Houghton Mifflin, 2002)

Stone, Peter, 'Internet consumer contracts and European private international law', *Information and Communications Technology Law*, 9 (2000): 5–15

Stoper, Emily and Emilia Ianeva, 'Democratization and women's employment policy in post-Communist Bulgaria', *Connecticut Journal of International Law*, 12 (1996): 9

Storey, Glenn R., 'The population of ancient Rome', *Antiquity*, 71 (1997): 966–78

Stover, William J., *Information technology in the Third World: Can I.T. lead to humane national development?* (Boulder: Westview Press, 1984)

Straus, J., 'Biodiversity and Intellectual Property', *AIPPI Yearbook*, 9 (1998): 99–128

Strayer, J.R., *On the Mediæval Origins of the Modern State* (Princeton: Princeton University Press, 1970)

Strickland, Matthew, 'Against the Lord's anointed', in George Garnett and John Hudson (eds), *Law and Government in Mediæval England and Normandy* (Cambridge: Cambridge University Press, 1994)

Strudwick, Nigel, *The administration of Egypt in the Old Kingdom: the highest titles and their holders* (London: Kegan Paul International, 1985)

Struve Catherine T., and R. Polk Wagner, 'Realspace sovereigns in cyberspace: Problems with the Anticybersquatting Consumer Protection Act', *Berkeley Technology Law Journal*, 17 (2002): 989–1041

Stubbs, William, *The Constitutional History of England* (4th edn, Oxford: Clarendon Press, 1906)

Suarez, Francisco, *Selections from three works: De legibus, ac deo legislators, 1612, Defensio fidei catholicae, et apostolicae adversus anglicanae sectae errores, 1613, De triplici virtute theologica, fide, spe, et charitate, 1621* trans. Gladys L. Williams, Ammi Brown and John Waldron (Oxford: Clarendon Press, 1944)

Sundquist, James L., *Constitutional Reform and Effective Government* (Washington: The Brookings Institution, 1992)

Sung, Lawrence M., 'Collegiality and Collaboration in the Age of Exclusivity', *DePaul Journal of Health Care Law*, 3 (2000): 411–39

Sunkin, Maurice and Sebastian Payne, *The Nature of the Crown: A Legal and Political Analysis* (Oxford: Oxford University Press, 1999)

Sunstein, Cass R., *Republic.com* (Princeton: Princeton University Press, 2001)

Susser, Bernard (ed.), *Approaches to the Study of Politics* (New York: Macmillan Publishing, 1992)

Szoke, Helen, 'The nanny state or responsible government', *Journal of Law and Medicine*, 227 (2002): S-1

Taafahi, Tauassa, *Governance in the Pacific: the dismissal of Tuvalu's Governor-General* (Canberra: National Centre of Development Studies, Australian National University, 1996)

Talmon, S., 'Recognition of Governments: An Analysis of the New British Policy and Practice', *British Yearbook of International Law*, 58 (1992): 231–97

Tarifa, Fatos, 'Quest for legitimacy and the withering away of utopia', *Social Forces*, 76 (1997): 437–74

Tassé, Roger and Maxime Faille, 'Online Consumer Protection in Canada: The Problem of Regulatory Jurisdiction', *Internet and E-Commerce Law in Canada*, 2 (2000–01): 41–8

Taylor, Arthur J., *Laissez-faire and state intervention in nineteenth-century Britain* (London: Economic History Society/Macmillan, 1972)

Taylor, Michael R. and Jody S. Tick, 'An incomplete picture. consideration of environmental laws to address problems that may arise from genetically engineered crops and food', *The Environmental Forum*, 20 (2003): 19

Teschke, Benno, *The myth of 1648: class, geopolitics, and the making of modern international relations* (London: Verso, 2003)

Thompson, Martyn P., *Ideas of contract in English political thought in the age of John Locke* (New York: Garland Publishing, 1987)

Tierney, Brian, *Religion, law, and the growth of constitutional thought, 1150–1650* (Cambridge: Cambridge University Press, 1982)

Tizard, Dame Catherine, *Crown and Anchor*; *the present role of the Governor-General in New Zealand* (Wellington: Government House, 1993)

Toepler, Stefan, 'From Communism to civil society? the arts and the nonprofit sector in Central And Eastern Europe', *Journal of Arts Management, Law and Society*, 30 (2000): 7–18

Trakman, Leon, *The Law Merchant – The Evolution of Commercial Law* (Littleton: F.B. Rothman, 1983)

Traunmüller, R. and K. Lenk (eds), *Electronic Government: First International Confrence, EGOV 2002, Aix-en-Provence, France, September 2002 Proceedings* (Berlin: Springer, 2002)

Trigger, Bruce G., *Early civilizations: ancient Egypt in context* (Cairo: American University in Cairo Press, 1993)

Tshuma, Lawrence, 'Hierarchies and Government versus Networks and Governance: Competing Regulatory Paradigms in Global Economic Regulation', Law, Social Justice and Global Development (1999) <http://elj.warwick.ac.uk/global/issue/2000-1/tshuma.html> (as at 22 January 2005)

Tsuji, Masatsugu, 'Transformation of the Japanese system towards a network economy', in Emanuele Giovannetti, Mitsuhiro Kagami and Masatsugu Tsuji (eds), *The Internet revolution: a global perspective* (Cambridge: Cambridge University Press, 2003)

Tucker, Robert C., *The Marx–Engels Reader* (New York: W.W. Norton and Co., 1972)

Tunstall, Ian, *Taxation and the Internet* (Pyrmont, Lawbook Co., 2003)

Twining, William, *Globalization and Legal Theory* (London: Butterworths, 1998)

Tyldesley, Joyce, *Hatchepsut: the female pharaoh* (London: Viking, 1996)

Ullmann, Walter, *The growth of papal government in the Middle Ages: a study in the ideological relation of clerical to lay power* (2nd edn, London: Methuen, 1965)

——————, 'This Realm of England is an Empire', *Journal of Ecclesiastical History*, 30 (1979): 175–203

United Nations Conference on Trade and Development, *UNCTAD World Investment Report 2000: Cross-border mergers and acquisitions and development* (New York: United Nations Conference on Trade and Development, 2000)

Vagts, Detlev F., 'State Succession: The Codifiers View', *Virginia Journal of International Law*, 33 (1993): 275–97

Vaidhyanathan, Siva, *Copyright and copywrongs: The rise of intellectual property and how it threatens creativity* (New York: New York University, 2001)

Vallamsetty, Udaykiran, Krishna Kant and Prasant Mohapatra, 'Characterization of E-Commerce Traffic', *Electronic Commerce Research*, 3 (2003): 167–92

Varga, Csaba, 'Transformation to Rule of Law From No-Law: Societal Contexture of the Democratic Transition in Central and Eastern Europe', *Connecticut Journal of International Law*, 8 (1993): 487–505

van der Veen, Cornelius, 'Facts and figures on Rhine pollution', *International Business Lawyer*, 9 (1981): 41–52

Vile, John R., *The Constitutional Amending Process in American Political Thought* (New York: Praeger, 1992)

Vito, Christine C., 'State biotechnology oversight: the juncture of technology, law, and public policy', *Maine Law Review*, 45 (1993): 329–83

Volckart, Oliver and Antje Mangels, 'Are the roots of the modern lex mercatoria really mediæval?', *Southern Economic Journal*, 65 (1999): 427–50

Wade, Sir Henry, 'The Basis of Legal Sovereignty', *Cambridge Law Journal* (1955): 172–97

Wade, Sir William, 'The Crown, Ministers and Officials: Legal Status and Liability', in Maurice Sunkin and Sebastian Payne (eds), *The Nature of the Crown: A Legal and Political Analysis* (Oxford: Oxford University Press, 1999)

Walbank, F.W., *The awful revolution: the decline of the Roman Empire in the West* (Liverpool: Liverpool University Press, 1969)

Walker, Clive, 'Review of the Prerogative', *Public Law* (1987): 62–84

Walker, Edward W., *Dissolution: sovereignty and the breakup of the Soviet Union* (Lanham: Rowman and Littlefield, 2003)

Walter, Bagehot, 'The English Constitution', in the *Collected Works of Walter Bagehot*, ed. Norman St John-Stevas (London: *The Economist*, 1974)

Walton, John K., *The Second Reform Act* (London: Methuen, 1987)

Walzer, Michael, *Just and Unjust Wars* (3rd edn, Plymouth: Plymbridge, 2000)

Warburton, David A., *State and economy in ancient Egypt: fiscal vocabulary of the New Kingdom* (Göttingen: University Press, Fribourg/Vandenhoeck and Ruprecht, 1997)

——————, *Egypt and the Near East: politics in the Bronze Age* (Neuchâtel: Recherches et Publications, 2001)

Waskan, Jonathan, 'De facto legitimacy and popular will', *Social Theory and Practice*, 24 (1998): 25–56

Watson, Alan, *Society and Legal Change* (2nd edn, Philadelphia: Temple University Press, 2001)

Watson, James and Sir Francis Crick, 'Genetical Implications of the Structure of Deoxyribonucleic Acid', *Nature*, 171 (1953): 964–7

Weber, Max, *The agrarian sociology of ancient civilizations*, trans. R.I. Frank (London: NLB, 1976)

——————, *The Protestant Ethic and the Spirit of Capitalism* trans. Talcott Parsons (London: Routledge, 1992)

Wedgwood, Ruth, 'The Internet and Public International Law: Cyber-Nations', *Kentucky Law Journal*, 88 (2000): 957–65

Weingast, Barry, 'The Economic Role of Political Institutions: Market Preserving Federalism and Economic Development', *Journal of Law Economics and Organization*, 11 (1995): 24–8

Weinstein, Samuel Noah, 'United States v. Microsoft Corp', *Berkeley Technology Law Journal*, 17 (2002): 273

Weiser, Philip J., 'Internet governance, standard setting, and self-regulation', *Northern Kentucky Law Review*, 28 (2001): 822–46

Weiss, Daniel H. and Lisa Mahoney (eds), *France and the Holy Land: Frankish culture at the end of the crusades* (Baltimore: Johns Hopkins University Press, 2004)

Weller, M., 'The International Response to the Dissolution of the Socialist Federal Republic of Yugoslavia', *American Journal of International Law*, 86 (1992): 569

Western, J.R., *Monarchy and Revolution – the English State in the 1680s* (London: Blandford Press, 1972)

Whitten, Ralph U., 'United States conflict-of-laws doctrine and forum shopping, international and domestic (revisited)', *Texas International Law Journal*, 37 (2002): 559–89

Wilhelmsson, Thomas, Salla Tuominen and Heli Tuomola (eds), *Consumer law in the information society* (Boston: Kluwer Law International, 2001)

Wilkes, H. Garrison, 'Plant Genetic Resources over Ten Thousand Years: From a Handful of Seed to the Crop-Specific Mega-Gene Banks', in Jack R. Kloppenburg, Jr. (ed.), *Seeds and Sovereignty: The use and control of plant genetic resources* (Durham: Duke University Press, 1988)

Williams, David, 'The Constitutional Status of the Treaty of Waitangi: an historical perspective', *New Zealand Universities Law Review*, 14 (1990): 9–36

Williams, John C., 'The role of the United States government in encouraging technological innovation', *Canada–United States Law Journal*, 15 (1989): 219–28

Williams, Nigel, 'European Parliament Backs New Biopatent Guidelines', *Science*, 277 (1997): 472

Wilson, Margaret, 'The Reconfiguration of New Zealand Constitutional Institutions: the transformation of Tino Rangatiratanga into political reality?', *Waikato Law Review*, 5 (1997): 17

Winterton, George, *Parliament, the executive and the Governor-General: A Constitutional Analysis* (Melbourne: Melbourne University Press, 1983)

——————, 'The evolution of a separate Australian crown', *Monash University Law Review*, 19 (1993): 1–22

Wittfogel, Karl A., *Oriental Despotism: A Comparative Study of Total Power* (New Haven: Yale University Press, 1957)

Wolf, Jonathan B., 'War games meets the Internet: Chasing 21st century cybercriminals with old laws and little money', *American Journal of Criminal Law*, 28 (2000): 95–117

Wolf, Martin, 'Will the nation-state survive Globalization?', *Foreign Affairs*, 80 (2001): 178–90

Wolfson, Joel Rothstein, 'Social and ethical issues in nanotechnology: Lessons from biotechnology and other high technologies', *Biotechnology Law Report*, 22 (2003): 376–96

Wolpe, Paul Root and Glenn McGee, '"Expert Bioethics" as Professional Discourse: The Case of Stem Cells', in Suzanne Holland, Karen Lebacqz and Laurie Zoloth (eds), *The Human Embryonic Stem Cell Debate: Science, Ethics, and Public Policy* (Cambridge: MIT Press, 2001)

Wonnell, Christopher T., 'The Noncompensation Thesis and its Critics: A Review of This Symposium's Challenges to the Argument for Not Compensating Victims of Legal Transitions', *Journal of Contemporary Legal Issues*, 13 (2003): 293–311

Woodward, Nicholas, *The management of the British economy, 1945–2001* (Manchester: Manchester University Press, 2004)

Woolliscroft, D.J., *Roman military signalling* (Stroud: Tempus, 2001)

Wriston, Walter B., *The Twilight of Sovereignty: How the information revolution is transforming our world* (New York: Scribner, 1992)

Wu, Timothy, 'Cyberspace Sovereignty? – The Internet and the International System', *Harvard Journal of Law and Technology*, 10 (1997): 647

Wulfstan of York, *An Werk Erzbischof Wulfstans von York – Die 'Institutes of Polity, Civil and Ecclesiastical'*, ed. K. Jost (Tübingen: A. Francke, 1959)

Yavitz, Laura, 'The WTO and the environment: the Shrimp case that created a new world', *Journal of Natural Resources and Environmental Law*, 16 (2001): 203–55

Yen, Alfred C., 'Western frontier or feudal society?: Metaphors and Perceptions of cyberspace', *Berkeley Technology Law Journal*, 17 (2002): 1207–63

Zaret, David, *Origins of democratic culture: printing, petitions, and the public sphere in early-modern England* (Princeton: Princeton University Press, 2000)

Zekos, Georgios, 'Internet or Electronic Technology: A Threat to State Sovereignty', *Journal of Information, Law and Technology*, 3 (1999), available at <http://elj.warwick.ac.uk/jilt/99-3/zekos.html> (as at 28 November 2003)

Zeller, Eduard, *Outlines of the History of Greek Philosophy*, trans. L.R. Palmer (13th rev edn, London: Routledge, 1948)

Zinder, Norton D., 'Patenting cDNA 1993: Efforts and Happenings', *Gene*, 135 (1993): 295–8

Index